Palgrave Studies in the History of Social Movements

Series Editors
Stefan Berger
Institute for Social Movements
Ruhr University Bochum
Bochum, Germany

Holger Nehring
Contemporary European History
University of Stirling
Stirling, UK

Around the world, social movements have become legitimate, yet contested, actors in local, national and global politics and civil society, yet we still know relatively little about their longer histories and the trajectories of their development. This series seeks to promote innovative historical research on the history of social movements in the modern period since around 1750. We bring together conceptually-informed studies that analyse labour movements, new social movements and other forms of protest from early modernity to the present. We conceive of 'social movements' in the broadest possible sense, encompassing social formations that lie between formal organisations and mere protest events. We also offer a home for studies that systematically explore the political, social, economic and cultural conditions in which social movements can emerge. We are especially interested in transnational and global perspectives on the history of social movements, and in studies that engage critically and creatively with political, social and sociological theories in order to make historically grounded arguments about social movements. This new series seeks to offer innovative historical work on social movements, while also helping to historicise the concept of 'social movement'. It hopes to revitalise the conversation between historians and historical sociologists in analysing what Charles Tilly has called the 'dynamics of contention'.

More information about this series at
http://www.palgrave.com/gp/series/14580

Jens Späth
Editor

Does Generation Matter? Progressive Democratic Cultures in Western Europe, 1945–1960

palgrave
macmillan

Editor
Jens Späth
Modern and Regional History
Saarland University
Saarbrücken, Germany

Palgrave Studies in the History of Social Movements
ISBN 978-3-319-77421-3   ISBN 978-3-319-77422-0   (eBook)
https://doi.org/10.1007/978-3-319-77422-0

Library of Congress Control Number: 2018941833

© The Editor(s) (if applicable) and The Author(s) 2018
This work is subject to copyright. All rights are solely and exclusively licensed by the Publisher, whether the whole or part of the material is concerned, specifically the rights of translation, reprinting, reuse of illustrations, recitation, broadcasting, reproduction on microfilms or in any other physical way, and transmission or information storage and retrieval, electronic adaptation, computer software, or by similar or dissimilar methodology now known or hereafter developed.
The use of general descriptive names, registered names, trademarks, service marks, etc. in this publication does not imply, even in the absence of a specific statement, that such names are exempt from the relevant protective laws and regulations and therefore free for general use.
The publisher, the authors and the editors are safe to assume that the advice and information in this book are believed to be true and accurate at the date of publication. Neither the publisher nor the authors or the editors give a warranty, express or implied, with respect to the material contained herein or for any errors or omissions that may have been made. The publisher remains neutral with regard to jurisdictional claims in published maps and institutional affiliations.

Cover illustration: © ullstein bild Dtl. / Contributor / Getty Images

Printed on acid-free paper

This Palgrave Macmillan imprint is published by the registered company Springer International Publishing AG part of Springer Nature.
The registered company address is: Gewerbestrasse 11, 6330 Cham, Switzerland

Series Editor Preface

Around the world, social movements have become legitimate—yet contested—actors in local, national and global politics and civil society; however, we still know relatively little about their longer histories and the trajectories of their development. Our series reacts to what can be described as a recent boom in the history of social movements. We can observe a development from the crisis of labour history in the 1980s to the boom in research on social movements in the 2000s. The rise of historical interests in the development of civil society—and the role of strong civil societies and non-governmental organisations in stabilising democratically constituted polities—has strengthened interest in social movements as a constituent element of civil societies.

In different parts of the world, social movements continue to have a strong influence on contemporary politics. In Latin America, trade unions, labour parties and various left-of-centre civil society organisations have succeeded in supporting left-of-centre governments. In Europe, peace movements, ecological movements and alliances intent on campaigning against poverty and racial discrimination—and discrimination based on gender and sexual orientation—have been able to set important political agendas for decades. In other parts of the world, including Africa, India and Southeast Asia, social movements have played a significant role in various forms of community-building and community politics. The contemporary political relevance of social movements has undoubtedly contributed to a growing historical interest in the topic.

Contemporary historians are not only beginning to historicise these relatively recent political developments, they are also trying to relate them to a longer history of social movements, including traditional labour organisations, such as working-class parties and trade unions. In the long term, we recognise that social movements are by no means a recent phenomenon and are not even an exclusively modern phenomenon, although we realise that the onset of modernity emanating from Europe and North America across the wider world from the eighteenth century onward marks an important departure point for the development of civil societies and social movements.

In the nineteenth and twentieth centuries, the dominance of national history over all other forms of history writing led to a thorough nationalisation of the historical sciences. Therefore, social movements have been examined traditionally within the framework of the nation state. Only during the last two decades have historians begun to question the validity of such methodological nationalism and to explore the development of social movements in comparative, connective and transnational perspectives considering the processes of transfer, reception and adaptation. Whilst our book series does not preclude work that is still being carried out within national frameworks (for clearly there is a place for such studies given the historical importance of the nation state in history), it hopes to encourage comparative and transnational histories on social movements.

At the same time as historians began to research the history of those movements, a range of social theorists—from Jürgen Habermas to Pierre Bourdieu, from Slavoj Žižek to Alain Badiou and from Ernesto Laclau and Chantal Mouffe to Miguel Abensour, to name but a few—have attempted to provide philosophical-cum-theoretical frameworks in which to place and contextualise the development of social movements. Although history has arguably been the most empirical of all the social and human sciences, it will be necessary for historians to explore further to what extent these social theories can be helpful in guiding and framing the empirical work of the historian in making sense of the historical development of social movements. Therefore, the current series is also hoping to contribute to the ongoing dialogue between social theory and the history of social movements.

This series seeks to promote innovative historical research on the history of social movements in the modern period since around 1750. We bring together conceptually informed studies that analyse labour movements, new social movements and other forms of protest from early modernity to the present. With this series, we seek to revive—within the context of historiographical developments since the 1970s—a conversation between historians on one hand and sociologists, anthropologists and political scientists on the other.

Unlike most of the concepts and theories developed by social scientists, we do not see social movements as being directly linked, a priori, to processes of social and cultural change, and therefore we do not adhere to a view that distinguishes between old (labour) and new (middle-class) social movements. Instead, we want to establish the concept of "social movement" as a heuristic device that allows historians of the nineteenth and twentieth centuries to investigate social and political protests in novel settings. Our aim is to historicise notions of social and political activism to highlight different notions of political and social protest on both the left and the right.

Hence, we conceive of "social movements" in the broadest possible sense encompassing social formations that lie between formal organisations and mere protest events. However, we also include processes of social and cultural change more generally in our understanding of social movements: This goes back to nineteenth-century understandings of "social movement" as processes of social and cultural change more generally. We also offer a home for studies that systematically explore the political, social, economic and cultural conditions in which social movements can emerge. We are especially interested in transnational and global perspectives on the history of social movements—and studies that engage critically and creatively with political, social and sociological theories—in order to make historically grounded arguments about social movements. In short, this series seeks to offer innovative historical work on social movements while also helping to historicise the concept of "social movement." It also hopes to revitalise the conversation between historians and historical sociologists in analysing what Charles Tilly has called the "dynamics of contention."

Jens Späth's edited volume, *Does Generation Matter? Progressive Democratic Cultures in Western Europe, 1945–1960*, synthesises insights from social-movement research with recent scholarship on political participation and mobilisation and applies it to the analysis of generations in Western Europe after 1945. Generational attributions have proliferated in recent years, especially in continental Europe, ranging from '45ers to '68ers to '89ers and all the way to Generation X. Significant progress has been made to move away from purely demographic understandings of "generation," particularly in the context of research by Anna von der Goltz, Lutz Niethammer, Mark Roseman and

viii   SERIES EDITOR PREFACE

Bernd Weisbrod (and his large Göttingen graduate school). However, our understanding of what the authors in this volume conceptualise as the "micro-politics" of generations—as well as the way in which their "historical experiences" were connected "to conceptual and everyday histories of democratic activism"—remains in its infancy. We also lack more systematically transnational and comparative analyses of these subjects.

This volume addresses these lacunae by providing us with a number of detailed and fascinating case studies about how "democratic elites" after 1945 constructed their experiences of democratic (re-)construction and generation as generational challenges and how they related to the period of the 1920s and 1930s. Inspired by "framing" approaches within social-movement research, the contributions highlight the constructed nature of generational narratives. "Generation" thus becomes an "open question" rather than a clearly delineated analytical concept. Therefore, this volume develops and finetunes influential work by Anselm Doering-Manteuffel, Dirk Moses, Udi Greenberg and Sean Forner, among others, who have emphasised the significance of the experiences of Weimar for the democratic reconstruction of Germany in the "Weimar Century" (Udi Greenberg).

The contributions broaden this perspective beyond Germany to include Italy and France, which experienced their own complex histories of continuity and rupture. Thus, overall the contributions sharpen our understanding for recognising not only the historicity of generational understandings. They also emphasise the ways in which popular and elite understandings of "democracy" and political engagement have their own histories and experiential contexts that are obscured by dominants political labels such as "pro-communist" or "anti-communist," "liberal' or "socialist." Thus, this volume provides us with a pre-history of our own times and a framework for understanding the transformation of popular politics and democratic engagement in the early twenty-first century.

Bochum, Germany   Stefan Berger
Stirling, Scotland   Holger Nehring

Acknowledgements

The origins of this volume go back to a conference organized by the editor at the German Historical Institute in Rome. The idea to publish selected papers presented at the conference, as well as additional papers, was developed afterward. That this idea was finally transformed into the present book happened thanks to a series of persons and institutions. First, the German Historical Institutes in Rome and Paris not only provided essential funding for the conference, they also generously supported translation and proof-reading services. Many thanks to Michael Matheus, Martin Baumeister and Stefan Martens for all of this. I am also grateful to my former colleague at the German Historical Institute in Paris, Steffen Prauser, for having individuated "generation" as the potential key issue of the book and for initial advice during the publication process. Gabriele Clemens at Saarland University gave me the opportunity to conclude the work offering further funding for proofreading services. Maike Jung, Markus Lay and Niels Grammes were indispensable with their linguistic and technical help while preparing the manuscript and the index. The two anonymous reviewers contributed to improve the quality of the project with their helpful comments. Molly Beck and Oliver Dyer, from Palgrave Macmillan, showed extraordinary professionalism in editing this volume and guaranteed that everything went smoothly. Finally, I thank the series editors, Stefan Berger and Holger Nehring, for having accepted this volume to be included into the Palgrave Studies in the History of Social Movements.

ix

CONTENTS

Part I   Does Generation Matter? Progressive Democratic Cultures in Western Europe, 1945–1960   1

1   Introduction: Generation as an Open Question   3
Jens Späth

2   Toward a New Political Culture? Totalitarian Experience and Democratic Reconstruction After 1945   29
Andreas Wirsching

Part II   Intellectuals, Science and Democracy   47

3   The Original 45ers: A European "Generation of Resistance"?   49
Dominik Rigoll

4   Continuity in Rupture: The Italian and German Constitutional Culture After 1945   71
Maurizio Cau

xii CONTENTS

5 Toward a New Political Science in Italy and West
Germany After 1945: Democracy, Politics
and Generational Change 93
Gabriele D'Ottavio

Part III Progressive Party Politics 117

6 Lost Generation? Nicolò Carandini, the Decline of New
Liberalism and the Myth of a New Europe 119
Christian Blasberg

7 Old and New Democracy: Placing the Italian Anomaly
in a European Context 151
Jan De Graaf

8 Inheriting Horror: Historical Memory in French
Socialists' and German Social Democrats' Fight
for European Democracy, 1945–1958 171
Brian Shaev

9 Two "Difficult Outsiders"? Anti-fascism, Anti-Nazism
and Democracy in Lelio Basso and Wilhelm Hoegner 197
Jens Späth

10 European Socialism and the French–German
Reconciliation 219
Christine Vodovar

11 Conclusions: Five Dimensions of Generation Around
1945 247
Jens Späth

Bibliography 257

Index 281

NOTES ON CONTRIBUTORS

Christian Blasberg is Lecturer for Contemporary History and European Studies at LUISS Guido Carli University, Rome, Italy. Furthermore, he is an occasional commentator on German and European Affairs on both Italian and international TV. He has studied at Heidelberg and Montpellier Universities and holds a doctorate in Contemporary History and Political Sciences. He has been visiting scholar at Montreal University, Canada, and has taught at Heidelberg University, Germany. His research is focused on the history of the European federalist idea and the twentieth-century conflict between democracy and totalitarianism. He has published extensively on these topics in various languages.

Maurizio Cau is Researcher at the German–Italian Historical Institute (ISIG) in Trento, Italy. His research interests focus on the history of contemporary European political thought and the history of Italian and German constitutionalism in the twentieth century. His publications include *Politica e diritto. Karl Kraus e la crisi della civiltà*, Bologna 2008; *L'Europa di De Gasperi e Adenauer. La sfida della ricostruzione*, Bologna 2011; *Geschichte und politischer Konsens. Übergänge der Nachkriegszeit (1945–1955)* (co-edited with G. Pallaver), Berlin 2014; and *L'età costituente. Italia 1945–1948* (co-edited with G. Bernardini, G. D'Ottavio, C. Nubola), Bologna 2017.

Jan De Graaf is Postdoctoral Fellow at KU Leuven, Belgium, where he is currently working on a research project on wildcat strikes as a pan-European phenomenon between 1945 and 1953 funded by the Research Foundation – Flanders. He obtained his doctorate from the University of

xiii

Portsmouth in 2015 with a comparative history of the post-war Czechoslovak, French, Italian, and Polish socialist and social democratic parties. A revised and expanded version of that thesis will be published by Cambridge University Press in 2018 under the title *Socialism Across the Iron Curtain: Socialist Parties in East and West and the Reconstruction of Europe after 1945.*

Gabriele D'Ottavio is Lecturer at Trento University, Italy, where he teaches International and European history. He has been DAAD-visiting fellow at Humboldt University (Berlin), visiting fellow at the European University Institute (Florence) and visiting fellow at the Goethe-University (Frankfurt am Main), and he is currently affiliated fellow at the Italian–German Historical Institute (Trento). His publications include *L'età costituente. Italia 1945–1948* (co-edited with G. Bernardini, M. Cau, C. Nubola), Bologna 2017; *Europa mit den Deutschen. Die Bundesrepublik und die europäische Integration* (1949–1966), Berlin 2016; and *Germany after the 2013 Elections: Breaking the Mould of Post-Unification Politics?* (co-edited with T. Saalfeld), Ashgate 2015.

Dominik Rigoll is Research Fellow at the Zentrum für Zeithistorische Forschung (ZZF) in Potsdam, Germany. Before joining the ZZF, he was lecturer at Friedrich-Schiller-Universität Jena, visiting fellow at Princeton University and Fernand-Braudel-Fellow at the Institut d'histoire du temps présent, Paris. His recent research deals with politics of internal security in Germany, right-wing and left-wing extremism in Germany and antagonist ways to "reconcile" France and Germany since the late nineteenth century. He is the author of *Staatsschutz in Westdeutschland. Von der Entnazifizierung zur Extremistenabwehr*, Göttingen 2013; and co-editor of *Der Antikommunismus in seiner Epoche. Weltanschauung und Politik in Deutschland, Europa und den USA*, Göttingen 2017.

Brian Shaev is Lecturer for International History at Leiden University, Netherlands. He completed a doctorate at the University of Pittsburgh and then was postdoctoral researcher at the University of Gothenburg and visiting scholar at the Max Planck Institute for European Legal History. He has published in *Contemporary European History* (2018), *French Historical Studies* (2018), and *International Review of Social History* (2016). He is co-editor of a book under contract, *Social Democracy and the History of European Competition Policy: Politics, Law and Regulation* and is co-organizer of a grant project "Welcome Home? Migrant Integration in European Cities from Historical Perspectives."

Jens Späth is Lecturer for Contemporary European History at Saarland University, Saarbrücken, Germany. He holds a doctorate from the University of Munich and was Research Fellow at the German Historical Institute in Rome. He has published extensively on nineteenth-century Italian and Spanish history and taught at SciencesPo in Nancy. Currently, he is working on socialism in France, Italy and Germany in the twentieth century. On this topic, he has published in *Docupedia-Zeitgeschichte* (2018), *Les socialistes français à l'heure de la Libération 1943–1947* (2016), *Contemporary European History* (2016), *Archiv für Sozialgeschichte* (2013) and *Diacronie. Studi di Storia Contemporanea* (2012).

Christine Vodovar is Lecturer for Contemporary History at LUISS Guido Carli University, Rome, Italy. She teaches Comparative History of European Political Systems and is specialised in Comparative and Transnational History of Mediterranean Socialism and Trade-Unionism as well as in the History of European Integration. Among her publications are "La Uil e l'Ugt, dal secondo dopoguerra all'ingresso della Spagna nella CEE" in *Ventunesimo Secolo. Rivista di studi sulle transizioni* (2016); "Socialistes et communistes, en France et en Italie à la Libération" in Noelline Castagnez et al., eds., *Les socialistes français à l'heure de la Libération. Perspectives française et européenne*, Paris 2016.

Andreas Wirsching is Director of the Institute for Contemporary History Munich – Berlin and Full Professor for Modern and Contemporary History at Ludwig Maximilians University in Munich, Germany. His research focuses, among other subjects, on the history of Germany and France during the twentieth century; the history of communism, fascism and national socialism; and German and European history since the 1970s. He has published among others *Vom Weltkrieg zum Bürgerkrieg? Politischer Extremismus in Deutschland und Frankreich 1918–1933/39; Berlin und Paris im Vergleich* (1999); *Abschied vom Provisorium. Geschichte der Bundesrepublik Deutschland 1982–1990* (2006); *Der Preis der Freiheit. Geschichte Europas in unserer Zeit* (2012); and *Demokratie und Globalisierung. Europa seit 1989* (2015).

ABBREVIATIONS

BLPSCE	Bureau de liaison des partis socialistes de la Communauté Européenne (Liaison Office of Socialist Parties of the European Community)
CDU	Christlich Demokratische Union (German Christian Democratic Party)
CGT	Confédération générale du travail (French General Confederation of Labour)
CNR	Conseil national de la Résistance (National Council of the Resistance)
COMISCO	Committee of the International Socialist Conferences
Co.S.Po.S	Committee for Political and Social Science
EDC	European Defence Community
ECSC	European Coal and Steel Community
EEC	European Economic Community
EPC	European Political Community
FRG	Federal Republic of Germany
FZO	French Zone of Occupation
GDR	German Democratic Republic
KPD	Kommunistische Partei Deutschlands (German Communist Party)
MFE	Movimento Federalista Europa (European Federalist Movement)
MLI	Movimento Liberale Indipendente and Movimento Liberale Italiano (Independent Liberal Movement)
MRP	Mouvement Républicain Populaire (French Christian Democratic Party)
MUP	Movimento di Unità Proletaria (Italian Proletarian Unity Movement)

xvii

xviii ABBREVIATIONS

NATO	North Atlantic Treaty Organization
NDR	Norddeutscher Rundfunk (Northern German Broadcasting Channel)
NSDAP	Nationalsozialistische Deutsche Arbeiterpartei (National Socialist German Workers' Party)
OSS	Office of Strategic Services (American Secret Service)
PCF	Parti communiste français (French Communist Party)
PCI	Partito Comunista Italiano (Italian Communist Party)
PdA	Partito d'Azione (Action Party, Italy)
PLI	Partito Liberale Italiano (Italian Liberal Party)
PR	Partito Radicale (Italian Radical Liberal Party)
PDSI	Partito Socialista Democratico Italiano (Italian Social Democratic Party)
PSA	Parti socialiste autonome (French Autonomous Socialist Party)
PSI	Partito Socialista Italiano (Italian Socialist Party)
PSIUP	Partito Socialista Italiano di Unità Proletaria (Italian Socialist Party)
PSLI	Partito Socialista dei Lavoratori Italiani (Italian Socialist Workers Party)
PSU	Parti Socialiste Unifié (French Unified Socialist Party)
PvdA	Partij van de Arbeid (Dutch Labour Party)
RPF	Rassemblement du peuple français (Rally of the French People)
SFIO	Section française de l'Internationale ouvrière (French section of Workers´ International)
SPD	Sozialdemokratische Partei Deutschlands (German Social Democratic Party)
SRP	Sozialistische Reichspartei Deutschlands (Socialist Reich Party)
UDN	Unione Democratica Nazionale (National Democratic Union)
UEF	Union of European Federalists

PART I

Does Generation Matter? Progressive Democratic Cultures in Western Europe, 1945–1960

CHAPTER 1

Introduction: Generation as an Open Question

Jens Späth

Several books that have appeared in the last two decades or so suggest a huge variety of different "generations" in the twentieth century: "the forgotten generation," "the lost generation," "the thrashed generation", "the 45ers", "the 68ers", "the 89ers", "the post-war generation", "the Baby Boomers,", "the millennial generation," and so on. Whether they are described with an adjective, a definite year or an object, these allocations suggest that everybody belongs or wants to belong to a certain generation that distances itself from others. Inclusion and exclusion have become crucial discourses within and between various generational groups all over the world when it comes to explaining political, economic and cultural new beginnings. In public perception and in self-representation, such specific generational groups—which are usually composed of individuals of similar ages with particular experiences, similar political ideas, social habitus and cultural practices—are supposed to establish the cultural hegemony of their point of view. At least, this is the classical definition of generational units since Karl Mannheim's ground-breaking article of 1928.[1] Generations can be interpreted first as projects offered for the

J. Späth (✉)
Universität des Saarlandes, Saarbrücken, Germany

© The Author(s) 2018   3
J. Späth (ed.), *Does Generation Matter? Progressive Democratic Cultures in Western Europe, 1945–1960*, Palgrave Studies in the History of Social Movements, https://doi.org/10.1007/978-3-319-77422-0_1

formation of communities; second as a place of longing with specific foundations of emotions; third as an obligation to pass on cultural values to the next generations; and fourth as a negotiation in the sense of a complex process in which many actors are involved.[2]

However, scholars disagree about how generations come into being, how they can be identified and what socialising effect they have over the lifetime of their members. First, while the graduate school of Göttingen University "Generationengeschichte. Generationelle Dynamik und historischer Wandel im 19. und 20. Jahrhundert" ("Generations in History. Generational Dynamics and Historical Change in the 19th and 20th Centuries")[3] and other European publications—including the Russian context—emphasize the role of political generations,[4] the US historiography gives more importance to consumer generations.[5] The latter is also more attentive to locating generational units by contextualising the cohort's size and its social demands, whereas analysing generation-conscious activists dominates the German debate.[6] In France and Italy, there seems to exist a more heterogeneous interest attached to both generational types including gender issues.[7] Generally, "generational identities have become more numerous, less politicized, less nation-specific and more consumer-orientated" in the course of the twentieth century.[8] Nevertheless, it has become even clearer through recent works that generations do not make history; instead they explain it to the society and to themselves. In other words, generations are no natural element of our societies; rather they are created in the media and popularized through communication.[9] Despite this broadening of perspectives for new categories and groups, it is striking to observe the high degree of nationalization and reinvention of generations in modern and contemporary history. Attempts to compare different national generations or to elaborate boundary-crossing, transnational generations still constitute an exception.[10]

In trying to fill this gap in the transnational component of political-generation formation, this collection of essays concentrates on one crucial moment of "the age of extremes" and on one specific generation: the year 1945 and its progressive politicians and intellectuals when the Second World War came to an end and was followed by the first one and a half decades of reconstruction in the post-war period. The book's working thesis is, of course, that age does matter in twentieth-century European history. Generational studies have mostly focused on the memory aspect, i.e. on how to come to terms with the past. Even though several decades ago Reinhart Koselleck had already emphasized the future as an autonomous category undetermined by past traditions,[11] research has mostly neglected and only recently begun to analyse how certain generational groups envisioned the future of their societies and Europe respectively, i.e. how to make sense of history by referring to past experiences when constructing a new democratic order.[12] This double-time perspective is exactly what most of the articles represented in this volume tackle. By focusing on ideas, plans and projects that were conceived, drafted and set in the interwar-period, during the Second World War and in the immediate post-war years up to the outbreak of the Cold War, they also question the dominating theses in historiography about Americanization, liberalization and Westernization in post-war Europe, shed more light on hidden transitions and reveal once more the participatory dimension of democratic politics.[13] Furthermore, considering the events from the decline of Nazi power from 1943 onward until the consolidation of the bipolar world of the Cold War allows one to break up the very German view on social history and experiences in the present literature.

The geographical focus lies on three Western European countries—Italy, West Germany and France—but is embedded in the broader European history and also considers the global dimension of the Cold War and its antagonists represented by the United States of America and the Soviet Union. Such an approach might be justified by saying that—despite its global importance—1945 had the most lasting effects on the European continent.[14] Some questions concerning the crucial moment addressed in this volume are these: How did the experience of autocratic government inform the way in which politicians developed new policies in Germany, France and Italy after the end of the Second World War? What conclusions did politicians draw from their experiences with totalitarianism? Did a new "generation" of leaders with shared democratic ideas gain the leading positions of their countries? Alternatively, did some of them already have experiences with democratic structures prior to the dictatorships? Was there any kind of exchange, transfer, or international collaboration, or did politicians operate exclusively within their particular national contexts? Finally, was the experience with totalitarian regimes kept alive in public memory and did people try to develop and implement progressive, forward-thinking ideas of social organization? Taking these central questions as a starting point, one can raise specific issues about each respective country, which reflect the contrast between occupation and collaboration in France, fascism and German-occupation in Italy, and National Socialism in Germany. What role did the two dictatorial experiences, namely first with fascism and then with National Socialism, play for Italy? In the case of France, one must bear in mind the experience of the popular front, the discrediting of the counterrevolutionary right by Vichy and the disappearance of the "deux France" after the Second World War. Regarding the Federal Republic of Germany and the GDR, it is important to explore further whether the resulting conflict between the two systems was of greater importance to their development than the previous experience with the Nazi dictatorship.

It is obvious that different generations were involved in the national processes of democratic reconstruction after the Second World War. The protagonists whose actions and ideas are at the centre of this volume are not necessarily all young men or members of the *Kriegsjugendgeneration* ("War Youth Generation"), identified by Ulrich Herbert as one out of three political generations in the twentieth century.[15] Nevertheless, these younger people, born between 1920 and 1933, play an important role because they had the chance to become active democratic politicians and intellectuals for the first time in their lives when the Second World War ended. Consequently, A. Dirk Moses describes these "forty-fivers" as a "generation between fascism and democracy."[16] But can we define these as a "new" transnational generation in terms of a strong common experience with totalitarian regimes? If we consider generations to be demographic categories and emotional communities distinguished and marked by political, military or economic events, and in the twentieth century by war and violence in particular, we can agree that some groups are more generational than others.[17] In other words, the number of people of similar ages who shared common experiences, political ideas and cultural practices was particularly large in the last century. This hypothesis seems to be evident when we look at the dominant generation of politicians after the Second World War, who were born before 1900. All of them had personal experiences from one or, in most cases, both world wars.

Generation building is a communicative process in which common experience can be used as a tool for mobilization in certain moments for particular aims. Having said that, we have to take into account the fact that experiences are often only interpreted retrospectively and a generational relationship constructed at intervals.[18] However, even if generations have been depicted as collective actors, only the most recent studies have started to do so with generations as collective communities of experience and to look closer at generational self-ascriptions and external ascriptions within which the biographical and social importance of war is particularly evident.[19] Generations might thus serve as a link between individual experiences and self-ascriptions, on the one hand, and political and social external ascriptions, on the other.[20] The term "experience" is undoubtedly the "softest and most resistant factor for analytic research" in historiography.[21] It is probably best to look for commonalities in background, environment, perceptions and belief systems. This includes new concepts—such as emotions, expectation and disappointment—as well as habitual stamps like asceticism and achievements.[22] Bernd Weisbrod reminds us to consider generationality as a "product of a historical negotiation process" that often overlooks more "silent" experiences. He also suggests overcoming national perspectives and focusing more on the generational link between experiences and expectations.[23]

Most of the following chapters make either demography or historical experience the central criterion for membership in a generation. In order to explore whether progressive political parties and intellectuals established a new democratic culture in Western Europe after 1945, these social movements' actors are connected in different ways to political generations in this volume: education, science and, primarily, policies of progressive political parties. This book does not aim at adding to our understanding of the impact, sequence, inter-dependence and changing hegemonies of generations by comparing the generation of 1945 with the generations of 1968 or 1989.[24] Of course, generations cannot explain the formation and success of social movements exclusively, but they can serve "as a heuristic and analytical tool for a better understanding" of the development of such movements.[25] The concept of generation is essentially fluid. As much as the post-war years should be understood as "open" history, so should the concept of generation be seen as an "open" question in space and time. Therefore, this volume asks what role generation played in the intellectual and political debates of 1945, i.e. whether it facilitated change, whether it served as source of solidarity and cohesion, and how post-war societies organized their time.

THE SECOND WORLD WAR AS CIVILIZATIONAL RUPTURE

By 1944–1945, inheritances from the past became visible to everybody in Europe and in the world: two world wars within less than 30 years, more than 80 million people dead and the civilizational rupture of the Holocaust with more than 6 million European Jews murdered by the Nazi machinery, not to mention all the other victim groups such as the disabled, homosexuals, Sinti and Roma, those affected by forced labour or native people in the colonized and occupied territories.[26] In addition to the misery of everyday life, intellectual cultural pessimism and the moral devastation of large parts of the population, "inheriting horror" seems to be an appropriate term to describe the situation of the entire European continent.[27] At the same time, the permanent state of emergency and everyday worries about the future suppressed a large debate and an analysis of the past.[28] Reconstruction was primarily a material task, but it also included a strong moral and symbolic dimension, first of all in re-establishing human dignity. When the Second World War ended, everything was on the move for a short moment in time. Many Left-wing politicians who had often joined the resistance movements against fascist and collaborating regimes believed that their historical hour had finally arrived. In their opinion, the different national societies were increasingly more ready for the establishment of a democratic socialism for overcoming the cleavage of the working class and for renouncing national sovereignty in favour of a European federation. The war ravages on the once-proud continent of the Enlightenment would raise the awareness of large parts of the population that the reason for all the evil was to be found in the capitalist and reactionary pre-war society. This progressive European social movement counted on cross-party cooperation and agreed on at least three principal goals: first, to build democratic structures from the bottom up; second, to facilitate political education and participation for wide masses; and third, to contain warmongering nationalism through a European peace-and-integration project. The numerous grass-roots movements that emerged out of the local, regional and national liberation committees or of the antifascist committees in 1944–1945 give manifold evidence of this period of essential willingness to experiment. However, most expectations and hopes of these politicians and intellectuals were dampened if not disillusioned because the allied victories did not concede any influence on administrative and governmental affairs to uncontrolled organizations. Contrary to the Soviet Union, the Western Allies—as well as the mostly majoritarian centre-right parties in Western Europe—opted for a new humbleness, a top-down stabilization and a piecemeal approach toward representative democratic systems.[29] When the disagreement among the four occupying forces over future German politics increasingly grew, the common antifascist paradigm collapsed rapidly and was overlaid by anti-communism in the Cold War and the German division.

Picking up these developments, this volume examines how progressive politicians in (West) Germany, France and Italy dealt with the new challenges and with what had gone wrong with democracy in the past. It argues that even after 1945 and despite all difficulties and limits, especially after the outbreak of the Cold War, there were transnational communalities within the progressive Western European sphere that were based on the actors' personal experiences with war and resistance against fascist regimes and gave impetuses for forward-looking politics, transnational cooperation and elements of a shared memory. A new democratic age was envisioned for Europe in which political parties and other interest groups dominated.[30] However, because it was not the progressive political parties that governed in Western Europe after 1945 (with the exceptions of the United Kingdom and Scandinavian countries), historiography has focused more on the majoritarian Christian Democratic and conservative parties, on the role of Christianity as moral guidance, on the importance of economic recovery and on the yearning for "normality."[31] Therefore, the authors in this volume seek to add to our understanding of what "democracy" meant within the political centre-left and how this was linked to the background of fascism and National Socialism.

Italy as the generic place of fascism and Germany, where the National Socialist movement first imitated the Italian model before overtaking it in its totalitarian structures, certainly constitute the most suitable comparative framework. To include the French progressive political sphere is exciting because France experienced several stages of political and social breaks in triplicate: as exile, as a country governed by a Popular front and as a territory partly occupied by the Nazis and partly controlled by the collaborating Vichy regime. It is particularly promising within the transitional period from totalitarian to democratic structures to look beyond the caesura of 1945 and to highlight the years from the end of the war until approximately 1960. This long-term perspective, which brings together pre- and the post-war history, will enable the reader to see considerable recourse to "European" ideas of the pre- and inter-war period. This raises several questions, e.g. Were any action concepts from the period of anti-fascist united fronts maintained after 1945, and, if so, which were they? What role did different generations and the very heterogeneous experiences of the emigrated in the respective host countries have? Can we talk across the board about a Westernization or Americanization of the progressive Western European politicians and intellectuals in light of numerous original European projects that were drafted in the first post-war years?[32] Were the ruptures between "West" and "East" solely the result of the two super powers enforcing their hegemony in their respective bloc, or were they to some degree already inherent in the pre-war and war experiences? Does the Cold War rupture not simplify the development of political culture in (Western) Europe, and weren't there a multitude of ruptures occurring within this period? Were not all attempts to find a "third way" between Western capitalism and Soviet socialism damned to fail because the majority of the people desired a "moral return to something safely known" rather than a "beginning of something new" in the post-war years?[33] What personal and ideal entanglements can we observe on a transnational level? Finally, how did (West) German, French and Italian Left-wing actors try to commemorate the violence and crimes of fascism between 1945 and 1960 ca?

This volume aims to contribute to a comparative and transnational history of the Western European political left in the second half of the twentieth century by connecting action with agency, i.e. structures and events with specific persons, groups and parties.[34] Referring to personal experiences before and during fascist regimes, it focuses on expectations, contributions to the (re-)construction of democracy and socio-political models for the future. In addition, it deals with memory discourses after 1945 and thus tries to take into consideration the process and entanglement character of the continuously changing democratic political programme that not only fed *ex negativo* on experiences with fascist regimes but also on concrete socio-economic and political-cultural situations before and after 1945. In addition to the past in the form of Koselleck's "Erfahrungsraum" ("space of experience"), the contributions not only consider the future with their "Erwartungshorizont" ("horizon of expectation"); through memory they also consider the presence of progressive politicians and intellectuals after the Second World War.[35] Similar to the first post-war period, there was an experience surplus that precluded, with its numerous individual memories, the expectation surplus as a motor of modern ideologies common to periods of peace. The comparative approach also allows for checking whether eventual generational (self-)descriptions by experience processing did not occur in contexts with considerable social differences.[36] Furthermore, it makes sense to separate the concrete experiences of war and resistance before 1945 from the retrospective experience processing, i.e. to distinguish between the concrete experience as "Erlebnis" and the retrospective procedure as "interpreted memory."[37]

INTRODUCTION: GENERATION AS AN OPEN QUESTION   11

Concerning the biographies, it will be interesting to examine in what way the different life experiences of different generations had communitarian effects.[38] A complementary question in many contributions is this: To what extent did parts of this progressive left operate policies for dealing actively with the past and found something like a collective cultural memory in France, Italy and West Germany? Certainly, within the context of an eventual Europeanization of memory, the authors notice different memories of the Second World War and of the Holocaust due to the diverse nature of both phenomena.[39] Changes of memory usually result in transformations of identity.[40] If we stress the ethic–moral value of resistance against arbitrary regimes as democratization movements, one could even talk about a moral responsibility for commemoration of progressive politicians and intellectuals, taking into account the fundamental role memory plays in the emergence of a political community.[41] Finally, memory discourses remind us to address also the fading out, the concealing or the conscious non-passing on of both levels and to indicate their interdependences.[42] Looking for an appropriate periodical end of this volume, one could think of 1956 because, after the reinforcement of the bipolar world and Stalin's death, the XXth Congress of the Soviet Communist Party carried out a programmatic reorientation in February that—in combination with the violent suppression of the Hungarian revolution in autumn of the same year—had considerable effects on the entire progressive Western European sphere. From a domestic point of view, in Western Germany and Italy the structural transition toward democracy and the mental acquisition of the republican constitutions was completed by the late 1950s, whereas France changed its constitution into a presidential system and proceeded from the Fourth to the Fifth Republic in 1958. Therefore, the end of the period under consideration has been fixed at 1960.

"OUT OF THE ASHES"?[43] DEMOCRATIC POLITICAL CULTURES IN WESTERN EUROPE AFTER 1945

Regarding the period under consideration, one can ask, "Should the year 1945 be regarded as maybe the deepest break with the past in world history in the twentieth century or as continuity in Germany, France and Italy in terms of how a democratic society was envisioned? Certainly, a mere re-establishment of the inter-war conditions was impossible. Concerning Western Germany, 1945 has become a metaphor for a new beginning and a successful democratization, as Hans-Ulrich Wehler has pointed out.[44] It includes the optimistic German myth of the "Stunde Null" ("Hour Zero") and the often-expressed desire for a tabula rasa even though many contemporaries interpreted the moment as a complete defeat. Others, such as the German economist and sociologist Alfred Weber, experienced their time as a "point of departure" and characterized this "sense of rebirth" as a "Nullpunkt" ("Zero Point").[45] Anselm Doering-Manteuffel identifies "transgenerational collective destiny" in the 1930s and 1940s and a past that had not gone by yet. In his eyes, these experiences of "strife, destruction and multiple traumata" explain why those two decades have become a "common element in culture of the European countries".[46] Although the three countries under consideration were governed for years or decades by totalitarian regimes (Italy for 23 years, Germany for 12 years, and France in parts for 4 years), all of them had previously had democratic and—in the French and German case—also republican experiences upon which they could build after the Second World War. It will be interesting to analyse their pre-war concepts of how to (re-)construct post-dictatorship democratic societies.

Looking at these transitions from one political system to another, political scientists usually focus on the political sphere while trying to include economic and social aspects too.[47] There have been three phases of transition from authoritarian to liberal-democratic political systems in the twentieth century. Starting with the American and French Revolutions, the first phase brought a general, equal and free franchise for roughly 30 countries. The "long" nineteenth century replaced absolute monarchies with constitutional monarchies or republics. It ended with the First World War and Mussolini's march on Rome, thus marking the beginning of an authoritarian countermovement that established fascist, authoritarian—corporative, populist and military—dictatorial regimes. The second phase, on which this book concentrates, witnessed transformations into democracies under Allied supervision in Western Germany, Austria, Italy, Japan and Latin America. The third and last phase can be seen in the period of the democratic transformations in Southern Europe starting in Portugal in 1974 and ending with the breakdown of the communist regimes in Eastern Europe in 1991.

Referring to our analytical term "democracy" and the period 1945–1960, the overall question is this: Did Western Europe moved toward a distinct new political culture after 1945 or toward different national political cultures? Therefore, conceptual and everyday histories of

INTRODUCTION: GENERATION AS AN OPEN QUESTION   13

democratic activism shall be connected to specific historical experiences. This includes issues of personal but also mental continuities and the efforts of post-war governments to handle their past.[48] Closely linked to this topic are categories such as democratization, the role of intellectuals, (re-) education, identity and the commemoration of the past, all of which gave rise to controversies after the war. That is why we should speak of a multiple past, an inhomogeneous civilization and several progressive political cultures. However, despite all heterogeneity, they shared common features. In Germany, France and Italy, all models of social and political progress after 1945, were based in the medium-term on democratic structures.[49] Democracy seemed to be attractive but also dangerous and somehow vague as far as concrete elements were concerned.[50] Nevertheless, there was a majority consensus on one issue that distinguished the three countries studied here from many other democracies in post-war Europe: Democracies in post-war France, Germany and Italy meant republics, as the constitutional referendum in Italy on 2 June 1946 demonstrated. Democratic republics were thought to be the best form of government in order to maintain the peace, as many intellectuals have stressed since Kant's theory postulated the connection between peace and republics. That is why, in most cases, social and economic models for the period after 1945 referred to ideas of a democratic peace (e.g. the Marshall plan). Concepts for a peaceful future were usually linked directly to socio-global ideas of order and, in our period, were characterized by the Cold War.[51] Fascism and National Socialism, war and genocide were often regarded as a civilizational break in which violence dominated moral values. To re-establish basic structures of a peaceful, pluralistic and democratic interaction was therefore among the main aims of many post-war intellectuals and politicians. "How to raise citizens in Europe after the Second World War", to fight for legitimacy, to defend the "inherently fragile nature of democracy" and, finally, to "make moral citizens" were not only concerns of the allied victory powers.[52] It is our interest here to see how citizens in France, Germany and Italy tried to create a new political culture and identity based on democratic and participatory values. Finally, it is important to consider how different scientific and constitutional cultures developed after 1945 and how "engaged democrats" of both the political and the intellectual sphere tried to make as much as possible out of the fluidity of the immediate post-war years as the Cold War began.[53]

A common, well-known and often studied type of this engagement was commemoration.[54] According to Stathis Kalyvas, we can observe four basic forms of collective memory after conflicts: these are exclusion, inclusion, contestation (such as the questioning of existent forms of government and society) and silence, each with corresponding forms of commemoration such as days of remembrance, debates and memorials.[55] Jörg Echternkamp and Stefan Martens recently reflected on the potential of Europeanizing the history of the Second World War.[56] Nevertheless, although European memory is one of conflicts and violence, it is also one of attempts to overcome these negative experiences by the meta-narrative of European rebirth. In a recent publication, Claus Leggewie mentioned both the Holocaust and the European Integration among the interlinked topics of a collective European memory.[57] In doing so, one always has to remember, of course, that individual experiences remain fundamentally disparate and generations are never monolithic. If we consider experiences to be social constructs that are constantly re-interpreted, it might be helpful to follow Dirk Moses' distinction between the "event" (*Erlebnis*) and the "experience" as "interpreted memory" in order to shift the focus of research on the processing of experiences.[58]

Usually, there are generational differences regarding the processing of historical events, e.g. some generations are more optimistic than others or have different backgrounds, meaning that their perception of the present time is characterized by socialization and emotions. One might ask, for example, who preferred not to discuss the Holocaust in the post-war period? Are there common European features of memory construction in these early times? French, German and Italian people did not only commemorate their experiences with totalitarian regimes, they also tried to establish structures to avoid a return of those dark years. Former soldiers in the four occupation zones of Germany, for example, were hoping for a better life and social recognition, whereas communists were eager to contribute actively to political reconstruction. Many of them were disillusioned not only by the denazification measures but also by the Russian occupation forces. Therefore, "victim" discourses, the integration of collaborators within collective experience processes and the impact of this integration within broader processes of coming to terms with the past have also to be taken into account.[59] The same applies to the permanently changing ways of social communication as a constant negotiation process after 1945, which were very important because the "what" and the "how" could be remembered or forgotten in specific spatial and temporal contexts.[60]

TOWARD AN INTEGRATED WESTERN EUROPEAN HISTORY

Adding the history of one nation-state to another is not enough in modern historiography. This also applies to social movements because we could define the progressive political parties, interest groups and intellectuals analysed in this volume. They were not limited to the territory of a nation-state even if for a long time they have been described and analysed within a dominant national framework. To detect transnational links of and between social movements as modernizers with global claims and utopias as well as key representatives of social conflict, the methods of comparison and entanglement are very important. Comparative historical research has at least five advantages over conventional national perspectives. First, it offers greater analytical distance to contemporary interpretations through specific questions. Second, it allows one to historicize dominant narratives such as democratization and Americanization. Third, it questions well-established causal chains, e.g. referring to fascism and National Socialism. Fourth, it invites verification of the importance of epochal thresholds. And fifth, it helps to sharpen our awareness of the actors' room for manoeuvres.[61] Transnational perspectives can help us to decentralize our point of view and to perceive territories not only as comparative units but also as mutually entangled components. To question why rather than how something happened will reveal common findings as well as divergences.[62] Consequently, all authors of these chapters have chosen a comparative approach and/or one of transfer, entanglements, relations and mutual perceptions covering the period between 1945 and 1960 and focusing on France, Germany and Italy.

Why does this volume confine itself to three countries of Western Europe while recent studies point us "towards a global history of social movements"?[63] The author of these lines is deeply convinced that scientists, especially those working in the humanities, should widen their horizon as far as possible in explaining political, social, economic and cultural developments. However, as Stefan Berger and Holger Nehring admit honestly in their inspiring recent volume, global approaches toward the history of social movements are still in their infancy.[64] Therefore, before arriving at the global level, solid "micro-studies" based on archival and printed sources are required that put parts of national narratives into a greater context and open up an integrated historical narrative through comparative and transnational perspectives. Europe as a transnational entity provides an excellent spatial area for transnational history because the nation-states on this continent are geographically among the closest of any area in the world. In addition, many states mean many boundaries, and the long tradition of exchange and transfer across the continent and beyond makes the argument even more valuable.[65] However, even in this tiny Europe, the entanglements and linguistic requirements are manifold, which might explain why we have only very little research that meets the requirements of a pan-European integrated history even today.[66] The articles collected in this volume try to make a start in such a historiographical approach in the core region of European integration, this core being France, West Germany and Italy—besides Benelux—which are three of the six founding members of the Rome Treaties in 1957. They refer to Europeanization concepts developed by Martin Conway, Ulrike von Hirschhausen and Kiran Klaus Patel and try to better connect two of the sub-periods of the twentieth century, i.e. the inter- and post-war periods, by examining ideas of democracy and democratization processes in Western Europe.[67]

The volume starts with an article by *Andreas Wirsching*. In his general overview, he analyses whether or not Western Europe moved toward a new political culture after 1945. Concentrating on France, Italy and West Germany, he confirms that there was "a deep cultural and political caesura" and that the genuine European roots of democratic reconstruction made a significant contribution to a different and more secular European narrative of history in the medium and long term. He identifies three aspects that favoured this political and intellectual shift in the countries under consideration in the second post-war period: the fundamental role of a generation born in the nineteenth century with older political traditions than those of totalitarianism; the tendency to overcome Nietzsche's "monumentalism," which was replaced by post-heroism and victimhood in order to liberate the European peoples from their past guilt; and, most importantly, for Wirsching, the ever increasing role of mass culture thanks to the economic boom, paid vacation and audio-visual mass media. Despite constitutional continuities, especially in France and Italy, the change of political culture compared to the bipolar extremism of the interwar period became evident everywhere in Western Europe after 1945. Contrary to the radical and extremist tendencies of the generation born around 1900, older politicians—such as Robert Schuman and Vincent Auriol, Luigi Einaudi and Alcide De Gasperi, Kurt Schumacher and Konrad Adenauer—grabbed the second chance they were offered by history and by the Allies. Apart from these common trends in Western Europe, there also existed considerable differences such as the role of communism in France and Italy due to resistance movements compared to their exclusion and social marginalization in Western Germany.

The second part of the volume is dedicated to selected fields of the new beginning in Western European political culture. Three authors examine key issues of democratization processes such as writing and historiography, constitutional culture and political sciences, comparing either the German–Italian or the Franco–German case. First, *Dominik Rigoll* puts a specific generation of intellectuals at the centre of attention. When the Western Allies assumed governmental control of Germany in 1945, they carried with them "White Lists" indicating names of Germans who were not compromised by the Nazi regime and should take over leading positions. In France, correspondingly, former Resistance fighters had entered the state apparatus 1 year before. Rigoll identifies this particular group of people as "original 45ers" and asks if we can characterise this generational unit as a "European generation of resistance." Most of its members were leaning to the political left, but there were also conservatives among them such as Adenauer in West Germany or de Gaulle in France. By using the term "45er" in its original but now forgotten meaning in historiography, Rigoll refuses to simply accept the by now dominant interpretation according to which the "45ers" were all members of the so-called Hitler Youth generation. Instead, he analyses the self-understanding of 11 prominent "original 45ers" such as Eugen Kogon and Jean Améry. Picking up the research of these "original 45ers" and that of the French historian Olivier Wieviorka since the late 1980s, he proposes a new conceptual approach to the history of this generational unit within a transnational perspective.

The next two chapters concentrate on law and political sciences as specific academic disciplines from a German–Italian comparative point of view. *Maurizio Cau* examines the constitutional culture north and south of the Alps stressing both the continuities and the ruptures in the second post-war period. He focuses on the constitution as an institution that had come under high pressure after decades of fascist rule. Cau argues that retracing the development of political thought on the State in sciences such as constitutional law reveals some hints about whether the political culture of the post-war period differed from or referred to the pre-war era. Questioning the "generational shift" and the "new beginning" of 1945, he stresses that there was rather a mixture of both distancing oneself from the past and upholding previous doctrines. Cau calls this phenomenon "multiple temporality" because the "timings of constitutional, cultural and social changes" often do not correspond with each other. Therefore, he suggests the formula of "continuity in rupture" to grasp this dichotomy between German and Italian constitutional experts before he asks how these ideas were implemented into new written constitutions.

Although law has been one of the basic academic disciplines since the foundation of universities in the Middle Ages, political science used to be taught within other disciplines such as law, history or economy throughout the nineteenth and much of the twentieth century. In his contribution, *Gabriele D'Ottavio* assesses the gradual consolidation of this field of study as a proper university discipline and the role it played in the democratization of former totalitarian societies in Italy and West Germany. By exploring the relevance of the generational issue within political science, he confronts the relationship between the discipline and various concepts of democracy. This also allows him to look critically at the generally accepted theses of "Americanization" and/or "Westernization" of Western European countries. He argues for distinguishing between both phenomena as a "cultural and intellectual process" on one hand and a "political goal" on the other. By first highlighting the role of the "three forerunners"—Gaetano Mosca, Karl Mannheim and Carl J. Friedrich—and then that of the new generation of Italian scholars such as Norberto Bobbio and Giovanni Sartori as well as German remigrants, including Arnold Bergstraesser and Karl Loewenstein, D'Ottavio shows how the cultural transfer from the US to Western Europe in political science after 1945 was generally filtered, mediated and even partially altered after 1945.

Whereas the second part of the volume focuses on generational changes within certain academic and intellectual groups, the last part is dedicated completely to progressive party politics covering the socialist, social democratic and the left-liberal sphere. To examine matters of generationality around 1945 within politically more coherent and left-oriented circles is particularly interesting and relevant because the historic chance and moment of the end of the Second World War seems to have been a unique opportunity to realize long-planned leftist projects for democratic societies after the political right had been discredited by fascism and National Socialism. In fact, it proved much more difficult to fulfill those hopes than left-wing politicians had expected, as is shown by the five following contributions. All of them analyse party politics from a comparative and/or transnational point of view. Thus, they provide first results for conceptualizing a particular Western European generation of socialism and left-liberalism by analysing how a transnational group of politicians coped with

INTRODUCTION: GENERATION AS AN OPEN QUESTION   19

the challenges of (re-)constructing democratic societies in the second post-war period. One could characterize this section as being about an outsider generation that aimed, but ultimately failed, to shape the political culture of the immediate post-war period in these countries: Their impact, it could be argued, came later, in the 1960s.[68]

Christian Blasberg employs the category of the "lost generation" and applies it to the Italian left-liberals, whose protagonist was Nicolò Carandini. Although the liberals had been a powerful group in Italy for decades since the foundation of the unified Kingdom in 1861, by 1945, and even more from 1947 onward, they were marginalized increasingly more between the bipolar Cold War party system with the communists and socialists on one side and with the Christian Democrats on the other. By assessing both Carandini's efforts to prepare centre-left concepts of a renewed social-liberalism in Italy and the impact of his international policy on the (Western) European political evolution after the war, Blasberg argues that the failure of Carandini's brand of new liberalism in Italy was, in a way, "counter-balanced by his commitment to the European idea." Thus, he stresses the Europeanist dimension of Carandini's action and thinking, which was first developed during his time as Italian ambassador in London from 1944 to 1947, and emphasizes that this unique intellectual was miles ahead of French and German national-liberal conservatives as far as supranational and federalist ideas were concerned. Following the political career of this particular personality of Italian post-war politics makes an important contribution to understanding of why many efforts of such left-oriented members of the "original 45ers"—to pick up Rigoll's topic again—failed in Western Europe after the Second World War. Establishing a truly new democratic society in Carandini's liberal vision raised the conflict between the "younger generation" and the "old liberals" that was decidedly in favour of the latter.

Clashes not only between younger and older generations but also between old and new concepts of democracy played out in the sphere of socialist internationalism as well. *Jan de Graaf* argues that they were not the old and well-known dichotomies of filo-communism versus anti-communism or revolution versus reform that distinguished Italian socialists from their Western European sister parties after 1945. Instead, the Italian socialists' very different idea about a new social and popular democracy as the ultimate goal placed the PSI, along with the Eastern European socialist parties, "outside of mainstream international socialism", as Guy Mollet put it in 1948. In his chapter, De Graaf explains the particular

20   J. SPÄTH

Italian way, with its profound socialist conviction, of overcoming an old bourgeois liberal society held responsible for more than two decades of fascism. He retraces the forerunners of this distinct Italian interpretation of democracy (Lelio Basso and Pietro Nenni) and highlights important elements such as preventing a counter-revolutionary fascism and the need for structural reforms, unity with communists and mass participation in government by the working classes in order to prepare society for the transition to socialism. Overall, he questions the characterization of Italian post-war socialism as "anomalous" and discusses the PSI within a pan-general European, not just Western European, context stressing the fact that Italian fascism, unlike fascism in most other European countries, had lasted for an entire generation and thus made a deeper impact than anywhere else.

Concentrating on the memory argument within the French–German context, *Brian Shaev* suggests that the socialist parties in both countries inherited the historical debts of their nations but used this memory of horror in their efforts to establish democracy. Furthermore, he shows how each party drew on the historical experiences of the other nation in analysing the trajectory of democracy in their own countries. Although the majority of memory studies have focused on national communities, there existed transnational efforts crossing national boundaries and stressing common experiences in the past and convictions for the future. Exploring this transnational dimension of European socialist memory is at the centre of Shaev's analysis. He relates his argument especially to discourses of the inter-war period that were crucial for French and German socialists in the transition toward post-war democracies. Presenting fresh evidence from archival sources, he questions both national master narratives, according to which there existed only distinct communist, socialist or Gaullist memories, and a "community of silence" in West Germany, respectively. He thereby makes an important contribution to broadening the approach of memory studies by also considering expectations of generational groups for the future. As Shaev can show, SFIO and SPD ideas and projects often had more in common with one another than with other political parties within their own nation. This was true, in particular, for the first generation of post-war socialist leaders until the late 1950s.

Another example of how to shift memory studies from their focus on the past toward future expectations follows in the chapter by *Jens Späth*. He compares the lives, ideas and actions of two prominent socialist politicians of the post-war period—Lelio Basso and Wilhelm Hoegner—who, despite their prominence, remained to a certain extent "outsiders" within their political parties. Referring to both the historical experiences of anti-fascism and the future project of democracy, he elaborates on some central parallels and differences between Italian socialism and German (but also Bavarian) social democracy and confirms that the history of Italian socialism after 1945 cannot be written without the history of the Soviet Union. Summarising first the generational communities to which Hoegner (born 1887) and the much younger Basso (born 1903) belonged, Späth outlines their experiences under fascism and National Socialism. As a second step, he discusses selected aspects of their political ideas and activities after 1945 focusing on the commemoration of the past on one hand and on theory and practice of democratic governments on the other. Although there existed important differences both in their background and in their concepts of democracy, one can define Basso and Hoegner as generationally close to each other because they both belonged to a generation of post-war European socialists who had a unique sense of history that drove them to transform anti-fascist experiences into the construction of democratic societies.

Making sense of history usually involves the issue of reconciliation. *Christine Vodovar* starts her contribution with a reflection on the Elysée Treaty of 1963 as one of the most important examples of official reconciliation documents. She makes the point that socialists in both West Germany and France took a very ambiguous attitude toward the ratification of the treaty: Although the SPD finally signed it after an important preamble had been added, the SFIO voted against it. In her chapter, Vodovar elaborates on some possible explanations for these divergences that seem to underline the mutual distrust of both parties more than a willingness for international cooperation between the former arch-enemies France and Germany. By alluding to different conceptions of peace and collective security as well as to interest calculations, she asks whether the wartime experiences and post-war expectations of French and German socialists mobilized both socialist parties after 1945 and created something like a distinct generation with a collective memory and a new political culture. Interestingly, she analyses not only the French and German socialist position before voting on the Elysée Treaty but also brings in the Italian socialist perspective as a "participant observer." This allows her to show that the efforts of all three parties in denying the principle of collective guilt were often counteracted by individual mistrust and even hostility.

Opening up comparative and transnational perspectives, the contributions show the potential and limitations of the generation concept and of Europeanizing the continent's history. Of course, future research should enlarge the perspective throughout all Western European states. It should also compare the contexts of the three Western European countries presented in this volume with examples from Middle and Eastern European such as the GDR, Czechoslovakia, Poland and Hungary where the real socialist governments not only claimed to be more democratic than the West but also could pick up their liberal and democratic traditions of one and a half centuries. Finally, global or colonial contexts also should be addressed. Nonetheless, this volume might serve as a contribution for research projects on integrated European history of the twentieth century and for breaking up the national framework in generational studies in the future.

NOTES

1. Mannheim, Karl. "Das Problem der Generationen." *Kölner Vierteljahreshefte für Soziologie* 7 (1928), 157–185, 309–330; reprinted as a single article in: Id. *Wissenssoziologie*, ed. by Kurt H. Wolff. Neuwied am Rhein: Luchterhand, ²1970, 509–565.
2. Gerland, Kirsten/Möckel, Benjamin/Ristau, Daniel. "Die Erwartung. Neue Perspektiven der Generationenforschung." In id., eds. *Generation und Erwartung. Konstruktionen zwischen Vergangenheit und Zukunft.* Göttingen: Wallstein, 2013, 9–25.
3. For further information, current projects and publications about the Göttingen graduate school, see: http://www.generationengeschichte.uni-goettingen.de/ (14.04.2017).
4. See Lovell, Stephen, ed. *Generations in Twentieth-Century Europe.* Basingstoke: Palgrave Macmillan, 2007.
5. Berghoff, Hartmut/Jensen, Uffa/Lubinski, Christina/Weisbrod, Bernd. "Introduction." In id., eds. *History by Generations. Generational Dynamics in Modern History.* Göttingen: Wallstein, 2013, 7. A recent example of the Anglo-American type is Parment, Anders. *Generation Υ in Consumer and Labour Markets.* London: Routledge, 2015.
6. See e.g. Carlson, Elwood. "Generations as Demographic Category. Twentieth-Century U.S. Generations." In Berghoff et al., eds. *History by Generations,* 15–37.
7. For France, see e.g. Andro, Gaïd. *Une génération au service de l'État.* Paris: Société des études robespierristes, 2015; Glazman, Wolf. *De génération en*

INTRODUCTION: GENERATION AS AN OPEN QUESTION   23

génération. Les enfants de la Shoah. Paris: Harmattan, 2009; Chauveau-Veauvy, Yves. *Génération AFN [Algérie 1956–1962].* Turquant: À Part du Temps, 2009; Fouque, Antoinette. *Génération MLF 1968–2008.* Paris: Des Femmes, 2008; for Italy e.g. Mori, Maria Teresa. *Di generazione in generazione. Le Italiane dall'Unità a oggi.* Rome: Viella, 2014; Latini, Carlo/ Vita, Vincenzo. *Il Sessantotto: un evento, tanti eventi, una generazione.* Milan: Franco Angeli, 2008; Capuzzo, Paolo, ed. *Genere, generazione e consumi. L'Italia degli anni Sessanta.* Rome: Carocci, 2003; Grandi, Aldo. *La generazione degli anni perduti. Storie di Potere Operaio.* Torino: Einaudi, 2003.

8. Lovell, Stephen. "Introduction." In id., ed. *Generations in Twentieth-Century Europe.* Basingstoke: Palgrave Macmillan, 2007, 11.

9. Bohnenkamp, Björn. *Doing Generation.* Bielefeld: transcript, 2014.

10. Jureit, Ulrike. *Generationenforschung.* Göttingen: Vandenhoek & Ruprecht, 2006, 35–39; as a positive exception, see Grace, Nancy M./ Skerl, Jenny, eds. *The Transnational Beat Generation.* New York: Palgrave Macmillan, 2012.

11. Koselleck, Reinhart. *Vergangene Zukunft – Zur Semantik geschichtlicher Zeiten.* Frankfurt a.M.: Suhrkamp, 1988.

12. The most recent literature review is Hölscher, Lucian. "Historische Zukunftsforschung – neueste Literatur." *Neue Politische Literatur* 61: 1 (2016), 47–62; see also his revised book *Die Entdeckung der Zukunft.* Göttingen: Wallstein, 2016; and the study of Seefried, Elke. *Zukünfte. Aufstieg und Krise der Zukunftsforschung 1945–1980.* Berlin: De Gruyter Oldenbourg, 2015.

13. See Levsen, Sonja/Torp, Cornelius, eds. *Wo liegt die Bundesrepublik? Vergleichende Perspektiven auf die westdeutsche Geschichte.* Göttingen: Vandenhoeck & Ruprecht, 2016, especially the introduction 9–28.

14. For a global perspective, see Buruma, Ian. *Year Zero: A History of 1945.* London: Atlantics, 2013.

15. Herbert, Ulrich. *Best. Biographische Studien über Radikalismus, Weltanschauung und Vernunft 1903–1989.* Bonn: Dietz, 1996, 42–45.

16. Moses, A. Dirk. *German Intellectuals and the Nazi Past.* Cambridge: Cambridge University Press, 2007, 55–73.

17. In addition to Mannheim's article, see Sirinelli, Jean-François. "Génération et histoire politique." *Vingtième Siècle* 22 (1989), 67–80; Nora, Pierre. "La génération." In id., ed. *Les Lieux de Mémoire. Vol. 3.* Paris: Gallimard, 1992, 931–971; Whittier, Nancy. "Political Generations, Micro-Cohorts and the Transformation of Social Movements." *American Sociological Review* 62 (1997), 760–778.

18. Stambolis Barbara. *Leben mit und in der Geschichte. Deutsche Historiker Jahrgang 1943.* Essen: Klartext, 2010, particularly 11–24.

24   J. SPÄTH

19. Möckel, Benjamin. *Erfahrungsbruch und Generationsbehauptung. Die "Kriegsjugendgeneration" in den beiden deutschen Nachkriegsgesellschaften.* Göttingen: Wallstein, 2014, 9.
20. Ibid., 387 f.
21. Daniel, Ute. "Die Erfahrungen der Geschlechtergeschichte." In Bos, Marguérite et al., eds. *Erfahrung: Alles nur Diskurs? Zur Verwendung des Erfahrungsbegriffs in der Geschlechtergeschichte.* Zürich: Chronos-Verlag, 2004, 59–69.
22. For the concept of disappointment, see Heinsohn, Nina/Moxter, Michael, eds. *Enttäuschung. Interdisziplinäre Erkundungen zu einem ambivalenten Phänomen.* Paderborn: Wilhelm Fink, 2016; Gotto, Bernhard. "Enttäuschung als Politikressource. Zur Kohäsion der westdeutschen Friedensbewegung in den 1980er Jahren." *Vierteljahrshefte für Zeitgeschichte* 62 (2014), 1–33; Gotto is also the project manager of "Enttäuschung im 20. Jahrhundert" ("Disappointment in the Twentieth Century") at the Institute for Contemporary History in Munich: http:// sofis.gesis.org/sofiswiki/Entt%C3%A4uschung_im_20._Jahrhundert._ Utopieverlust_-_Verweigerung_-_Neuverhandlung (10.04.2017).
23. Weisbrod, Bernd. "Generation und Generationalität in der Neueren Geschichte." *Aus Politik und Zeitgeschichte* 8 (2005), 3–9, quotations 8.
24. This has been addressed e.g. by Horn, Gerd-Rainer/Kenney, Padraic, eds. *Transnational Moments of Change. Europe 1945, 1968, 1989.* Lanham, MD: Rowman & Littlefield, 2004.
25. Berger, Stefan/Nehring, Holger. "Introduction." In id., eds. *Towards a Global History of Social Movements.* Basingstoke: Palgrave Macmillan, 2017, 20.
26. Cf. Kershaw, Ian. *To Hell and Back: Europe 1914–1949.* London: Penguin Books, 2015.
27. Cf. Brian Shaev's contribution in this volume.
28. On Germany, see Reichardt, Sven/Zierenberg, Malte. *Damals nach dem Krieg. Eine Geschichte Deutschlands 1945 bis 1949.* Munich: DVA, 2008; in a global perspective, Buruma, *Year Zero.*
29. See, with evidence from Schumpeter to Churchill, Nolte, Paul. *Was ist Demokratie? Geschichte und Gegenwart.* Munich: C.H. Beck, 2012, 284–293.
30. For the legacy of the European ideas of non-communist resistance-members on European integration, see Heyde, Veronika. *De l'esprit de la Résistance jusqu'à l'idée de L'Europe. Projets européens et américains pour l'Europe de l'après-guerre (1940–1950).* Brussels et al.: P. Lang, 2010.
31. See e.g. Kalyvas, Stathis. *The Rise of Christian Democracy in Europe.* Ithaca: Cornell University Press, 1996; Sack, Daniel. *Moral Re-Armament: The Reinventions of an American Religious Movement.* New York: Palgrave

INTRODUCTION: GENERATION AS AN OPEN QUESTION   25

Macmillan, 2009; Durand, Jean-Dominique, ed. *Christian Democrat Internationalism, vol. 2: The Development 1945–1979: The Role of Parties, Movements, People*. Brussels et al.: P. Lang, 2013; Großmann, Johannes. *Die Internationale der Konservativen. Transnationale Elitenzirkel und private Außenpolitik in Westeuropa seit 1945*. Berlin: De Gruyter, 2014; Grabas, Christian/Nützenadel, Alexander, eds. *Industrial Policy in Europe after 1945. Wealth, Power and Economic Development in the Cold War*. Basingstoke: Palgrave Macmillan, 2014.

32. For Germany, see Doering-Manteuffel, Anselm. *Wie westlich sind die Deutschen? Amerikanisierung und Westernisierung im 20. Jahrhundert*. Göttingen: Vandenhoek & Ruprecht, 1999; Angster, Julia. *Konsenskapitalismus und Sozialdemokratie: die Westernisierung von SPD und DGB*. Munich: Oldenbourg, 2003; for Europe as a whole, see De Grazia, Victoria. *Irresistible Empire: America's Advance Through Twentieth-Century Europe*. Cambridge, MA: Harvard University Press, 2005; and Stephan, Alexander, ed. *The Americanization of Europe. Culture, Diplomacy, and Anti-Americanization after 1945*. New York: Berghahn, 2006.

33. Müller, Jan-Werner. *Contesting Democracy. Political Ideas in Twentieth-Century Europe*. New Haven: Yale University Press, 2011, 129.

34. See e.g. Raphael, Lutz. *Imperiale Gewalt und mobilisierte Nation. Europa 1914–1945*. Munich: C.H. Beck, 2011 for a consequently comparative study. On recent transnational approaches, see Patel, Kiran Klaus/ Reichardt, Sven, eds. *The Dark Side of Transnationalism: Social Engineering and Nazism, 1930s–40s*, Special Section of *Journal of Contemporary History* 51: 1 (2016).

35. Koselleck, Reinhart. *Vergangene Zukunft. Zur Semantik geschichtlicher Zeiten*. Frankfurt a.M.: Suhrkamp, 1988, 349–375.

36. Möckel, *Erfahrungsbruch und Generationsbehauptung*, 28.

37. Moses, *German Intellectuals*, 56.

38. Mannheim, *Problem der Generationen*, 544.

39. Pakier, Malgorzata/Strath, Bo, eds. *A European Memory? Contested Histories and Politics of Remembrance*. New York, Oxford: Berghahn, 2010.

40. Cf. Assmann, Aleida. *Erinnerungsräume. Formen und Wandlungen des kulturellen Gedächtnisses*. Munich: C.H. Beck, 1999; Assmann, Aleida/ Frevert, Ute, *Geschichtsvergessenheit/Geschichtsversessenheit. Vom Umgang mit deutschen Vergangenheiten nach 1945*. Stuttgart: DVA, 1999; Assmann, Aleida. *Der lange Schatten der Vergangenheit. Erinnerungskultur und Geschichtspolitik*. Munich: C.H. Beck, 2006.

41. Margalit, Avishai. *The Ethics of Memory*. Cambridge, MA: Harvard University Press, 2002.

26   J. SPÄTH

42. Uhl, Heidemarie. *Zivilisationsbruch und Gedächtniskultur das 20. Jahrhundert in der Erinnerung des beginnenden 21. Jahrhunderts.* Innsbruck et al.: Studien-Verlag, 2003; Kalyvas, Stathis. "Cuatro maneras de recordar un pasado conflictivo." *El Pais*, 22.11.2006.

43. This is how Kershaw, *To Hell and Back*, 470–522, describes his last chapter about the end of the Second World War.

44. Wehler, Hans-Ulrich. *Deutsche Gesellschaftsgeschichte, Vol. 5: Bundesrepublik und DDR 1949–1990.* Bonn: Bundeszentrale für politische Bildung, 2009, 185–191.

45. Forner, Sean. *German Intellectuals and the Challenge of Democratic Renewal. Culture and Politics after 1945.* Cambridge: Cambridge University Press, 2014, 1. A thorough overview of the debate on 1945 has been written by Kleßmann, Christoph. "1945 – welthistorische Zäsur und „Stunde Null". Version: 01.0." In *Docupedia-Zeitgeschichte* 15.10.2010, http://docupedia.de/zg/1945 (10.04.2017).

46. Doering-Manteuffel, Anselm. *Das doppelte Leben. Generationenerfahrungen im Jahrhundert der Extreme.* Stuttgart: Franz Steiner, 2013, 4, 16.

47. Merkel, Wolfgang. *Systemtransformation. Eine Einführung in die Theorie und Empirie der Transformationsforschung. 2nd revised and enlarged edition.* Wiesbaden: VS Verlag für Sozialwissenschaften, 2010, 15–19.

48. Exemplary for West-Germany, see Frei, Norbert. *Vergangenheitspolitik: die Anfänge der Bundesrepublik und die NS-Vergangenheit.* Munich: C.H. Beck, 2012.

49. Nolte, Paul. *Was ist Demokratie? Geschichte und Gegenwart.* Munich: C. H. Beck, 2012; Müller, Jan-Werner. *Contesting Democracy. Political Ideas in Twentieth-Century Europe.* New Haven, CT: Yale University Press, 2011.

50. Conway, Martin/Depkat, Volker. "Towards a European History of the Discourse on Democracy. Discussing Democracy in Western Europe 1945–60." In Conway, Martin/Patel, Kiran Klaus, eds. *Europeanization in the Twentieth Century: Historical Approaches.* Basingstoke: Palgrave Macmillan, 2010, 134–144.

51. See Dülffer, Jost, ed. *Frieden durch Demokratie? Genese, Wirkung und Kritik eines Deutungsmusters.* Essen: Klartext-Verlag, 2011, especially the contributions by Kater, Thomas. "Am Anfang war Kant? Über Demokratie, Republik und Frieden." 17–34 and by Müller, Tim B. "Frieden durch Demokratie? Intellektuelle im Dienst der US-Regierung vom Zweiten Weltkrieg zum Kalten Krieg." 147–166.

52. See Levsen, Sonja. "Authority and Democracy in Post-War France and West Germany (1945–1968)." *Journal of Modern History* 89 (2017), 812–850.

53. The term "engaged democrats" was introduced by Fröhlich, Claudia/ Kohlstruck, Michael. "Einleitung." In id., eds. *Engagierte Demokraten: Vergangenheitspolitik in kritischer Absicht.* Münster: Westfälisches Dampfboot, 1999, 14–18.

INTRODUCTION: GENERATION AS AN OPEN QUESTION   27

54. Good introductions offer Erll, Astrid/Nünning, Ansgar, eds. *A Companion to Cultural Memory Studies*. Berlin/New York: De Gruyter, 2010, and Sierp, Aline. *History, Memory, and Trans-European Identity: Unifying Divisions*. New York: Routledge, 2014.
55. Kalyvas, *Cuatro maneras*.
56. Echternkamp, Jörg/Martens, Stefan, eds. *Der Zweite Weltkrieg in Europa. Erfahrung und Erinnerung*. Paderborn: Schöningh, 2007. English translation: *Experience and Memory. The Second World War in Europe*. New York/Oxford: Berghahn, 2010.
57. Leggewie, Claus (with Anne-Katrin Kang). *Der Kampf um die europäische Erinnerung. Ein Schlachtfeld wird besichtigt*. Munich: C.H. Beck, 2011.
58. Moses, *German Intellectuals*, 56.
59. Some of these topics were addressed by Robert Dale, Christiane Kohser-Spohn and Richard Bessel at a conference in Munich in 2011 on "Enttäuschungen im 20. Jahrhundert" ("Disappointments in the Twentieth Century"); see the conference report by Nadine Recktenwald in: H-Soz-Kult, 02.02.2012, <http://www.hsozkult.de/conferencereport/id/tagungsberichte-4035> (10.04.2017).
60. Winter, Jay. "Thinking about Silence." In Ben-Ze'ev, Efrat/Ginio, Ruth/Winter, Jay, eds. *Shadows of War. A Social History of Silence in the Twentieth Century*. Cambridge: Cambridge University Press, 2010, 3–31.
61. Levsen/Torp, eds. *Bundesrepublik*, 20–28. Especially interesting for the German–Italian context is the chapter by Gatzka, Claudia Christiane. ""Demokratisierung" in Italien und der Bundesrepublik. Historiographische Narrative und lokale Erkundungen". In ibid., 145–165.
62. See the reflections of Espagne, Michel/Kreienbaum, Jonas/Cooper, Frederick/Conrad, Christoph/Ther, Philipp. "Forum II: How to Write Modern European History Today? Statements to Jörn Leonhard's JMEH-Forum." *Journal of Modern European History* 14: 4 (2016), 465–491.
63. Cf. Berger/Nehring, eds. *Towards a Global History*.
64. Ibid., 3.
65. Horn/Kenney, eds. *Transnational Moments*, xiv.
66. Especially interesting is the article by Martin Conway/Volker Depkat, Towards a European History of the Discourse of Democracy: Discussing Democracy in Western Europe, 1945–60, in: id./Kiran Klaus Patel (eds.), Europeanization in the Twentieth Century. Historical Approaches, Basingstoke: Palgrave 2010, pp. 132–156.
67. See the introduction by Hirschhausen, Ulrike von and Patel, Kiran-Klaus, 1–18, and the conclusion by Conway, Martin, 271–277, in the same volume.
68. See Nehring, Holger. "Generation" as a Political Argument in West European Protest Movements during the 1960s." In Lovell, ed. *Generations*, 57–78.

CHAPTER 2

Toward a New Political Culture? Totalitarian Experience and Democratic Reconstruction After 1945

Andreas Wirsching

The comeback of democracy after 1945 was, to some extent, surprising. Democracy in continental Europe seemed to be doomed to failure in the 1930s. All European democracies had tremendous difficulties adapting themselves to the problems caused by the Great War. These problems concerned public finances, industrial relations, social security, unemployment, distress and, last but not least, the enduring question of an international peace settlement that was stable and just at the same time. By the end of the 1930s, first Italy, then Germany, had fallen victim to fascism and National Socialism, and even in France democracy was strongly endangered.[1] There was widespread resentment among the middle classes, which were partly tempted to give support to extra-parliamentary right-wing leagues. Some historians have seen the Vichy regime in continuity to that anti-parliamentarianism of the 1930s.[2] Others have stressed the stunning and spectacular defeat of 1940, which caused the breakdown of the Republic and the transition to an authoritarian or even fascist regime.[3]

A. Wirsching (✉)
Institut für Zeitgeschichte, Munich, Germany

© The Author(s) 2018
J. Späth (ed.), *Does Generation Matter? Progressive Democratic Cultures in Western Europe, 1945–1960*, Palgrave Studies in the History of Social Movements, https://doi.org/10.1007/978-3-319-77422-0_2

In any case, the deep crisis of democracy and of parliamentarianism in the interwar period left, at first glance, little hope for restoring democracy in the near future. Durable democratic reconstruction required, in fact, a deep political and cultural caesura in Western Europe.

In this chapter, I will argue that there *was* such a deep caesura; a caesura that went far beyond the military and political turnaround of 1944–1945 but that affected the depth of Western European political culture. At the same time, there remains the question: To what extent this was a genuinely *European* process, or to what extent was European democracy the benefit of American superiority and the large influx of aid that came from this superiority? I make an argument for taking into account the *European* roots of the democratic reconstruction without denying, of course, that this reconstruction was only possible under the military and political umbrella of the US. In my opinion, the main transformation resulted from a secular shift in how Europeans perceived their history and how they perceived themselves as actors in this history. To put it differently, it was a profound change in the narrative by which Europeans saw their own role in history. This narrative was more or less completely re-written after 1945 and gave a rather new orientation to politicians and intellectuals but also to ordinary people.

I concentrate my remarks on a comparison of the three countries in question during this conference: Italy, France and West Germany. In addition, I discuss three aspects that converged to bring about the change of the narrative in these countries after 1945. First, I speak of the crucial role of a democratic generation that had its roots in the nineteenth century. Against the background of the age of totalitarianism, those people were able to revive older political traditions and give them a new shape fitting into the specificities of the post-war situation. Second, I will speak of the trend toward post-heroism. Third, I speak of the role of mass culture. These three elements—generation, post-heroism and mass culture—converged to bring about a profound change of historical and political narrative in the three countries.

THE ROLE OF A DEMOCRATIC GENERATION ROOTED IN THE NINETEENTH CENTURY

At first glance, however, there was, Germany left aside, a strong trend toward political and constitutional continuity in Western Europe. The constitutional monarchies that had existed before the war, like Great

Britain, Norway, Denmark, Sweden, Belgium and the Netherlands, continued to exist after 1945, and the system of parliamentary monarchy was revived. "France, too, returned to the pre-war political system."[4] In many respects, the Fourth Republic resembled the Third Republic with its weak governments and a powerful parliament that was dominated by individuals rather than by the weakly organized parties. Even in Italy there was a clear tendency toward reconstructing the pre-fascist order. After the referendum of 1946, the republican constitution of 1948 resulted in a political system that was relatively similar to that which preceded fascism.[5]

However, these constitutional continuities in Western Europe were embedded by a political culture that was dramatically shifting compared to the political atmosphere of the 1920s and 1930s. Between the wars, European political culture revealed a dangerous tendency toward a bipolar structure. As is well known, this tendency favoured the extremes. Against the background of mounting social and economic problems, the political extremes—communism, fascism and National Socialism—propagated and claimed simple solutions. Moreover, they propagated these simple solutions by scapegoating political opponents. They revealed their totalitarian character by their penchant to moralize political and structural antagonisms. Political opponents were to be seen exclusively as truly *enemies* or *criminals* according to Carl Schmitt's concept of the political as a civil war. Such a concept, with its absolute distinction between friend and foe, excluded any rational parliamentary politics; but when the mounting pressure of political problems was overwhelming, governments and parliaments with pseudo-religious clarity and the seductive language of the extremes suggested an easy way out.[6]

If this system of friend and foe was made absolute, no middle ground, then no option between the extremes remained available. From this perspective, the political struggle required a rigid "either/or" mentality. To escape from the camp of one abominated and abhorred enemy, it was necessary to opt for the other camp. Georges Valois, the French fascist and admirer of Mussolini, put it this way in 1923: On the ruins of the old liberal Europe, communism and fascism alone fought for the future of the continent. Moreover, it was only a sort of European fascism that would be able to save the Western civilization from being destroyed by "Asian" bolshevism. "Two powers are at work – the one in the steppe, the other in the Romanic country. Both embody the total intellectual and practical negation of all democratic values. But Lenin is the dictator of barbarism, while Mussolini is the dictator of civilization."[7]

This coercion to choose between good and evil, between friend and foe, characterized the bipolar, totalitarian structure of the interwar period. And this coercion increasingly threatened to close any middle ground of plurality and compromise. This bipolar structure strongly affected the room to manoeuvre of those political forces that were willing to follow parliamentary rules and democratic practice. Indeed, we can say that three of the four great political currents of the nineteenth century—i.e. liberalism, socialism and conservatism—were strongly affected by the maelstrom of the bipolar, totalitarian structure of the time. Nothing needs to be said about the downfall of liberalism between the wars.[8] However, in the Weimar Republic, for example, alongside the liberal pillar, the conservative pillar eroded equally from 1928 onward. The appeal of the extremes and the escape into radicalism required more convincing answers. This mechanism was also dangerous for social democrats and reformist socialists. They remained incessantly under fire by the communists and other representatives of the extreme left. Socialists who stayed firm to the norms of democratic constitutionalism remained, in the eyes of Moscow, traitors before they became "social-fascists" as of 1929.

There is ample evidence now that the generation born around 1900 was the most vulnerable to the temptations of totalitarian thinking. Its members constituted a large part of élites and followers alike of political extremism. As fascists and Nazis, they enjoyed, under the respective regimes, extremely bright career opportunities, and more than once they succumbed to the temptations of quick and easy power.[9] For the communists, however, the generational leitmotiv remained "anti-fascism" and resistance, persecution and exile.[10] Therefore, the categories of "friend" and "foe" were reinforced by war and terror. After 1945, however, the ideologically founded bipolarity, which was so typical for the interwar period, was quickly fading away. Many fascists, Nazis and collaborators, it is true, remained unmolested by justice and found their place in the post-war democracies. Some of them made even a new civil career. However, as to the renegotiation of the political system, the extreme right remained more or less completely de-legitimized. It had no relevant political voice in the reconstruction of democracy even though overtones of militant anti-communism were never absent. A *political* comeback of former fascists and Nazis was precluded.[11]

Thus, in post-war Europe the radical and extremist tendencies and their representatives, mostly belonging to the generation born around 1900, were politically quieted down and socially integrated. At the same time, the generation of pre-war democrats now got their second chance. After 1945, this older generation, born during the last third of the nineteenth century, took the lead in the reconstruction of politics. Without entering here into a general discussion of the controversial concept of generation,[12] some remarks seem to be necessary. There is ample evidence that for the generation of those who were born between circa 1860 and 1885, it was easier to accept democracy and pluralism than it was for the younger one. If their members belonged to the educated middle class, their mental and social background was clearly the classical liberalism of the nineteenth century and its claims for political reason and rational discourse. If they belonged, on the contrary, to the working classes, their political mentalities were marked by the success of the European working-class movement before 1914. This success privileged a sort of "revisionist" and pragmatic attitude along with a strong optimistic feeling of "progress." Both pragmatism and optimistic belief in progress boosted a policy of evolutionary improvement. "We, the old generation," remarked Friedrich Ebert in 1922, "do not become impatient if progress is not as fast as we hoped for."[13]

This concept of a "rational" and evolutionary policy was rooted in a biographical and psychological disposition. Members of this generation had established themselves socially and professionally long before 1914. Their beliefs were already consolidated when the First World War began turning the world upside down. In terms of firm convictions and material conditions, they were much more independent than their younger compatriots and could therefore much more easily deal with the shocks of war and revolution.[14]

In West Germany, France, and Italy, almost all leading politicians of the first post-war years had been born before 1900. This was true for Konrad Adenauer, Kurt Schumacher, Theodor Heuss, Léon Blum, Vincent Auriol, Robert Schuman, Henri Queuille, Luigi Einaudi, Attilio Piccioni, Enrico De Nicola and, of course, Alcide de Gasperi. Almost all of them were politically active before the advent of war and dictatorship. And after having spent many years in political isolation or even under arrest, this generation got their second chance. It profited from the window of opportunity and—in the German case—from the favour of the Allies.

With this generation taking the lead, post-war political culture became dominated by a tinge of nineteenth-century traditions.[15] Even in those countries, where the crisis of democracy had been deepest—in Germany, Italy and France—convinced democrats had also been at work. And liberals, social and Christian democrats had succeeded in conserving their political traditions in the teeth of totalitarian rule and throughout the horrors of war and dictatorship. The result was a sort of second "recasting bourgeois Europe," to borrow a term Charles Maier applied to the first post-war period from 1919 to 1925.[16]

In France and Italy, this recasting bourgeois Europe initially took the form of "tripartism" and included the communist party. This political alliance between communists, socialists and Christian democrats was sealed under the sign of resistance experience. Heterogeneous and short-lived, it may be seen as a typical consensus transition from a period of dictatorship, occupation and repression to a period of new democratic stability. At the same time, it highlighted an important difference between the political cultures of France and Italy on one hand and West Germany on the other: This difference concerned the role of communism.

Flushed with its victories in the combats of the Résistance and in the Resistenza, communism emerged as a major force in Western European politics. Resistance prestige was one reason for its new importance; another was its control of organized labour, which it had—to a large extent—wrested from the more moderate, socialist-oriented trade-union leaders during the war years. Finally, the economic hardships of the years 1943–1946 encouraged the spread of communist influence. However, poverty alone was never the chief reason for the appeal of communism. It depended rather on its mystique, its power to inspire devotion and sacrifice among its adherents. This was especially true of intellectuals and of young people. And these were two groups who generally knew communism only in the moderate and patriotic guise it had assumed during the war years. Therefore, in the immediate post-war years, communists could achieve excellent results at the polls. In the first general election in France held in October 1945, they emerged on the top with more than a quarter of the votes.[17]

In Germany, the situation was different and unique: Here, convinced communists had an option to go to the Soviet zone and to work there for their personal utopia. In West Germany, however, the remaining communists were banned from the old/new political élites. At the beginning, harbouring new illusions as to the coming revolution, West German communists met very soon with the well-known cycle of disappointment and exclusion, political erosion and social marginalization. But, contrary to the interwar period, the expanding economy offered new options of social integration to disillusioned communists. As a precondition, they of

TOWARD A NEW POLITICAL CULTURE? TOTALITARIAN EXPERIENCE...   35

course had to give up their political aspirations. In the words of Till Kössler, revolutionary cadres *might* at least become citizens of the Federal Republic of Germany.[18]

After tripartism had broken up in 1947, the reconstruction of democracy became more and more linked to Christian democracy, which in itself was a strong innovation of party systems. In Italy, the Democrazia Cristiana was the heir of the Popular Party of the short democratic period of 1919–1922. In France, there had been forerunners in the 1920s and 1930s, but as a strong political force French Christian democracy was an almost new invention and more or less a completely new phenomenon after 1945. In Germany, the Christian Democratic Union was the first political party in German history that offered a common platform to political Catholicism *and* protestant conservatism.[19]

Christian democracy could appeal to the electorate through a very specific profile. That profile combined Christian values with the offer of reconciliation, which was so badly needed by societies traumatized and divided by the war. Although the Christian democrats were hostile to the idea of class struggle, they were far from having a purely capitalistic approach. Catholic social thought was deeply pledged to a harmonistic concept of society. Elements of that concept were social solidarity, the idea of a strong intervening state that would and could guarantee social security. At the same time, Christian democrats were strongly anti-communist, a necessary precondition to win confidence among the middle classes. At any rate, in France and Italy, many conservatives voted for Christian Democrats as the least objectionable of the mass formations considering that their own political parties had largely disappeared because of their sympathies for fascism.

The successful reconstruction after 1945 was largely due to the concurrence of political traditions, generational imprints and the military and political state exception that followed the American hegemony over Europe. But the fragility of this historic window of opportunity could be seen by the strong criticism expressed toward the new model of a multiparty parliamentary democracy in the making. This criticism articulated itself definitely in generational terms. Obviously, the new post-war politicians were the old ones. Therefore, in France, the old guard of the Third Republic did not succeed in convincing the French public of the adequacy of the Fourth Republic. In Germany, the attack of the "youth" against the "old" was sometimes worded in the well-known elements of anti-party and anti-parliamentarian sentiment. Journals like the *Frankfurter Hefte* or

Der Ruf denounced the tendency to fall back on concepts of a centralized mass democracy with its rule of parties: "Those parties resurrected from the bankrupt Weimar Republic, with their 'old men' who have been shipwrecked before are anachronistic."[20]

I added the above-mentioned quote because it shows us the strong political and mental tensions that were at work in the immediate post-war period. These tensions give us an idea of how uncertain the prospects of democracy were in 1945. It was not only a question of political parties and parliamentary functions that lay at the root of democratic stabilization. To strengthen its position in the long run, the new democratic order needed cultural "soft powers," and that brings me to my second point.

POST-HEROISM

I have stressed the fact that, after 1945, we can observe a definite farewell to the ideological bipolarity that had so deeply influenced the interwar period and was now overcome by the consensus of an older generation of politicians: These politicians had suffered themselves from the many forms of repression and violence coming from that ideological bipolarity that only knew friend and foe.

In one sense, however, the historical experience of the age of totalitarianism was present and at the same time rewritten. That is to say, from now on it was important to stand on the morally right side. Until the Second World War, a form of collective memory had dominated in Europe that may be called "historical monumentalism," to borrow Friedrich Nietzsche's famous phrase. In a monumentalistic conception of history, Nietzsche says that history "belongs above all to the man of deeds and power, to him who fights a great fight, who needs models, teachers, comforters".[21]

This mode of remembrance, aiming at heroes and feats, invoked the great men of the nineteenth century: Napoleon Bonaparte, Garibaldi, and Bismarck to name just a few. After having been so terribly perverted by fascism and Nazism and after the horrors of the Second World War, the heroic narrative lost its spell. Instead, Western Europe entered the phase of post-heroism according to the phrase coined by German political scientist Herfried Münkler.[22] In all three countries under consideration, the narrative of heroism came to an end. What was developing, instead, was a new narrative, the narrative of victimhood.

This was even true for Germany. In the immediate post-war era, most Germans could not help considering themselves as victims. And the narrative of their own national destiny as a history of victimization dominated the public discourse. The 8th of May—"this gloomy day of deepest humiliation," as the *Frankfurter Allgemeine Zeitung* commentated in 1955—primarily represented suffering and destruction, surrender and allied occupation.[23] Ten years after the war, West German politicians, journalists and historians continued to put the "sea of misery"[24] caused by the end of war into the centre of commemoration. Keywords continued to be "ruin" and "capitulation," "expulsion" and "chaos."[25] It was only by the late 1960s that the remembrance of *German* suffering started to fade and German *victims* and the Holocaust entered the collective memory.[26]

By claiming victimhood, peoples and individuals demonstrated moral purity. This was the most important aspect of the German conversion from a community of perpetrators to a community of victims. Only by considering themselves as victims could they conserve, as it were, a good conscience. Even more important was the question of victimhood for those societies that were torn apart between fascism, collaboration and resistance. The role of France during the war, for example, could be regarded in a threefold way: as collaborator, resister or victim.[27] It was only by the 1980s that France finally came to accept its first role as collaborator. During the immediate post-war period, however, the roles of *La France–Résistante* and *La France–Victime* were the only ones by which the moral dignity of the nation could be upheld and democracy restored. Thus, "la villemartyre" Oradour-sur-Glane, whose population had been massacred by the Germans in 1944, became a sort of representative victim for the whole nation.[28]

The situation was similar in Italy. After 1943, anti-fascist forces succeeded in forging a collective memory that remained dominant for a long time. They created the narrative of Italy having fallen victim to Mussolini's fascism and to Germany's Nazism. By putting the blame for the war exclusively on Mussolini, this narrative implied a re-dimensioning of Italian responsibility and a glorification of the Italian people in the struggle against Nazi Germany and its fascist allies.[29]

In moral terms, condemning war criminals and leaving the people alone was the easiest way out, and the story of victimization and self-victimization might be further explicated. But what is important here is the fact that continental Europe obviously needed a historical narrative that liberated its peoples from past guilt. This self-conception constructed a new perception of history in which the role of the victim was placed in the centre. I think it is fair to say that without such a switch to victimhood, the European post-war democracies could hardly have been built. Only the victim status promised legitimization and avoided any sort of moral responsibility. This construction of a new collective memory had, of course, little to do with historical reality. But it was a necessary cultural element for stabilizing the new democracies. To quote Alon Confino, "Remembering is not about getting the past right; it is often about getting it wrong, thus making the present bearable." It was in this sense that victimhood even became a "pillar of national identity" (Alon Confino).[30]

Mass Culture

In addition to the construction of this new interpretive pattern, which, by invoking collective suffering and victimhood, promised the survivors of dictatorship social belonging and moral self-esteem, economic development paved the way for stabilization. After the economic boom of the 1950s and 1960s, a new kind of society developed in Western Europe that was marked by higher standards of living, more leisure time, a return to privacy and new forms of mass culture. This brings me to my third point dealing with the question of how much modern mass culture contributed to the stabilization of a new post-war democratic order. I tend to see in these developments an important, maybe even the most important, element of democratic life after 1945. Thus, let me make a few remarks on that.

It seems clear that the use of time in modern mass culture tends to depoliticize the people. The individual suffers a lack of time to devote to political matters, to trade-union organization, or to charitable work, and so on. The surplus of time becomes a factor of demand on the market of mass culture. However, at the same time it is converted into a lack of time that would be needed for civic and political activities. If the impact of leisure becomes stronger, less time can be spared for political and civic participation.[31]

An important key term, in this respect, was "paid vacation." Already in the 1930s, the first regulations of paid vacation were introduced. In France, for example, the government of the popular front, which came into power in 1936, faced a strong strike movement in the summer of that year. It finally granted 1 week paid vacation to the workers, which had a tremendous impact. For the first time in history, many thousands of families, mainly from the Paris region, headed to the south of France to spend a short vacation on the Mediterranean coast.[32]

In Germany, the Nazi propaganda used the longing of the masses for vacation to establish the so-called *Kraft durch Freude* ("Strength Through Joy") organization, providing for many thousands to have vacations, for the first time in their lives, in the Black Forest, at the North or Baltic Sea, even in Italy.[33]

At their epoch, these events had an important symbolic and propagandistic value. However, in general it was only a sort of forerunner of those vacation habits that were to come after the War. In 1956, all Frenchmen gained a third week of paid vacation, and in the early 1960s, some companies even granted a fourth week. At that time, the French enjoyed the longest annual vacation period in all of Europe. In West Germany, most federal constitutions postulated the wage-earner's right to paid vacations. Some constitutions even decreed a minimum of paid days off, normally about 12 working days. Finally, in 1963, a federal vacation law was passed. Therefore, in practice there was a strong tendency toward European convergence in vacation regulations and habits. In the 1960s, about one third of the population would take holidays.[34]

In addition, they would do so increasingly in their own car. The possession of a car equalled an extremely meaningful symbol: It was a symbol of having gained time and achieved individual mobility and even freedom. Cars became probably the most important element of the mass culture of the 1950s and 1960s. To possess a car promised the enlargement of the limits of space and time and allowed for a more individualized lifestyle. Moreover, it was a strong symbol for the "American" way of life, which was so much admired by many Europeans.[35]

A second keyword of the modern mass culture concerns the media. Historically, there had been a first breakthrough of modern mass media, which took place at the end of the nineteenth century. With literacy levels coming close to the total of the population in the developed countries, there was a great boom of magazines, series, popular novels, illustrated papers and so on. After the Second World War, there was a further push of mass media, which at the same time changed the structure of the media more or less completely. That was the beginning of the era of audio-visual media, which in fact caused a sort of disjunction between media consumption and literacy.[36]

It was only by the end of the 1950s that radio and increasingly TV became mass media in the strict sense of the word. The basic developments were about the same in all Western European countries, even if one had to consider some differences. Television profoundly changed the

40 A. WIRSCHING

structure of the media and of mass culture. Image and tone—and with them the "cult of distraction," about which the German writer Siegfried Kracauer had already complained in the 1920s—now arrived in the private living room. Within a very short period, television became a form of mass media for the whole population. In the face of the TV program, social and economic inequality ceased to play a role. The farmer, the white-collar worker or the business manager all watched the same program.[37]

That was, of course, a new form of cultural levelling that was strongly criticized by many European intellectuals. They considered the new tendencies as the evil sign of Americanization.[38] Even if the phenomenon of cultural Americanization and the discussion of it were well known before 1945, there is no doubt that European societies underwent a particularly strong cultural transformation after the war. In France, for example, some observers spoke of a new French Revolution: a cultural revolution that catapulted the country from its socio-economic and cultural backwardness into modernity.[39] Thus, while General Charles de Gaulle challenged American predominance in Europe politically, the American way of life and the American style of consumerism were shaping the French landscape.

It is no coincidence either that de Gaulle strongly criticized the development that put in danger, as he thought, the "individualistic way of life that many generations of Frenchmen had followed as farmers, craftsmen, merchants and rentiers." Now that individualistic way of life was being replaced by a new form of uniformism: Commerce, de Gaulle wrote in his memoirs,

> was carried out in identical supermarkets, with rows of shelves and imperious advertising. Everyone's house now resembled a cell in some nondescript block. Grey anonymous crowds travelled in public transportation. Even leisure now was collective and regimented: meals efficiently served in canteens; cheers in unison from the grandstands of sports stadia; holidays spent in crowded sites among tourists, campers, and bathers laid out in rows; day or evening relaxation at fixed hours for families in identical apartments, where before bedtime everyone simultaneously watched and heard the same broadcasts on the same wavelengths.[40]

Although many people, especially among the young generation, indulged in the new possibilities and experiences of leisure and consumption, criticism of American-style consumerism came from all intellectual camps. In contrast, in face of the dynamics of social and cultural change, it became more and more difficult, if not impossible, to resist the new society. Accordingly, a sort of tacit acceptance began to be seen among European intellectuals who had, by the 1970s come to the forefront. To quote another French voice, which is quite typical of that attitude, Jean Marie Domenach, the editor of the influential magazine *Esprit*, wrote in 1960: "Ten years before, we were still able to look down upon the snack-bars, the supermarkets, the strip-teases, and the whole acquisitive society. By now, all this has more or less established itself in Europe. This society is not ours but it may be the society of our children."[41]

CONCLUSION

Coming to the end, I would like to stress that democratic reconstruction after 1945 implied much more than condemnation of war criminals, constitutional change, and the revival of parliament and parties. These elements, together with the reinstatement of the rule of law were, it is true, the indispensable political and legal preconditions for any form of democratic perspective. However, what was also needed was a political culture that gave a firm ground to the political and constitutional changes. In this context, a new conception was crucial for how history was to be interpreted after the anguish caused by dictatorship and after the horrors of war and civil war; what was needed was a new idea of what role Europeans might play in their shattered continent ruined by history. The idea that most European people were, in fact, not heroes anymore but victims of war and dictatorship contributed to forming a long-lasting narrative that helped to mentally overcome the past and gave a meaning to the present.

Finally, the expansion of the economy and the development of a consumer society must not be underestimated. In fact, every political regime in the twentieth century—democracies and dictatorships alike—sought legitimization through consumption and economic well-being. After 1945, it was the first time in history that this legitimization was achieved in large parts of Europe. Even if it may sound trivial, this helped West Europeans to accept democracy in their everyday lives: to accept democracy as social practice, as a lifestyle – nearly in the same sense that Tocqueville had described American democracy more than a century ago.[42]

42   A. WIRSCHING

Notes

1. Raphael, Lutz. *Imperiale Gewalt und mobilisierte Nation. Europa 1914–1945.* Munich: C.H. Beck, 2011; Payne, Stanley G. *A History of Fascism 1914–1945.* Madison, WI: University of Wisconsin Press, 1995.
2. Wirsching, Andreas. *Vom Weltkrieg zum Bürgerkrieg? Politischer Extremismus in Deutschland und Frankreich 1918–1933/39. Berlin und Paris im Vergleich.* Munich: De Gruyter Oldenbourg, 1999.
3. Jackson, Julian. *France. The dark years, 1940–1944.* Oxford: Oxford University Press, 2001.
4. Sassoon, Donald. "Politics." In Fulbrook, Mary, ed. *Europe since 1945.* Oxford: Oxford University Press, 2000, 14–52, at 18.
5. Cf. ibid., 19; Focardi, Filippo. "Reshaping the Past. Collective Memory and the Second World War in Italy, 1945–55." In Geppert, Dominik, ed. *The postwar challenge. Cultural, Social, and Political Change in Western Europe, 1945–58.* Oxford: Oxford University Press, 2003, 41–63, at 49 f.
6. Cf. Wirsching, *Weltkrieg.*
7. "Deux pouvoirs en exercice, l'un dans la steppe, l'autre au pays latin, sont la négation totale, intellectuelle et pratique, de toutes les valeurs démocratiques: mais Lénine est. dictateur de la barbarie, tandis que Mussolini est. dictateur de la civilisation." Valois, George. "Les Commentaires de Clovis." In id., ed. *L'homme qui vient. Philosophie de l'autorité, 2nde edition.* Paris: Nouvelle Librairie Nationale, 1923, 9.
8. Jones, Larry Eugene. *German liberalism and the dissolution of the Weimar party system (1918–1933).* Chapel Hill: University of North Carolina Press, 1988.
9. As a case study Herbert, Ulrich. *Best. Biographische Studien über Radikalismus, Weltanschauung und Vernunft 1903–1989.* Bonn: Dietz, 1996; Wildt, Michael. *Generation des Unbedingten. Das Führungskorps des Reichssicherheitshauptamtes.* Hamburg: Hamburger Edition, 2002, esp. 46–52; Kurzlechner, Werner. "Die Gestapo-Elite als Generationseinheit. Eine biographische Analyse der politischen Sozialisation Himmlers, Heydrichs und Bests." In Schulz, Andreas/Grebner, Gundula, eds. *Generationswechsel und historischer Wandel.* Munich: De Gruyter, 2003, 121–147.
10. Epstein, Catherine. *The last revolutionaries. German communists and their century.* Cambridge, MA: Harvard University Press, 2003.
11. See Frei, Norbert. *Vergangenheitspolitik. Die Anfänge der Bundesrepublik und die NS-Vergangenheit.* Munich: C.H. Beck, 2012; Herbert, Ulrich. "NS-Eliten in der Bundesrepublik." In Loth, Wilfried/Rusinek, Bernd-A., eds. *Verwandlungspolitik. NS-Eliten in der westdeutschen Nachkriegsgesellschaft.* Frankfurt a.M./New York: Campus, 1998, 93–115; Wirsching, Andreas. "Politische Generationen, Konsumgesellschaft, Sozialpolitik. Zur Erfahrung von Demokratie und Diktatur in

TOWARD A NEW POLITICAL CULTURE? TOTALITARIAN EXPERIENCE... 43

Zwischenkriegszeit und Nachkriegszeit." In Doering-Manteuffel, Anselm, ed. *Strukturmerkmale der deutschen Geschichte des 20. Jahrhunderts.* Munich: De Gruyter, 2006, 43–64, at 47.

12. See Schulz, Andreas/Grebner, Gundula, eds. *Generationswechsel und historischer Wandel (Beihefte der HZ 36).* Munich: De Gruyter, 2003; esp. the editors' introduction, 1–23; Reulecke, Jürgen, ed. *Generationalität und Lebensgeschichte im 20. Jahrhundert.* Munich: De Gruyter Oldenbourg, 2003; Jureit, Ulrike/Wildt, Michael, eds. *Generationen. Zur Relevanz eines wissenschaftlichen Grundbegriffs.* Hamburg: Hamburger Edition, 2005.

13. Quoted in Braun, Bernd. "Die „Generation Ebert"." In Schönhoven, Klaus/Braun, Bernd, eds. *Generationen in der Arbeiterbewegung.* Munich: Oldenbourg, 2005, 69–86, at 77.

14. See, for example, Friedrich Meinecke's development in: Meineke, Stefan. *Friedrich Meinecke. Persönlichkeit und politisches Denken bis zum Ende des Ersten Weltkrieges.* Berlin/New York: De Gruyter, 1995, 308.

15. As a case study Wirsching, Andreas. "Demokratie als „Lebensform." Theodor Heuss (1884–1963)." In Hein, Bastian/Kittel, Manfred/Möller, Horst, eds. *Gesichter der Demokratie. Porträts zur deutschen Zeitgeschichte.* Munich: Oldenbourg, 2012, 21–35.

16. Maier, Charles. *Recasting bourgeois Europe. Stabilization in France, Germany and Italy in the decade after World War I.* Princeton: Princeton University Press, 1975.

17. Cf. Becker, Jean-Jacques. *Histoire politique de la France depuis 1945.* Paris: Armand Colin, 1989, 16; Lagrou, Pieter. "Beyond Memory and Commemoration. Coming to Terms with War and Occupation in France after 1945." In Geppert, Dominik, ed. *The postwar challenge. Cultural, Social, and Political Change in Western Europe, 1945–1958.* Oxford: Oxford University Press, 2004, 65–91, at 76–78; Focardi, *Reshaping the Past,* 50–56.

18. Kössler, Till. *Abschied von der Revolution. Kommunisten und Gesellschaft in Westdeutschland, 1945–1968.* Düsseldorf: Droste, 2004.

19. Cf. Focardi, *Reshaping the Past,* 55–61; Masala, Carlo. "Die Democrazia Christiana 1943–1963. Zur Entwicklung des partito nazionale." In Gehler, Michael/Kaiser, Wolfram/Wohnout, Helmut, eds. *Christdemokratie in Europa im 20. Jahrhundert/Christian Democracy in 20th Century Europe/ La Démocratie Chrétienne en Europe au XXe Siècle.* Vienna/Cologne/ Weimar: Böhlau, 2001, 348–369; Béthouart, Bruno. "Le Mouvement Républicain Populaire. L'entrée des catholiques dans la République française." In ibid., 313–331. For the Christian Democratic Party see Lappenküper, Ulrich. "Zwischen „Sammlungsbewegung" und „Volkspartei." Die CDU 1945–1969." In ibid., 385–398, at 385–388;

44   A. WIRSCHING

Bösch, Frank. *Die Adenauer-CDU. Gründung, Aufstieg und Krise einer Erfolgspartei 1945–1969.* Stuttgart/Munich: DVA, 2001.
20. Böttcher, Karl Wilhelm. "Die junge Generation und die Parteien." *Frankfurter Hefte* 3 (1948), 756–761, at 757: "Die aus der Konkursmasse von Weimar wiederauferstandenen Parteien mit ihren ,alten Männern', die schon einmal Schiffbruch erlitten haben, sind ein Anachronismus."
21. Cf. Nietzsche, Friedrich. *Untimely Meditations.* Cambridge: Cambridge University Press, 1997, (Orig. *Unzeitgemäße Betrachtungen. Vom Nutzen und Nachtheil der Geschichte.* Leipzig, 1874.), 67; see Schilling, Rene. *Kriegshelden. Deutungsmuster heroischer Männlichkeit in Deutschland 1813–1945.* Paderborn: Schöningh, 2002; Naumann, Michael. *Der Strukturwandel des Heroismus. Vom sakralen zum revolutionären Heldentum.* Königstein/Ts.: Athenäum, 1984.
22. Münkler, Herfried. "Heroische und Postheroische Gesellschaften." *Merkur. Deutsche Zeitschrift für europäisches Denken* 61 (2007), 742–752.
23. Dombrowski, Erich. "8. Mai 1945." *Frankfurter Allgemeine Zeitung,* 07.05.1955.
24. Friedmann, Werner. "Reifeprüfung im Mai." *Süddeutsche Zeitung,* 07./08.05.1955.
25. Freund, Michael. "Die Wochen, die ein Jahrtausend zerstörten." *Die Zeit,* 05.08.1955.
26. Cf. Wirsching, Andreas. "8. Mai und 27. Januar 1945. Zwei Tage der Befreiung?" In Conze, Eckart/Nicklas, Thomas, eds. *Tage deutscher Geschichte. Von der Reformation bis zur Wiedervereinigung.* Munich: DVA, 2004, 239–255; Hurrelbrink, Peter. *Der 8. Mai 1945. Befreiung durch Erinnerung. Ein Gedenktag und seine Bedeutung für das politisch-kulturelle Selbstverständnis in Deutschland.* Bonn: Dietz, 2005; Margalit, Gilad. *Guilt, suffering, and memory. Germany remembers its dead of World War II.* Bloomington: Indiana University Press, 2010.
27. Cf. Lagrou, *Beyond Memory and Commemoration*; Meyer, Henning. *Le changement de la « culture de mémoire » française par rapport à la Deuxième Guerre mondiale à partir de trois « lieux de mémoire »: Bordeaux, Caen et Oradour-sur-Glane.* (Augsburg: 2006).
28. Ibid.
29. Focardi, *Reshaping the Past*, 41.
30. Quoted in Williard, David. *Adopting victimhood. Heroism cannot define European post-World War II memory. Confino gives Tyler lecture (2005).* In web.wm.edu/news/archive/index.php?id=4397 (25.05.2013); see also Confino, Alon. *The work of memory. New directions in the study of German society and culture.* Urbana: University of Illinois Press, 2002; Confino, Alon. *Histories and memories of twentieth-century Germany.* Bloomington: Indiana University Press, 2005.

TOWARD A NEW POLITICAL CULTURE? TOTALITARIAN EXPERIENCE... 45

31. Cf. with further details Wirsching, Andreas. "Massenkultur in der Demokratie. Zur Entwicklung von Kultur und Gesellschaft in der Bundesrepublik und Frankreich nach 1945." In Miard-Delacroix, Hélène/ Hudemann, Rainer, eds. *Wandel und Integration. Deutsch-französische Annäherungen der fünfziger Jahre.* Munich: Oldenbourg, 2005, 379–396; Maase, Kaspar. *Grenzenloses Vergnügen. Der Aufstieg der Massenkultur 1850–1979.* Frankfurt a.M.: Fischer, 1997.
32. Cf. Seidman, Michael. *Workers against Work. Labor in Paris and Barcelona during the Popular Fronts.* Berkeley, CA: University of California Press, 1991, 271–280.
33. See Weiß, Hermann. "Ideologie der Freizeit im Dritten Reich. Die NS-Gemeinschaft „Kraft durch Freude"." *Archiv für Sozialgeschichte* 33 (1993), 289–303.
34. Cf. Boyer, Marc. *Histoire du tourisme de masse.* Paris: Presses universitaires de France, 1999, 79; Rauch, André. *Vacances en France. De 1830 à nos jours, 2nde edition.* Paris: Fayard, 2001, 97–131; Schildt, Axel. *Moderne Zeiten. Freizeit, Massenmedien und „Zeitgeist" in der Bundesrepublik der 50er Jahre.* Hamburg: Christians, 1995, 180–208.
35. Schildt, *Moderne Zeiten,* 194; Hütter, Hans Walter/Rösgen, Petra, eds. *Endlich Urlaub! Die Deutschen reisen. Begleitbuch zur Ausstellung im Haus der Geschichte der Bundesrepublik Deutschland.* Cologne: Dumont, 1996, 54–58; Rauch, *Vacances en France,* 154.
36. Cf. Zeldin, Theodore. *France 1848–1945. Intellect and Pride,* Oxford: Oxford University Press, 1950, 144, 203 f.; Delporte, Christian. "Au miroir des médias." In Rioux, Jean-Pierre/Sirinelli, Jean-François, eds. *La culture de masse en France de la Belle Époque à aujourd'hui.* Paris: Fayard, 2002, 305–351; Schildt, Axel. "Der Beginn des Fernsehzeitalters. Ein neues Massenmedium setzt sich durch." In id./Sywottek, Arnold, eds. *Modernisierung im Wiederaufbau. Die westdeutsche Gesellschaft der 50er Jahre.* Bonn: Dietz, 1993, 477–492.
37. Cf. Kracauer, Siegfried. *Das Ornament der Masse.* Frankfurt a.M.: Suhrkamp, 1963, at 311.
38. Cf. Wirsching, *Massenkultur,* 395 f.; Roger, Philippe. *Rêves et cauchemars américains. Les États-Unis au miroir de l'opinion publique française (1945– 1953).* Arras: Presses Universitaires du Septentrion, 1996.
39. Ardagh, John. *The new French Revolution.* New York: Harper & Row, 1969; see also Kuisel, Richard. *Seducing the French. The dilemma of Americanization.* Berkeley: University of California Press, 1993.
40. Quoted in Kuisel, *Seducing,* 146.
41. Domenach, Jean-Marie. "Le modèle américain." *Esprit* 28 (1960), 1219– 1232, at 1221.
42. Cf. Wirsching, *Demokratie als Lebensform.*

PART II

Intellectuals, Science and Democracy

CHAPTER 3

The Original 45ers: A European "Generation of Resistance"?

Dominik Rigoll

When the American troops pushed their way onto German soil in the final months of the Second World War, the occupying officers depended not only on an "Arrest Categories Handbook" to help them identify and detain individuals who were considered potentially dangerous. Some also carried with them a "White List of Persons in Germany Believed to be Anti-Nazi or Non-Nazi," which in December 1944 comprised some 1500 people. Among them were former politicians such as Konrad Adenauer but also civil servants, journalists, and members of all sectors of state and society.[1] By means of targeted recruiting, which could also could favour returned emigrants and "exonerated persons" willing to participate in the reconstruction, the Western Allies wanted to ensure that the approximately 55,000 civil servants subject to an employment ban were replaced by "persons who, by their political and moral qualities, are deemed capable of assisting in developing genuine democratic institutions in Germany", as foreseen by the Potsdam Agreement from 2 August 1945.[2] In the early phase of denazification, the replacement of the "totalitarian elite" by a much smaller "potential counter-elite" representing its "political

D. Rigoll (✉)
Zentrum für Zeithistorische Forschung, Potsdam, Germany

© The Author(s) 2018 49
J. Späth (ed.), *Does Generation Matter? Progressive Democratic Cultures in Western Europe, 1945–1960*, Palgrave Studies in the History of Social Movements, https://doi.org/10.1007/978-3-319-77422-0_3

antithesis"[3] seemed possible because Germans were only allowed to occupy key positions at local and regional levels.

When the beginning of the Cold War in 1947 made the division of Germany into a communist and a non-communist zone increasingly more likely, all the followers and even many offenders were allowed to return to their previous positions under the condition that they distance themselves from National Socialism and keep away from neo-Nazi groups. Especially in the Federal Republic of Germany, founded in 1949, the return of the old elite was so broad that many of those who had been recruited during the denazification period felt politically (re-)marginalized and even endangered by a "re-Nazification" of state and society. At the same time, they started to call themselves the "45ers." Now and again, the research quotes from journalist and Buchenwald survivor Eugen Kogon. In 1954, he lamented in the *Frankfurter Hefte* that outsiders recruited after the war had long been pushed out by offenders and followers who had been reinstated or promoted after the enactment of the so-called "131er law" in 1951: "All too many of the 131ers have already roundly defeated all too many of the 45ers."[4] Indeed, in the second half of the 1950s, when the Federal Army recruited many of the 150,000 soldiers fired in 1945, the de--Nazification of the state was almost completely reversed.

The moniker "45er" or "1945er," however, was not simply a self-designation; it was also used by the opponents. The right-extremist theologian Herbert Grabert, for instance, who continued to be denied a position at a West-German university despite the 131er law, still railed in the mid-1960s against the "45ers" and their program of political renewal.[5] When he was imprisoned by the British in 1953 as a result of the so-called Gauleiter Conspiracy, Joseph Goebbels' former aide Werner Naumann was reminded of practices "from the 45er years"[6] and thus from the time of denazification and reconstruction. In 1961, the journalist Hermann Behr still characterized the "men who started for us" as the "so-called '45ers'."[7] This series of references can be easily extended.

In historiography, the terminology did not catch on. Lutz Niethammer represents an exception. He expressed in 1973 the still-valid desideratum that the research should undertake a "quantitative analysis of names, positions, ancestral traits" of the "45ers."[8] Even though two volumes with (auto-)biographical portraits of some of the protagonists of the early reconstruction period were published by journalists in 1979 and 1981, the designation "45er" does not appear in either of these books.

THE ORIGINAL 45ERS: A EUROPEAN "GENERATION OF RESISTANCE"? 51

As at least some German readers might already know, however, the theatre critic Joachim Kaiser coined the term in a completely different way in 1989. In a volume of essays edited by historian Martin Broszat, Kaiser associates the "45ers" with an entire age group, which was also his own: the so-called Hitler Youth generation. As representative members of the "45er generation," Kaiser—who in 1945 had been a 16-year-old *Hitlerjunge* himself—singled out Günter Grass and Jürgen Habermas. Both men claim that the year 1945 was a watershed for them, even though neither became politically active until the 1950s.[9]

Although the "old" 45er concept certainly continued to appear from time to time,[10] the "Kaiser 45ers" have since then completely supplanted the "Kogon 45ers." As a rule, specialist research and newspapers alike followed historian Dirk Moses, who adopted the terminology recommended by Kaiser at the end of the 1990s and at the same time stressed the significance of the followers and wartime children born between 1918 and 1934 to the West-German liberalization processes.[11]

In France, however, many more people than in Germany could claim in 1944–1945 that they represented a "counter-elite" that was opposed to those who had collaborated with the Nazis during the war. This might help explain why historians started to analyse the post-war careers of what Olivier Wieviorka calls the "génération de la Résistance. In 1989, Wieviorka asserted in a much-quoted article that the German occupation contributed for many French to a kind of political "new beginning" in illegality and thus to the genesis of a generation. Although the 'generation of resistance,' unlike the front generation of the First World War, recruited from among all age groups, its "generational consciousness" was above all directed against that "parental generation" that had not been able to protect the nation in 1940. Considerably more important than age for generational formation, however, was the way the "debacle" of 1940 was interpreted and what specific actions followed from it: Whoever risked taking a step in the direction of illegal engagement distinguished himself in a fundamental way from the rest of the population. After the war, the resistance experience not only culminated in a "resistance discourse" of "national unity" that stood out from both Vichy as well as the Third Republic; a "resistance practice" was also established that was particularly opposed to classical party politics (unless one once belonged to the clandestine structures of the PCF or the SFIO).[12] This aversion not only resulted in a pronounced engagement in nonpartisan organizations with

52   D. RIGOLL

the aim of affecting fundamental social transformation; it is also possible to notice a specific voting behaviour beyond the left–right axis that extended into the 1980s. Still, the former resistance fighters rarely vociferously presented themselves as the representatives of a "generation." Instead, public discourse about the resistance and its political legacy was either influenced by the communists or the Gaullists.

Whereas in France the impact and the role of former resistance fighters in the political life of the 1940s and 1950s has been explored since the publication of Wieviorka's article,[13] German case studies so far have largely concentrated on the contribution of former emigrants or anti-fascists to memory politics and other forms of *Vergangenheitsbewältigung*. The author of this chapter recently made a first attempt to employ the original usage of the 45ers concept as an analytical tool to better understand the development of the German political scene, especially between 1945 and 1980 but also in the 1980s and 1990s. As in France, even though public discourse is dominated by political parties open to both former fascists and anti-fascists, it is often possible to identify "45er discourses" between the lines and "45er practices" inside of the parties themselves or in the state institutions.[14]

In this chapter, the focus will not be on the political actions of the "Kogon 45ers" but rather on the question of their self-understanding as a "strategic group" in West German post-war politics and even as an integral part of a European "generation of anti-Nazis" that defined itself less in terms of the birth years of its members than according to the role that they played in the "European civil war" and in the democratic beginning after 1944–1945. Emphasis will be placed on how the first "original" 45ers perceived and conceived themselves in hindsight as members of a distinct political group beyond considerations of ideology, age or even national origin. The chapter therefore does not treat any one "generation in itself" that still requires investigation but rather much more a "generation for itself" resulting from the communicative construction of generationality.[15] Viewed from this perspective, the 45ers can be interpreted as a "generational unit" that defined itself in political opposition to the members of the "generational unit" that had, in one way or another, supported Nazi politics in Germany or Europe.[16]

Because the conceptual history of the original terms "45ers" is still in its nascence, I will only concentrate on two books published in 1961 and 1979. In both books, "Kogon 45ers" ruminate on the post-war years, on the political hopes connected with the liberation of Europe from Nazism and on how many of them remained unfulfilled. First, I will discuss *Die zornigen alten Männer. Gedanken über Deutschland seit 1945*, a collection of essays published in 1979 by the former communist and *Weltbühne* journalist Axel Eggebrecht. Second, I will take a closer look at the work of one of the "old men": Jean Améry. Améry is especially interesting because he not only writes as a Vienna-born Jew who was an incisive observer of Western Germany until his suicide in 1979. He was also an intellectual who remained in his Belgian exile after the war and aligned himself politically with the French model.

Ten West-German Perspectives on the Years After 1945

In his book, *The Indignant Old Men,* journalist Axel Eggebrecht collects the "thoughts about Germany since 1945" from Eugen Kogon, Wolfgang Abendroth, Wolf Graf von Baudissin, Ossip K. Flechtheim, Walter Fabian, Heinrich Böll, Fritz Sänger, Heinrich Albertz, Bernt Engelmann and Jean Améry.[17] Although the 45er concept does not come up in any of the essays and interviews, the volume should nevertheless be understood as a kind of last gasp of the 45ers consistent with Kogon's sense. The preface remarks that the "feeling of rebellious solidarity" among the contributors is not only attributable to the "shared experience" of Nazi resistance and the new beginning but also to the "ever new bitter experiences" up to the present. The book, in fact, appeared in a context because the 45ers in Kaiser's sense had already provided the most avidly adopted "keywords for the intellectual situation of the times", as the title of a 1979 edited volume—which is also frequently consulted by historians—by Jürgen Habermas put it. Yet on the liberal conservative side of the political spectrum, *Flakhelfer* (anti–aircraft warfare helpers)—such as Hermann Lübbe, who we now know had joined the NSDAP in 1944 as a teenager—also set the tone.[18] What political objectives link *The Indignant Old Men* to the year 1945? Do they understand themselves as having been a "counter elite" to the "totalitarian elite" or even a "new generation of democratic politicians"? How do they assess their role in the development of West-German democracy in the early post-war years and later?

Who were "the indignant old men"? Ossip K. Flechtheim, Wolfgang Abendroth and Eugene Kogon worked as political analysts after the war; Axel Eggebrecht, Walter Fabian, Fritz Sänger, Bernt Engelmann and Jean Améry were journalists. Wolf Graf Baudissin, who contributed an interview to the volume, was imprisoned by the British as a high-ranking German officer and was among the few democratic reformers of the German military after the war before being reassigned in 1961 from the Bonn Defence Ministry to the NATO headquarters in France. Heinrich Albertz was a politician in the SPD and occupied for a brief period the office of mayor of Berlin in 1966–1967 before falling out of favour with his own party. The only real famous individual was the writer Heinrich Böll, who had been awarded the Nobel Prize in 1972 and, like Baudissin, was only interviewed.

Eleven biographical sketches, the contents of which presumably came from the authors themselves, provided information about their lives in an appendix to the volume.[19] Améry (born 1912) wrote as an emigrant, Auschwitz survivor and member of the Belgian resistance. Abendroth (born 1906) wrote as a representative of the radical-left resistance group *Neu Beginnen* (New Beginning) but also as a Gestapo prisoner and veteran of the notorious penal division 999, where he had fought for 2 years before joining the partisans in Greece shortly before the country's liberation. Kogon (born 1903) wrote as a survivor of the Buchenwald concentration camp, where—after several imprisonments by the Gestapo in the preceding years—he was interned between 1939 and 1945. The fact that he was affiliated with the anti-democratic right as a young man is not mentioned in his sketch, just as he appears to have spoken very little in general about his early political activity. Flechtheim (born 1909), who came from a Jewish family, was also a member of the *Neu Beginnen*; after imprisonment, he went into exile in the United States where he worked on Franz Neumann's *Behemoth* before returning as a lieutenant colonel with the American army. Fabian (born 1902) took flight from the Nazis as a socialist to France and to Switzerland, returning to Germany from the latter country not until 1957. He was the only one of the contributors who emphasized the fact that while he experienced "relief" in 1945, he was also filled with "profound scepticism from the first hour.".[20] Sänger's (born 1901) contribution was from the perspective of a social-democrat journalist who had been under a professional ban for several years during the Third Reich before finding employment as a correspondent in Berlin, among other places, at the *Neues Wiener Tagblatt* and being hired by the resistance to head the national wire service in the period immediately after Hitler's defeat. Albertz (born 1915) had been detained numerous times as a member of the Confessing Church. Finally, Engelmann (born 1921) wrote as a survivor of the concentration camps Dachau and Flossenbürg

THE ORIGINAL 45ERS: A EUROPEAN "GENERATION OF RESISTANCE"? 55

where he had been detained because of his resistance activities in 1942 and 1944. Before this, during the time between his *Abitur* in 1938 and when he was injured in 1942, he had been a member of the German army.

At 58, Engelmann—who is now known to have been an ardent unofficial Stasi collaborator[21] in the 1980s—was the youngest contributor. Although given his birth year of 1921 he could have been counted among the "Kaiser 45ers"; his anti-fascist engagement and his detention in a concentration camp as a young man clearly distinguished him from most of his peers. At first glance, the contributors only appear to have their age in common. Far more relevant, however, was their indignation about the fact that West Germany so little resembled the Germany toward which they had worked after the end of the war. In addition,, there was the bitter disappointment over politicians such as Konrad Adenauer. Against the background of the Cold War and the renazification of personnel, the latter supposedly stripped the CDU (the founding of which still involved Kogon) of its early reform program—not only with respect to the permanent disarmament and denazification of the country but also with regard to the democratization of political processes and the nationalization of the economy.

This interpretation is supported by the interviews that were included in the volume from Baudissin (born 1907) and Böll (born 1917), who neither participated in any kind of resistance activity nor experienced persecution. In his interview, Böll even admitted that he at first naïvely left 'the democracy between 1945 and 1948–1949' "in the hands of the Allies.".[22] The fact that Eggebrecht would have liked to add a contribution of the author and poet Luise Rinser, whose attitude toward National Socialism was likewise contradictory, can also be interpreted along these lines. In all three cases, the editor appears to not only find their potential exoneration with respect to the questionnaire significant but also, and perhaps most importantly, their consistent advocacy before the republic's founding of a relatively radical denazification and democratization in the spirit of the new-beginning framework.

Eggebrecht himself emphasized in a radio interview that the publisher was against Rinser because he wanted to stay true to the title on which the NDR radio program was based: They were "indignant old men," not indignant "people" or "citizens."[23] In fact, the first 45ers included a number of women, many of whom were later pushed out again as "Yankee floozies" (*Amischicksen*).[24] The White List also mentioned key female political figures such as Helene Wessel and Christine Teusch, and among

56   D. RIGOLL

Hermann Behr's "men who started for us" were also counted female Social Democrats such as Annemarie Renger and Louise Schröder.[25] The political pressure to conform that weighed on these women was no doubt even greater than among the men.

Whereas Rinser and Böll were engaged in West Germany's development as journalists and writers, Baudissin's democratic engagement, unlike many of his comrades, first consisted in coming to terms in 1945 with the end of his career and the opening up a small pottery workshop with his wife. In his interview, which is sober and does not seem very indignant compared to the other contributions, he relates how he first had to be convinced by German Chancellor Adenauer to build a "democratically appropriate" army together with a greatly incriminated military. Nonetheless, both political parties soon had to recognize that "with an overly forward-looking program" like the "citizens in uniform," "no votes were to be won". For this reason, Baudissin was reassigned 1961 to the staff of the Allied forces in Fontainebleau near Paris, and the reform was not finally implemented until the SPD appointed a defence minister in 1969.[26]

Although Baudissin conveyed a certain satisfaction for the—albeit belated— application of his reform ideas, Kogon's assessment of West Germany was by contrast less favourable. At the very beginning of his contribution, he expresses his firm conviction that there was a "real chance" in 1945 to achieve "a state formation in the West with an aspect of idealism": "There was no food, clothing, accommodations, heating, not to mention schools or educational tools, yet those with ties to the Nazis were denied decision-making positions from the start and it was precisely for this reason that every possibility of new development could be weighed, discussed, planned, proposed and possibly enacted." He notes that it was the hour of those Germans who risked, "in collaboration with the prudent individuals of the occupational authorities", "reinforcing the undertaking, whose influence was supposed to extend far into the future, with an expansive ethics of humanity.". At the time of the 1970s, however, the most feared developments ultimately did not come to pass, although it appeared to him as "almost an oddity" that the un-incriminated persons "politicians, professors, and journalists" of his era "felt that an all-encompassing sensibility would follow after the shock of total defeat, giving rise to a productive fantasy for working on behalf of a new social reality.". In the East, the Soviets and the communist remigrants allowed the new beginning to result in a dictatorship. In the West, there were still

THE ORIGINAL 45ERS: A EUROPEAN "GENERATION OF RESISTANCE"? 57

the lingering "congenital defects" leading to an effective overturning of denazification. This often led to a situation where, even in 1979, the same "experts or their family members" continued to occupy positions "in the parties, the administration, the economy, organizations, schools and the army" who "took away the spontaneity and momentum of our social renewal" from the beginning.[27]

Just how this social renewal might have taken place is described not only by Kogon and Baudissin but also by the other "indignant men" partly autobiographically, partly analytically, although consistently without any specific evidence. Eggebrecht emphasizes, among other things, the numerous misunderstandings that developed from the start between the 45ers and most of the population:

> We were in fact convinced that our critical posture would be mirrored throughout the population; this was hardly the case, however. Finally speaking openly and publicly about Nazism after such a long silence, we were thought to be vindictive and opportunistic backers of the occupational powers. But this is precisely what we were not – on the contrary, we opposed many of the measures of the military authorities, often successfully. And we never entertained thoughts of beheading all Nazis as if we were rabid Jacobins – not even figuratively. No, today I'm quite sure that we were much too conciliatory.[28]

Flechtheim wrote that he and his peers had "not only hoped for a comprehensive democratization of all public life," but they had also been prepared "to accept the economic, land and educational reforms undertaken by the occupational powers and the anti-fascists." The Cold War and the reincorporation of the NS functionaries were the reason why not only the conservatives, but soon also the Godesberg SPD, first oriented themselves over the years to addressing the needs and resentments of the incriminated persons and followers: "Not class warfare, but community!" was the cry.[29] Sänger, who, after briefly working for the Americans, rose to become the head of the German press service in 1947, makes similar observations. When the German press service was transformed into the German press agency in the 1950s, Sänger supposedly resigned his post because of pressure from the CDU. He was thus a victim of one of the many displacement processes in journalism, which, according to Sänger, led to a situation where "the editing boards of all press organizations" were forced to work with new hires who "effectively lacked any personal history."[30]

Engelmann describes how "the ruling Christians" in Bavaria consistently made life difficult for him "in a democratic and social manner" as one of the few journalists interested in uncovering earlier political scandals. The *Bundesprüfstelle für jugendgefährdende Schriften* (Federal inspection authority for writings posing a risk to young people), founded in 1949 to protect underage citizens from "glorifications of war" and "racial hatred," had been directed over the years by a member of the "old guard." This particular official, for instance, did not have the *Protokolle der Weisen von Zion* or the *Landser* booklets removed from the store shelves but instead supposedly pornographic works from authors such as Günter Grass. Even "horrifying documentary films" about the concentration camps and other reports about the Third Reich, which "might undermine children's trust in the state," were limited to viewers 18 years and older.[31]

Abendroth partially blames personnel developments like these for the radical, often politically naïve, voluntarism of the West-German 68ers. Naturally, these West Germans "lacked any shared conceptions" and were "largely adolescent in many of their actions.". For indeed, "Where could the students have even obtained their own clear social and social-historical notions? Where were they supposed to have found their models for their actions?" Given that "most professors refused rational discussion and most of the authorities did not behave any better," the students "demanded from the few 'left' professors among us that we provide them with plans – which we after all must have known about – for a social, political and scientific revolution, here and now." When they were told that "no such plans existed, the students first 'occupied' our institutes of all places, because, in their eyes, we had failed." Even though these developments "not only greatly troubled him psychologically, but also physically," the protests in his view gave "all of the 'old folks'" new hope after years of isolation and defamation.[32] Albertz's discussion goes in an entirely different direction. He regrets that for himself and for other political leaders "the most important means of engaging with the students" remained for a long time "the police and the intelligence service," even though, as he now recognized, it was not possible to rely on their situational assessments.[33]

The word "generation" does not appear in any of the contributions. This might be due to the fact that the Kogon 45ers actually considered themselves to be a morally and politically superior "counter elite" and were still cognizant that they represented a tiny minority compared with the "totalitarian elite." Or to use Mannheim's words: In the German case, the "generational unit" that had supported or accepted Nazism after 1933 and therefore experienced 1945 as a defeat, not a liberation, was so vast that speaking of "generations" only made sense for members of this majority. This might not only explain the political and analytical success of the Hitler Youth generationality but also that of the First World War youth generationality. The members of this latter generation were born around 1900 and largely contributed to the success of the Nazi party in the 1930s and 1940s. What's more, after having recovered from the humiliation of the denazification, they were also instrumental to the West German "success story" of the 1950s and 1960s. During this last period, the former anti-Nazis had to choose: They either buried their 45er project of radical renewal and adapted it to the needs of the majority (Kogon speaks of becoming "uninspired, bossy old hands of democracy"[34]), or they remained true to it and suffered political and intellectual marginalization – at least until some were "discovered" as role models by the so-called 68ers.[35]

JEAN AMÉRY: A TRANSNATIONAL LOOK BACKWARD

Did the 45ers in Kogon's sense also exist in a comparable form in other countries that were involved in the Second World War? Jean Amérys contribution to Axel Eggebrecht's volume supports this thesis. "Whoever had fought against Hitler," Améry writes at the beginning of his article, "was our friend; whoever had been on the side of the monster was our enemy. That's how simple everything seemed to us. Americans, Englishmen, Frenchmen, Russians, liberals, militant Catholics and Protestants, socialists, communists: They were all equally welcome as our comrades."[36] In contrast, Améry added a "parenthesis" to the text, explaining: "What I have to present here is based on the fact that I, together with others like me, did not experience the days of liberation in war-ruined Germany but in Western Europe, where the fight against Nazism was always *national* at the same time." Furthermore, contrary to many, German people in Western Europe "had a roof over our heads" and "something to eat." Because of this, "when I conjure up the memory of 1945 I am distinguishing myself radically from most of the contributors to this volume."[37]

Améry expressed despair over his contribution, evocatively, entitled "Spoken into the Wind," not only with regard to the Federal Republic but also in reference to the West-German leftists with whom he felt a kinship since beginning to participate in national debates in the 1960s—about the

60   D. RIGOLL

way to cope with the NS past as well as in regard to many other political issues. Améry blamed himself and his peers for making three mistakes. First, those who experienced fascism first-hand as victims or resistance fighters failed to enlighten young people about ordinary fascism: "We didn't talk about everyday life under the Nazis. Instead, we shrilly screamed 'Danger! Fascism!' when an ill-bred minister of economics [i.e. Ludwig Erhard] called the leftist intellectuals 'pinschers.' The young people screamed along with us. It is not their fault that they lost sight of all proportions." Second, those who stood in 1945 for the new beginning wrongly assessed the needs of the population: "Despite all the evidence, we convinced ourselves that the nation was unhappy about the restorative trend" in the Cold War, even though in West Germany it "not only integrated and partly even rehabilitated the old Nazis and reactionaries of every variety" but also "consumable prosperity." Third, many 45ers did not distance themselves fast and clear enough from their ancient soviet ally: "The Nazis in Germany and the collaborationists in France, Belgium, and Holland" never could have "regained a strong position if we, for our part, had not been compromised on the one hand by a 'socialism'" in the East "to which we understandably but rather unwisely remained loyal."[38]

Améry nevertheless appealed to the reader to show understanding for the political missteps that he, and many of his fellow former members of the anti-Hitler coalition, took: "We were, I hope, not stupid. But we were miserably informed and besides that, my skull ached. Also, we were not free of a victory euphoria that no doubt appears comical today. Perhaps we had done nothing more than distribute flyers that were as foolishly conceived as they were ineffective. But this, so we believed, gave us the right to march in rank and file with the defenders of Stalingrad and the British and American soldiers who had landed in Normandy." And while many in the West already feared that in Hitler one had probably "slaughtered the wrong pig," Améry and his peers "were still living within the mentality of the Resistance" and "stopped our ears" when

> someone told us of the bitter fights that had been fought, still during the war, between the right and left wings of the resistance movements [...]. We lived in the illusion of a 'Popular Front' that embraced all of the democratic forces, from a bourgeois but upright Babbitt [the protagonist of a novel of the same name by American author Sinclair Lewis, D.R.] to an Ivan Ivanovitch [the protagonist of a novel of the same name by Soviet author Antonina Koptjajewa, D.R.] who was zealously attending the ideology courses of the Communist Party.[39]

Although the project of a radical new beginning was a tremendous failure from his standpoint, Améry obviously continued to hold onto his view from that time that the members of the anti-Hitler coalition were bound together by more than just their opposition to the Third Reich:

> The resistance, so it seems to me, was borne by the *elan vital* of a *leftist* view of politics, even when it was nationally tinged. I have in mind not only French Gaullism but also – and this may stir violent objections – the conservative German resistance against Hitler, which reached its climax on July 20, 1944. [...] Today, more than three decades later and now in full knowledge of the concrete situation, without any illusions, I still persist in believing that their deepest motives, which they certainly would not have wanted to declare and were also hardly aware of, fit the world view of the Left; but only on condition that we are prepared to revise the concept and by the term 'Left' no longer mean an attitude towards the problem of economic hegemony but essentially a radical humanism.[40]

Whether Améry already thought this way in 1945 cannot be explored within the scope of this article. Nonetheless, a similar interpretation can already be found in his essay, "Birth of the Present," which concerns the "Forms and formations of Western civilization since the end of the war" in 1961.[41] Although cultural production was one of his central concerns, Améry also indirectly examines political developments in the chapters on Germany, France, Great Britain and the United States.

Already in the introductory chapter, "1945 – looking for Europe" ("1945 – Auf der Suche nach Europa"), Améry is only able to come up with "a few honourable but provisional attempts" in post-war Germany "to reconnect to a world from which the country was cut off 12 years earlier, [and] a few names like Eugen Kogon, Rudolf Pechel, Walter Dirks." For un-incriminated Germans like the three named here, it was "extremely difficult" "to catch up to the rest of Europe and become acquainted with names like Emmanuel Mounier, Stephen Spender, Julian Huxley, Jean Rostand." By and large, there had simply been "no internal fundament" in Germany "upon which to build a cultural superstructure"—at a time when not only Améry himself, but also renowned émigrés such as Thomas Mann, "did not even fleetingly entertain the idea of returning." France, by contrast, was in Améry's eyes "a country where, not for the first time, decisions about Europe were being made; the only country that met the post-war period head on with a solemn exertion of spiritual energy."[42]

62   D. RIGOLL

Améry even directly attributes the success of John Paul Sartre's existentialism to the resistance. Through "their mere existence" "all citizens have as much potential to be heroic as they do to be potentially security-obsessed bourgeoisie or potential traitors," which "offered the French individual for the first time since Verdun a grand opportunity for self-realization.". While in France, "a person was confronted with a choice as a result of the resistance movement" to define "what was good for him and what was evil"; for members of other nations there was an option to retreat behind their "soldierly duty to conceal and, when necessary, to say: I did not want this." Only against this backdrop is it possible to understand why "Sartre's philosophy had its stirring effect on a generation that had to spend its formative years in the world of resistance, attentism and collaboration."[43]

The "national significance of resistance," he writes, was for this reason not militaristic but "political and, even more so, psychological." The resistance made it possible for France to present itself in 1945 as a "victor nation." And "it produced a thoroughly authentic popular front, for even if the diverse conservative, liberal, socialist, communist resistance circles occasionally feuded with each other in illegality, they were nevertheless a united front in their opposition to their adversary. A communist worker who fled his deportation train on route could always expect to find a place to hide with a liberal barrister or a pensioned Gaullist officer." Indeed, even the "actual historical role" of Charles de Gaulle was "leftist," even though politically he must be counted as a "figure of the right," "perhaps even the extreme right," but at a minimum "conservative-Catholic, authoritarian, tradition-bound and militaristic."[44]

Still, an "optical illusion" was at play in the ostensible "leftist trend of the resistance" because this trend "was only concerned with the collective fight, and not with a vision of the future. Its contradictions must have been obvious as soon as an attempt was made to preserve it within the peaceful reality of the Fourth Republic." On one hand, this was due to structural continuities and continuities in personnel in state and society; on the other, it was related to the population's distaste for revolution:

> While the elite on the left dreamed with great clairvoyance of the complete restructuring of the country and discussed this restructuring with such unprecedented intensity that one could say that it was truly a delight to be alive, the old guard reconstituted itself in the economic and political classes, in industry, in the army and in administration. And while those at the spiri-

tual apex operated with partly mythical, partly abstract concepts of a people moved to revolution, the mass of the actual population was moved to achieve what it wanted everywhere and always: to live and work in relative harmony – amicably and in peace.[45]

Contrary to Western Germany, France was nurtured "spiritually from the myth of resistance" immediately after the end of the war. Politically, however, not only were the communists such as Aragon and Gaullists such as André Malraux marginalized during the Cold War, but so was the tiny resistance party that Sartre had founded with Buchenwald survivor David Rousset in 1948. Afterward, Sartre became known as the "compagnon de route" of the Communists, whereas Rousset—along with Malraux and his friend Eugen Kogon—participated in the anti-Communist and CIA-financed "Congress for Cultural Freedom." From Améry's perspective, "the most interesting novels, most beautiful films, the most intelligent essays" actually came out of France during the Cold War, but as "a creative nation of sustaining ideas of the West," the country passed on its responsibility to the United States.[46]

And what about West Germany? Although in France the former resistance fighters undoubtedly continued to set the tone intellectually as Gaullists, *compagnons de route* or communists, the "tiny minority" in West Germany in 1945 that "would have been capable and called on to meet the difficult challenge of a German revolution at least *post festum*" fell into "a state of dull resignation and impotent frustration": "Since the struggle against the pervasive residue of Nazism within the body politic was determined to be superfluous, untimely and harmful because it distracted from anti-communist crusade, and, moreover, since at least one of Hitler's actions, the war in Russia, was being silently justified, they knew not to exert their influence, felt distraught and as if they had been cheated of their victory." If they were not members of the Communist Party, "who found a sorry substitute for political gratification in the mere fact of the Soviet expansion" and the GDR, they "grudgingly retreated." As far as the majority of the population was concerned, if they did not conform to the predominant discourse, they were soon considered "suspicious individuals, extravagant intellectuals, loose cannons, troublemakers and knaves without a fatherland." Only a handful of authors of the so-called "lost generation" surrounding Heinrich Böll and Hans Werner Richter would have been able to have some kind of impact on the "new beginning"— without, however, "participating in a contemporary historical process" with their audience as the "resistance literature" in France, despite its political defeat, had succeeded in doing: "Because there were no (or too few, too limited) records that concerned forming a concept of the German future during Nazi rule, the writers were not able to supplement the 'No' to the Hitler regime with a 'Yes' to a political vision of a German future."[47]

It is thus hardly surprising that Améry was not even able to come up with a handful of West Germans when putting together in 1955 a volume of 60 people entitled *Portraits of Famous Contemporaries*. Nevertheless, for the chapter "Engaged, Enraged," which was the only one dedicated to political issues, he expressly selected those personalities that could be deemed 45ers. The range of portraits extended from Ilja Ehrenburg and Jean-Paul Sartre to Arthur Koestler and André Malraux and Lord Richard Coudenhove-Kalergi, the conservative founder of the pan-Europe movement. Just as he was 6 years later in the *Birth of the Present*, Améry is interested in continuities and discontinuities between the political actions of his protagonists before and during the Second World War. Coudenhove-Kalergi, for instance, wrongly hoped that after 1945 that he would be able to successfully follow up on his failed European project of the interwar period. When the Cold War intensified in the 1950s, the "triumph of 1949" (the founding of the Council of Europe) proved to be "premature."[48]

Do Améry's observations bear out the fact that, at least in the self-perception of its members, there was something resembling a European "generation of resistance" that was finally only articulated in decidedly different ways between the various countries? When looking at the interpretations presented by Améry in 1955, 1961 and 1979, it is indeed possible to discover several parallels to Wieviorka's 1989 analysis. Certainly, Améry stresses that his position as an emigré is "radically different" from that of the West-German contributors. However, he insists thereafter on using the transnationally understood "we." This "we" appears to signal identification with the military objectives and the political agenda of the anti-Hitler coalition. Améry also refers to the tension between the dominant discourse and the experience of the minority that Wieviorka identified when analysing the "génération de la Résistance." Finally, the conflict between political demands and real disappointments—which represents the essence of all the contributions to *The Indignant Old Men*—was treated by Wieviorka in a volume of interviews from 1995 with the descriptive title *Embarking on a Career. From the Resistance to the Conduct of Power*.[49]

The Original 45ers as a Transnational Generational Unit

The similarities between Améry and Wieviorka notwithstanding, the exiled intellectual presents a more differentiated use of the term "generation." Looking back in 1961, Améry identifies a "generation which had to spend its decisive years in the world of resistance, attentism and collaboration."[50] Thus, he recalls that the Second World War (and the attendant "European civil war") not only gave birth politically to a "generation of resistance" but also to at least two other opposed "generational units" whose members reacted in a very different and even antagonistic way to the same series of events. Whereas one generational unit was active in support of the axis powers, the other tried to remain neutral. As Karl Mannheim writes: "Within any generation there can exist a number of differentiated, antagonistic generational units. Together they constitute an 'actual' generation precisely because they are oriented towards each other, even though only in the sense of fighting one another."[51]

In Western Germany, the direct "antagonists" of the 45er minority were a mass of Nazi offenders and followers who returned to their previous positions (or something similar) during the 1950s due to the Cold War and the founding of a communist Germany that professed to represent the "anti-fascist" experience as a whole. Of course, the Federal Republic was also full of people who were opposed to National Socialism. However, in contrast to the party dictatorship that developed in the East, where communist 45ers remained in positions of power until the 1980s as members of a "generation of distrustful patriarchs,"[52] their communist and non-communist Western counterparts were obliged to either merge their political projects with those of the other generational units or risk marginalization. In the case of leading politicians such as Konrad Adenauer, but also Willy Brandt, the 45ers completely distanced themselves from their own generational unit, and—to win over the majority of the population to democracy—they ultimately oriented themselves toward the interests of their former rival generational unit.

In France, the starting point was entirely different. Because the 45ers were much more numerous here than in Germany and could draw on the necessary authority, they were actually able to implement a broad range of ideas from the reform program of the Conseil National de la Résistance (CNR) in the years between the liberation and the breakup of the "popular front" in 1948 (such as the Sécurité Sociale). Whereas the "old" parties

66   D. RIGOLL

gained the upper hand in the Fourth Republic and the *Epuration* was also largely rescinded, the former resistance fighters played a role nearly everywhere in the institutions, parties and organizations of the country— not as "45ers" or even as "Résistants" but as Gaullists, Christian Democrats, communists and socialists.[53]

An exemplary case worth pointing to is that of Stéphane Hessel, whose biography can be interpreted, like Améry's, as the one of a European 45er. Born in Berlin in 1917, Hessel became naturalized French citizen in 1939. After the occupation of France, he joined General Charles de Gaulle in London and entered the Resistance. After the war, he became an observer to the editing of the Universal Declaration of Human Rights in 1948. When the political projects connected with the declaration failed during the Cold War, Hessel went into diplomatic service as a Gaullist. He only again acknowledged his lifelong association with the CNR program after entering retirement, his convictions "not having fundamentally changed" since the 1940s.[54] At the same time, he emphasized how important the experience had always been to him in the resistance and in the Buchenwald concentration camp, where Kogon, with whom he enjoyed a lifelong friendship, had saved his life. In any case, this is how Hessel represents it in his autobiographical writings.[55] Resource-rich biographies of this and other European "Kogon 45ers" still remain to be written. The historicization of the 45er phenomenon as a whole might then represent a second significant analytical step.

NOTES

1. See Wuermeling, Henric L. *Die weiße Liste. Umbruch der politischen Kultur in Deutschland 1945*. Frankfurt a.m./Berlin: Ullstein, 1988, 22.
2. Quoted from Hanhimäki, Jussi M./Westad, Odd Arne, eds. *The Cold War: A History in Documents and Eyewitness Accounts*. Oxford/New York: OUP, 2004, 53; see also Krauss, Marita. *Heimkehr in ein fremdes Land. Geschichte der Remigration nach 1945*. Munich: C.H. Beck, 2001, 9–15.
3. Edinger, Lewis J. "Post-totalitarian Leadership. Elites in the German Federal Republic." *The American Political Science Review* 54: 1 (1960), 58–82, here: 58.
4. Kogon, Eugen. "Beinahe mit dem Rücken zur Wand." *Frankfurter Hefte* 9 (1954), 641–645, here: 642.
5. Grabert, Herbert. *Sieger und Besiegte. Der deutsche Nationalismus seit 1945*. Tübingen: Verl. d. Dt. Hochschullehrer-Ztg., 1966, 66.

THE ORIGINAL 45ERS: A EUROPEAN "GENERATION OF RESISTANCE"? 67

6. Naumann, Werner. *Nau Nau gefährdet das Empire?* Göttingen: Schütz, 1953, 91.
7. Behr, Hermann. *Vom Chaos zum Staat. Männer die für uns begannen 1945–1949.* Frankfurt a.M.: Verl. Frankfurter Bücher, 1961, 132.
8. In: Dorn, Walter L. *Inspektionsreisen in der US-Zone. Notizen, Denkschriften und Erinnerungen aus dem Nachlass.* Stuttgart: DVA, 1973, 7 f.
9. Kaiser, Joachim. "Phasenverschiebungen und Einschnitte in der kulturellen Entwicklung." Broszat, Martin, ed. *Zäsuren nach 1945. Essays zur Periodisierung der deutschen Nachkriegsgeschichte.* Munich: Oldenburg, 1990, 69–74, here: 73 f.
10. For example, as a chapter heading in the book Michael Kogon edited of his father's writings; Kogon, Eugen. *Gesammelte Schriften, Vol. 6.* Weinheim/Berlin: Beltz Quadriga, 1997, 83.
11. Moses, Dirk. "The Forty-Fivers. A Generation between Fascism and Democracy." *German Politics and Society* 17 (1999), 94–126; id. *German Intellectuals and the Nazi Past.* Cambridge: CUP, 2007.
12. Wieviorka, Olivier. "La génération de la résistance." *Vingtième Siècle* 22 (1989), 111–116.
13. See Lachaise, Bernard, ed. *Résistance et politique sous la IVe République.* Bordeaux: Presses Univ. de Bordeaux, 2004.
14. Rigoll, Dominik. *Staatsschutz in Westdeutschland. Von der Entnazifizierung zur Extremistenabwehr.* Göttingen: Wallstein, 2013; on the 45ers concept, see especially 21–27; see also id. "Den Wald vor lauter Bäumen. Jean Améry und die Niederlage der 45er." In Bielefeld, Ulrich/Weiss, Yfaat, eds. *Jean Améry. "...als Gelegenheitsgast, ohne jedes Engagement".* Munich: Wilhelm Fink, 2014, 105–118.
15. See also Weisbrod, Bernd. "Generation und Generationalität in der neueren Geschichte." *Aus Politik und Zeitgeschichte* 8 (2005), 3–9.
16. Mannheim, Karl. "Das Problem der Generationen." *Kölner Vierteljahrshefte für Soziologie* 7 (1928), 157–185, 309–330, here: 311; for the English translation, see: Mannheim, Karl. *Essays on the Sociology of Knowledge, vol. V.* London: Routledge, 1998, 163–195.
17. Eggebrecht, Axel, ed. *Die zornigen alten Männer. Gedanken über Deutschland seit 1945.* Reinbek: Rowohlt, 1979; the following citation is on 7.
18. Habermas, Jürgen, ed. *Stichworte zur 'geistigen Situation der Zeit', 2 vols.* Frankfurt a.M.: Suhrkamp, 1979; Lübbe, Hermann. "Fortschritt als Orientierungsproblem." In Podbewils, Clemens, ed. *Tendenzwende? Zur geistigen Situation der Bundesrepublik.* Stuttgart: Klett, 1975, 9–24.
19. See Eggebrecht, *Männer*, 280–286.
20. Ibid., 165 f.

68   D. RIGOLL

21. *Die Welt*, 19.06.2004.
22. See Eggebrecht, *Männer*, 104.
23. See *Fragen an den Autor*, Saarländischer Rundfunk 2, 17.02.1980, 38:30 min.
24. See Garner, Curt. "Remaking German democracy in the 1950s. Was the civil service an asset or a liability?" *German Politics* 6 (1997), 16–53.
25. See Wuermeling, *Weiße Liste*, 284, 294; Behr, *Männer*, 315 f., 53.
26. Eggebrecht, *Männer*, 209, 217.
27. Ibid., 74, 89.
28. Ibid., 11 f.
29. Ibid., 31, 61.
30. Ibid., 229 f., 334.
31. Ibid., 241, 251, 256.
32. Ibid., 158.
33. Ibid., 198 f.
34. Kogon, *Beinahe*, 41 f.
35. See Rigoll, Dominik. "Erfahrene Alte, entradikalisierte Achtundsechziger. Menschenrechte im roten Jahrzehnt." In Weinke, Annette/Frei, Norbert, eds. *Towards A New Moral World Order? Menschenrechtspolitik und Völkerrecht seit 1945*. Göttingen: Wallstein, 2013, 182–192; Spernol, Boris. *Notstand der Demokratie. Der Protest gegen die Notstandsgesetze und die Frage der NS-Vergangenheit*, Essen: Klartext, 2008.
36. In: Eggebrecht, *Männer*, 259.
37. Ibid., 260.
38. Ibid., 275 f., 265, 268.
39. Ibid., 259 f.
40. Ibid., 261 f. [emphasis in original].
41. Améry, Jean. *Geburt der Gegenwart. Gestalten und Gestaltungen der westlichen Zivilisation seit Kriegsende*. Olten/Freiburg: Walter, 1961.
42. Ibid., 12 f., 17.
43. Ibid., 27 f., 39.
44. Ibid., 26 f., 55.
45. Ibid., 27, 55.
46. Ibid., 25, 41, 66.
47. Ibid., 176, 179, 188, 192.
48. Améry, Jean. *Karrieren und Köpfe. Bildnisse berühmter Zeitgenossen*. Zürich: Thomas, 1955, 143.
49. Wieviorka, Olivier. *Nous entrerons dans la carrière. De la Résistance à l'exercice du pouvoir*. Paris: Editions du Seuil, 1995; see also id. "Le poids de la Résistance dans la vie politique de l'après-guerre: Réalité ou illusion rétrospective? Essay de questionnement." In Lachaise, ed. *Résistance*, 11–24.

THE ORIGINAL 45ERS: A EUROPEAN "GENERATION OF RESISTANCE"? 69

50. Améry, *Geburt*, 39 ("eine Generation, die in der Welt von Résistance, Attentismus, Collaboration ihre entscheidenden Jahre verbringen mußte").
51. Mannheim, *Essays*, 187.
52. Gibas, Monika. "'Bonner Ultras', 'Kriegstreiber' und 'Schlotbarone'. Die Bundesrepublik als Feindbild der DDR in den fünfziger Jahren." In Satjukow, Silke/Gries, Rainer, eds. *Unsere Feinde. Konstruktion des Anderen im Sozialismus.* Leipzig: Leipziger Universitäts-Verlag, 2004, 75–106, here: 92; see also Epstein, Catherine. *The Last Revolutionaries. German Communists and Their Century.* Cambridge, MA: Harvard University Press, 2003; id. "The Politics of Biography: The Case of East German Old Communists." *Daedalus* 128: 2 (1999), 1–30.
53. See Lachaise, Bernard. *La Résistance dans les parcours des délégués départementaux du RPF*; Buton, Philippe. *La PCF et la Résistance sous la IVe République*; Castagnez, Noelle and Morin, Gilles. *Résistance et socialisme: Brève rencontre*; Béthouart, Bruno. *La place de la Résistance dans le MRP sous la IVe République*; all in: Lachaise, ed. *Résistance.*
54. Hessel, Stéphane. *Engagiert Euch!* Berlin: Ullstein, 2011, 37.
55. See id. *Tanz mit dem Jahrhundert. Erinnerungen.* Berlin: Arche, 2011, 120.

CHAPTER 4

Continuity in Rupture: The Italian and German Constitutional Culture After 1945

Maurizio Cau

DEFINITION OF THE FIELD OF RESEARCH

History, as Walter Benjamin pointed out in a preparatory note of the thesis, *Über den Begriff der Geschichte* (*On History*), is marked by moments in which "tradition is broken showing the roughness and spikes that offer a foothold to those who want to proceed."[1] In the history of European politics, the period after the Second World War represented a similar moment of break up, in which the birth of new institutional experiences led to the decline of established constitutional and political traditions.

Vittorio Emanuele Orlando underlined this concept in a passage of the speech given in March 1946 in front of the Consulta Nazionale ("National Consultation"), which was entrusted to pave the way to a new institutional setup and which was fully aware of being on the threshold of a new age:

> If we could cast our eyes over the walls of the spiritual prison where we are banished, then we would see a sight of boundless, frightening, historical greatness. The events ahead of us, whose approach explains the past terrible

M. Cau (✉)
Fondazione Bruno Kessler, Istituto Storico Italo-Germanico, Trento, Italy

© The Author(s) 2018   71
J. Späth (ed.), *Does Generation Matter? Progressive Democratic Cultures in Western Europe, 1945–1960*, Palgrave Studies in the History of Social Movements, https://doi.org/10.1007/978-3-319-77422-0_4

thirty years of war and destruction, [...] represent [...] one of those turning points in the history of humanity which label the eras into which it is divided. By comparison, even the memory of the French Revolution of 1789 diminishes. This is a time when [...] we switch from one era to another [...]. These are the changeovers of ages, of historical eras. Now we are witnessing this great event: a new type of State that is being prepared. The Nation State, whose making took several centuries, is transforming in its very essence. [...] It may still take centuries of struggling, fighting and suffering, but it is the age that is changing.[2]

Naturally, the collapse of totalitarian regimes started a complex process of reconstruction that was to involve the constitutional structures and political cultures of Italy and Germany right to the foundations. For the branch of learning concerning the Constitution in both countries, the change in the political and regulatory setup of the late 1940s constituted a breach of considerable significance, which put the whole experience of concepts and themes, built up over the previous decades in juridical doctrine, under considerable pressure. From this point of view, the science of constitutional law is a vantage point not only to understand the evolution of thought on the State gained over the years of reconstruction but also to check how the culture of the post-war period can compare, by distancing itself or recovering some of its roots, with the previous constitutional era.

This view can provide starting points of considerable interest about the role the experiences of the past had in the organization of mid-twentieth century democratic systems and on the generational shift that took place from the mid-1940s onward between rupture and continuity. Regarding the generational aspect, not only the registry data are important. As will be shown, in the reconstruction of the postwar constitutional culture the generations of young scholars who had studied during the antidemocratic regime had a central role, but what deserves more in-depth analysis are the reference paradigms of the new actors of political and legal sciences. In the Italian case, in particular, the dialogue took place directly with part of the legal culture developed during the years of Fascism.

In this chapter, the development of these processes will be followed from a comparative perspective. The two situations—the German and the Italian[3]—were different in many ways, and their comparison with the past and revival of democratic models happened along lines that did not always travel side by side. Likewise, these cases each have similar elements, and it is worth reflecting on such considerations here.

In general terms, the transition from a dictatorial regime to a Republican system constituted a "new beginning", but immediately after the war "the new and the old mingled" inevitably.[4] The decisive action of distancing from the past, which both countries considered to be paramount for strengthening the new constitutional experiment, did not actually prevent the doctrinal knowledge developed in the previous era from continuing to show its influence.

CONTINUITY IN RUPTURE: DRAGGING THE CULTURAL MODELS OF THE PAST INTO THE POST-WAR ERA

In the so-called "age of reconstruction," there is frequent osmosis, sometimes marked by conflict, between different historical periods. The vicissitudes of post-war Italian and German science of constitutional law confirm that the timing of how constitutional processes are defined do not always coincide with the timing of fruition concerning the juridical question. Thus, from the point of view of the evolution of juridical culture, the post-war period is an age of multiple temporality, in which the processing of past historical experience is viscous and in which the timings of institutional, cultural and social changes are often out of phase with each other. This irregular pulsating of historical time leads to some reflections on the classical theme of the historiographical survey, i.e. that of the relationship between continuity and rupture in the evolution of cultural models.

If it is true that "in all the transitions of history [...] the boundaries between regimes are rendered malleable by the fact that slow-moving currents and fields of action and of thought overlap and interact with others in turbulence,"[5] then the relationship between continuity and rupture that took shape during the post-war period cannot be conceived as a static connection between separate phenomena but should rather be interpreted as the dialectical nexus that binds different layers of historical time. Continuity and change do not exclude each other; rather, it is in the change and interweaving between "resistance" and "survival" that continuity shows.[6] It is not surprising, therefore, that in German and Italian science of constitutional law during the years of reconstruction, the new and the old mixed together showing quite noticeable signs of cultural continuity among the different constitutional eras.

Among the most common rhetorical figures used in public speaking to describe this moment of switching to a new era is the expression "anno zero" (meaning "year zero" in English, which becomes "Stunde Null" in German). This expression intends to pinpoint a precise time of birth of a new political era, in which the forces of change are unleashed, thus allowing the glimpse of an image of a future ready to unfold on a completely new basis. This popular metaphor therefore suggests the idea of a time reset and emblematically describes the rupture that specific events impose on the course of events. However, this image is ill suited within the constitutional framework. Indeed, as has been pointed out recently, "institutions and juridical systems are mainly based on their own petrified past. They pile up their historical background in stages, then they reject and change it thus gaining their own specific stability through the slowness of the intrinsic processes of reorganization."[7]

The German Case

In the German case, the comparison between the juridical discipline and the new constitutional order was made through the recovery and the partial update of the fund of concepts developed by the *Staatslehre* of the Weimar Republic in the past. This comparison confirms the existence of a distinctive time lag between the implementation of the new institutional framework and the definitive setting of new models of understanding of the entire body of laws. Immediately after the collapse of the Nazi (totalitarian) regime, the efforts to redefine the concept of State by reorganizing it into a new philosophic and political body[8] did not have a significant impact on constitutional and juridical studies, which continued within the statist paradigms that had characterized much of the legal debate during the interwar period. In the post-war period, the main currents of *Staatslehre* were characterized thusly: "albeit in different ways and to different degrees, by the statist orientation, by the reaffirmation of the controversy over formalism and by the stubborn defence of the juridical body against any sociological contamination."[9]

In Germany, the *Neubeginn* (New Beginning) involved neither the direct resumption of the democratic experience interrupted in 1933 nor a real re-establishment of state order. The choice between "Restauration" and "Neubeginn" was not a real alternative to the point that the launch of a democratic experience, which was not new at all, involved the retrieval of a significant part of the legal and professional heritage of the Weimar period, all of which took place under the aegis of the Allied forces in the name of preservation of the German State as a legal subject. Unlike what

CONTINUITY IN RUPTURE: THE ITALIAN AND GERMAN CONSTITUTIONAL... 75

happened in the aftermath of the First World War, the contribution of constitutional law science was limited; the *Staatsrechtslehre*, the most important discipline of the *Staatswissenschaften*, was—after all—in a state of instability and bewilderment. Many of the key figures of the Weimar Republic were at the end of their career (Hans Triepel, Gerhard Anschütz, Richard Thoma, Gustav Radbruch); others were no longer active in Germany (as in the case of Hans Kelsen, who remained in the U.S. after the emigration of the 1930s, or Hermann Heller, who died in exile); and those most compromised by Hitler's regime were caught up in the process of denazification (the most affected were Carl Schmitt, Otto Koellreuter, Ernst Rudolf Huber and Reinhard Hoen). Others (such as Erich Kaufmann, Walter Jellinek, Hans Nawiasky and Gerhard Leibholz) chose instead to return from exile in order to contribute to the rebirth of the German State.[10]

The purge involving a large part of German society did not produce excessive shocks within the scientific community of public law representatives. Except for the most obvious cases, German juridical science accepted the "strategy of silence" as shared by German society. Thus, it favoured the widespread reinstatement of jurists who were more or less directly implicated with the former regime. The soft approach, which (at the resumption of its activity) the *Vereinigung der deutschen Staatsrechtslehrer* (Association of German Constitutional Law Professors) reserved for the so-called *Mitläufer* (fellow travellers), shows—especially when compared with the harsh criticism reserved for the colleagues who had chosen to continue their activities in the GDR—the widespread desire of many jurists to leave behind a past impossible to conjure up again and which needed to be exorcised by opening wider channels of cooperation with the new democratic State. In 1949, Richard Thoma, the 75-year-old President of the *Vereinigung*, as work was resumed after 18 years of inactivity, is quoted as saying, "the task of our association was and is to serve the constitutional life of a national community that aims toward unity, legality and freedom while providing, at the same time, the correct interpretation and harmonious improvement of the juridical framework of a State subject to the democratic rule of law. When the State subject to the rule of law was suffocated and buried, our association did not comply, but ceased its activities. Now we can proudly begin again."[11]

Despite their closeness to the past regime, many of the main constitutional and juridical figures—formed in Germany in the 1930s (for example Theodor Maunz [1901–1993], Hans Peter Ipsen [1907–1998], Ulrich

Scheuner [1903–1981] or Ernst Forsthoff [1902–1974])—were soon reinstated within the scientific community to become a point of reference for the progress of German juridical science, progress that was, however, slow to come as is testified by the studies produced in the late 1940s. A more cautious approach to the new constitutional framework was generally preferred to the argumentative zeal of the *Methodenstreit* (methodological debate), thus indicating that, for most of the scholars of constitutional law science, the priority was a return to an active contribution to the revival of a State subject to the rule of law.

Not surprisingly, the most characteristic feature of the *Staatslehre*, disclosed straight after the war, was its own "theoretical abstinence"[12] engendered by the virtual stoppage imposed on the discussion of the constitutional issue by the Nazi ideology. Indeed, the development of the political debate in Nazi Germany around the concepts of *Führer* and *Volk* made the jurisdictional arguments, established previously during the Weimar Republic, useless including those more open to statist and conservative trends. The years under the heel of the National Socialist Party were a period of deep crisis for the studies of constitutional law science; thus, the revival of the *Staatsrechtslehre* after the war had to remain disjointed from the previous experience. On the contrary, it was possible to establish a line of continuity directly with the Weimar period and with the *Richtungsstreit* (ideological dispute), the principles of which were laid down in the first decade of the twentieth century.[13]

The absence of theoretical reference models pushed German science to look back at the concepts defined at the time of the Weimar Republic. This reinterpretation of the past developed through a twofold approach. Whereas the constitutional model derived from the 1919 *Novemberrevolution* continued to cast negative shadows over the new institutional path leading to the Federal Republic, the *Staatsrechtslehre* was more partial to the anti-formalist doctrines defined in the 1920s to fuel the rethinking of the concept of State, even in that markedly different context.[14]

For German constitutionalism, ready to retreat on the conceptual positions of the Weimar tradition, the 1950s did not represent a period of great creativity from the theoretical point of view.[15] In post-war Germany, the constitutional and juridical debate became polarized around two schools of thought, composed by younger scholars but both an expression of the cultural issues that had emerged in the period of the Weimar Republic. The first, strongly linked to statist positions, was represented by

CONTINUITY IN RUPTURE: THE ITALIAN AND GERMAN CONSTITUTIONAL...   77

experts who had grown up around Carl Schmitt; the second, bound to a mainly pluralist vision of the constitutional dynamic, was supported by the group of scholars trained in Rudolf Smend's seminars on constitutional theory.[16] The debate, during the German postwar period, was among different cultural options more than among opposite generational blocks.

The group representing Schmitt's school of thought—which included Ernst Forsthoff, Werner Weber (1906–1975), Hans Schneider (1912–2010) and, at a later date, also admitted Ernst-Wolfgang Böckenförde (1930-), Roman Schnur (1927–1996) and Helmut Quaritsch (1930–2011)—was strongly orientated toward accepting Carl Schmitt's decision-making paradigm that was used to openly criticize the initial results of the new constitutional season: from the definition of fundamental rights such as *Wertordnung* (set of values) up to the building of the juridical system. On the contrary, Smend's school of thought—represented by Konrad Hesse (1919–2005), Horst Ehmke (1927–2017), Peter von Oertzen (1924–2008), Ulrich Scheuner (1903–1981) and Wilhelm Hennis (1923–2012)—reintroduced the pluralist model of *Integrationslehre* proposed by Smend himself in the 1920s. Despite following the ideal path originating from the constitutional experiences of the Weimar years, the democratic perspective and that concerning the Atlantic Pact, within which Smend's group carried out its research, involved going beyond and abandoning the conservative and the statist components of Smend's thought that, in the 1950s, underwent a change of direction in a democratic perspective.[17] The direction in the field of humanities developed and defined by Smend in his Berlin years exercised a considerable influence not only on the scientific debate in the German Federal Republic (for example, the developments of dogmatism on fundamental rights) but also on the activity of the *Bundesverfassungsgericht* (Federal Constitutional Court) itself, where frequent references to the Weimar theories of Smend and of Leibholz himself were present.[18]

Indeed, what was taken up from the constitutional interwar period constituted the anti-positivist direction, which, although of different conceptual bases, united Schmitt's and Smend's theories in the 1920s.[19] For Kelsen's normativism there was no room: Positivism, particularly in the pan-legalistic form expressed by Kelsen, was accused of having favoured the unchallenged rise of the Nazi regime and was in fact dismissed from the conceptual horizon of the post-war *Staatsrechtlehre*. Indeed, it was not before the 1980s that a renewed interest was expressed in the formalist theories of the Austrian jurist. The other major figure from the Weimar

78   M. CAU

period, absent from the post-war scenario, was Hermann Heller, whose *Staatslehre*—published posthumously in 1934 and oriented toward the definition of a doctrine based on a State subject to the rule of law—reappeared in circulation only at the beginning of the 1960s. Despite the strong defence of the democratic Weimar paradigm, or perhaps precisely because of this, Heller's line of thought, characterized by a unique methodological syncretism and oriented toward a new foundation on the basis of a sociological doctrine of the state,[20] enjoyed a belated rediscovery, which exerted an influence more in political than in constitutional science.[21] Cultural continuity between Weimar and Bonn shows how the deep break in political order that followed the end of Nazism did not imply a generational break in Germany. The fault in the postwar debate was not generational but doctrinal.

THE ITALIAN CASE

The Italian context shows that much of legal science has remained anchored, to a great degree, to the legal tradition of the past when compared with the flexibility shown by Political Science to adapt to the new constitutional framework. The scheduling of the theoretical models of juridical science did not follow the new historical period in a straight line but often clashed with it. Indeed, the doctrinal foundations that were to permit Italian juridical science, at least where it was shrewder to support the implementation of the constitutional design, were derived from the cultural season rooted in the debate of the late 1930s. Those scholars of the juridical doctrine, who at the beginning of the 1940s had proved to be ahead of their time (for example, Mortati, Giannini, Crisafulli, Miele and Lavagna), to a great extent paved the way for juridical thinking of the new time, engaging in an often heated confrontation with a significant number of other members who continued to think as if, in actual fact, a shift to a new constitutional time had never taken place.[22]

"Everything has been destroyed, how can we build it up again?" asked Orlando in 1946.[23] To answer this question, Italian science of constitutional law followed two different directions: The first was aimed at the resumption of the liberal paradigm of the State with legal status at the root of the tradition of constitutional law science in pre-Fascist times[24]; the second, on the contrary, followed the path of reviving the theories, produced in a sort of Italian *Methodenstreit*, which had animated the debate on the science of constitutional law in the late 1930s and early 1940s. A

CONTINUITY IN RUPTURE: THE ITALIAN AND GERMAN CONSTITUTIONAL... 79

few years before, some of these scholars had tried through lively debate to find an answer to the crisis of the State already documented many years before by Santi Romano. It was precisely this debate that prevented the post-conflict recovery from happening in the same ideological void that had characterized post-Nazi Germany.

In the Italian case, therefore, the abandonment of the Fascist ideological and cultural apparatus did not involve the complete dismissal of scientific experiences gained during the years of the dictatorship. The juridical views mostly involved with the fallen regime, such as that of Carlo Costamagna in defence of a "comprehensive" view of the relations between State and society or that of Sergio Panunzio—which was aimed at boosting an idea of corporatism with a clear statist contour—were dropped without means of appeal. However, much of the most recent juridical debate was used to found the new course of studies but in a different institutional and cultural context.[25]

In Italy, the division into groups and schools of thought was less clearly defined than in Germany.[26] From the perspective of the ability to adapt to the new institutional context, it is possible to identify two groups, neither one internally homogeneous either for holding the same political convictions or for doctrinal orientations. On one side were the "Great Brooders of the Thirties," as they were nicknamed by Grossi,[27] such as Costantino Mortati (1891–1985), Vezio Crisafulli (1910–1986), Giovanni Miele (1907–2000), Carlo Esposito (1902–1964), Carlo Lavagna (1914–1984) and Massimo Severo Giannini (1915–2000); on the other were the supporters of a constitutional science still anchored to a traditional layout of the juridical line of thought and of the sovereignty of the State with legal status represented by Vittorio Emanuele Orlando (1860–1952), Oreste Ranelletti (1868–1956), Emilio Crosa (1885–1962), Antonio Amorth (1908–1986) and Amedeo Giannini (1886–1960).[28]

As shown by the records data, the generational element was important. Apart from Amorth, the ones who defended the dogma of the legal science of liberal age were the protagonists of that age. In the Italian postwar legal culture, the existence—using Mannheim's words—of different "generational links" are in the meantime cause and effect of the acceleration of the historical and political dynamics. These generational blocks do not express identical and homogeneous positions but lie on mainly common values and generational perspectives. It is the confirmation of the idea according to which historical and social change, discontinuous in itself, has on individuals different effects depending on the moment in life in which they find themselves.[29] The legal scholars who had reached full scientific maturity at the advent of Fascism, or the young scholars who had studied during the years of Fascism, define two generations that are different not only for records data; they also evaluate differently the key events that between the end of the 1930s and the half of the 1940s subverted the political national and international order.[30]

Until the completion of the constitutional design, which happened in the early 1960s, the confrontation of these two diverse doctrinal and generational orientations—one pointing to the need for overcoming the theoretical residues of the *Rechtsstaat* by basing the Constitution on new theories, the other strongly linked to the dogmatic traditional doctrine hostile to the redefinition of the relationship between politics and law as suggested in the new Constitution[31]—was one of the main features of Italian juridical science.

From the more strictly theoretical–doctrinal point of view, the Italian scene of constitutional law developed instead substantially along two trends: on one hand was the normativist current, sensitive to the influence of Kelsenism and present in the original line of thought of Crisafulli and, more awkwardly, of Esposito; on the other was a trend more sensitive to the political and sociological dimension of constitutionalism that from Duguit and Hariou leads, through the institutionalism of Santi Romano, to the line of Mortati.[32] In many ways, indeed, the Italian doctrinal background is very different from that of the German, where the formalism of the Kelsen framework was ostracized up to the end of the 1970s.

On the topic of dragging past cultural models into the new constitutional framework, Mortati's work is a kind of symbolic hinge linking three different historical periods. It has been written that this "marks the defeat of a certain doctrinal tradition, but also its reestablishment by a troubled process of transformation, which brings new juridical issues into the Republican Constituent Assembly."[33] Mortati's "third way" positions itself in the "theoretical space between tradition and revolution"[34] and originates from the late 1930s in the quest for a theoretical model capable of starting a discussion with a new historical form to be assumed by the modern State and gradually admitting politics into its juridical dimension. Within this framework, the concept of "prescriptive vocation of the Constitution," which was to develop into Mortati's doctrine in 1940, was retrieved. Mortati's doctrine symbolized the way that was to be trodden by the traditional State toward becoming a constitutional State subject to the rule of law and the rebirth of the social sphere that, according to the new constitutional order, was to influence the agendas of the science of constitutional law after the Second World War.[35]

Conceptualization of the party as a constitutional instrument of social differentiation and, consequently, the formulation of a theory of a State understood as a teleologically oriented political body are just two of Mortati's nodal points that became part of the constitutional theory aimed at overcoming the hypostasized vision of the traditional liberal State and contributing to the definition of the "constitutional" version of the State subject to the rule of law.

The development of Mortati's theories is perhaps the clearest confirmation that, also in Italy, "the transition from one political regime to another did not take place despite the persisting of layers and elements of continuity, but, at least partially, precisely because of this persistence".[36]

THE PROCESS OF CONSTITUTIONAL IMPLEMENTATION AND THE POINT OF VIEW OF LEGAL SCIENCE

To put the new constitutional structures into practice, it was necessary that the extremely programmatic character of the Constitutions of the post-war period, featuring a strong orientation to the future, should be followed by solid actions for their implementation. If on one hand the publication of constitutional texts ended a period of transition between different legal regimes, on another it ushered in a new one that was linked to how the new constitutional plans were turning out.

In both Italy and Germany the attitude of legal science toward the new constitutional structure presented a dichotomy, the result of a rather sharp division between strongly critical trends and openly favourable tendencies regarding the constituent process and its effective implementation. In the Federal Republic, where those belonging to the legal profession taking part in the constituent phase had been numerically low and programmatically not very effective, disappointment was not slow to appear[37] over a constitutional plan that on paper was of a "provisional" nature, as should be remembered.

The group of scholars who followed the decision-maker theories developed by Schmitt in the Weimar period were openly critical toward the new constitutional plan, which was considered an expression of an "excess of power" of the *Parlamentarischer Rat* (Parliamentary Council) and a lack of "strength of political organization." Among the most vocal opponents of the *Grundgesetz* (Basic Law) was Werner Weber who, in terms not too far from those used by Carl Schmitt, attacked the Bonn Charter during the inaugural lecture at the University of Göttingen. This charter was marked by a distinct lack of democratic legitimacy and undermined by the interference of the allied forces, which would have effectively prevented the full deployment of German sovereignty.[38] In Weber's analysis, the system of parliamentary representation—restricted within party dynamics—would confirm the weakness of a State that basically had no sovereignty, a result of the weakening of the powers of the executive and the deadly processes of "legalization of politics" and "politicization of justice" emblematically represented by the new system of constitutional justice. Weber's arguments resumed in tone and content Schmitt's traditional set of theories, thus updating the issues under discussion. The newly built Republic was then analysed through the conceptual grid of Weimar decision-making, which did not stop exercising its influence in the doctrinal context of the post-war period.

The views of Ernst Forsthoff were equally sharp. Forsthoff, in the name of the recovery of decision-making and institutionalist components of the Schmidt tradition, was critical toward the lack of sovereignty and authority that the Constitution of the Federal Republic of Germany seemed to reveal.[39] Although Forsthoff considered himself "bound to the system made up of laws and regulations," he made no secret, as he observed the historical evolution of the State subject to the rule of law first-hand, of his fondness of the "ideal type" of *Rechtsstaat*, which was threatened by the new-born German Republic with its programme of social rights ratified in the *Grundgesetz*. By the fact that the State, subject to the rule of law, gave a firm guarantee in the classical sense according to the tradition of Mohl, Stahl and Mayer, Schmitt's pupil, Forsthoff, petitioned for the "institutional supremacy" of the *Rechtsstaat* ("rule of law") over the social State outlined in the basic law of the German Federal Republic. By projecting a conception of regulation typical of the past theoretical heritage onto the German Republic of the time, Forsthoff ultimately aimed at excluding all forms of normativism not only from the system of values ratified on a constitutional level but from the very idea of a social State subject to the rule of law.

The position of Hans Peter Ipsen was more conciliatory. By giving his total support to the new constitutional order, he gave up those elements of his own set of theories, which adhered to authoritarian ideology. Although Ipsen did not avoid discussing the more sensitive issues bequeathed by the *Grundgesetz* (from the democratic legitimacy of the

CONTINUITY IN RUPTURE: THE ITALIAN AND GERMAN CONSTITUTIONAL... 83

BRD to the problem of the normativism of basic rights up to the actual coordinates of the Social State Principle), he sided with the *Grundgesetz*, which was perceived as an instrument that could be improved but also able ultimately to guarantee the democratic development of the country.[40]

It can be seen by the comments of most of the German *Staatsrechtslehrer* that they accepted wholeheartedly the new political and constitutional order. Without giving way to over-enthusiasm and not failing to point out the problematic aspects of the path to implement the constitutional plan, a substantial number of the members of the *Vereinigung der deutschen Staatsrechtslehrer* (from Triepel to Leibholz, from Mangoldt to Nawiasky) began to sketch the first outlines of the allegiance to the new constitutional order, which over the decades would become a fundamental value shared by many in the German legal world.[41]

In general, the art of commentary on the Constitution, which in the Weimar period had been an integral part of the *Richtungsstreit*, did not give rise to a particularly lively doctrinal comparison. The sessions of the *Vereinigung der deutschen Staatsrechtslehrer* themselves, when compared with those of the preceding age, took place in a more relaxed and scientifically less turbulent atmosphere.[42] The ability of constitutional law science to guide constitutional life was by now showing the first signs of weakness, which would be confirmed after the start of the activities of the *Bundesverfassungsgericht*.

In Italy, too, the science of constitutional law, which had played a large, though not central, part in constitutional activity, did not fail to make its voice heard in those complex years of implementation of the constitutional plan. In particular, it is well known that voices of criticism did not fail to rise up and attack the new constitutional structure and its delayed implementation.

The traditional doctrine, which had witnessed the construction of a constitutional model, which in many ways did not reflect the doctrine itself, gave a very lukewarm welcome to the Charter of '48. Through a recovery "of the aseptic legal method", it substantially endorsed "bringing a default action against the Constitution itself.".[43] The "reconversion" to the new democratic order happened, therefore, in many cases, along the cultural lines expressed in the past, although it suitably updated to make them compatible with the new direction taken by politics and to guide possible future developments. As has been pointed out by historians when criticizing the weakness of the constitutional project, many lawyers believed "they had room for manoeuvre in order to be able to direct the project towards results other than those which the country then actually experienced. Furthermore, they thought that they could do this, both by exerting pressure on the constituents through what they wrote [...] and by means of the more effective weapon that they had in their possession, namely interpretation".[44]

During the first term of legislation, "a tension between old and new involving the Constitution" was created.[45] Among the elements subject to most criticism coming from traditional legal science, the concept of sovereignty certainly stands out. Everyone, from Orlando to Crosa, from Amedeo Giannini to Amorth, moved in defence of the supremacy of the State around which the Italian doctrine of the State subject to the rule of law had been built and which the sovereignty of the people, considered by some scholars to be an element alien to the Italian legal tradition, openly questioned.[46] The insufficient involvement of lawyers in the preparatory phase of the constitutional text was, at least for many in Italian science of constitutional law, one of the causes of the inadequacy of the new constitutional structure, the ambitions of which hid obvious shortcomings in terms of normativeness of rights. This group of Italian scholars of the science of constitutional law did not merely condemn the shortcomings of the new-born Republican system; they tried to hinder its coming to life by trying "to put the still fluid situation of the reborn Italian democracy back on the tried and tested tracks of the model of the State subject to the rule of liberal law.".[47]

Taking advantage of the phase in the first half of the 1950s during which the Constitution failed to be implemented, traditional legal doctrine attempted to restore the centrality of the State by harnessing the constitutional novelties ratified by the Charter according to the interpretation dear to the liberal school. In those years, the Supreme Court also followed a similar path. The jurisprudence of the Court, broadly in line with the interpretation of traditional doctrine, helped to delay the full application of constitutional principles as was shown by the well-known sentence of February 1948, which distinguished between perceptive and directive provisions.[48]

The jurists who were more open to the new theories introduced by the new-born institutional model took a stand against the interpretation which, in the midst of transition, aimed at removing legitimacy from the new theories on which the constitutional State was based. Thus, the principle of the sovereignty of the people, the constitutional role of the parties and the recognition of the normativeness of constitutional rights were the subject of specific attention on the part of constitutional law science, which was more open to the constitutional bases expressed by the Charter. This is also the case for Mortati, Crisafulli, Lavagna, Esposito and Barile who, despite their differing doctrinal positions, made great efforts toward the actual implementation of the constitutional principles and an understanding of the Charter to assure it a sound development.

The background of constitutional science in the early 1950s was therefore rather inhomogeneous. On one side the representatives of the traditional legal school were arrayed, and on the other were those people who, since the 1930s, had aimed at reforming Italian legal culture.[49] Crisafulli remarked rather controversially during the 1950s: "With very few exceptions it did not seem that the latest doctrine had made a real effort to comply with the new principles set out by the Constitution on the relationship between State and society and, as a consequence, on the position and juridical importance of the people in the system in force at the time [...] Certain statements in the constitutional text seemed to be a real nuisance in a doctrinal routine."[50]

An unusual position was taken by Piero Calamandrei after the Constitution came into force. He had contributed wholeheartedly to the preparatory work on the Charter; however, after its enactment he found himself criticizing first the short-sightedness of the Constitutional text, which was unable to look ahead and give rise to a real social revolution and then the laziness of a juridical and political culture weakened by "discontinuance" and by conformity. Driven by the belief that the Constitution paved the way for the future situation much more than did the completion of a process of transformation, he waited feverishly for the constitutional transition to happen and for the juridical inheritance belonging to the previous rule of authority to be wound up. As we know, this only happened from the time when the Constitutional Court was established in 1956. Calamandrei's remark was this: "Only now that the Republic is about to start working can we begin to feel that it is not going to collapse".[51]

Conclusion

At times of political and institutional upheaval, the function of juridical science can be considered twofold. On one hand, according to Calamandrei, it manages "to settle the ground and remove the debris of revolution"[52];

in contrast, it is called upon to determine the structure of the new constitutional buildings, maybe even recovering some of the old beams. In this organization and redefinition within the juridical field, the cultural and institutional experiences of the past inevitably exert a weighty influence.

The examination of some parts of Italian and German constitutional culture after the war has revealed how the new direction taken by post-war democratic constitutionalism has distanced itself considerably from the past. It is also clear that there has been a recovery and an updated re-proposal of doctrinal stylistic methods and cultural models, which are the offspring of this constitutional past with which the "new beginning" intended to make a sharp break. Although they both stem from very different political conditions that evolved during the post-war period, Italy and the Federal Republic of Germany have traced similar growth curves in many respects, and their comparison allows the highlighting of several "constants" that help to understand the role that the re-working of past experiences has played in the building of post-war cultural and institutional models.

The evolution of understanding in the area of post-war constitutional science shows how much the breakaway elements are actually interwoven with those that are more strictly continuative. The main theory groups, on which the science of constitutional law has been remodeled—both for Germany and for Italy—are in fact projections or extensions of cultural experiences that have arisen or come to maturity over the previous decades. In the case of Germany, in which there had not been a real generational break, there has been a considerable re-proposal of the interpretation of the Weimar debate, partly readapted to the new political context and without some of the scientific options that had been discredited by the evolution of recent national history. In the case of Italy, however, the comparison has been between two different generational fronts, which are witness to the persistence (and the resistance) of the liberal kind of juridical tradition and the emergence of a doctrinal front varied in its methodology and offspring of the debate, which had livened up juridical science in the later years of the dictatorship.

In both situations, therefore, the building of new scientific prospects has occurred based on the re-thinking of past theories, which have maintained their value despite the passing of the institutional set-up in which they were born and have continued to exert their influence in the early years of the new constitutional orders.

NOTES

1. Benjamin, Walter. *Sul concetto di storia*, ed. by Gianfranco Bonola/Michele Ranchetti. Bologna: Il Mulino, 1997, 86.
2. Orlando, Vittorio Emanuele. *Discorsi parlamentari*, ed. by Fabio Grassi, Bologna: Il Mulino, 2002, 681–683. On Orlando's role at the Costituente see Pombeni, Paolo. *Vittorio Emanuele Orlando: il costituente, in Vittorio Emanuele Orlando: lo scienziato, il politico e lo statista.* Soveria Mannelli: Rubbettino, 2003, 33 f.; Quaglioni, Diego. "Ordine giuridico e politico in Vittorio Emanuele Orlando." Carta, Paolo/Cortese, Fulvio, eds. *Ordine giuridico e politico: esperienze lessico prospettive.* Padua: Cedam, 2008, 3–25.
3. A clarification is necessary: The examination of the German case is limited to the experience of the Federal Republic because of the profound differences that the political, constitutional and doctrinal developments had in the two states, which rose from the ashes of Hitler's Germany. The FRG and the GDR gave rise to two very different systems of public law oriented toward the pursuit of antithetical political goals and resting on premises that were incompatible. The history of constitutional culture in the two Germanies is therefore a history of radically parallel experiences, the details of which cannot be discussed here. The focus therefore falls solely on the West-German experience, the most directly comparable to the Italian case.
4. Grossi, Paolo. *Scienza giuridica italiana. Un profilo storico 1860–1950.* Milan: Giuffrè, 2000, 289.
5. Petri, Rolf. "Transizione." *900. Per una storia del tempo presente* 12 (2005), 11.
6. On the relationship between continuity and durability of the lines of change, see Lepsius, Mario Rainer. "Die Bundesrepublik Deutschland in der Kontinuität und Diskontinuität historischer Entwicklungen: Einige methodische Überlegungen." Conze, Werner/Lepsius, Mario Rainer, eds. *Sozialgeschichte in der Bundesrepublik Deutschland. Beiträge zum Kontinuitätsproblem.* Stuttgart: Klett-Cotta, 1983, 16 ff.
7. Stolleis, Michael. *Geschichte des öffentlichen Rechts in Deutschland*, vol. IV. Munich: C.H. Beck, 2012, 25; see also Rückert, Joachim. "Kontinuitäten und Diskontinuitäten in der juristischen Methodendiskussion." Acham, Karl/Nörr, Knut Wolfgang/Schefold, Bertram, eds. *Erkenntnisgewinne, Erkenntnisverluste. Kontinuitäten und Diskontinuitäten in den Wirtschafts-, Rechts- und Sozialwissenschaften zwischen den 20er und 50er Jahren.* Stuttgart: Franz Steiner, 1998, 128–155.
8. The opening up of German political science to the Anglo-Saxon tradition and the efforts of Hannah Arendt to redefine the foundations of political action are two emblematic examples of this attitude.

88   M. CAU

9. Portinaro, Pier Paolo. "Una disciplina al tramonto? La Staatslehre da Georg Jellinek all'unificazione europea." *Teoria politica* 1 (2005), 19.

10. For a deeper examination of the general trends of post-war *Staatslehre* and the biographical profiles of the main figures of the science of constitutional law of the period, refer to Günther, Frieder. *Denken vom Staat her. Die bundesdeutsche Staatsrechtslehre zwischen Dezision und Integration 1949–1970*. Munich: Oldenbourg, 2004, 112–211; Stolleis, *Geschichte des öffentlichen Rechts*, vol. IV, 115–145; Bülow, Birgit von. *Die Staatsrechtslehre der Nachkriegszeit (1945–1952)*. Berlin: Berlin-Verl. Spitz, 1996; Möllers, Christoph. *Der vermisste Leviathan. Staatstheorie in der Bundesrepublik.* Frankfurt a.M.: Suhrkamp, 2008.

11. Thoma, Richard. "Vorwort." *Veröffentlichungen der Vereinigung der Deutschen Staatsrechtslehrer.* 1950, 8.

12. Möllers. *Der vermisste Leviathan*, 31.

13. On the line of continuity between the thought of the early twentieth century, the Weimar *Staatslehre* and the juridical culture of the Federal Republic, see Schefold, Bertram. "Geisteswissenschaft und Staatsrechtslehre zwischen Weimar und Bonn." In Acham/Norr/Schefold, eds. *Erkenntnisgewinne, Erkenntnisverluste*, 566 f.

14. Five different schools of thought can be recognized firing the debate on the Weimar Republic: (1) the classical positivist line of thought represented by eminent scholars, although not always sharing the same methodological positions (such as Thoma, Anschütz, Preuss, Triepel and Radbruch) and by the supporters of normativism of the Viennese school of Kelsen; (2) the anti-positivist field with the doctrines of Carl Schmitt (characterised by decision-maker traits) and of Rudolf Smend (who adopted the methodology in the humanities with the support of jurists such as Kaufmann, Holstein and Leibholz); and (3) the *Staatslehre* of Heller (favorable toward the integration between juridical thought and sociological methods). The literature on this subject is vast; thus, for a general overview, see Stolleis, Michael. *Geschichte des öffentlichen Rechts*, vol. III. Munich: C.H. Beck, 2002.

15. As pointed out by Frieder Günther, for the *Staatslehre* "the fifties were not a decade of exciting modernization, but a period of retreat with little inclination to innovation and largely conservative"; Günther, Frieder. "Ein Jahrzehnt der Rückbesinnung. Die bundesdeutsche Staatsrechtslehre zwischen Dezision und Integration in den Fünfziger Jahren." In Henne, Thomas/Riedlinger, Arne, eds. *Das Urteil Lüth aus (rechts-) historischer Sicht. Die Konflikte um Veit Harlan und die Grundrechtsjudikatur des Bundesverfassungsgerichts*. Berlin: Berliner Wissenschaftsverlag, 2005, 305.

CONTINUITY IN RUPTURE: THE ITALIAN AND GERMAN CONSTITUTIONAL... 89

16. For a detailed examination of the composition of the two groups and of the different doctrines, please refer to Günther. *Denken vom Staat her*, 112–190 and Schefold, *Geisteswissenschaft und Staatsrechtslehre*, 581–599.

17. On the "rupture in continuity" occurring within Smend's school of thought and on the gradual abandoning of the statist horizon see Günther, Frieder. "Ein Jahrzehnt der Rückbesinnung." In Henne/Riedlinger, eds. *Das Urteil Lüth*, 308–310. Among the key figures who promoted the shift of the *Integrationslehre* toward a more responsive answer to Republican issues, Gerhard Leibholz played a major role. His first reflections in the Weimar period on representation as the foundation of political forms also revealed a certain degree of diffidence, if not a clear disinclination, toward the paradigms of the Republican model; see Schefold, *Geisteswissenschaft und Staatsrechtslehre*, 575–580.

18. See ibid., 585–590.

19. Both cases were orientated toward a conservative line of thought that did not hide an open hostility toward the democratic republican option. It is significant that, during the years of the reintroduction of democracy in Germany, the theoretical choices in the Weimar period sided more openly in defence of democracy (therefore Kelsen's and Heller's school of thought), remained on the edges of the constitutional and juridical debate while it was actually the model of Smend's *Integrationslehre*—put together in the 1920s and based on anti-liberal and anti-democratic prejudices— that was elevated to be at the core of the new democratic State.

20. For an in-depth understanding of Heller's doctrine produced by the relational study between historical materialism, philosophical anthropology and cultural sciences, see Henkel, Michael. *Hermann Hellers Theorie der Politik und des Staates. Die Geburt der Politikwissenschaft aus dem Geiste der Soziologie*. Tübingen: Mohr Siebeck, 2011; Llanque, Marcus, ed. *Souveräne Demokratie und soziale Homogenität. Das politische Denken Hermann Hellers*. Baden-Baden: Nomos, 2010.

21. Among the post-war "heirs" of Heller's *Staatslehre* it is worth remembering scholars of major relevance such as Martin Drath, former assistant lecturer in Frankfurt of Heller himself, who exerted a great influence on the first Senate of the *Bundesverfassungsgericht* from 1951. Also, the line of thought of Wolfgang Abendroth, who at the beginning of the 1950s left constitutional science for political science, moved closer to Heller's position.

22. On the cultural context in which the new constitution was implemented, see Bartole, Sergio. *Interpretazioni e trasformazioni della Costituzione repubblicana*. Bologna: Il Mulino, 2004, 41 ff.

23. Orlando, *Discorsi parlamentari*, 667.

24. Fioravanti stressed that "the presence of the tradition of constitutional law science, and more specifically, the presence of those traditional jurists formed during the liberal period, did not end at all during the Fascist period. After the fall of the regime, leading figures such as Santi Romano, and especially Vittorio Emanuele Orlando, tried to influence and to determine the constitutional and juridical trend and somehow to interpret the events leading to the establishment of the new political system and a new constitution"; Fioravanti, Maurizio. "Dottrina dello Stato-persona e dottrina della Costituzione. Costantino Mortati e la tradizione giuspubblicistica italiana." Galizia, Mario/Grossi, Paolo, eds. *Il pensiero giuridico di Costantino Mortati*. Milan: Giuffrè, 1990, 165.

25. Historians have pointed out that "the theory of the 'parenthesis', which ties the threads of the methodological discussion to the pre-Fascist period or to the theory of rupture, indicating the collapse of the dictatorship as the turning point towards the new constitutional science, can be more realistically confronted, part of Italian doctrine having been "neutralized" and another having been surpassed, by a more interesting and modern line of thought that sprang from the intense debate itself which took place during the authoritarian period after the collapse of the liberal State"; Lanchester, Fulco. *I giuspubblicisti tra storia e politica. Personaggi e problemi nel diritto pubblico del secolo XX*. Torino: Giappichelli, 1998, 65.

26. For in-depth research on the academic and doctrinal geography of postwar studies on constitutional law in Italy, see ibid., 113–120; Gregorio, Massimiliano. "Quale costituzione? Le interpretazioni della giuspubblicistica nell'immediato dopoguerra." *Quaderni Fiorentini per la storia del pensiero giuridico moderno* (2006), 35.

27. Grossi, *Scienza giuridica italiana*, 290.

28. Naturally the two sides were not rigidly defined and opposed to each other; for example, see Esposito who, from his position of "positivist critic," clearly stressed the dangers of an unbalanced Constitution within its values; see Esposito, Carlo. *La Costituzione italiana. Saggi*. Padua: Cedam, 1954, 17 ff.; on this point, see Fioravanti, Maurizio. "Profilo storico della scienza italiana del diritto costituzionale." In Labriola, Silvano, ed. *Valori e principi del regime repubblicano, 1. II, Sovranità e democrazia*. Rome/Bari: Laterza, 2006, 152.

29. See Cavalli, Alessandro. "Generazioni." In *Enciclopedia delle Scienze Sociali*, vol. IV. Rome, 1995, 237–242.

30. The Italian legal culture of that age complies with Fogt's definition of political generation: "A political generation is composed by members of an age group or cohort that – confronting certain key events – take a similar aware position towards ideas and values of the political order in which they grew"; Fogt, Helmut. *Politische Generationen. Empirische Bedeutung und theoretisches Modell*. Opladen: Westdeutscher Verlag, 1982, 21.

CONTINUITY IN RUPTURE: THE ITALIAN AND GERMAN CONSTITUTIONAL...   91

31. The views expressed by Vittorio Emanuele Orlando on this matter are emblematic; see Quaglioni, *Ordine politico*, 12–25.
32. See Rimoli, Francesco. "I manuali di diritto costituzionale." *Rivista Trimestrale di Diritto Pubblico* 4 (2001), 1412 f. The constitutional model of the Weimar Republic had played a relevant role during the Italian *Costituente*, and despite all the legal culture 'classics' produced in the 1920s in Germany, only Kelsen's studies on pure legal theory were retained, omitting the ones on democracy and parliament, whereas the more explicit works by Schmitt, Heller, Smend and Leibholz, specifically on the relation between law, society and constitutional order, were neglected for a long time; see, on this point, Ridola, Paolo. "Gli studi di diritto costituzionale." *Rivista Trimestrale di Diritto Pubblico* 4 (2001), 1262.
33. Fioravanti, *Dottrina*, 48.
34. Ibid., 49.
35. For a discussion of Costantino Mortati's constitutional theory, please refer to Galizia/Grossi, eds. *Il pensiero giuridico*; Galizia, Mario, ed. *Forme di Stato e forme di governo: nuovi studi sul pensiero di Costantino Mortati.* Milan: Giuffrè, 2007; Zagrebelsky, Gustavo. Premessa, quote, VII–XXXVII.
36. Petri, *Transizione*, 23.
37. On the reactions to the *Grundgesetz*, which came to a head within the German *Staatslehre*, see Stolleis. *Geschichte des öffentlichen Rechts*, vol. IV, 125–145; on the reaction of the general public to the basic law, see Bommarius, Christian. *Das Grundgesetz. Eine Biographie*. Berlin: Rowohlt, 2009, 9 ff.
38. Weber, Werner. *Weimarer Verfassung und Bonner Grundgesetz*. Göttingen: Fleischer, 1949. The critical positions of Weber were repeated in substance in id. *Spannungen und Kräfte im Westdeutschen Verfassungssystem.* Stuttgart: Vorwerk, 1951, to be partially revised a few years later in id. *Die Verfassung der Bundesrepublik in der Bewährung.* Göttingen: Musterschmidt, 1957.
39. Forsthoff, Ernst. *Lehrbuch des Verwaltungsrechts, vol. 1, Allgemeiner Teil.* Munich: C.H. Beck, 1950, 100 ff.; see also id. *Einleitung zum Bonner Grundgesetz.* Heidelberg: Rothe, 1953.
40. Ipsen, Hans Peter. *Über das Grundgesetz.* Hamburg: Univ., 1950.
41. The current-affairs journalism of Mangoldt, one of the fathers of the *Grundgesetz*, was particularly widespread. He contributed several times in major law journals of the time to illustrate and establish scientifically the reasons for the constituent; see Mangoldt, Hermann von. "Zum Beruf unserer Zeit für die Verfassungsgebung." *Die Öffentliche Verwaltung* (1948), 51 ff.; id. "Die Grundrechte." *Die Öffentliche Verwaltung* (1949), 261 ff.; id. "Grundrechte und Grundsatzfragen des Grundgesetzes Bonner." *Archiv für öffentliches Recht* 75 (1949), 273–290.

42. For a review of the activities of the *Vereinigung* in the years of the Democratic revival, see Ipsen, Hans Peter. *Staatsrechtslehrer unter dem Grundgesetz – Tagungen ihrer Vereinigung, 1949–1992.* Tübingen: Mohr Siebeck, 1993.
43. Lanchester, Fulco. "I costituzionalisti italiani tra Stato nazionale e Unione Europea." *Rivista Trimestrale di Diritto Pubblico* 4 (2001), 1084.
44. Gregorio, *Quale costituzione?*, 857.
45. Lanchester, *I costituzionalisti italiani*, 1086.
46. For a discussion on the doubts of Capograssi over the forms of twentieth-century constitutionalism, on the suspicions of Orlando about the process of constitutional rationalization of power, on the embarrassment of Ranelletti over the discipline of the parties or on the diffidence of Crosa and Amorth about the acceptance of the sovereignty of the people, see Gentile, Francesco/Grasso, Pietro Giuseppe, eds. *Costituzione criticata.* Naples: Edizioni Scientifiche Italiane, 1999; Gregorio, *Quale Costituzione?.*
47. Gregorio, *Quale Costituzione?*, 863.
48. One of the critics who was most aware of the consequences that the decisions of the Supreme Court would have had concerning the definition of a system to guarantee the rights of freedom was Calamandrei; see Calamandrei, Piero. *Scritti e discorsi politici*, vol. II, ed. by Norberto Bobbio. Florence: La Nuova Italia, 1966, 467 ff.
49. Gregorio wrote: "In the aftermath of 1948, the panorama of Italian legal culture did not offer a sound, homogeneous reference paradigm, helpful in the interpretation of the Constitution. On the contrary, the science of constitutional law oscillated between longstanding mistrust and opening up, although not supported either by a shared theoretical framework or by a practical and reliable development strategy and implementation of the Charter"; Gregorio, *Quale Costituzione?*, 912.
50. Crisafulli, Vezio. "La sovranità popolare nella Costituzione italiana." *Scritti in memoria di Vittorio Emanuele Orlando*, Vol. I. Padua: Cedam, 1955, 407–463.
51. See Galante Garrone, Alessandro. *Calamandrei.* Milan: Garzanti, 1987, 264–282.
52. Calamandrei, *Scritti e discorsi politici*, vol. I, 67 f.

CHAPTER 5

Toward a New Political Science in Italy and West Germany After 1945: Democracy, Politics and Generational Change

Gabriele D'Ottavio

INTRODUCTION

Even before 1945 in Germany and Italy, there were solid traditions of political studies, the origins of which can be traced back to the late nineteenth century or even earlier.[1] However, these traditions did not consider politics as a separate field of study but rather as a topic that had to be taught in other disciplines such as history, law or economics. This is also why the plural form, "political sciences", was preferred to the singular. In both Germany and Italy, disciplinary legitimacy and full institutionalization of Political Science, intended as a specialized social science, were not achieved before the late 1960s and early 1970s.[2]

The main aim of this study is to assess how and to what extent the establishment of a modern Political Science after 1945 in Italy and West Germany, respectively, should be considered as a break with the past. The analysis will look not only at the relationship between the homegrown traditions of political studies and the new Political Science that emerged in

G. D'Ottavio (✉)
Department of Sociology & Social Research, University of Trento, Trento, Italy

© The Author(s) 2018   93
J. Späth (ed.), *Does Generation Matter? Progressive Democratic Cultures in Western Europe, 1945–1960*, Palgrave Studies in the History of Social Movements, https://doi.org/10.1007/978-3-319-77422-0_5

the 1950s and 1960s; it will also consider the role played by the challenge of building a lasting democratic political system in Italy and Germany after the experience of the Second World War. In fact, in both Italy and West Germany the establishment of Political Science as a distinct academic discipline seems to have been highly dependent on the course of political developments on the one hand, while, in contrast, it contributed to shaping these developments. The relevance of the generational issue for understanding the history of West German and Italian political sciences after 1945 will also be explored. In this regard, the analysis will illustrate how some of the leading figures of the first and second generations of political scientists envisaged the relationship between Political Science and democracy: What should the scope of the new Political Science be about? To what values and to what political and cultural paradigms should it refer? What conceptions of democracy have they marshaled? In this context, the concept of "generation" will be linked to some specific political and intellectual experiences shared by the members of the two national communities of political scientists. For the Italian case study, the analysis will point to the connection between the active role played by some scholars in the *Resistenza* and the adoption, after 1945, of a positivistic approach to the study of politics. As far as Germany is concerned, the focus will be on the very specific generation of the so-called "remigrants" (*Remigranten*): scholars who had made a name in the social sciences during their exile and returned home as spokespersons and interpreters of the American scheme to educate European toward liberal democracy.

By considering the common and distinctive features that marked the development and institutionalization of the discipline in West Germany and Italy, respectively, after 1945, the analysis will finally discuss the different ways the supposed "Americanization" and/or "Westernization" took place in the field of political sciences. The main goal here is to point out the difference between "Americanization" and "Westernization" as a cultural and intellectual process and "Americanization" and "Westernization" as a political goal. The analysis shows that it is difficult to downplay the American impact on the history of Political Science in Italy and Germany after the Second World War, above all if we consider both the impressive political and financial support given in the 1950s and 1960s. However, even if the assumption is correct that the American impact was central to the development and institutionalization of the new Political Science both in West Germany and Italy, it seems that the cultural transfer from the US to Western Europe after 1945 was more generally filtered and mediated, if not even altered, by the contribution and interference of other factors and actors.

Three Snapshots of Three Forerunners: Gaetano Mosca, Karl Mannheim and Carl J. Friedrich

Let us start with three snapshots that, beyond the image conveyed by some leading political scientists, allow a more realistic and comprehensive picture of the complex relationship between the pre-existing traditional political studies and the development, after 1945, of the "new" Political Science in both Italy and Germany. One of the most common limitations encountered in history of this discipline is the highly self-referential nature of the existing literature, which often depicts the development of Political Science as triumphantly "switching from utopia to science, from the clever intuitions of 19th century authors to the methodological rigour of contemporary Political Science."[3] This consideration, as will be clarified later, is especially true in Italy, whose case has been studied less than that of Germany.

A long-term historical perspective should be favoured. Therefore, the first snapshot goes back to 1896 when Gaetano Mosca (1848–1941) published his well-known essay *Elementi di scienza politica*.[4] In the late 1930s, the last version of this work (1923) was translated into English and published in the United States and in Great Britain under the title *The Ruling Class*.[5] Many exponents of the discipline still consider the essay to be one of the founding texts of modern Political Science.[6] However, Mosca's attempts, although only hinted at, to solve some fundamental theoretical and methodological issues in order to establish Political Science as a separate discipline had very little follow-up in the short to medium term.

The second snapshot focuses on *Ideology and Utopia* (1929) by Karl Mannheim (1893–1947) who was born in Hungary but became a naturalized German citizen.[7] Particularly, in the third chapter—entitled *The Prospects of Scientific Politics: The Relationship between Social Theory and Political Practice*—he singles out, among the tasks of the sociology of knowledge (*Wissenssoziologie*), solving "a problem which has always gone unanswered: [...] why we have not yet witnessed the development of a science of politics," and he goes on to say that "in a world which is permeated by a rationalistic ethos, as it is our own, this fact represents a striking

96 G. D'OTTAVIO

anomaly."[8] He also addresses the question "why is there no Science of Politics," referring to the reason why Science of Politics did not exist as a subject that could be considered "scientific" by its standards and by its achievements, again putting forward his argument of the social conditioning of thought. In particular, Mannheim identifies, among "the great difficulties which confront scientific knowledge in this realm", the extreme fluidity of politics and thus the great difficulty for observers to free themselves from having "a partisan view through his evaluations and interests" and, consequently, to rationalize the constraints of the "political and social currents" of his time on his "way of thinking":

> *[...] Furthermore, and most important, is the fact that not only is the political theorist a participant in the conflict because of his values and interests, but the particular manner in which the problem presents itself to him, his most general mode of thought including even categories, are bound up with general political and social undercurrents.[9]*

Evidently, the historical place that Mannheim was referring to was not the US, where Political Science, understood and applied as an empirical science, was already established within the field of social sciences,[10] but the Weimar Republic of the late 1920s.[11] In 1929, that world might have seemed to breathe a "rationalist ethos", but – as Thomas Mann forecast in 1918, German society proved to be blinded by irrationalism. The failure of the "Weimar laboratory" and Hitler's rise to power made it all the harder for those avant-garde scholars, such as Mannheim, to give political science a rational basis. For racial and political reasons, many scholars were forced to decamp to the United States, or, as in Mannheim's own case, the United Kingdom.[12]

Especially in the German case study, the evaluation of the relations between the homegrown traditions of political sciences and the new Political Science, which emerged after 1945, becomes even more complex if we consider the cultural 'interactions' between the old continent and the US. In this regard, the German political scientist Alfons Söllner has shown that many German scholars who were forced to emigrate during the Nazi regime not only managed to build ordinary careers as political or social scientists in American universities; they returned to Germany after the end of the Second World War and offered their help to the American authorities during the occupation period, thus contributing significantly to the emergence of a German political science as a distinct academic discipline.[13] Some of them—Otto Kirchheimer (1905–1865), Herbert Marcuse (1898–1979) and Franz Neumann (1900–1954)—were even recruited as analysts by the American Secret Service Office of Strategic Services.[14] The case of the famous scholar, Carl J. Friedrich, is a particularly interesting example.[15] He studied under Alfred Weber at the University of Heidelberg, where he graduated in 1925 and received his doctorate in 1930. However, already in 1926 he worked as a lecturer in Government at Harvard University, and when Hitler came to power in 1933 he decided not to quit the United States and become a naturalized citizen. He was then appointed Professor in Government at Harvard University in 1936. After the Second World War, he served as Constitutional and Government advisor to the Military Governor of Germany, General Lucius D. Clay. From this position, he played a key role in the work leading up to the drafting of the Basic Law and, more generally, in Germany's denazification and democratization program of occupied Germany. On his return to the United States in 1948, he soon became one of the preeminent spokespersons of the theory of Totalitarianism organizing a series of conferences and publications that raised the term to a key category in modern politics debates.[16] He served then as president of the American Political Science Association in 1962 and of the International Political Science Association from 1967 to 1970. Friedrich's experience certainly represents an extreme case but, as we will see later in this analysis, he was not the only German émigré who, on one hand, became accustomed to the practice of the American political science and, on the other hand, brought with him a different academic tradition and contributed to a more critical self-understanding of American political theory.

These three snapshots are a good representation of what, at first glance, may seem to be a contradiction. Although both Italy and Germany could boast strands of political studies, which had their origin in positivism and could not only interact with American Political Science but also influence it deeply, the claim of a Political Science, intended as an autonomous discipline, remained the prerogative of a very small number of scholars. This alleged contradiction finds a full explanation when considering the dominant cultural paradigms for political studies, in the early 1900s in Germany and Italy, where these studies were strongly influenced by juridical theories of the state (*Staatswissenschaften*) and by anti-empirical approaches such as idealism and historicism.[17] In the Italian case, the highly critical

98   G. D'OTTAVIO

judgment expressed by Benedetto Croce about these new trends is emblematic: "What kind of political empirical science could this be if, instead of being subordinate to historical knowledge and preserving the results [....] it could be imposed on history as a construction of abstractions, generalities, preconceptions and prejudices?"[18]

As Norberto Bobbio remarked, the main obstacle that hindered the first generation of political scientists in establishing a modern Political Science, intended as an "applied" science, in Italy was

> that dominant, hegemonic trend, almost an official guideline that, as soon as it is slightly shaken by a contrasting tendency, takes over again and makes every other thought that does not conform appear heretical, false and foreign, characterized by a certain mannered spiritualism, sometimes speculative, sometimes only rhetorical and anti-pedagogical, capable of excommunicating positivism, empiricism, materialism, utilitarianism, wherever they appear, as vulgar, narrow-minded, mercenary and impure philosophies.[19]

The advent of Fascist regimes brought an ever increasing ideologisation into the cultural and academic world, especially in Germany where it resulted in what Peter Gay called "the largest transfer of intelligence, talents and knowledge that has ever happened"[20] and implied a further step backward from the perspective of a "new rationalism" that, as hinted at by Mannheim, was one of the essential requisites for establishing a real "scientific" approach to the study of society and politics.

In fact, it was only after 1945 that the problem of the relative backwardness of Political Science and, more generally, of social sciences all over the old continent, especially in the countries that lost the Second World War, acquired a completely new political, cultural and generational value that was able to encourage, rather than hinder, the search for a solution to this problem. With regard to this, it is sufficient to mention how the formation of the first national professional associations of Political Science, the establishment of the first chairs of Political Science, the birth of specialized journals and, finally, the emergence of a, albeit fluid, "professional ideology" that was largely sympathetic to the idea of giving a more empirically oriented character to Political Science, were all phenomena that arose in West Germany and in Italy after 1945 and, in particular, in the period between the early 1950s and the first half of the 1970s.[21]

Italy: A New Generation of Political Scientists

Some subsequent representations provided by some exponents of the discipline propose two very different ways of looking at the development of a new Political Science after 1945 in Germany and Italy, respectively. More precisely, whereas in Germany there is a tendency to emphasize the essentially political nature of the causes, which brought about the establishment of Political Science in Italy after the end of the Second World War, as was noted in particular by Damiano Palano, "the history of Political Science has been conducted by focusing almost exclusively on the methodological aspect."[22] It is worth reading and comparing two short passages in which two well-known leading figures in the discipline—Hans Maier (for Germany) and Norberto Bobbio (for Italy)—each face the question of the revival of modern Political Science in Germany and Italy at the beginning of the 1960s. In particular, for Maier mainly political–pedagogical reasons prevailed at first:

> *The desire to immunize the public, especially the young generation of students, against the effects of totalitarianism and the will to make a contribution to the stabilization of democratic life through political education and thereby save the Federal Republic from the fate of the Weimar Republic.*[23]

Bobbio's analysis seems instead much more focused on methodological aspects:

> *The birth, or rather, the rebirth of this science can be dated to the first issue of the magazine "Il Politico" (1950), directed by Bruno Leoni, who also taught State Doctrine. In Pavia in 1950, for the inauguration of the academic year, Leoni gave his opening speech Political Science and political action, alleging that too many political problems had been removed from scientific analysis. [...]. In 1952, the magazine "Studi politici" appeared at the University of Florence. In the first issue, Giovanni Sartori published an article called* Political Science and Retrospective Knowledge, *which is already in itself a programme for the renewal of political studies. The following year in the same magazine, there was another article entitled* Philosophy of Politics and Empirical Science of Politics, *in which he argued that empirical science would have to make its way by freeing itself from the subjection to ideologies, on the one hand, and to political philosophy, on the other.*[24]

This diversity of approach can also be seen, furthermore, in some following studies that were published in the 1980s. For example, according to Luigi Graziano:

100   G. D'OTTAVIO

A historical reconstruction of the events that led to the "revival" of political studies in Italy from the 50s and 60s should be based on four groups of factors. The first factor has to be seen in the conscious effort of some distinguished scholars, which aimed at saving this tradition of studies from the decline that it had fallen into, and at building Political Science as a subject in its own right, methodologically and substantially distinct from more established subjects such as Public Law, Historiography and Political Philosophy [...].[25]

Whereas, as far as the German case is concerned, for Arno Mohr:

Rarely has a scientific discipline been sponsored in such a persistent way as Political Science in West Germany after 1945. It has not detached spontaneously from other disciplines, but rather its birth is due to a political decision.[26]

Although both Graziano and Mohr actually resist the temptation to give monocausal explanations regarding the revival of Political Science, recognizing the presence of different factors,[27] it is clear that in balancing out and weighing the various driving forces, the Italian scholar focuses primarily on the theoretical and methodological aspects, whereas the German openly states in the introduction to his book that his main purpose is to show that in the Federal Republic the rediscovery of Political Science was fundamentally a political product (*ein politisches Kind*).[28]

This diversity of perspectives has a strong historical foundation that allows us to grasp the first important difference concerning both the mechanisms and the leading figures who triggered the process of re-establishment of Political Science in the two countries under discussion. In particular, the political constraints in Italy, especially those coming from outside the country, did not take such definite shape as in the Federal Republic. However, this is not to deny their existence. To understand the importance of political aspects in the process of re-establishment of Political Science in Italy, it is enough to refer briefly to the debate on the future of the faculties of Political Science that arose soon after the Second World War.[29] This debate hinged mainly on the question of the measures to be taken against the people who, in one way or another, were involved with Fascism. A document of November 1945 of the *Consulta nazionale* was significant in this regard in that it showed a "scheme of legislation for the abolition of the faculties and degree courses of Political Science" put forward by then current Minister of Education Arangio Ruiz, which says: "Besides, it was clear that the faculties of Political Science were created by Fascism, not so much in the interests of science as in its own, which was obvious when the *communis opinio* rose up to demand their abolition after the collapse of Fascism."[30]

In fact, in the aftermath of the Second World War, not all faculties of Political Science in Italy fell into the same disrepute. In particular, compared with the other five faculties of Political Science that had been established during a period of 20 years (at the Universities of Milan "Cattolica", Padua, Pavia, Perugia, Rome), the "Cesare Alfieri" of the University of Florence, besides being the only one that could boast of a glorious tradition in the field of political studies dating back to the end of the previous century, had also been relatively less affected by Fascism.[31] It was exactly because it conformed less to the regime and this proved decisive with respect to the resolution of the academic Senate on 5 January 1945, endorsed by the Education Minister De Ruggiero, by which the reconstitution of the faculty in Florence officially became the Cesare Alfieri Faculty of Political and Social Sciences. The decision not to abolish but to support the specification of Cesare Alfieri as a school of excellence through reform was the expression of a clear political will to break with the recent past rather than an attempt to pick up the threads of a tradition of political studies hitherto for a minority and which Fascism had helped to break up.

The portraits emerging from a first attempt to reconstruct the prosopographic profile of the main characters of the revival of Political Science in Italy are even more significant. Amongst these, the figures of Norberto Bobbio (1909–2004), Bruno Leoni (1913–1967), Giuseppe Maranini (1902–1969) and Giovanni Sartori (1924–2017) must be remembered. The first two both played active roles in the *Resistenza*. Norberto Bobbio joined militant antifascism in 1939 and took part in the founding of the Venetian division of the Action Party in October 1942 where he remained as a member until 1946.[32] Bruno Leoni, in contrast, was called to arms in 1944 and took part in the war of liberation and was even decorated with a cross for military valour, by decree of the Ministry of Defence, for the following reason: "As a volunteer for missions of combat in territory occupied by the enemy, he carried out numerous and risky operations during intense, daring and bold activity, facing considerable dangers and responsibility (period of service, 1944–April 1945)."[33]

The biography of Maranini presents more contradictory elements.[34] Strongly opposed in his academic career by an establishment that did not like his antiformalist attitude, Maranini managed to obtain a university chair in Constitutional History at the newly established Faculty of Political Science in Perugia only thanks to the personal intervention of Mussolini who appointed him *per chiara fama* (for his renown),in 1933, probably giving way to pressure from Maranini's father who was an old friend of

102   G. D'OTTAVIO

Mussolini. As time passed, even Maranini turned away from Fascism. He was concerned by the racial laws that threatened to deprive him of his post (his mother was Jewish), and he became increasingly sceptical about the "restorative" bent of the regime. Already at the outbreak of the war, Maranini began to move back closer to the socialist inspiration of his youth. In all three cases mentioned, the approach to Political Science came relatively late, when they were already well-established scholars in academic circles, in particular, Bobbio and Leoni in the field of Philosophy of Law and Maranini as a historian of Constitutional Law. In contrast it is obvious that their approach to Political Science cannot be understood only from their common interest in the theory of science and positivistic methodology applied to the study of law, in the first place, and politics, in the second place. Although they all started from very different philosophical and theoretical positions (Bobbio reconnected with Kelsen's formalism, Leoni with the American empiricism and Maranini with the theorists of the élite), all three ended by seeing an almost identical correspondence between positivistic methodology and democracy actually promoting a Political Science in favour of political modernization in Italy. In the case of Bobbio, the cultural approach was social-liberal and progressivist[35]; in the case of Leoni, it was inspired by economic liberalism[36]; and in the case of Maranini, it was liberal-élitist.[37] The latter distinguished himself by taking a strongly critical position over the transformation of democracy into "particracy" (*partitocrazia*).[38]

The first chair of "Political Science" in Italy, however, went to the younger Giovanni Sartori, whose biography, if only because of his age, does not make it possible to establish the existence of any connection between his political stance during the fascist regime and his subsequent professional success in academic circles.[39] Born in 1924, Sartori was appointed to the post on the Cesare Alfieri faculty of Political Science in Florence in 1957 and moved on to a professorship only in 1966. In this respect, the autobiographical memory of the battle fought and finally won by Giovanni Sartori against an academic world hostile to the idea of introducing Political Science as a teaching subject is striking as well as indicative of the specific way in which leading Italian figures of that time portrayed the history of Political Science in terms of a heroic undertaking:

> *It was, although I'm not quite sure, the year of Our Lord 1954 (or maybe 1955). I felt lost, but since, at that time, I was a brave or rather very stubborn little teacher, I decided to face the lion in his den. I asked for an appointment with Carlo Antoni and got it. In those years, the Italian university was*

TOWARD A NEW POLITICAL SCIENCE IN ITALY AND WEST GERMANY...   103

governed by the Board of Education where Antoni presided over the faculty of Political Science and, therefore, their changes of charter (the introduction of new subjects). My faculty, the "Cesare Alfieri" of Florence had asked for the change of charter of Political Science more than anything else to get rid of a nuisance (my nagging), but I knew perfectly well that none of my colleagues would have lifted a finger. So, I had to go to Antoni. I held him in great esteem as a scholar, but I knew he was a strict follower of Croce for whom Political Science was an anathema. [....] I had nothing to lose so I came out with this: "Professor, you teach philosophy of history, a subject that, according to Croce, should not exist anymore than Political Science. Please allow another non-existent person to work alongside you." I cannot say that I saw Antoni laugh, but he certainly smiled. The agreement was made over that remark. Antoni, who was a gentleman, had the amendment to the charter passed by the Board. In 1956, the University of Florence appointed me to the post of Political Science. I remained rather small and on my own for several years [....].[40]

Giovanni Sartori, who started off in history of philosophy and considered Political Science as an empirical way of thinking that was able to defuse the ideological charge of politics, undoubtedly proved to be more aware of the limitations of the subject compared with the other "noble fathers" of Italian Political Science, especially with regard to the problem of defining the autonomy of "politics" as the object of analysis, on one hand, and the relationship between the philosophical premises and the prescriptive contents of political analysis on the other. In this context, the two articles that appeared in the first two issues of the journal *Studi politici* in 1952 and 1953, respectively—"*Scienza politica e conoscenza retrospettiva*" ("Political Science and Retrospective Knowledge") and "*Filosofia della politica e scienza empirica della politica*" ("Philosophy of Politics and Empirical Science of Politics")—fit rather well. Even more to the point was the publication in 1957 of his most famous work, *Democrazia e definizioni* ("Democracy and Definitions"). Starting from the premise according to which "there is no 'real' democracy without ideal democracy [...] the descriptive definition of democracy is inseparable from its prescriptive definition", Sartori developed a long and learned excursus on the notion of democracy and its definitions in Western political thought to lay the groundwork for a political analysis of democratic functioning.[41] Giovanni Sartori was also the editor of the *Antologia di Scienza Politica*, which was also the first systematic statement of mainstream Political Science (mainly American) to the Italian public.[42] It was significant, however, that this work came out only in 1970.

West Germany: The Role of Remigrants

In the Federal Republic, too, the rebirth of Political Science was promoted by leading figures, most of whom were outside the academic world, which was involved with the regime or had more or less come to terms with it. However, what makes the German question different from the Italian one is the influence of the geopolitical situation on the development of the discipline. After the end of the Second World War, the revival of Political Science and, more generally, of social sciences in the Federal Republic was directly encouraged by the Allied Forces, especially the Americans, and secondly by political parties, above all the SPD. Here, the snapshot that best captures the American influence is one that comes from the conference of Waldleiningen, near Frankfurt, in September 1949.[43] This meeting was organized, thanks to the region of Hesse (one of the three *Länder* placed under American military occupation), and attended by several exponents of the academic and political world, who, in fact, started off the development of this subject in the universities.[44] Concerning this, it is significant that in Hesse was also appointed the first chairs of Political Science (*Politische Wissenschaft*) outside of the traditional academic circles. These appointments were given to proven anti-fascists such as Wolfgang Abendroth (1906–1985),[45] who would later become one of the leading exponents of Marxist-inspired Political Science; Eugen Kogon (1903–1987),[46] who had shared with the future leader of the SPD, Kurt Schumacher, his traumatic experience as a prisoner in the concentration camp of Buchenwald; and Carlo Schmid (1896–1979),[47] who was a well-known leading member of German Social Democracy.

As already pointed out, a key role in the process of the re-establishment of German Political Science was played by the so-called *Remigranten* (remigrants), a large group of scholars who, under the Nazis, had been forced to emigrate abroad for racial or political reasons and during their exile had managed to establish themselves in the field of social sciences, especially in the American academic scene.[48] Back in their home country at the end of the war, some of these scholars became interpreters and spokesmen for both of the intentions of the occupying forces, (re-)converting and educating the Germans to democracy.[49] Among the most prominent representatives, Arnold Bergstraesser (1896–1964), Ernst Fraenkel (1898–1975), Carl-Joachim Friedrich (1901–1984)—who, however, never left his chair at Harvard—Otto Kirchheimer (1905–1965), Karl Loewenstein (1891–1973), Franz L. Neumann (1900–1954) and

Joachim Ritter (1903–1974) must be remembered. Their analysis, too, concentrated mainly on democracy, a topic that became the focus of post-1945 Political Science and on which the promoters of the Waldleiningen conference had planned to lay the groundwork for political studies in Germany.[50] To reflect on representative democracy and on its dynamics meant above all to look with a critical eye at the failure of Weimar and the tragedy of the Nazi regime (which was put on the same level as the Stalinist regime as far as "totalitarianism" was concerned) but also to put forward Western political systems as models for the political class and for public opinion. Therefore, this meant identifying not only the weaknesses but also the strengths of the democracy to be consolidated. The choice of these topics reflected the need to learn from personal experience and from that of others. In contrast, if the approach was mainly historical and institutional, the aim was mostly pedagogical.[51]

In this context, it is worth focusing briefly on the work of Arnold Bergstraesser and Ernst Fraenkel, both marked by the experience of exile and their professional success as political scientists in the United States. They were both inter-disciplinary in their approach. Under their guidance, respectively, at the University of Freiburg and the resurrected *Hochschule für Politik* in Berlin, known as the Otto-Suhr Institute from 1957 onward, scholars such as Hans Maier, Hans-Peter Schwarz, Kurt Sontheimer and Karl-Dietrich Bracher were trained. The contributions of Bergstraesser (1896–1964) and Fraenkel (1898–1975) are particularly significant for the way they conceived Political Science and worked out the relationship between Political Science and democracy. In particular, both pointed to the originality of Political Science as being the result of the converging of different disciplines and methods. Bergstraesser defined Political Science as *synoptische Wissenschaft* (1961), Fraenkel as *Integrationswissenschaft* (1960). The other element common to the two authors was, however, to present German Political Science mainly as a science at the service of democracy (*Demokratiewissenschaft*) and therefore within a concept of the discipline where the empirical part was clearly subordinate to the normative one. In contrast, although they both had American democracy as a point of reference, Bergstraesser and Fraenkel ended up spreading two very different normative models of democracy in that they were based on the selection of those characteristics that corresponded more closely to their respective visions of society: "liberal-conservative" (in the first case) and "social-pluralistic" (in the second case).[52] Their story is rather significant. On one hand, it is a good example of the "Westernizing" effect and, in particular, the "Americanizing" effect on German Political Science, which was made evident by the connection established between Political Science and the basic values of Western democracy (in this case, American). In contrast, it shows the variety and, at times, the contradictory nature of the processes of reception and transmission of Western models by some established scholars.

The question of funding from overseas must be addressed separately. This is an issue that, especially in recent years, has been an important area of research for tackling the subject of intellectual hegemony in the United States.[53] In particular, recent studies have brought to light the role played, especially from the beginning of the 1960s, by several well-known American philanthropic foundations, notably the Ford Foundation and the Rockefeller Foundation.[54] By founding research, study programs abroad, and other forms of cooperation, these gave a fundamental thrust to the development of modern political science on the Old Continent. Cultivated public opinion in Western Europe was likewise gradually sensitized to political thinking based on liberal democratic values. By way of the Congress of Cultural Freedom in particular, the United States supported a number of journals with clearly anti-communist sympathies: "*Der Monat*" in Germany, "*Tempi Moderni*" in Italy.[55] Some of these soon became special forums of political debate as to the transformations of western European politics. The lodestone orienting this massive operation of cultural diplomacy was the conviction that the social sciences had a precious role to play in modernizing political thought and guiding European democracy in its confrontation with international communism. It is possible to argue that the resources invested by the United States in the Federal Republic were far greater than those invested to promote Political Science in Italy. Here, too, the reasons for this disparity are easily traceable to the distinctive geopolitical importance of the Federal Republic as an outpost of the Western world and as the main stake in the context of the Cold War. In this perspective, it is not surprising that most of these funds flowed into the city of West Berlin to support the *Institut für Politikwissenschaft*, in particular, and the afore-mentioned *Hochschule für Politik* attached, from the late 1950s, to the newly established *Freie Universität zu Berlin*.[56] There is no space here to go into this subject because the area of funding and, more generally, of direct intervention both from private foundations and from government agencies would lead us to focus attention on many other leading figures, mostly outside traditional academic circles (in Italy, for example, the Olivetti Foundation, the

Committee for Political and Social Science [Co.S.Po.S], the Cattaneo Institute and the Mulino publishing group of Bologna come to mind), which promoted the development of political and social science.

"Americanization" or "Westernization"? Rethinking the Political, Generational and Empirical Turn

It would be simplistic or even misleading to explain the post-1945 development of Political Science in Italy and West Germany only from the defeat in the Second World War onward, or rather as a mere product imported from the United States, as has happened in the German case.[57] This is especially so in Italy where the belief of having taken part in the war on the other side, through the *Resistenza*, lasted for a long time, especially in "high" academic circles. Moreover, the process of adaptation to Western thought continued to be greatly influenced by an academic environment that was hostile, for both corporative and cultural reasons, to the introduction of Political Science and this in fact contributed to the delay of its institutionalization. Actually the struggles of Italian political science for its very existence against well-established disciplines were long lasting. In this context, it is significant that even in 1967, Sartori had to fight against the use of the term "Political Sciences" in the plural,[58] whereas the first public competition for university professorships in Political Science came about only in 1970.

The contribution of scholars with a historical–philosophical or a juridical education was remarkable. However, instead of facilitating the recognition of Political Science as a separate field of study, interaction with exponents of related subjects probably ended up by impeding it. As Bobbio remarked in 1969: "While it is clear that lawyers have not noticed Political Science, historians know it exists but do not give it much credit [...]".[59] In contrast, not even the leading figures in the revival of Italian Political Science after 1945 could boast a specialized training. Moreover, because they all had different training and skills, this helped to create an image of great fragmentation within the subject.

In addition to neglecting the role of earlier traditions of political studies, a general application of the concepts of "Westernization" and/or "Americanization" to the issue of Italian Political Science would not even allow the understanding of the strong relationship between the evolution of political thought and the developments of the national political system over the 1950s and 1960s. In particular in the first decade, attention was focused mainly on the issue of the Constitution and, especially, on the issue of its alleged betrayal, whereas in the second half of the 1960s, the new debate on the party system took shape along lines that were at least partly due to developments in the national political system. It is known that the debate took shape around the two concepts of the "imperfect two-party system" (Galli)[60] and "polarized pluralism" (Sartori),[61] notions that reflected or even suggested two different ways of interpreting the shift to the *centro-sinistra* (center-left) and, in particular, the anti-system nature of the *Partito Comunista Italiano* (PCI, Italian Communist Party).

Similar considerations on the explanatory value of concepts, such as "Westernization" and "Americanization,"[62] and their limits may also be extended to the case of Germany, albeit with some significant differences. In Germany, the processes of maturation and institutionalization of modern Political Science, which began in the aftermath of the Second World War, were more rapid than in Italy thanks to the contribution of the *Remigranten*, who undoubtedly favoured the adaptation of German political thinking to the reality of Western democracy.[63] In contrast, not even in Germany were these processes straightforward or fully accepted in academic circles. In fact, if we were to end the analysis at the Waldleiningen Conference, the historical understanding of how the debate on the revival of Political Science in Germany, which continued afterward, would suffer greatly. Following along the sequence, there are two other conferences, one in Königstein (1950)[64] and one in Frankfurt (1952),[65] during which the opposition of a substantial part of the German academic world of neo-humanist inspiration became clear. Moreover, this was supported by the Conference of University Chancellors of West Germany, which openly challenged the plan to introduce Political Science as a teaching subject in that it was considered alien to the German university tradition.[66] In this context, the intercession of Karl Loewenstein, an emigrant who from the early 1930s had taught Political Science at Amherst College in Massachusetts, proved decisive. On one hand, he put in a good word for the new subject; in contrast, he claimed that a simple "transplant" from the American context to the German one would be neither necessary nor desirable.[67]

The same role played by the *Remigranten* therefore precludes a description of the process of cultural transfer from the United States in terms of mere "Americanization." Although inspired by the American model of Political Science, which considered the discipline as a form of knowledge whose aim was mainly that of creating guidelines for those in government, their approaches and research methods too were greatly affected by earlier traditions of political studies. In particular, when scholars of the first decade of the twentieth century talked about "theory," they nearly always meant political philosophy. Their interest (and that of their students) in the *Ideengeschichte* became ever more important starting from the conviction that new ideas for the building of new "theories" and the discovery of ethical-political principles could be derived from the doctrines of the past. Therefore, in many cases, as shown by the examples of Bergstraesser and Fraenkel, the putting into practice of Political Science offset the required balance between empiricism and normativism, sometimes even ending up claiming that Political Science was a science of evaluation although open to different interpretations.

To sum up: There is no doubt that the emergence of modern Political Science has led, in both Italy and Germany, to a process of adaptation to Western thought and that this process has been largely influenced by the political and intellectual hegemony of the US. In contrast, it is equally true that a generic application of concepts, such as "Westernization" or "Americanization", to the development of Italian and West German Political Science would not allow either the complete grasp of the role of earlier traditions of political studies or of the various political and cultural currents around which some schools of thought of Political Science were built or of the choice of issues on which Political Science focused its attentions. Neither would the various political cleavages, methodological and generational—which in the field of political and social sciences have perhaps been the real engine of scientific progress—be grasped, nor would the different ways in which Western and American models of political systems have been acknowledged, adopted and spread by various scholars. Finally, it would be impossible to understand the reasons for which the cycles of institutionalization and consolidation of modern Political Science have been faster in West Germany than in Italy, although not in line with developments in American post-war Political Science. Concerning this, it is significant that at the very moment in which German political scientists were rediscovering the importance of political theory (meaning political philosophy, which is the conceptual and analytical contribution that modern political thought could offer to address the major issues of contemporary politics), American Political Science, inspired by the behavioural revolution, appeared ever more oriented toward formalization and statistic–quantitative research.[68]

This last point is important to understand the way the supposed "Americanization" or "Westernization" of the Federal Republic of Germany and Italy took place in the field of Political Science. Moreover, here we come to the distinction we must make between "Americanization" and "Westernization" as a cultural and intellectual process on one side and "Americanization" and "Westernization" intended as a political goal on the other side. Even if it is difficult to separate the two dimensions, it is noteworthy that the outcomes of political Westernization and of intellectual Americanization, respectively, turned out to be in some respects different, if not even contradictory. Somewhat paradoxically, the political influence exerted by the US in shaping West German and Italian Political Science toward a Western democratic–oriented Political Science prevented them, at least in the formative phase, from becoming more similar to American Political Science, which was much more empirical and much less normative than in the past. In other words, political Westernization prevented intellectual Americanization. When the 'behavioral revolution' eventually took place also in West Germany and Italy, domestic factors—such as the political, cultural and generational changes of the early 1970s—played an important role too in shaping the 'Americanization' of German and Italian Political Science. Somewhat paradoxically again, this 'empirical turn' took place when some of the political and cultural paradigms on which the Italian and German post-1945 Political Science had been refounded were again called into question including a certain way of understanding the relationship between Political Science and democracy.

NOTES

1. Maier, Hans. "Die Lehre der Politik in den deutschen Universitäten vornehmlich zum 16. bis 18. Jahrhundert." In Oberndörfer, Dieter, ed. *Wissenschaftliche Politik. Eine Einführung in Grundfragen ihrer Tradition und Theorie.* Freiburg: Rombach, 1962, 59–116; Bleek, Wilhelm/ Lietzmann, Hans J., eds. *Schulen der deutschen Politikwissenschaft.* Opladen: Leske + Budrich, 1999; Bobbio, Norberto. *Saggi sulla scienza politica in Italia.* Rome/Bari: Laterza, 1969; Palano, Damiano. *Geometrie del potere. Materiali per la storia della scienza politica italiana.* Milan: Vita e pensiero, 2005.

2. Mohr, Arno. *Politikwissenschaft als Alternative: Stationen einer wissenschaftlichen Disziplin auf dem Wege zu ihrer Selbständigkeit in der Bundesrepublik Deutschland 1945–1965.* Bochum: Studienverl. Brockmeyer, 1988; Pasquino, Gianfranco/Regalia, Marta/Valbruzzi, Marco, eds. *Quarant'anni di scienza politica in Italia.* Bologna: Il Mulino, 2013.

TOWARD A NEW POLITICAL SCIENCE IN ITALY AND WEST GERMANY... 111

3. Palano, *Geometrie del potere*, 14–15.
4. Mosca, Gaetano. *Elementi di scienza politica*. Turin: Bocca Editori, 1896.
5. Mosca, Gaetano. *The Ruling Class*, translation by Kahn, Hannah D. Edited and revised, with an Introduction by Arthur Livingston. New York/London: McGraw-Hill Book Company, 1939.
6. On the role of Gaetano Mosca as founding father of modern Political Science, see Bobbio, Norberto. *Gaetano Mosca e la scienza politica. Discorso inaugurale dell'anno accademico 1959–60*. Rome: Accademia Nazionale dei Lincei, 1960; Lombardo, Antonio. "Sociologia e scienza politica in Gaetano Mosca." *Rivista italiana di scienza politica* 2 (1971), 297–323; Fisichella, Domenico. "Alle origini della scienza politica italiana. Gaetano Mosca epistemologo." *Rivista Italiana di scienza politica* 3 (1991), 447–470.
7. Loader, Colin. *The Intellectual Development of Karl Mannheim*. Cambridge: Cambridge University Press, 1985; Woldring, Henk E.S. *Karl Mannheim: The development of his thought: Philosophy, sociology, and social ethics, with a detailed biography*. New York: St. Martin's Press, 1987.
8. Mannheim, Karl. *Ideology and Utopia*. London: Routledge, 1997, 98.
9. Ibid., 103 f.
10. Farr, James/Seidelman, Raymond, eds. *Discipline and History. Political Science in the United States*. Ann Arbor: University of Michigan Press, 1993.
11. Blomert, Reinhardt. *Intellektuelle im Aufbruch. Karl Mannheim, Alfred Weber, Norbert Elias und die Heidelberger Sozialwissenschaften der Zwischenkriegszeit*. Munich/Vienna: Hanser, 1999.
12. Palmier, Jean-Michel. *Weimar in Exile: The Antifascist Emigration in Europe and America*. London: Verso, 2006.
13. Söllner, Alfons. *Deutsche Politikwissenschaftler in der Emigration*. Opladen: Westdeutscher Verlag, 1996.
14. Laudani, Raffaele, ed. *Franz Neumann, Herbert Marcuse e Otto Kirchheimer. Il nemico Tedesco. Scritti e rapporti riservati nella Germania nazista (1943–1945)*. Bologna: Il Mulino, 2012.
15. On the figure of C.J. Friedrich, see Lietzmann, Hans J. "Carl Joachim Friedrich. Ein amerikanischer Politikwissenschaftler aus Heidelberg." In Blomert, Reinhard/Eßlinger, Hans Ulrich/Giovannini, Norbert, eds. *Das Institut für Sozial- und Staatswissenschaften zwischen 1918 und 1958*. Marburg: Metropolis-Verlag, 1997, 329–347.
16. Lietzmann, Hans J. *Politikwissenschaft im „Zeitalter der Diktaturen": die Entwicklung der Totalitarismustheorie Carl Joachim Friedrichs*. Opladen: Leske + Budrich, 1999.
17. On this see, for example, Bleek, Wilhelm. *Geschichte der Politikwissenschaft in Deutschland*. Munich: C.H. Beck, 2001 and Palano, *Geometrie del potere*, for the German and the Italian case, respectively.

112 G. D'OTTAVIO

18. Quoted in Bobbio, Norberto. "Teoria e ricerca politica in Italia." *Il Politico* XXV (1961), 217.
19. Bobbio, Norberto. *Profilo ideologico del Novecento italiano.* Turin: Einaudi, 1969, 3 f.
20. Gay, Peter. "Weimar Culture. The Outsider as Insider." In Fleming, Donald/Bailyn, Bernard, eds. *The Intellectual Migration. Europa and America, 1930–1960.* Cambridge: Cambridge University Press, 1969, 12.
21. For an analysis extended also to the British and French cases, see D'Ottavio, Gabriele. "Democracy in Transition. The Development of a Science of Politics in Western Europe after 1945." In Pombeni, Paolo, ed. *The Historiography of Transition. Critical Phases in the Development of Modernity (1494–1973).* New York/London: Routledge, 2016, 183–198.
22. Palano, *Geometrie del potere*, 15.
23. Maier, Hans. "Zur Lage der politischen Wissenschaft." *Vierteljahreshefte für Zeitgeschichte* 3 (1962), 227.
24. Bobbio, Norberto. "Politische Theorie und Forschung in Italien." In Stammer, Otto, ed. *Politische Forschung.* Cologne/Opladen: Westdeutscher Verlag, 1960, 65 f.
25. Graziano, Luigi. "Per una storia della scienza politica." In id., ed. *La scienza politica in Italia. Bilancio e prospettive.* Milan: Franco Angeli, 1984, 21 f.
26. Mohr, Arno. *Politikwissenschaft als Alternative: Stationen einer wissenschaftlichen Disziplin auf dem Wege zu ihrer Selbständigkeit in der Bundesrepublik Deutschland 1945–1965.* Bochum: Studienverlag Brockmeyer, 1988, 9.
27. In particular, for Graziano, the other three "groups of factors" to be considered have to do with "the economic and social development of Italian society," "the processes of political democratization, economic rationalization and secularization of society which have accompanied it," [... and] "the external influence, especially the impact of American Political Science and the behavioural movement", cfr. Graziano, *Per una storia della scienza politica*, 21 f.
28. Mohr, *Politikwissenschaft als Alternative*, 9.
29. Lanchester, Fulco, ed. *Passato e presente delle facoltà di Scienze politiche.* Rome: Giuffrè, 2003.
30. Consulta nazionale, Schema di provvedimento legislativo. Soppressione della facoltà e dei corsi di laurea in scienze politiche, 12 novembre 1945, http://www.senato.it/documenti/repository/leggi_e_documenti/raccoltenormative/27%20%20Consulta%20Nazionale/Documenti/Prov. leg.N.040%20del12%20novembre%201945.pdf. (19.11.2014).
31. On this, see Rogari, Sandro. "Il "Cesare Alfieri" da Istituto a Facoltà di Scienze Politiche." In id., ed. *L'Università degli Studi di Firenze, 1924–2004.* Florence: Leo S. Olschki, 2004, 677–739; Di Nucci, Loreto. *Nel*

cantiere dello Stato fascista. Rome: Carocci, 2008; Comparato, Vittor Ivo/ Lupi, Regina/Montanari, Giorgio Eduardo, eds. *Le scienze politiche. Modelli contemporanei.* Milan: Franco Angeli, 2011.

32. Bobbio, Norberto. *Autobiografia*, ed. by Alberto Papuzzi. Rome/Bari: Laterza, 1997, 41 f.
33. On Bruno Leoni, see the special issue of *Il Politico*: Scaramozzino, Pasquale, ed. *Omaggio a Bruno Leoni. Il Politico*, 1969.
34. On Giuseppe Maranini, see Capozzi, Eugenio. *Il sogno di una costituzione. Giuseppe Maranini e l'Italia del Novecento.* Bologna: Il Mulino, 2008.
35. Lanfranchi, Enrico. *Un filosofo militante. Politica e cultura nel pensiero di Norberto Bobbio.* Torino: Bollati Boringhieri, 1989. Salvadori, Massimo L. "Il liberalismo di Bobbio tra etica, politica e progresso sociale." In id., ed. *Liberalismo italiano. I dilemmi della libertà.* Rome: Donzelli, 2011, 153–168.
36. Masala, Antonio. *Il liberalismo di Bruno Leoni.* Soveria Mannelli: Rubbettino, 2003.
37. Frosini, Tommaso Edoardo. *Maranini e la costituzione tra mito e realtà*, *introduzione a G. Maranini, Il mito della costituzione.* Rome: Ideazione, 1996, 3–44.
38. Griffo, Maurizio. "Sull 'origine della parola, partitocrazia'." *L'Acropoli* 4 (2007), 396–409.
39. On Sartori's contribution to the modern Political Science, see Pasquino, Gianfranco, ed. *La scienza politica di Giovanni Sartori.* Bologna: Il Mulino, 2005.
40. Sartori, Giovanni. "Norberto Bobbio e la scienza politica." *Rivista Italiana di scienza politica* 1 (2004), 10.
41. Sartori, Giovanni. *Democrazia e definizioni.* Bologna: Il Mulino, 1957, VI.
42. Sartori, Giovanni, ed. *Antologia di scienza politica.* Bologna: Il Mulino, 1970.
43. *Die politischen Wissenschaften an den deutschen Universitäten und Hochschulen. Gesamtprotokoll der Konferenz von Waldleiningen vom 10. und 11. September 1949*, ed. by Hessisches Ministerium für Erziehung und Volksbildung. Frankfurt a.M.: Verlag Neue Presse, 1950.
44. On this, see Mohr, *Politikwissenschaft als Alternative*, 97–113.
45. Balzer, Friedrich-Martin/Bock, Hans Manfred/Schöler, Uli, eds. *Wolfgang Abendroth. Wissenschaftlicher Politiker. Bio-bibliographische Beiträge.* Opladen: Leske + Budrich, 2001.
46. Habicht, Hubert, ed. *Eugen Kogon – ein politischer Publizist in Hessen. Essays, Aufsätze und Reden zwischen 1946 und 1982.* Frankfurt a.M.: Insel Verlag, 1982.
47. Weber, Petra. *Carlo Schmid: 1896–1979. Eine Biographie.* Munich: C.H. Beck, 1996.

114   G. D'OTTAVIO

48. Söllner, Alfons, ed. *Zur Archäologie der Demokratie in Deutschland, vol. 1: Analysen politischer Emigranten im amerikanischen Geheimdienst, 1943–1945.* Frankfurt a.m.: Europäische Verlagsanstalt, 1982; Id., ed. *Zur Archäologie der Demokratie in Deutschland, vol. 2: Analysen von politischen Emigranten im amerikanischem Außenministerium, 1946–1949.* Frankfurt a.m.: Europäische Verlagsanstalt, 1986; Id. "Normative Westernization? The Impact of Remigres on the Foundation of Political Thought in Post-War Germany." In Müller, Jan Werner, ed. *German ideologies since 1945.* New York: Palgrave Macmillan, 2002, 41–60.

49. Buchstein, Hubertus. *Demokratiepolitik. Theoriebiographische Studien zu deutschen Nachkriegspolitologen.* Baden-Baden: Nomos, 2011.

50. On this, see also Bauerkämper, Arndt. "Demokratie als Verheissung oder Gefahr? Deutsche Politikwissenschaftler und amerikanische Modelle 1945 bis zur Mitte der sechziger Jahre." In id./Jarausch, Konrad H./Payk, Marcus M., eds. *Demokratiewunder. Transatlantische Mittler und die kulturelle Öffnung Westdeutschlands 1945–1970.* Göttingen: Vandenhoeck & Ruprecht, 2005, 253–280.

51. Caciagli, Mario. "Il dibattito politologico nella Repubblica Federale Tedesca." *Rivista italiana di scienza politica* 6 (1976), 564.

52. Oberndörfer, Dieter, ed. *A. Bergstraesser: Weltpolitik als Wissenschaft. Geschichtliches Bewußtsein und politische Erziehung.* Cologne/Opladen: Westdeutscher Verlag, 1965; Fraenkel, Ernst. *Das amerikanische Regierungssystem. Eine politologische Analyse.* Cologne/Opladen: Westdeutscher Verlag, 1960.

53. On this, see, for example, Krige, John. *American Hegemony and the Postwar Reconstruction of Science in Europe.* Cambridge, MA: MIT Press, 2006; and, with particular regard to the German case study, see Mauch, Christof/Patel, Kiran Klaus, eds. *The United States and Germany during the Twentieth Century.* Cambridge/New York: Cambridge University Press, 2010.

54. Cfr. Berghahn, Volker R. *America and the Intellectual Cold Wars in Europe. Shepard Stone between Philantropy, Academy, and Diplomacy.* Princeton: Princeton University Press, 2001; Gemelli, Giuliana. *The Ford Foundation and Europe (1950's–1970's).* Brussels: European Interuniversity Press, 1998; Tournès, Ludovic, ed. *L'Argent de l'influence. Les foundations américaines et leurs réseaux européens.* Paris: Autrement, 2010.

55. Coleman, Peter. *The Liberal Conspiracy. The Congress for Cultural Freedom and the Struggle for the Mind of Postwar Europe.* New York: Free Press Collier Macmillan, 1989.

56. Rausch, Helke. "«Allemagne, année zero?». Dénazifier et democratiser (1945–1955)." In Tournès, ed. *L'Argent de l'influence*, 34 f.

57. Arndt, Hans-Joachim. *Die Besiegten von 1945. Versuch einer Politologie für Deutsche samt Würdigung der Politikwissenschaft in der Bundesrepublik Deutschland.* Berlin: Duncke & Humblot, 1978.
58. Sartori, Giovanni. "La scienza politica." *Il Politico*, 1967, 688–701.
59. Bobbio, *Saggi sulla scienza politica in Italia*, 17.
60. Galli, Giorgio. *Il bipartitismo imperfetto. Comunisti e democristiani in Italia.* Bologna: Il Mulino, 1967.
61. Sartori, Giovanni. *Parties and Party Systems: A Framework for Analysis.* Cambridge: Cambridge University Press, 1976.
62. For an analysis of these terms with particular regard to the German case study, see Schildt, Axel. *Zwischen Abendland und Amerika. Studien zur westdeutschen Ideenlandschaft der 50er Jahre.* Munich: Oldenbourg, 1999; Doering-Manteuffel, Anselm. *Wie westlich sind die Deutschen? Amerikanisierung und Westernisierung im 20. Jahrhundert. Amerikanisierung und Westernisierung im 20. Jahrhundert.* Göttingen: Vandenhoeck & Ruprecht, 1999; Schildt, Axel. *Annäherungen an die Westdeutschen. Sozial und kulturgeschichtliche Perspektiven auf die Bundesrepublik.* Göttingen: Wallstein Verlag, 2011.
63. In particular, the National Association of Political Science (*Deutsche Vereinigung für die Wissenschaft von der Politik*, from 1959 *Deutsche Vereinigung für politische Wissenschaft*) was created in 1951. Its reference magazine came out of the revived *Zeitschrift für Politik* (in existence since 1908) and the *Politische Vierteljahresschrift* (in existence since 1960). From 1957 to 1961, the number of chairs for the teaching of Political Science more than doubled from 13 to 27. See Lepsius, Mario Rainer. *Denkschrift über die Lage der Soziologie und Politikwissenschaft. Im Auftrag der Deutschen Forschungsgemeinschaft.* Wiesbaden: Franz Steiner, 1961.
64. *Über Lehre und Forschung der Wissenschaft von der Politik. Gesamtprotokoll der Konferenz von Königstein im Taunus vom 15. Und 16. Juli 1950*, ed. by Hessisches Ministerium für Erziehung und Volksbildung. Frankfurt a.M.: Verlag Neue Presse, 1950.
65. On the conference in Frankfurt, see Mohr, *Politikwissenschaft als Alternative*, 122–124.
66. Ibid.
67. Cfr. Loewenstein, Karl. "Über den Stand der politischen Wissenschaften in den Vereinigten Staaten." *Zeitschrift für die gesamte Staatswissenschaft* 2 (1950), 349–361.
68. Narr, Wolf-Dieter/Naschold, Friedrich. *Theorie der Demokratie.* Stuttgart: Kohlhammer, 1971.

PART III

Progressive Party Politics

CHAPTER 6

Lost Generation? Nicolò Carandini, the Decline of New Liberalism and the Myth of a New Europe

Christian Blasberg

"If you don't know us, look at our socks; we are the Radicals of Count Carandini," was the refrain of a popular song circulating for some time in post-war Rome. Presumably, the lyrics were a deformation of an older fascist chant. Ironically alluding to the elegant clothing style – with white (some say red) socks – of a certain group of bourgeois intellectuals, it also named the most prominent representative of this group, Count Nicolò Carandini.[1] Not many politicians could claim to be mentioned in such folkloristic chants—and probably they were better off without it because usually the lyrics were not too flattering. And not only: Another slogan, a free interpretation of Marx presumably created by Ennio Flaiano around the high times of the "friends of Il Mondo" in the late 1950s[2]: "Landowners of the world unite – the lands to the Carandini!", frames even more ironically the socio-political features—and contradictions—of this northern Italian nobleman, who had not been born rich but in 1926 had become co-owner of the Torre in Pietra estate near Rome, being the main milk producer for the capital by the 1930s.[3]

C. Blasberg (✉)
LUISS School of Government, Rome, Italy

© The Author(s) 2018
J. Späth (ed.), *Does Generation Matter? Progressive Democratic Cultures in Western Europe, 1945–1960*, Palgrave Studies in the History of Social Movements, https://doi.org/10.1007/978-3-319-77422-0_6

119

In political terms, Carandini was often called the "red Count," alluding to his left-leaning ideas, which seemed to contrast his social position. Indeed, according to Giovanni Spadolini's memory, the antifascist journalist Mario Missiroli had coined another characterization of Carandini as an "English-style conservative" right after the Count's most important programmatic speech in September 1944.[4] It is thus difficult to find a coherent definition: He may be characterized as a left-wing conservative liberal, certainly a unique character among the emerging political elite of post-war Italy—and perhaps one who chose the wrong political family. "It's a pity that your socialism is what it is [...],", he once told socialist leader Pietro Nenni, "[...] because if it were different I would be a socialist."[5]

Despite, or rather because of, this uniqueness, Carandini is remembered as a second-rank politician who preferred sticking to a set of higher political ideals, if necessary renouncing public office, rather than inclining to political contingencies and swimming on the tide of socio-cultural tendencies.[6] This gives his political curriculum a certain sense of being unaccomplished and transformed him from one of the most promising political leaders of a generation, ready to take responsibility for the democratic reconstruction of the country in the immediate post-fascist period, into a niche intellectual with a somehow enigmatic charisma in the first decades of the Republic.[7] With a little disrespect one might easily tend to stigmatize him as a privileged part-time politician and occasional publicist who, from a 'mainstream' point of view (whether it is Christian democrat or communist), engaged in cranky Byzantine disputes and long-lost battles, cultivating an idealism that increasingly set itself apart from the realities of the political evolution in Italy. Meanwhile, Carandini held representative positions such as President of *Alitalia* airlines (1948–1968).[8]

Nonetheless, Carandini's unaccomplished political career is closely linked to the destiny of Italian liberalism in the first post-war decades. He played a role in both the decline of the classical liberal doctrine between 1943 and 1953 and the intellectual preparation of the centre-left concept in the next decade, although without managing to trigger a comeback of liberalism within this scheme. Thanks to his years as ambassador in Great Britain between 1944 and 1947, however, all these shortcomings in domestic politics were overshadowed by an intense sensibility for the international and European implications of all national political concepts. In this wider panorama, Carandini differed sharply from the conservative national-liberalism that prevailed in France or Germany until the beginning of the 1950s.

He instead regarded a renewed social-liberalism as a necessarily supranational and federalist doctrine that would be able to break up the ideological
polarization of Europe and the world. This Europeanist dimension of his
political thinking and action has been undervalued in historical research,
although it seems to be the decisive linkage uniting the various and partly
contradictory aspects which characterize the personality. This chapter suggests a reassessment of his impact first on Europe's and second on Italy's
political evolution. The failure of his New Liberalism in the Italian political
reality may, in a certain sense, be counter-balanced by his commitment to
the European idea.

THE LEADER AND THE GODFATHER

From the very beginning of his political activity, which he started rather
late around the age of 30 years, and mostly due to his marriage in early
1926 to Elena, daughter of Luigi Albertini (the former director of the
Corriere della Sera, who had been ousted by the fascists few months
before), Carandini cultivated an elitist attitude. First, he identified with
the minority of Italians who chose not to follow or fit themselves in the
fascist regime[9]; later, when anti-fascism assumed a broader national consensus, he stood with the few survivors of the bourgeois-liberal tradition
in its purest forms, the "Italy of reason."[10] "We are liberals [...]", Carandini
wrote in his first clandestine pamphlet, *Primi Chiarimenti*, circulated in
Rome since 1 May 1943, 3 months before the fall of Mussolini, "[...] and
we don't feel any need to correct this qualification of ours by accentuating
adjectives towards chromatic tendencies and graduations that could promise us, [...] a broader and more immediate popularity."[11]

Carandini took the risk of being unpopular. He understood "being liberal" in the revolutionary climate of the increasingly post-fascist era would
be a confession almost as daring as "being fascist." Wasn't the liberal State
widely blamed for having generated and supported fascism? Didn't the
catastrophe the country was facing in those months reveal the failure of
the entire history of unified liberal Italy since the *Risorgimento*, thus
implying the need to re-build the State from its very roots? To claim citi-
zenship for his New Liberalism within the landscape of post-fascist Italy,
Carandini had to stress that it was "[...] an antifascist position and qualification of which we claim the merits and accept the consequences and
risks."[12] Only an intransigent antifascism, he believed, could give liberalism the legitimacy to dare a comeback and claim spiritual leadership of the

Italian society as well as an educational mission to guide it toward democracy. "The new liberalism [...]," Gerardo Nicolosi writes, "[...] forges itself in antifascism, and even more in the resistance."[13]

This new liberal elite implied also a clear generational consciousness. Carandini saw himself as "[...] part of a mature and proven generation which, having known freedom when this supreme good had been the natural fellow and essential exigency of life, thereafter had to assist to its repudiation operated by the improvisation of an unreasonable and unprepared faction [...]".[14] Thus, no rupture with the liberal past, because one's own life experience went back far enough to remember better days before fascism, was worth being taken as a starting point for the construction of post-fascist Italy. However, as Nicolosi further observes "[...] a rupture was claimed towards the old liberal guard, except the 'masters' [...],", first among them Benedetto Croce. Only very few of these old "masters" of liberalism could claim a clean record of antifascist moral integrity and therefore were considered as still being able to provide their precious services to the reconstruction of democracy.[15]

The assistance and guidance by the older "masters" was held as indispensable. *Primi Chiarimenti* and the second pamphlet published by Carandini in late August 1943, *Realtà*, mirrored perfectly Croce's ideas for a new reformed liberalism and the role it would have to assume in post-fascist Italy: "[...] we do not aim, for now, at the reconstruction of that 'liberal party' [...]" with an economic program, like the other antifascist groups were about to build up by that time – prematurely, according to Carandini. "We want to renounce deliberately on our immediate affirmation as a party [...]," he explained, "[...] because what drives us is accelerating [...] the movement towards the spiritual and political emancipation of the country, which must be the only motivation of the day [...]." Carandini further admitted that, "We do not possess a panacea program for all economic, social, political, national and international problems, that the new world still keeps hidden and will not reveal before the crisis is ripened in which the war will have to resolve [...]."[16] This was exactly what Croce had intended with his idea of a 'pre-party': acting directly through the existing institutions—which were still the institutions of liberal Italy created at the time of the *Risorgimento*—to create a broad sociocultural consensus for the spirit of freedom as a moral precondition for any further political reconstruction and democratic distinction of economic doctrines in the country.[17] Liberalism as a religion for the people, as Croce had designed it in his 1932 *Storia d'Europa nel Secolo Decimonono*.[18]

However, Carandini's devotion to the "master" knew some limits. He appreciated the philosopher's reformist socio-economic ideas of the early 1940s, although he was less convinced by his "action-plan," which was aimed at instigating the Royal Court to take the initiative for the destitution of Mussolini. Carandini did not share the liberal "secession" of the *Partito d'Azione* (PdA) at the end of 1942, but he might well have done so if the PdA had not adopted its policy of "republican priority."[19] However, his decision to address public opinion well before the fall of Mussolini, and to gather younger anti-fascists such as Leone Cattani and Mario Pannunzio—some of them 10 or more years his junior and therefore without experience of pre-fascist liberalism—in the *Movimento Liberale Italiano* (MLI),[20] was nonetheless a barely veiled step toward the creation of an organized liberal party in contrast to what Croce and the "elders" wanted and despite Carandini's own assertions in *Primi Chiarimenti*.

Consequently, after July 25th the men of the MLI considered the Monarchy to have exhausted its institutional duty and decided that King Victor Emanuel III now had to lay power in the hands of the democratic forces of anti-fascism. The decision by Croce and other "old liberals" (in particular Alessandro Casati) in August 1943 to accept the Badoglio government and to exclude the younger liberals from leadership of the constituting *Partito Liberale Italiano* (PLI), however, marked their disapproval of the "youngster's" too brisk approach and generated in Carandini a greater consciousness for the need to transfer power into the hands of a generation of which he himself (at 50 years old) was already a "senior."[21] "I appreciated the work of the old men in this first period of half-government [...]," he would write in 1945 after the liberation of the North, "[...] but I think we need to renew courageously, to find new men with fresh energies [...]." His choice, though, was everything but enthusiastic considering the enormous and difficult challenges of reconstruction reserved for those who would govern Italy. Nevertheless, he concluded, "Neither the old nor the young are prepared for this superhuman task. So it's worth anyway trying with the young."[22]

During the German occupation of Rome, Carandini had emerged as one of the leading democratic politicians in Italy. Communications with Croce had been interrupted since the liberation of Naples in late September, and Carandini became the de facto leader of the PLI in Rome, which was now enforcedly dominated by new men of the younger generation. After the resignation of the older Casati, he also represented the liberals within

124   C. BLASBERG

the clandestine Roman *Comitato di Liberazione Nazionale* (CLN).[23] Constantly running the risk of being arrested like some of his colleagues (notably Pannunzio, director of *Risorgimento Liberale*, who escaped by pure luck being executed at the Fosse Ardeatine),[24] Carandini could claim a perfect record of antifascist and patriotic resistance by the time of the liberation of Rome in June 1944, thus making him inevitably one of the most credited politicians of post-fascist Italy.[25]

When the new CLN government was formed, Carandini was considered the highest ranked liberal politician after Croce and was thus offered the Ministry of Agriculture, not only in recognition of his expertise in this field but also because "[...] he has a very good influence on Bonomi, whom he could prevent from making errors, and he knows how to deal with those on the left [...]."[26] In the end, he stepped back in favour of older liberals like Casati, considering instead the organization and unification of the PLI a priority where he wanted the young and, as he believed, more progressive-minded liberals to prevail.[27] However, after 2 months Croce resigned and convinced a reluctant Carandini to take his Ministry without portfolio, a position reserved to the six leaders of the CLN parties in order to assure their loyalty to the government.[28]

He now was equal to Togliatti, Saragat and De Gasperi, and crown prince Umberto considered him the key figure in the institutional conflict because he seemed to be the only one capable of bridging the rift between the moderate forces, mostly in favour of a popular referendum, and the intransigent republicans on the left.[29] However, it was this mediating attitude that exposed Carandini increasingly more to conflicting suspicions on either side of the CLN parties. Most of all, the monarchist "old guard" of the liberals, such as Vittorio Emanuele Orlando, suspected him—interpreter of Croce's "agnostic" position—to be a camouflaged republican.[30] The institutional question inevitably inflamed the conflict between prefascist liberal notables, monarchists and local patrons who claimed their right to a broad representation within the new PLI and through the party to gain more influence on the CLN, and the Carandini-led generation of younger liberals open for institutional reform.[31]

The already mentioned programmatic speech held by Carandini on 3 September 1944 at the Brancaccio Theatre was thus intended—not without a certain naivety—to put a halt to these tendencies, cement his position as leader of the PLI and clearly define its ideological position as a young, progressive and anti-totalitarian party in equal competition with the mass parties. It would instead prove to be a clamorous miscalculation

LOST GENERATION? NICOLÒ CARANDINI, THE DECLINE OF NEW... 125

of the political games played inside and outside of the CLN and the PLI. Moreover, it was to be the turning point of his domestic political career. The PLI, according to Carandini, represented the pure liberal tradition with its inherent progressivism: "The new liberal generations [...]," he claimed, "[...] intend to affirm their right to serve liberty and justice according to a renewed inspiration." He attacked all conservative and purely monarchist tendencies, "[...] the first germ of national discordance [...]" that tried to undermine the renewal of the PLI and the legitimacy of the CLN to lead the country through the post-fascist transition period.[32] All kinds of dictatorship, right or left, were firmly refused, but Carandini also warned that the political parties "[...] Today [...] all plead for freedom, but not all intend tomorrow to make the same use of it."[33] Nonetheless, he maintained that a compromise between liberalism and the revolutionary ideologies in a "[...] fair composition, an advanced democracy [...]" would be possible. The containment of condensed individual powers by "[...] a rigorous system of brakes, of controls, of sanctions is necessary [...]" even though not beyond the limits of the need for an individualist expression of life. The State, Carandini continued, "[...] should be required to ever more discipline and to ever better direct this flow of individual impulses. In addition, the communists and socialists surely have something to teach us on this path. For this we progressive liberals [...]," he concluded, "[...] look without apprehension on communism, entered to share governmental responsibility; for this we look without distrust on socialism, assuming the same responsibility."[34]

These theses were sufficient for being perceived as an imminent danger to the safeguard of broader individual interests in the reconstruction process. The leader of Italian liberals had proposed a set of rather socialist ideals, which clearly overshadowed the many holy principles of a traditional liberalism, which Carandini's address had well confirmed. However, by reaching the hand of reconciliation to both sides of the CLN area—and condemning everything existing outside of it—Carandini gave reason for distrust to all. Most of all, Carandini's stance on the institutional question, leaving the choice between the Monarchy and the Republic open to individual conscience after the liberation of the North and giving priority to the guarantees for freedom and progressive democracy, must have alarmed the promoters of the Monarchy, who were traditionally represented by the Liberal Party.[35]

Only a few weeks after the speech, Carandini was appointed Italian ambassador to London, apparently at the proposal of the British ambassador to Rome, Noel Charles, a supporter of the Italian Monarchy. Thus, it is not a surprise that the Royal Court more than welcomed the decision as we know from the diaries of the Royal Minister Falcone Lucifero. He mentions a meeting with Umberto, who authorized him to communicate to the Foreign Ministry "[…] that he is very, very satisfied about the designation of Carandini to London. Also before [me] leaving [the room] he repeats it, for that I shall not forget it."[36] Was this joy at the success of a secret plan to kick Carandini upstairs?[37] In fact, Elena Carandini believed that "[…] there were monarchist interests behind the removal of Nicolò from the party and from Italy. He had been explicit: Saving the monarchy only if unquestionably wanted by the majority of the Italians in a plebiscite, with absolute priority for the democratic interest. So, one cannot count on Carandini."[38]

The liberals of the PLI, too, did not want to count on Carandini. Instead of mediating between moderate and revolutionary parties within the CLN, the younger leadership began to realize that the PLI was to play the role of a hinge between the CLN itself and the forces outside of it, most notably the Monarchy and the conservatives surrounding it, if it wished to avoid the risk that this ambience would mess about with the remnants of fascism. Carandini was urged to accept the diplomatic mission abroad, even though he felt disgruntled about leaving his governmental position and the leadership of the party in which he saw himself as an indispensable element of cohesion. "At the end I complied, with the pact that every month I will come to Rome […]," he stated, believing that "[…] It will be a mission of few months, because I have no intention to be a career ambassador."[39]

In the end, the mission to London lasted for almost 3 years until October 1947. Carandini did indeed try to keep in close contact with the PLI, but he had to acknowledge his progressive alienation from a leading role in it, mainly at the hands of the same younger generation whose position he had defended against the return of the "old liberals."[40] This became strikingly evident at the end of 1945: Carandini's attempts, through various letters sent from London, to convince Cattani, now Secretary General of the PLI, to abstain from provoking a governmental crisis and breaking the CLN alliance were deliberately ignored. Carandini had lost his role as a doyen of the young liberals. Cattani considered the ambassador simply out of touch with domestic politics in Italy and thus too incompetent to participate in these affairs.[41]

Few time later, all hopes of both a progressive turn of New Liberalism as well as a generational change in liberal leadership vanished. For the elections of 2 June 1946, Croce had convinced the four "old men" of Italian liberalism to lend their faces as promoters of the liberal electoral alliance, *Unione Democratica Nazionale* (UDN): Orlando, Nitti, the consumed Bonomi, and himself. Against their expectations, based on believing that the broad middle class was still devoted to the liberal values of the *Risorgimento*, they were not able to trigger much enthusiasm among moderate voters, and the results were correspondingly disappointing: 6.9% at the national level. Personal animosities among the old liberal leaders, which had been inherited from the past, made the rest: Nitti, who could hardly walk, is said to have commented that "advanced age to some affects the legs, to others the brain,"[42] clearly referring to Orlando who had been mocking Nitti's health condition.

However, Croce still considered Carandini his potential successor despite the increasing discrepancy between the philosopher's exigency for unity among all liberals and Carandini's claims for an open articulation and debate between the various tendencies within the PLI, which was a petty dispute if considered in its substance.[43] However, "The position of Croce concerning the party-form was diametrically opposed to the one of Carandini [...]," as Luca Riccardi analysed.[44] The discord between the two men would intensify during the summer of 1946 and lead to a cooling-down of their relations from that point onward, especially when Carandini decided to leave the party in early 1948 after a last attempt to convince Croce that his idea of liberal unity at all costs had failed. Concerning their reaction in opposition to the new monarchist right-wing leadership of the PLI, Carandini and Croce split: The philosopher blamed his disciple for abandoning the battlefield; the disciple accused his master of making himself the jumping jack of anti-liberal interests.[45] Their relationship was never completely restored in Croce's last years.[46]

However, although Croce had made some adjustments to his early reformist ideas of 1942[47] and had adapted himself to the "centrist" turn of Italian politics between 1945 and 1948—notably by overcoming his hostility to Christian Democracy and refusing to consider Communism just an economic doctrine that was potentially compatible with liberalism[48]— Carandini would defend Croce's early ideas for a long time. To keep this faith, he had to gradually distance himself from the PLI, preferring isolation in Italian politics after his return from London. His last "chance" to return to public office had been De Gasperi's offer to make him Foreign Minister in 1947. Nevertheless, the ambassador refused the offer when he was faced with the refusal by the PLI leadership and Croce to support another tripartite government including the Communists, and the signature of the Peace Treaty.[49] He could have been an independent, technical Minister who did not represent any party, but yet a nostalgic loyalty to his former political home and its master prevailed on that occasion.[50] This loyalty would default a year later when he experienced a rupture with the party, which, in reality, had been long overdue.

THINKING EUROPE

When Nicolò Carandini appeared for the first time in front of an audience of the *Movimento Federalista Europeo* (MFE) in January 1948, a new direction in his political activity had begun.[51] Only a few days before he had left the Liberal Party in bitterness because it had made an electoral alliance with the right-wing populist movement *Uomo Qualunque*.[52] New Liberalism had been relegated to a mere cultural phenomenon without a real impact on national political affairs. The scary escalation of the conflict between the USA and the Soviet Union in the preceding months, which was threatening to degenerate into a global war and causing tensions close to civil war in Italy, had led him instead to the conviction that the political battle to contrast this new conflict scenario had to be fought beyond the national level, on the international stage, and—according to the *Ventotene Manifesto*—while establishing a highly integrated federal European state system before pursuing national ideological designs.[53]

Already during his participation in the peace negotiations in London, Paris and New York throughout 1945 and 1946, Carandini had learned that Italy as victim of the victorious powers was not the main problem to be addressed but rather it was that swooning Europe as a whole, winners and losers alike, had become the chessboard of two overpowering world-players with little regard for ancient national interests in continental affairs.[54] Differently from his master, Croce, he had accepted his country's status as a defeated nation and its inability to influence the terms of the Treaty directly, which he knew would be tough. "If France, Yugoslavia, Greece are jealous about our rehabilitation, we need to satisfy them, throw them a bone to gnaw at, show that Italy has paid."[55] He believed that the Italian accession to the United Nations and, in consequence, the chance to revise the Treaty with more friendly-minded neighbours would give less importance to national sacrifices.[56] Only the Trieste question kept troubling Carandini, who didn't want to recognize any Yugoslav claims, even though he defined himself as "[...] the denial of nationalism [...].".[57] However, at Trieste Italy defended freedom against totalitarianism, not one national interest against another. In any case, Italy's future depended on its capacity to gain its neighbour's confidence, and the Peace Treaty was an obstacle on this path that needed to be removed as soon as possible and at any cost.

As ambassador, Carandini had tried to gain the confidence of Great Britain, the most European among the "Big Three," by overcoming a hostile atmosphere in London during the first period of his stay when Italians were still often considered enemies despite their efforts to show their democratic creed. Re-establishing British goodwill towards Italy was fundamental because Great Britain was to be the natural future leader of a free Europe. Carandini was confident that "England today is tired, tomorrow will be exhausted, but it will repose, revitalize and will take up its course again. And we with her."[58] The importance of this task even made him decline the highest ministerial offers at home for the post-liberation government in 1945 (the PdA favoured him as the best possible Prime Minister).[59] Working for the European idea abroad seemed to be a more useful way for him to serve his country's interest than running government at home. In London, he believed himself to be at the spot where the destinies of the new European order would be decided.

Post-war France, under the leadership of Charles de Gaulle, worried him instead. The French, he noted in March 1945, "[...] don't see anything but France and they see it bigger than it actually is. They do not seem to me renewed or animated by a broad European spirit. They want to be at any cost what they cannot be any more." He was pleased about the friendly French attitude toward Italy but complained that this sympathy was "[...] without a special interest, without conviction. [...] France alone doesn't count any more, [...] it now depends on the friendships it will manage to conquer for itself and on the solidarities it will be able to merit."[60] However, purging the country of its Pétainist past would be a heavy burden on the way to this rehabilitation, he thought, because the Maréchal "[...] had with him ninety percent of the Frenchmen. Thus, process against France."[61]

Carandini did not seem to have any particular attitude toward Germany despite his personal friendship with former ambassador Ulrich von Hassell (executed in 1944 for his involvement in the Stauffenberg plot against

Hitler) in the 1930s.[62] As an anti-fascist, Carandini simply saw the country as the main enemy if Nazism had not been definitively uprooted and the people re-educated to democracy. This process, though, was to happen without resorting to a new racism directed against the Germans, even in the light of the horrors committed by them. Nevertheless, his admiration for democratic traditions excluded Germany as a competitor of Great Britain and France. Even in later years, he would remain rather emotionless when faced with the German problem and the need to grant it a place in his federative European design. He never shared Croce's traditional predilection for the German culture nation.[63]

Until 1945, European integration had been for Carandini mainly a question of balance between the continent's components. A close French–Italian or "Latin" axis, he believed, was needed to counterbalance German demographic strength. Likewise, he was initially confident that Eastern European states, such as Poland and Czechoslovakia, would be able to balance their independent existence against the predominance of the Soviet Union, which he wanted to see as a protector for them and not as an occupier. He believed that "[…] a global Anglo-Russian-American directorate can be a good medium and self-neutralizing mixture [...]."[64] The principle of mediation wherever conflict lines occurred was the guiding principle of Carandini's political design, thus mirroring his personal inclination to avoid siding with one or the other party as long as a liberal basic consensus was respected.

Even when the atmosphere in international relations hardened in the following years, Carandini did not renounce his conciliatory ideas and refused to accept the reality of bipolarization. A convinced supporter of the Anglo–American socio-constitutional model while refusing soviet-style dictatorship and collectivism, he nevertheless separated the question of ideological preferences from that of an international peace and security order. By 1947, the idea of a mediating *Third Force* became his lead concept for the solution of the entire complex of intertwined problems from the domestic to the global level. "We want a 'Third Force' in Italy [...]," he declared at the *Third Force* Congress in Milan in April 1948, "[...] for that Italy becomes an element of 'Third Force' in Europe, so that Europe may rise to be the 'Third Force' in the world."[65] However, although *Third Force* had become a fashionable idea all over Europe, particularly in France due to the socialist-led Ramadier government, Carandini represented a much more liberal variant of the concept and worked in Italy on removing the socialist monopoly from the idea.[66]

In early 1948, he was still convinced that Great Britain—the traditional embodiment of liberalism in the world—would not be subdued by the USA and would soon arise from its economic difficulties, placing itself as a powerful third alternative between the two superpowers. He even believed that Great Britain, led by the Labour government and as leader of a European Federation, would manage to assume a position that could gain confidence within both blocks, the capitalist and the communist.[67] The socio-economic policy adopted by the Attlee government was, as he assured at the MFE meeting in January 1948, "[...] for sure the most mature, balanced and closest to satisfy the opposed exigencies of liberty and discipline that baffle the European conscience."[68]

Even after the Prague Coup in February, Carandini still believed that the Cold War would be nothing but a short-lived phenomenon of international tension. A process of community building was underway in both Western and Eastern Europe as a precondition for further integration, which was to occur naturally after the end of "[...] this absurd state of warlike peace [...]." The driving force in the West was the Marshall Plan imposed by the USA; in the East it was the network of bilateral agreements between the USSR and the smaller nations conquered at the end of the Second World War, which, according to Carandini, had the positive effect of creating "[...] a pool of nations in the area of Europe most exposed to nationalistic disruptions [...]"—a community of sovereign nations that by choice had temporarily accepted Soviet protection and was therefore coequal, actually even advanced, compared with any western community. A de facto federation in the East, as Carandini saw it, needed to be equalled by a federation in the West. The two European partial communities were then much more likely to bind together then a multitude of fragmented nations as had existed before the war.[69]

On this conciliatory theory of Europe as a *Third Force*, even though it left some open questions about his realistic perception of the situation in the Eastern part of the continent, Carandini nevertheless became the leading figure of European federalism in Italy and was commissioned to preside over the Italian delegation at the European Congress at The Hague in May 1948, although he would do so without any representatives from the national government or parliament.[70] He then toured Italy in order to promote the results of the summit and the idea of a Council of Europe that, according to Carandini, could be only an embryonic body on which to build up further political institutions of the supranational European federation. Inspired by Luigi Einaudi, he argued that "[...] the healing

132   C. BLASBERG

revolution will not come until the paralyzing myth of the untouchable national sovereignties will have been dared to be crushed [...]", and warned that "[...] an economic federation doesn't arise, doesn't live, doesn't last if it isn't preceded and guaranteed by a substantial political federation."[71]

In October, the Italian weekly *L'Europeo* depicted him as the "Apostle of European Federalism,"[72] and De Gasperi entrusted him with the organization of an international Congress of the *Union of European Federalists* (UEF) at Palazzo Venezia in Rome in November. Here, however, some fundamental changes in his views became evident. In the debate about the Atlantic Pact, he now accepted the functional approach of Italian membership in this Western alliance led by the USA even though this was detrimental to Western European credibility if it wanted a rapprochement to the East and to the real chances of Europe becoming a *Third Force*. The Cold War, escalating with the Berlin blockade, seemed to have been accepted as a lasting state of the international scenario at the time, thus justifying a deeper protective interference by the USA in Western Europe. Talking instead about the role of Great Britain in the future European setup, Carandini was now rather disappointed about the Euro-sceptic turn of the Labour government, which seemed anything but willing to assume that kind of leading role as a mediator between East and West that the former ambassador had designed for it.[73]

It even came to a diplomatic incident when Carandini claimed that Great Britain had to find its political and economic integration within a European Federation, "[...] abandoning its 'separatism', even though it is impossible to pretend that it, bound to its empire as it is, can fully participate in the federation. Altogether, the pan-European politics presumes British collaboration, but cannot be a reflection of the particular exigencies of British politics." After some loud protesting by British delegates, Carandini continued claiming "[...] that Great Britain has to dissipate the impression that she wants to build herself a military defence at Europe's dispenses [...]." Now the British delegation left the conference hall and only hours later could be convinced to return.[74] The times of the "Anglomania," for which he had often been criticized, were definitely over. He even avoided meeting British representatives at social events when not necessary.[75]

Although Great Britain lost Carandini's favour, France had constantly gained his consideration since 1947. Léon Blum's *Troisième Force* campaign designing a simple triangular system of European democracy threatened from both sides, American capitalism and Soviet communism,[76] fit perfectly with Carandini's idea. The reality of a *Troisième Force* government gathering all democratic forces against Communists and Gaullists alike seemed to be the model for what he had in mind regarding Italy. Paul Ramadier's assertions at The Hague Congress about the potential weight of an independent and united Europe for a world-peace order were explicitly highlighted by Carandini, and by 1950—after the launch of the Pleven Plan—he had to recognize "[...] to France the merit to have clearly seen and conceptualized [...]" the problem of a common, supranational defence structure including Germany.[77]

By that time, Carandini seems to have clearly accepted the reality of the Cold War, which had grown evident with the Korean War. Any ideal of a European neutralism, a Europe as *Third Force* equally distanced from both superpowers, had become invalid when confronted with the threat of Soviet aggression and the acknowledgement that the Eastern European Community of States was not an autonomous actor in a multitude of international communities drifting naturally toward a united Europe but a mere extension of the USSR. "Neutral is who, disposing of a real and terrifying force, abstains from using it a priori, reserving to put it on the scales at an opportune moment in order to paralyse the conflict moods between third parties [...],", he explained at another federalist meeting at the end of 1950 in Rome. However, because Europe did not have these forces at its disposal, neutrality "[...] is not what Europe wants for itself and what the world expects from Europe."[78]

Consequently, Carandini remained a strong supporter of the two main West-European projects, the Coal and Steel Community (ECSC) and the European Defence Community (EDC), even though he did not agree with the functionalist approach of Jean Monnet. Indeed, he continued insisting that "[...] facing the military and economic problem without making it precede by a political solution means turning the natural order of things upside down, making the problem unsolvable from the very start and waste the energies spent for it."[79] Most of all with regard to the spiny question of the EDC, a political union would guarantee peaceful admission of Germany into this West-European Community without fears of its new hegemonic ambitions.[80] By 1954, he reminded, in *Il Mondo*, that a refusal by France and Italy to ratify the EDC Treaty "[...] would mean the failure of all the conciliatory politics of Adenauer already accused by the nationalists to have betrayed the promise [...] to give to the German people equality of status in Europe

134   C. BLASBERG

[…]," and a severe danger for the democratic process in that country.[81] Consequently, the end of the EDC, and with it the European Political Community (EPC), marked another turning point for Carandini. French Prime Minister Mendès France, who had been an ideological inspiration for Italian social liberals before, ceased to be a prospective partner for Carandini due to his presumed responsibility for the failure of the European project.[82]

Although Carandini's rapprochement toward Germany itself would remain cautious and rational, he nonetheless had much more emotional access to the Germanic world thanks to his role in the 1946 De Gasperi–Gruber agreement about the question of South Tyrol and Trentino. Negotiating as ambassador of Italy with the Austrians, Carandini had shot down Austrian claims for an outright restitution of the two provinces (assigned to Italy in 1919) in exchange for granting them an autonomous status. This attempt for a policy of devaluation of frontiers had been one of the few Italian successes in the complex of the Peace Treaties.[83] The region, however, remained troublesome, and at the end of the 1950s Carandini intervened with several articles in *Il Mondo* in which he defended the Italian position against the nationalistic claims of the German-speaking population in the two provinces.[84] Germany and "Germanness" in general would, in Carandini's sub-consciousness, always remain mystically linked to a sense of inferiority in democratic education and liberal spirit, whereas France and especially Great Britain remained the traditional champions of democracy and freedom despite all nationalistic and isolationist tendencies.

A Friend of "Il Mondo"

Already around 1948 and 1949, however, Carandini had become increasingly pessimistic about the possibilities for him to influence public opinion in Italy. After the failure to gain support for New Liberalism, his European message met nationalistic and interest-driven incomprehension by his countrymen who preferred to align in a defeatist attitude with the USA in NATO or appeal to the United Nations for the restitution of old colonies rather than understand the need for Italy to cede its sovereignty to a European Federation. "It seems that everything appears to the Italians in a deforming mirror […],", he desperately complained in early 1949, "[…] every gentleman crossing the peninsula has his own undulated mirror, concave or convex as it may be, and it seems that he enjoys bending the simple line of truth into a thousand antics, to confuse the others and put himself in safety from logic and the discomforts that go along with it."[85] If the Italians didn't want to follow him, he reasoned, he had to follow them while trying to avoid the worst degenerations on their erroneous path.

Despite the deceptions he experienced in his domestic and international commitments, Carandini would continue to engage in politics but with a lower profile and less idealistic ambition than before his revelation concerning the perception of his political positions. It was a kind of return to the ideal roots of 1943, an attempt for a new start in an even more restricted ambience, when he created the *Movimento Liberale Indipendente* (MLI) together with his friend Mario Ferrara in June 1948. The aim was to gather the dissidents of the PLI to set up a *Third Force* among the democratic lay parties in Italy.[86] The project failed, not for the least part, because of its leader's sheer lack of physical presence in the movement's activities due to his multiple commitments on many different stages— European federalism, *Alitalia*, the ICF Bank, the SIOI— which consequently lead to him spending long periods abroad. Pushed by Ferrara in 1951, Carandini decided to re-integrate the MLI back into the ranks of the Liberal Party, which in the meantime had expelled its most reactionary elements. On the PLI's Unification Congress in December 1951, the "Carandinians" would finally assume their role as a constituted "liberal left" tendency.[87]

In addition, this new liberal idyll revealed itself to be built on feet of clay. Faced with the threat of a rising neofascist–monarchist front after the administrative elections of 1952, Carandini would abandon the *Third Force* initiative that had been part of the agreement between his group and the PLI and adhere to the much discussed "fraud-law" of 1953,[88] which gathered the lay parties around the Christian Democrats in an attempt to safeguard their centrist majority amidst the awarding of parliamentary seats to the winning coalition—a clear deviation from Carandini's former purpose overtly directed against Christian Democracy but justified in times of general danger for the very survival of democracy.[89]

Carandini ran for parliament in Milan in 1953 but failed to be elected by just a handful of votes, whereas the only elected liberal candidate in this constituency would be Giovanni Malagodi, who had joined the PLI only a few months earlier and was renowned for his outstanding expertise on economic questions. Soon he would become Secretary General of the party and Carandini's main antagonist.[90] The two men had opposing conceptions of centrism beleaguered by anti-system forces but were in need of support from their ranks in order to have a majority: Malagodi excluded any opening towards the Socialists while not hesitating, on the other hand, to vote with the Monarchists and the Neofascists where opportune; Carandini did not accept any indulgence toward the extreme right but considered a dialogue with the Socialists possible provided that they were to detach from the Communists. Faced with Malagodi's attempt to suppress autonomous tendencies within the PLI and lead it in dictatorial manner toward an "economic right"—not too dissimilar from Croce's concept of liberal unity in 1946—Carandini and his followers, who were mainly made up of the same group of antifascist intellectuals with whom he had founded the party in 1943, retired from the direction and led a ferocious internal opposition, thus preluding a new split.[91]

Most of all it was Malagodi's involvement with the industrialist's association *Confindustria* that caused Carandini's concern. Between 1954 and 1955, *Il Mondo*, under the direction of Pannunzio, led a violent campaign against Malagodi in defence of the original and pure liberalism independent from economic or social interests and located in the centre of politics. Since 1949, *Il Mondo* had been the unofficial organ of the MLI first and the "liberal left" thereafter and thus was the main public communication medium for Carandini, who used it to recall the spiritual guidance and witness of the old "masters"—Croce, Einaudi, Francesco Ruffini and even Giovanni Giolitti—to safeguard liberalism.[92] The Secretary's continuous attacks on the centrist government and even his own liberal ministers were, according to Carandini, proof that "[...] organized interests [...] have preferred choosing as instrument and shield the P.L.I. occupying and distorting it [...] from its universal mission to their particular ends. Which explains why the right honourable Malagodi had to adopt [...] contradictory politics [...]" to serve the economic interests behind him.[93] "The noble party of Croce and Einaudi [...],", *Il Mondo* stated in early 1955, "[...] has been leased (perhaps not even acquired) by Assolombarda" (the influential industrialists' association in Lombardy).[94]

It was, however, a novelty for Carandini to use polemic personal attacks as he did in the case of his dispute with Malagodi even though—or perhaps because—he had been favouring the economist's accession to the party after the Liberal Unification Congress of 1951 and, at the PLI-Congress of 1953, had carelessly acclaimed his economic laissez-faire-program, not realizing its contradictions with the centre-left political program, which included also a share of state intervention in the economic sphere.[95] Polarizing the conflict and claiming the reasons of liberalism for his "liberal left" tendency, he now wanted "[...] to avoid, at any cost, with any sacrifice, that malagodism and liberalism become synonyms, that the liberal party [...] slips fatally to the extreme right [...] in the desolate company of the monarchic-missino [neofascist] alliance."[96] Seeing the Liberal Party, which he still considered to be in part his own creature, slip out of his hands for a second time seemed to have embittered him even more than the failure of 1948.

The circumstances of the December 1955 split of the PLI, however, were different because this time the "liberal left" had taken more than a year to prepare and organize a follow-up project, which would become the Partito Radicale (PR). Compared with the limited attempts of the (second) MLI, the PR would be an outright political party with all its structural features and would gather adherents from a wider and culturally more influent area of lay democracy such as former actionists and European federalists (Ernesto Rossi), socialists (Leo Valiani, Guido Calogero), *Unità Popolare* (Leopoldo Piccardi) and republicans (Mario Boneschi). Furthermore, the conflict within the PLI had also triggered a split by the liberal youth organization with the "young liberal left" (Marco Pannella) playing an active part in the construction process of the PR, thus making it an element of generational transition with Carandini and his friends becoming the "old guard."[97]

Already, since the times of the (second) MLI, Carandini had taken much care to gather young liberals—such as Eugenio Scalfari, Marco Pannella, Giovanni Ferrara or Stefano Rodotà—who would all play an imminent intellectual role in the Radical Party and in Italian politics in general throughout the following decades but, in the act of the party's dissolution in 1962, would often dismiss the positions of their older leader Carandini as too moderate.[98] The turning point of his radical experience were the 1958 elections, which resulted in a debacle for the PR. Carandini tried to justify the Radicals' political alignment oriented against Clericalism and Communism at once: "[...] we have to continue [...],", he addressed the young radicals, "[...] being active promoters of a 'republican front' that includes the democratic parties, that refuses communist style frontism and stands, despite temptations and compliance, in opposition to Christian Democracy."[99] However, his classical *Third Force* rhetoric could no longer convince a generation that had well understood the impossibility of

138   C. BLASBERG

building up a democratic alternative to the DC in Italy without scratching at the social–communist door. Such a rupture with the anti-communist credo was the proposal made by Carandini's disciple Marco Pannella, who soon became the leader of a new "radical left."[100]

Carandini instead was too bona fide in the harmonious political virtues and intellectual capacities of the new party. At the second PR-Congress in 1961, he noted "[…] the absence of any ambitious competition of tendencies of any compromise behind the scenes, of any personal competition,"[101] although many contrasts had already erupted among its various components. A few months later, the "Piccardi case" brought a fragile equilibrium to collapse. Remaining faithful to his anti-fascist principles, Carandini could not accept the presence of a man in his party whose participation in Italian–German racial congresses in the late 1930s had been proven by historian Renzo De Felice.[102] His resignation from the PR in March 1962—alongside his old companions Pannunzio, Cattani and Libonati—marks the end of his political commitment in Italian domestic affairs. After the end of its radical incarnation, New Liberalism, as understood by Carandini, dispersed in a multitude of reformist niche drifts partly represented by Christian Democracy, partly by Socialism and other political forces, and it would never again unite into one distinctive doctrine.

Around the turn of the decade, the attention of Carandini's contributions in *Il Mondo*—in 1956 he had become co-owner of the weekly—had focussed more than ever on the international scene, especially after the Suez Crisis and the Khrushchev ultimatum of 1958. He had to accept the bipolarization of the world and sided decisively with an occidental point of view, the democratic West being the only credible agent of his anti-fascist and anti-totalitarian creed. Especially in his own country, however, he saw a widespread inclination toward relativizing the global totalitarian threat. Initiatives, such the Italian Foreign Minister's invitation to Nasser for a visit in Rome in early 1958, represented, in Carandini's view, nothing but a chance for Moscow to rupture the occidental solidarity,[103] and every reproach of imperialism addressed to the USA or Great Britain in their opposition to the Egyptian dictator were unfounded after the successful decolonization process operated by these two countries, each playing its role.[104] Remarkably, he even seemed to have revised his own three-level model of the mediating *Third Force* he had made a case for 10 years before. He now criticized the Italian "[…]

LOST GENERATION? NICOLÒ CARANDINI, THE DECLINE OF NEW... 139

fascination for special missions and mediations [...],", which was, if based on such insufficiencies as represented by the weak Italian democracy, just a "[...] squalid pretext for an expansion of influence [...] of an occult ambitious flavour."[105]

This pessimistic assessment of Italy was also extended to Europe. A direct agreement between the USA and the USSR, Carandini wrote in 1960 when distension seemed to substitute escalation in the Cold War, was most desirable because "[...] in the absence of a Europe still wrapped in its antique quarrels and for its divisions unable to make clear at least what it wants, only these two powers together are able to guarantee a peace of which today nobody knows in whose hands it lies."[106] None of his articles in *Il Mondo* ever dealt with the European Community founded in 1957 with the Roman Treaties. It was not the federal politically united Europe he had imagined, and the British as well as the East European absence made it incomplete with France, again under De Gaulle, which was not willing to enlarge it or increase its supranational character. Because a triangular world order was out of all realistic perspective, a bipolar order balanced by the nuclear equilibrium, the hope for a peaceful coexistence with more mutual confidence between the two superpowers, and with a subordinated Europe firmly protected by the US nuclear shield remained Carandini's grand design. His series of articles, published in *Il Mondo* in spring 1960 about the main conflict areas of the world under these bipolar conditions, ended in May with a pathetic homage to the USA and its might while the U2 incident put a temporary end to the signs of distension.[107]

Carandini, however, saw both the Berlin Wall Crisis of 1961 and the Cuban Missile Crisis a year later as a proof of the substantial stability and security of the international system, showing on one hand unveiled admiration for the reactive capabilities of the USA under Kennedy without, on the other, addressing any irrational critique toward the Soviet Union, which instead just played its responsible role in a game that it was aware it could never win. Carandini's last articles in *Il Mondo* were a general analysis of the world's new situation in spring 1963 after the Cuban Crisis, concluding with another enthusiastic adhesion to the United States as the ideal world leader and democratic model. His exaltation of the USA was probably even more flattering for the virtues of this new champion of freedom and progress than his ancient admiration for Great Britain in the 1940s and before had ever been.[108]

CONCLUSION

Did Carandini represent a lost generation in the sense of the impact possibilities of his political ideas after the Second World War? We have seen a history of continuous failures and re-adaptations of his thought on the evolutions of the post-war world ending in the acknowledgement that the principal pillars of his original ideological construction—a liberal–democratic Italy integrated into a federated Europe as mediator on a global level between a capitalist and a communist community—had not come true. Italy's liberal-democratic constitutional order was in the early 1960s besieged by clerical (partly inclining to open the doors to a neo-fascist revival) and communist forces with democratic socialism caught in the trap between the two and the residual fringes of liberalism, which bowed on one side to industrialist interests and dissolved into an intellectual Byzantinism and cranky animosities on the other. Europe was not a supranational political union devaluating its inner frontiers—the persisting nationalist difficulties in South Tyrol put Carandini's main diplomatic achievement in question—but it was at best a very first step in a process that promised to become much longer then he had thought in the late 1940s and would surely outlive his generation. The world, instead of a being peaceful multipolar system of self-neutralizing communities, depended on the responsible goodwill of two opposing leaders to shy away from annihilating the other for fear of being annihilated themselves.

Carandini had reason to be pessimistic about his generation's opportunities to see things change: In Italy liberation from the clerical-communist deadlock occurred only in the early 1990s—20 years after his death—and resulted in an even deeper crisis of those socially advanced liberal–democratic values he had advocated. The next fundamental step on the way to a politically united Europe would be achieved only in 1992 with the Maastricht Treaty, still far from what he had in mind and even in trouble since the Euro crisis. The bipolar world order based on nuclear balance could not have been a long-lasting solution; although it remained stable throughout his lifetime, it began to crumble into a multipolar system marked by a new climate of nationalism and cultural suspicion and nuclear multilateralism in the late 1980s. Here it is interesting to observe that Carandini, although not imagining the downfall of the Soviet Union, had started, since the early 1950s, to hint at China's future possibilities as a third superpower and to warn against the diffusion of nuclear armament to countries other than the USA and the USSR.[109]

However, Carandini was a positive thinker by nature who was able to see in every setback those aspects that could transform a defeat into a new chance. This became evident in the way he identified with and took advantage of his diplomatic mission to London even though it evidently had been a manoeuvre to cut short his domestic political career. He did not resign in bitterness faced with the unexpected harshness of the Peace Treaty but saw the long-term chances for his rehabilitating country in a de-nationalized world order. For long, he kept faith in a revival of social liberalism, renounced easy exits for a personal political advantage, and instead made many attempts to re-launch it even in the most desperate circumstances such as in 1948 and again in 1955. When "his" Europe—failed with the end of the EDC project and the consolidation of the East–West division after 1956, he made this global order a virtue even though he had feared such a scenario back in 1946.

In all this Carandini felt it a mission to connect Italy with the world. In a certain sense, his activity as President of *Alitalia* since 1948 might have boosted his perspective in interpreting the fortunes of his country from an almost external point of view. The frequent flights to the USA and longer stays there in the 1950s and 1960s, which came along with his position, surely contributed decisively to developing an almost naïve admiration for the outstanding capabilities of the superpower, of which he already had appreciated the democratic tradition long before. Thus, it was easier for him to overcome his frustrated Europe-centred perspective with Great Britain as a leading agent. Overall, Carandini's commitment to any kind of progress can be retraced not only in the political and social spheres but also in the technical one as is shown in his fascination for the development of new aircraft technology, which he tried to acquire for *Alitalia* in order to make it a leading international air company.[110]

This was a sense of progressiveness inherited from the nineteenth century, though. Moreover, this might lead us to the aspect in which Carandini really belonged to a lost generation. His generational "trap" lay in those few years in his youth in which he had the chance to get to know the old liberal system of Cavourian Italy and the spirit of idealism in its elites before the fascist era, not as a negative model to be abandoned in its substance but as an immovable groundwork that just needed to be reformed and modernized. Politicians of his own generation, such as Togliatti or De Gasperi, would have been even more successful after 1943 if their experience of pre-fascist liberalism had been substantially negative, not impressed by idealism. Carandini's younger long-time political companions, Cattani and Pannunzio, shared his belief in social liberalism but were much more influenced by a realism developed in opposition to fascism as their first political experience. Especially Cattani often took care to differentiate his reasons from those of Carandini even though on first glance their careers through the Liberal and later the Radical Party seemed to have gone in parallel. Nevertheless, although Carandini needed to pursue a grand vision to motivate his political decisions, Cattani's action, although tending to a certain moral abstraction, was driven by a meticulous detail analysis of the given circumstances.[111]

It is true that we have noted the rupture in Carandini's attitude that occurred by 1948–1949 and, in a certain sense, that he would accommodate the unavoidable tendencies of his times from then on, thus acknowledging his inability to go against the tide and becoming aware that he had totally overestimated the democratic maturity of his fellow citizens. His second attempt with the PLI after 1951, as well as the acceptance of the bipolar world order, showed this on different levels. Even the much older Croce, one might conclude, proved more of a realist than Carandini, who only some years later would take the same street as his master, whom he had criticized for distancing from his own ideals before 1948. In reality his devotion to the master was always relative, and we may presume that well before 1943 he had already acquired autonomous thought equilibrated between Croce, Einaudi, Luigi Albertini (his admired father-in-law, for whom he felt indebted to carry on the political heritage after his death in 1941) and other intellectuals. It would, in this regard, be of some interest to learn more about the early personal contact between Carandini and these intellectuals during the fascist years just as it would be to learn about Carandini's readings and about the development of his political ideas in general in his early years. For the time being, this must remain the duty of further research.

However, whatever may have been the roots of Carandini's thought—it might have seemed idealistic, too progressive or also backward-oriented for his time and may have contributed to his marginalization in domestic and European affairs plus he might seem of doubtful representativeness for a well-founded social consciousness because of his privileged social position—contradictions between his political purposes and his professional activities can indeed not be denied. With the distance of several generations and in the light of more recent developments on all three of the levels on which he focused his attention, a reconsideration of the complex structure of his ideas and guiding principles seems to be overdue, especially if considering the ethical inspiration and global vision that constituted the starting point for all of his political thought and action.

Notes

1. Pannella, Marco. "La sera non andavamo in Via Veneto." *Il Foglio*, 27.08.2009. It is presumed that communist Giancarlo Pajetta invented the rhyme.
2. http://www.pasolini.net/luoghiPPP_caffeRosati-Roma.htm (01.02.2013).
3. Longo, Oddone. "Breve storia della bonifica di Torre in Pietra, 1926–1944." In id., ed. *Albertini, Carandini. Una pagina della storia d'Italia*. Venice: IVSLA, 2005, 51–74.
4. Riccardi, Luca, ed. *Nicolò Carandini. Il liberale e la Nuova Italia [1943–1953]*. Florence: Mondadori, 1992, 6 (prefazione di Giovanni Spadolini).
5. Filippone-Thaulero, Giustino. Diario 1944–1945 di Nicolò Carandini. Nuova Antologia 2145 (31.03.1945), 228.
6. Riccardi, *Nicolò Carandini*, 9.
7. Quaglieni, Pier Franco. Nicolò Carandini. Centro Pannunzio Web site: www.centropannunzio.it/mondo/NicoloCarandini.html (22.03.2013).
8. He was furthermore president of the SIOI (Italian Society for International Organization) and president of the *Istituto di Credito Fondiario* Bank; see Blasberg, Christian. "Nicolò Carnadini." In *Dizionario del Liberalismo Italiano. Tomo II*. Soveria Mannelli: Rubbettino, 2015, 247–251.
9. Benedetto Croce ironically stated: "On 40 million Italians, the antifascists are 40, inevitably they know and meet each other." See: *La Repubblica*, 22.02.1990.
10. Lanaro, Silvio. "Nicolò Carandini politico liberale." In Oddone, Longo, ed. *Albertini, Carandini. Una pagina della storia d'Italia*. Venice: IVSLA, 2005, 76.
11. Carandini, Nicolò. *Primi Chiarimenti. Movimento Liberale Italiano*. Rome, 1943.
12. Ibid.
13. Nicolosi, Gerardo. "Il nuovo liberalismo." In Grassi Orsini, Fabio/ Nicolosi, Gerardo, eds. *I liberali italiani dall'antifascismo alla Repubblica*. Soveria Mannelli: Rubbettino, 2008, 249.
14. Carandini, *Primi Chiarimenti*.
15. Nicolosi, *Il nuovo liberalismo*, 250.
16. Carandini, *Primi Chiarimenti*.
17. Setta, Sandro. *Croce, il liberalismo e l'Italia postfascista*. Rome: Bonacci, 1979, 14–26; see also Jannazzo, Antonio. *Croce e il prepartito della cultura*. Rome: Carucci, 1987.
18. See the last edition of Croce's work: Galasso, Giuseppe, ed. *Benedetto Croce: Storia d'Europa nel secolo decimonono*. Milan: Adelphi, 1999.
19. "...the 'religion of liberty' by Croce had been serving to keep alive and educate souls and intelligences...," writes Novelli, Claudio. *Il Partito d'Azione e gli italiani. Moralità, politica e cittadinanza nella storia*

144 C. BLASBERG

repubblicana. Milan: La Nuova Italia, 2000, 8, "... but in particular to the young liberal socialists it seemed insufficient from the point of view of political commitment and the concrete action to take against the regime ...."

20. De Giorgi, Maria, ed. *Il Movimento Liberale Italiano (Roma 1943–1944)*. Galatina: Congedo, 2005.
21. Carandini Albertini, Elena. *Dal terrazzo. Diari 1943–1944*. Bologna: Il Mulino, 1997, 17 f. (entry of 19.08.1943).
22. Filippone-Thaulero, Giustino, ed. "Diario 1944–1945 di Nicolò Carandini." *Nuova Antologia 2146* (1983), 177; Carandini wrote further: "The country needs to feel governed. The renewal has to come from above."
23. *Risorgimento Liberale* mentioned him on 27.07.1944 as having been the "President of the Clandestine National Council" of the PLI.
24. On Pannunzio, see: Cardini, Antonio. *Mario Pannunzio. Giornalismo e liberalismo. Cultura e politica nell'Italia del Novecento (1910–1968)*. Naples: Edizioni scientifiche italiane, 2011.
25. Carandini Albertini, *Dal terrazzo*, 56–58 (04.11.1943).
26. Carandini Albertini, Elena. *Passata la stagione.... Diari 1944–1947*. Florence: Passigli, 1989, 20 (09.06.1944).
27. Ibid., 21 (09.06.1944); the southern, mainly Neapolitan branch of the PLI was led by Renato Morelli and 31-year-old Giovanni Cassandro, both close disciples of Croce; Carandini's predominant role in the early organizational stages of the PLI has been highlighted by: Pallini, Renato. "Vita organizzativa e diffusione territoriale del PLI." In Grassi Orsini, Fabio and Nicolosi, Gerardo, eds. *I liberali italiani dall'antifascismo alla Repubblica*. Soveria Mannelli: Rubbettino, 2008, 109–130.
28. On 13 July, Carandini—faced with the request by Croce—"[...] eschewed this office and proposes Soleri, liberating him from the Treasury. He doesn't see how to be useful in this ministry disempowered from the start." Only after another visit to Croce on 20 July and the refusal by Enrico De Nicola did he accept (Ibid., 33, 35 [13 and 21.07.1944]).
29. Ibid., 40 (01.08.1944); Umberto, at a meeting with Carandini on 1 August, is said to have told him: "If the choice will be for the Republic, dear Carandini, you shall be sure that I will be a good republican like you [...]."
30. Vittorio Emanuele Orlando was intent on modifying the program of the Liberal Party "[...] which is not the one of Croce and Carandini, who are not clear about the institutional question." See Lucifero, Falcone. *L'ultimo Re. I diari del ministro della Real Casa, 1944–1946*. Milan: Mondadori, 2002, 114 (31.08.1944).
31. Carandini Albertini, *Passata la stagione* ..., 39 (06.08.1944); the quote refers to the old liberal senator Alberto Bergamini and Raffaele De Caro, leader of the southern *Partito della Democrazia Liberale*.

LOST GENERATION? NICOLÒ CARANDINI, THE DECLINE OF NEW... 145

32. Carandini, Nicolò Paolo. "Il partito liberale e i problemi italiani." *Risorgimento Liberale*, 04.09.1944; he though defended the integration of the monarchist Partito Democratico Liberale into the PLI as a first step "[...] on the way of a simplification of our political life, a way on which the most advanced democratic nations have preceded us [...]," referring with much evidence to Great Britain.
33. Ibid.
34. Ibid.
35. Ibid.; "I have been indicated by certain press as the head of the republican faction within the Liberal Party [...]," Carandini said, not denying this; but instead of tending to either position, "[...] we don't ask the adherents of our party if they are republicans or monarchists. We ask them if they [...] have the intention to fight [...] for freedom in the future political assemblies in which the Italians will be called to deliberate about the institutional form of the state."
36. Lucifero, *L'ultimo Re*, 140 (03.10.1944).
37. The thesis cannot be proven with certainty; Lucifero himself seems to have been convinced by Carandini's purpose to keep the Monarchy, if wanted by popular decision and in a democratic regime, thinking of him and De Gasperi as possible successors of Prime Minister Bonomi. See ibid., 178 (27.10.1944).
38. Carandini Albertini, *Passata la stagione* ..., 61 (21.10.1944).
39. Lucifero, *L'ultimo Re*, 142 (04.10.1944).
40. "That my person is now aside is a good thing...", Carandini thought already in December 1944, "[...] I encumbered the street to the others." Filippone-Thaulero, Giustino. "Diario 1944–1945 di Nicolò Carandini." *Nuova Antologia* 2144, 348 (27.12.1944).
41. Blasberg, Christian. "La crisi del PLI. I liberali tra CLN e qualunquismo." In Monina, Giancarlo, ed. *1945–1946. Le origini della Repubblica*. Soveria Mannelli: Rubbettino, 2008, 178.
42. Andreotti, Giulio. *Visti da vicino. Volume 2*. Milan: Rizzoli, 1982, 46.
43. B. Croce to N. Carandini, 09.07.1946. Archivio Centrale dello Stato [ACS], Carte Carandini, file 17.
44. Riccardi, *Nicolò Carandini il liberale*, 87.
45. See: Blasberg, Christian. *Die Liberale Linke und das Schicksal der Dritten Kraft im italienischen Zentrismus, 1947–1951*. Frankfurt a.M.: P. Lang, 2008, 97–106.
46. "I don't allow myself in no way to think that you might not have listened to your conscience [...]," Croce wrote to Carandini many months after his split from the party, "[...] but I think that your intellect this time did not well advise your good will." B. Croce to N. Carandini, 30.12.1948. ACS, Carte Carandini, file 18.

47. Croce's 1942 notes for a political "program" were published only in 1966: "Croce politico." *Il Mondo*, 01.03.1966.
48. Setta, Sandro. *Croce il liberalism e l'Italia postfascista*. Rome: Bonacci, 1979, 27–41.
49. Carandini Albertini, Elena. *Le case, le cose, le carte, Diari 1948–1950*. Padua: Il Poligrafo, 2007, 166 (31.08.1948).
50. Carandini Albertini, *Passata la stagione...*, 273–275 ("Fine gennaio" 1947).
51. Carandini Albertini, *Le case, le cose, le carte*, 66 (25.01.1948).
52. For the *Uomo Qualunque* movement, see: Setta, Sandro. *L'Uomo qualunque, 1944–1948*. Bari/Rome: Laterza, 2000.
53. The most recent edition: Spinelli, Altiero/Rossi, Ernesto, eds. *Il Manifesto di Ventotene*. Milan: RCS Quotidiani, 2011.
54. Riccardi, 54 f.; after a colloquium with Ernest Bevin in summer 1945, Carandini "[...] is convinced that our destiny does not depend so much on the English, but on the complex general politics of peace which is in the hands of America. But in the big bargain, it could cede to Russia on the point of Italy in compensation for positions in the Pacific or other." See Carandini Albertini, *Passata la stagione....* 152 (29.08.1945).
55. Filippone-Thaulero, NA n. 2145, 194.
56. According to Leone Cattani, Carandini considered the Peace Treaty "[...] unjust and wrong, but he thinks that one couldn't have obtained more and that in the current conditions he thinks it's wiser to accept, reserving to try and make oneself worthy in the best way within UNO." See De Felice, Renzo "L'Italia postfascista vista da Parigi e da Londra. Pagine di diario di Leone Cattani, febbraio-marzo 1947." *Storia Contemporanea* XV (1984), 1009 (10.03.1947).
57. Filippone-Thaulero, NA n. 2145, 206 (26.02.1945).
58. Ibid., 210 (02.03.1945).
59. Ibid., 214 (09.03.1945); 225 (28.03.1945); Leo Valiani favoured Carandini as the next Prime Minister after the liberation "[...] because he was above the melee, appreciated in the anglo-saxon world and disinterested." See Altarocca, Claudio. "Carandini. Un "conte rosso" per De Gasperi." *La Stampa*, 11.06.1994.
60. Filippone-Thaulero, NA n. 2145, 215 (13.03.1945).
61. Carandini Albertini, *Passata la stagione...*, 129 (04.06.1945).
62. Cabona, Maurizio. "'Mio nonno cercò invano di dividere Duce e Führer'." *Il Giornale*, 06.05.2006.
63. Carandini Albertini, *Le case, le cose, le carte*, 166 (31.08.1948).
64. Filippone-Thaulero, NA n. 2145, 200 (14.02.1945).
65. Mercuri, Lamberto, ed. *Sulla ,Terza Forza'*. Rome: Bonacci, 1986, 59 f.
66. Blasberg, *Die Liberale Linke*, 124–135.

LOST GENERATION? NICOLÒ CARANDINI, THE DECLINE OF NEW... 147

67. Ibid., 136.
68. Carandini, Nicolò. "L'Inghilterra e l'Europa." *Iniziativa Socialista*, 27.01.1948.
69. Mercuri, *Sulla ,Terza Forza'*, 60–65; Carandini showed indulgence towards the USSR, whereas he accused the USA of not having given the necessary guarantees to the Soviets in order to allow them to accept Marshall-Plan aid.
70. Varsori, Antonio. "Il Congresso dell'Europe dell'Aja (7–10 maggio 1948)." *Storia Contemporanea* 21 (1990), 478.
71. Carandini, Nicolò. *L'Unità Europea e il Congresso dell'Aja. Discorso tenuto alla Manifestazione federalistica di Firenze, 13 giugno 1948*. Rome: Athenais, 1948, 10.
72. [n.a.] "Carandini l'apostolo." *L'Europeo*, 10–17.10.1948.
73. *Iniziativa Socialista*, 11.11.1948.
74. [n.a.] Solo la Federazione europea può risolvere la questione tedesca. *La Voce Repubblicana*, 12.11.1948; the British delegation on that occasion was led by Miss Frances L. Josephy, a liberal activist for European Federalism.
75. Carandini Albertini, *Le case, le cose, le carte*, 483 (16.06.1950).
76. Blum, Léon. "La troisième force internationale." *Le Populaire*, 06.01.1948.
77. Carandini, Nicolò. *Responsabilità Europea. Discorso tenuto al Teatro Sistina di Roma il 4 novembre 1950 a chiusura della campagna per la petizione in favore di un Patto d'unione federale europea*. Rome: Emer, 1950, 9 f.
78. Ibid., 11.
79. Ibid., 12; Carandini would thus be instrumental behind De Gasperi's initiative for a European Political Community (EPC) in May 1952; see Risso, Linda. *The [Forgotten] European Political Community, 1952–1954*. EFPU Conference Paper, 2004.
80. "It's necessary to offer to Germany the occasion we are able to offer it, that is its trustful acceptance within a solid family of not daunted peoples where she can develop her great virtues and see corrected her brutal defects"; see Carandini, *Responsabilità Europea*, 15.
81. Carandini, Nicolò. "L'occasione offerta." *Il Mondo*, 25.05.1954.
82. An Italian analysis of Mendès France's role in the failure of the EDC in: Brizzi, Riccardo. *Il governo Mendès France*. Bologna: CLUEB, 2010.
83. On the De Gasperi-Gruber agreement, see: Steininger, Rolf. *Autonomie oder Selbstbestimmung? Die Südtirolfrage 1945/46 und das Gruber-De Gasperi-Abkommen*. Innsbruck et al.: Studienverlag, 2008.
84. Carandini, Nicolò. *The Alto Adige. An Experiment in the Devaluation of Frontiers*. Rome: Ed. Il Mondo, 1958.

148   C. BLASBERG

85. Carandini Albertini, *Le case, le cose, le carte*, 224 (27.01.1949).
86. Blasberg, *Die Liberale Linke*, 170–180.
87. Blasberg, *Die Liberale Linke*, 417–519.
88. About the so-called "fraud-law" ("legge truffa"), see: Quagliariello, Gaetano. *La legge elettorale del 1953. Dibattiti storici in Parlamento.* Bologna: Il Mulino, 2003.
89. Carandini, Nicolò. "Cosa vuole quest'Italia?" *Il Mondo*, 28.06.1952.
90. Carandini explained his candidacy in Milan with the will "… to give to the list […] an equilibrium and an appeal to all the currents of a liberalism that […] is not all launched towards the right-wing or towards certain economic super-interests." N. Carandini to B. Villabruna, 24.03.1953. ACS, Carte Carandini, file 21.
91. Blasberg, Christian. "Liberali per il centrosinistra: Radicali e Democrazia liberale." *Ventunesimo Secolo 7*: 1 (2008), 62–67.
92. Carandini, Nicolò. "Il tempo delle scelte." *Il Mondo*, 20.09.1955.
93. Carandini, Nicolò. "Una grave disavventura." *Il Mondo*, 05.07.1955.
94. Taccuino. *Il Mondo*, 08.03.1955.
95. Orsina, Giovanni. *L'alternativa liberale. Malagodi e l'opposizione al centrosinistra.* Venice: Marsilio, 2010, 29.
96. Carandini, *Una grave disavventura.*
97. Blasberg, *Liberali per il centrosinistra*, 67.
98. Zanuttini, Annalisa. "L'organizzazione del partito radicale (1955–1962)." In Vallauri, Carlo, ed. *L'arcipelago democratico. Organizzazione e struttura dei partiti italiani del centrismo (1949–1958).* Rome: Bulzoni, 1979.
99. Carandini, Nicolò. "L'appello dei giovani." *Il Mondo*, 10.06.1958.
100. Un articolo del radicale Pannella: la 'sinistra democratica' e il PCI. *Paese Sera*, 22.03.1959.
101. Carandini, Nicolò. "La polemica radicale." *Il Mondo*, 06.06.1961.
102. De Felice's revelations about Leopoldo Piccardi had first appeared in: De Felice, Renzo. *Storia degli Ebrei Italiani sotto il Fascismo.* Turin: Einaudi, 1961.
103. Carandini, Nicolò. "Italia smaniosa." *Il Mondo*, 04.03.1958.
104. Carandini, Nicolò. "I pericoli dell'inazione." *Il Mondo*, 29.07.1958. Taken "[…] anti-imperialism in terms of democratic affirmation […]", Carandini claimed, "[…] we, at least we, have to remind that the United States and England are democracy itself, are the best that democracy was able to give in the modern world."
105. Ibid.
106. Carandini, Nicolò. "Un filo tra l'Oriente e l'Occidente: Lo spirito di Camp David." *Il Mondo*, 16.02.1960. Interestingly, Carandini now appreciated the diplomacy of mutual state visits by ideologically opposed leaders including the Italian President Giovanni Gronchi's visit to Moscow.

107. Carandini, Nicolò. "Un filo tra l'Oriente e l'Occidente: Energica America." *Il Mondo*, 31.05.1960.
108. See: Carandini, Nicolò. "I tre mondi in crisi. Il conto sulle dita." *Il Mondo*, 15.01.1963; Carandini, Nicolò. "L'occhio dell'America. Acheson risponde." *Il Mondo*, 16.04.1963; Carandini, Nicolò. "L'occhio dell'America. I piani di McNamara." *Il Mondo*, 23.04.1963.
109. Carandini, Nicolò. "Un filo tra l'Oriente e l'Occidente. L'altra faccia della terra." *Il Mondo*, 17.05.1960.
110. Carandini, Nicolò. "Un filo tra l'Oriente e l'Occidente: Energica America." *Il Mondo*, 31.05.1960; see also numerous short films on keywords: 'Nicolò Carandini' and 'Alitalia' by Istituto Luce, available at: http://www.archivioluce.com/archivio/.
111. A confrontation between Carandini and Cattani is well illustrated by Renzo De Felice in his edition of Cattani's diaries during a trip to France and Great Britain in early 1947: De Felice, Renzo. "L'Italia postfascista vista da Parigi e da Londra: Pagine di diario di Leone Cattani, febbraio-marzo 1947." *Storia Contemporanea* XV (1984), 973–1014.

CHAPTER 7

Old and New Democracy: Placing the Italian Anomaly in a European Context

Jan De Graaf

The trials and tribulations of the post-war Italian Socialist Party (*Partito Socialista Italiano* [PSI]) attracted much bewilderment amongst its (Western) European sister parties. Reporting back from the January 1947 PSI congress, at which the party saw its anti-communist right wing break away, the Belgian socialist Victor Larock noted how the proceedings had been marked by the "afterbirth of fascism." All the foreign delegates had been "unanimous," he explained, that "traces of fascism" had shone through in "the violent tone and wording of the interventions, the clear presence of hired clappers, [and] the contempt for the minority despite continuous invocations of democracy." Not that the secessionist minority was free from "fascist manners" itself, continued Larock. For he had learned that "many young followers of [Matteo] Matteotti [one of the main leaders of the breakaway party and the son of the famous Giacomo Matteotti, the socialist leader of the opposition to Mussolini who was murdered in 1924] are proponents of direct action." Some of these youngsters had even armed themselves and "gone underground."[1]

J. De Graaf (✉)
KU Leuven, Leuven, Belgium

© The Author(s) 2018   151
J. Späth (ed.), *Does Generation Matter? Progressive Democratic Cultures in Western Europe, 1945–1960*, Palgrave Studies in the History of Social Movements, https://doi.org/10.1007/978-3-319-77422-0_7

Both in its internal struggles and its outward radicalism, therefore, Italian socialism presents an altogether different proposition from what we tend to associate with socialist and social democratic parties during their post-war "golden age."[2] In fact, historians have often described it as an "anomaly" in the otherwise more benign picture of reformist, anti-communist and governmental (Western) European social democracy.[3] It would take Italian socialism decades to recover from its "two fatal years" of 1947–1948,[4] during which the PSI split, found itself removed from the government and suffered disastrous losses in the parliamentary elections of April 1948. Consequently, the Italian socialists would not lead a national government until the 1980s.

This chapter represents an attempt to place the post-war history of the PSI in a broader, pan-European context. It will show that we can make a lot more sense of the politics of and views taken by the Italian socialists if we compare them with their counterparts in Eastern Europe. To be sure, the socialist and social democratic parties in post-war Eastern Europe only had a short life span because these parties had all been forced into mergers with the communists by 1948. Yet, the political agenda put forward by the Eastern European socialists and social democrats closely resembled that of the post-war PSI. Much of this revolved around the question of democracy. Except for Czechoslovakia, where parliamentary democracy had survived during the inter-war years, all the countries in Eastern Europe had also experienced prolonged periods of right-wing authoritarian or fascist rule. This had left their socialists with a distinct belief that practicing democracy in the old bourgeois–liberal model would always end up in dictatorship in countries like theirs. In its place, they advocated a "new democracy" ("socialist democracy" or "popular democracy" were also used in this context), which involved a real reckoning with the fascist past as well as efforts to teach the popular masses democracy from the bottom up.

This focus on renewal was personal as much as political. In fact, the Italian socialists and their Eastern European comrades frequently defined themselves quite explicitly against (some of) the foremost leaders of the interwar European socialist and social democratic parties, especially against those leaders who had sought accommodation with the capitalist system or the bourgeois parties. In the tense atmosphere of the early Cold War, they increasingly felt that these old stalwarts of interwar socialism, many of whom still played a significant role within their respective parties and within the international socialist movement, were making all the same mistakes. The heated debates between the post-war European socialist and social democratic parties were thus in many ways a struggle between an old generation of socialist leaders and a set of mostly younger challengers who had emerged from a lengthy fight against right-wing dictatorships.

NEW DEMOCRACY

So, what was meant by "new democracy"? In the words of its foremost Italian protagonist—Lelio Basso, PSI Secretary General in 1947–1948—it was "a politics of ever new conquests which affect the structure of the old state and crumble its bureaucratic-military apparatus, placing new arms or new powers in the hands of the working-classes."[5] This neatly captures two of the key dimensions of new democracy. On one hand, it was about transforming the structures of capitalist society to such an extent as to prepare it for a transition to socialism. This was to be achieved through "structural reforms" (a much-beloved notion amongst the post-war Italian socialists, as we will see) within the framework of the capitalist economy, however, unlike loathed reformism, never to strengthen capitalism's resolve. On the other, it was about extending the working-class' grip on power in the struggle with the Right. With the threat of a renascent fascism still looming large in countries such as Italy, that struggle could only be won if all workers gained class consciousness through participation in public life. Until then, Basso wrote as leader of a party that was still represented in government: "We don't consider the current regime in Italy to be a truly democratic regime."[6]

True democracy would never be realized, however, without the fulfillment of a third and crucial pre-condition of new democracy—the political unity of the working class. Whereas countries such as Britain and the Soviet Union might be so fortunate to see (the majority of) their workers united within a single party, both wings of the labour movement commanded considerable strength in continental Europe. To prevent communists and socialists from being played off against each other by reactionaries yet again, it was imperative that they presented a united front. This was the rationale for the PSI to agree a "unity of action pact" with the Italian communists in October 1943, which renewal in 1946 sparked all the problems—the party split, the ostracism from government and the decade spent in the shadows of communism—now associated with its supposed anomaly. However, instead of dwelling on these already well-documented issues once more,[7] I will now turn to considering the three distinguishing features of new democracy in more detail.

Ends and Means

Right from the liberation, the PSI's understanding of democracy was conditioned by its fear of fascism returning to Italy and Europe. In one of the first documents the newly constituted PSI published, it claimed to be democratic in "ends as well as means" but immediately added that "against the reactionary threat, it would not hesitate to call upon the workers to crush with revolutionary violence every neo-fascist attempt to block the people from the road of legality."[8] With their country in a state of near civil war for the first years after liberation,[9] this sort of rhetoric reflected the fright of those right-wing bands still roaming the countryside. Yet as the centre-left government gradually established control over the situation, it quickly became obvious how strongly perceived reactionaries performed even within the boundaries of bourgeois legalism and democratic constitutionalism. The coming of the Cold War and the commensurate increase of American interference in Italy only further added to the belief that a fascist take-over was imminent.

In what was perhaps a symptom of the revolutionary "euphoria" capturing many European socialist parties in the immediate aftermath of the Second World War, the Italian socialists initially pronounced fascism dead.[10] According to Pietro Nenni—the PSI's Secretary General between 1943 and 1946, together with Basso, the most important party leader in the period under review in this article—fascism was "finished as an organization, dead as an ideology and buried under the rubble it had generated as a movement" in August 1944.[11] With reactionary forces also being on the back-foot, it was now a matter of dealing with those capitalists and agrarians who had backed fascism. Before long, however, it became clear that these groups "still had many cards to play."[12] At a November 1944 inter-regional meeting of the PSI in Northern Italy, it was claimed that it was a big mistake to think that the introduction of socialism would not be opposed by powerful interests and obscure conservative forces, the survival of which would "inevitably lead to new fascisms, new wars [and] new catastrophes."[13]

By that time, Nenni himself had also completely changed his mind on the magnitude of the challenge facing democracy in post-war Italy. Writing in the party daily, he argued that reactionary forces, after an initial period of confusion and disbandment, had reorganized under the banner of a constitutional and monarchical neo-fascism. To make matters worse, these reactionaries were already wielding influence on some sectors of the anti-fascist front. Armed with a liberal and democratic discourse and with a good deal of scare-mongering about the "Bolshevik" danger emanating from the communists and the socialists, they were exerting "an irresistible attraction" on the liberal and Christian democratic parties. This amounted to "the historical problem" of democracy in Italy. Would the centrist parties be able to guarantee a Constituent Assembly operating in freedom and legalism, or would the popular masses and the proletarian avant-garde be forced to open it up "by other means"?[14]

It was this dilemma of either working with parties with questionable sympathies, or preparing for a wholesale revolutionary take-over, that shaped socialist politics during the following months. Having left the Bonomi Government in November 1944 on account of it curbing the competencies of the revolutionary liberation committees whilst handing reactionary elements free rein,[15] the PSI abandoned its self-proclaimed "intransigence"[16] to return to power in June 1945. Speaking to workers in Milan, Nenni insisted that the party had not re-entered the coalition with "the old social democratic illusion" according to which it was possible to change the objective social and political conditions of the country from within government. However, with "the tissue holding the nation together" in rapid decay, the socialists had to step in to prevent those forces that would plunge the country into a new civil war from seizing power.[17] Under these circumstances, the PSI adopted a strategy of relaxation. As Nenni pointed out during a Central Committee meeting, a repeat of the events of 1919 was to be avoided at all costs.[18] That meant holding on to the coalition with the Christian democrats and forsaking support for any industrial radicalism at least until the elections to the Constituent Assembly could breathe fresh life into Italian democracy.

Yet, even before the elections had taken place, some socialists were expressing doubts as to the transformative potential of a popular vote in post-war Italy. Already in mid-1945, Basso was writing that it would be a "dangerous delusion" to attribute "miraculous virtues" to the Constituent Assembly. By themselves, electoral rallies "could not give a democratic conscience to a people that never had one," and the experience of 1919–1922 had demonstrated that "no legal institute, no law [and] no parliamentary form could substitute for the democratic education of a people."[19] To be sure, a considerable part of the working class (particularly in the industrial North of the country) had gained political maturity through its involvement in the anti-fascist resistance, but there were still enormous crowds that could easily be captured by reactionary propaganda.

These fears were not allayed by the mixed results of the June 1946 elections. Even if the PSI was delighted that a republic was established in the Italian constitutional referendum, the slight margins by which a monarchy so intimately linked to fascism was defeated formed a cause of real concern.[20] And although the socialists could be pleased about becoming larger than the communists in the Constituent Assembly, the two parties combined were lacking more than 1 million votes for an overall parliamentary majority. That reduced the PSI to another stint as "shock absorber" between the communists and the Christian democrats within a new centre-left coalition.[21] Quickly realizing that the socialists could not possibly win from that position, Nenni was asking his fellow party leaders existential questions by August 1946: "Should we, like [socialists] in many countries, make an alliance with Christian Democracy?" "Or should we instead enter into a left-wing bloc founded on an alliance between socialists and communists?"[22]

The fact that the PSI chose the latter alternative inspired some heated debates about the nature of democracy with the parties of Western European social democracy. In the first months of 1947, the international office of the PSI was still satisfied that it had managed to convince most of its sister parties that their united-front politics should not be confused with fusionism.[23] Yet, this mutual understanding rapidly began to unravel as the Cold War turned hot for the first time during summer 1947. The pronunciation of the Truman Doctrine being followed so swiftly by the Left's exclusion from government in Italy evoked huge fears of a "Greek scenario" (e.g. reactionary forces establishing a dictatorship backed by American military might) amongst Italian socialists. By August, Basso was complaining during an international socialist gathering that the Western Europeans knew very little about the problems of Italy where "the solution could only be socialism or fascism."[24]

Who *did* understand were the Eastern European socialists and social democrats. Themselves part of "new democracies," they had claimed all along that countries without a longer democratic tradition needed "different weapons" to protect themselves from the threat of a renascent fascism.[25] The concomitant application of police-state methods and violations of strict democratic procedures were then necessary evils to achieve the higher goal of bringing socialism to their under-developed electorates. As one Rumanian social democrat put it during the first post-war International Socialist Conference: "We have learnt to see that the war was a result of the failure of the German and Italian masses to fight reaction; we do not

OLD AND NEW DEMOCRACY: PLACING THE ITALIAN ANOMALY... 157

want to make the same mistake, or allow a Rumanian Hitler to climb to power on universal suffrage."[26]

During the last months of 1947, the PSI came ever closer to accepting this logic. Already during the spring, the socio-political situation in post-war Poland had received some very favourable coverage in *Avanti!*[27] and excellent relations were to develop between the Italian and Polish socialists during the coming months. As delegations of the two parties met first in Warsaw (August–September), then in Rome (November), there were intense murmurings about the imminent establishment of a "Socinform" for left-wing socialists who were fed up with Western European domination of the international socialist movement.[28] Matters between Italian and Polish socialism on one hand and Western European social democracy on the other came to a head at the late 1947 International Socialist Conference in Antwerp. Whereas the Western Europeans were beginning to ask serious questions of the methods used by socialists in government across Eastern Europe,[29] the Italians and Poles rather focused on recent developments in France. Nenni underscored the danger of counter-revolution in present-day Europe. Apart from Greece, where counter-revolution was already triumphant, this threat was strongest in France and Italy. However, whereas the PSI at least presented a united front with the communists, the French socialists had actually made things worse by breaking the unity of the working class at this crucial time. Under no circumstances, Nenni concluded, could "Italy become a second Greece."[30]

Within the post-war international socialist movement, however, the Italian socialists and their Eastern European comrades were fighting a losing battle. The amendment (full of references to a putative counter-revolutionary danger in Western Europe) to the draft resolution on world peace proposed by Italian and Polish socialists at Antwerp was defeated by 14 votes to 3 (with only the Hungarian social democrats supporting the amendment).[31] The final rupture came 2 months later, when the communists, backed by their social democratic–coalition partners, grabbed power in Czechoslovakia during the February 1948 Prague Coup. Because the response to "this crime" against "the principles of Democratic Socialism" had immediately been declared "an acid test of sincerity" by the British Labour Party, the Italian socialists "shocked" Western European social democracy by sending a congratulatory telegram to the leaders of the Czechoslovakian social democrats.[32] Looking back on these events and the subsequent break with Western European social democracy, however, Basso noted that the question as to whether democratic methods had been followed during the Czechoslovakian and the other Eastern European take-overs was really irrelevant. What mattered was whether socialists recognized that the proletariat had "the right to wrest power from the hands of the dominant class and construct a new social order."[33]

COMPLETE CIRCLE

The Italian socialists were adamant that the old dominant class had lost every moral right to rule their country. After the bourgeoisie had plunged Italy and Europe into the abyss of dictatorship and war, they insisted, there was no way for socialists to work with its political representatives ever again. As Nenni wrote in one of his first tracts after the liberation, the country now stood before a clear choice: "Either a government of workers acting in the interest of workers, or a bourgeois government disguising under a thin veil of parliamentary democracy an effective economic dictatorship." With fascism, he argued, the bourgeoisie had completed its "historical circle." It had neither a programme nor the energies to re-invent itself. There was no point rebuilding Italy, then, if it was not going to be a socialist Italy.[34] Yet, as the socialists were soon to find out, the Italian and (Western) European bourgeoisie were more resilient than many had expected at Zero Hour.[35] This prompted the PSI to a reconsideration of the mistakes that had seen bourgeois democracy give way to fascism rather than socialism during the interwar period.

The lessons were twofold. The first and foremost was that the bourgeoisie could not be entrusted with the defence of democracy in countries such as Italy. After all, fascism had not been the result of a "band of adventurists" or the "betrayal of the monarchy" but instead of "the economic and political deficiencies of our bourgeoisie."[36] For the PSI, the inter-war period had conclusively demonstrated that the Italian bourgeoisie—despite all its lofty language regarding democracy—was quite willing to throw in its lot with reactionary or fascist forces if it considered its economic interests threatened by the working class. According to Nenni, fascism had been "the most extreme manifestation" of the bourgeoisie's "chronic incapacity" to understand the needs of the people. From Crispi to Mussolini, Italy had been sacrificed to the interests of the dynasty, the landowners and the industrialists. Rather than doing anything to improve the lives of workers, these groups had spent billions on wars in futile attempts to resolve the internal contradictions of their system.[37] In the same vein, Basso explained how bourgeois society, its riches drained by the

First World War, had taken recourse to dictatorship to restore its economic pre-dominance in large parts of continental Europe. To halt the historical process of the working class becoming the ruling class, "conservative forces, capitalist classes, reactionaries, [and] monarchists" had "instigated and supported fascism in Italy, Germany, Spain, Hungary etc." With the continent in even bigger ruins now than after the First World War, it was "truer than ever that a bourgeois restoration in Europe could only mean new fascisms [and] new wars."[38]

Accordingly, the post-war socialists always felt uneasy about having to operate within the strict confines of bourgeois democracy (or "bourgeois legalism" as they preferred to describe it).[39] Whilst still in government, party leaders would often point to the fragility of democracy in its current form. As *Avanti!* director Sandro Pertini put it at the April 1946 congress of the PSI, "Fascism has shown that freedom, if it does not have those social reforms associated with socialism at its core, can be obliterated in the space of an afternoon."[40] After the party had been removed from power, however, its judgments on bourgeois democracy became more clear-cut. Speaking of "the Italian problem" at a meeting of European socialists, Basso described it as "having no bourgeois democrats."[41]

Once again, this kind of reasoning shows striking similarities with the arguments some Eastern European socialist and social democratic parties were putting forward to defend their uncompromising line toward bourgeois parties. Claiming a democratic bourgeoisie was lacking in their countries, they often contrasted their situation with that of the British Labour Party. If Labour was to lose power, one Hungarian social democrat argued, that would at worst result in the introduction of socialism in Great Britain being delayed until the next election. If, in contrast, "the old reactionary classes would re-take power in Hungary, there would not be enough trees in Bakony Forest for their counter-revolutionary regime to hang all the true democrats and socialist workers from."[42] The "British card" was also played in the debates between pro-communists and anti-communists within the PSI. At its mid-1945 National Council, Pertini reproached Giuseppe Saragat, the future leader of the secessionists, for being disingenuous in claiming that there was no longer a danger of violent reaction returning to Italy. An "educated man" such as Saragat should have based his views not only on the situation in Britain and some other countries but also on "the objective Italian situation." Above all, he had forgotten that "we are emerging from a dictatorship imposed by violence, that Germany is emerging from a dictatorship imposed by violence and that a dictatorship imposed by violence still exists in Spain."[43] He might well have included countries such as Bulgaria, Hungary, Poland and Rumania into this equation.

Sharing their diagnosis that no durable democratic arrangement could be reached with the bourgeoisie in countries lacking a democratic tradition, the PSI applied the same medicine as its Eastern European sister parties: a united front with the communists. This was linked to the second big lesson of the interwar period i.e. that divisions on the Left had allowed fascists to divide and conquer. In a report the party leadership published in April 1945, it argued that without the unity of the working class no truly democratic politics were possible. The "tragic experiences of the past in both Italy and Germany, in both France and Spain" had taught them that "every struggle between communists and socialists plays into the hands of the reaction."[44] For the sheer magnitude of its consequences, the struggles between communists and social democrats in Weimar Germany especially captured the imagination of the Italian socialists. Expressing his delight that nobody within the PSI supported a politics based on the old slogan of "neither revolution, nor reaction" anymore, Nenni warned that fighting the communists on the Left would see "us end up like German social democracy, i.e. little by little absorbed by reactionary elements."[45] Likewise, Pertini pointed to the dangers of forgetting about the aims of the working class whilst cooperating with right-wing parties within the government. It was imperative that socialist ministers questioned every measure taken as to its merits for the working class because "the shadow of Noske hangs above our comrades in government."[46]

Whereas the foremost role of the communist–socialist united front was thus to operate as a bulwark against a resurgent Right, it was also intended to keep the communists on the democratic path. Pertini already hinted at this when he argued it was the function of the PSI "to defend the democratic conscience within the working-class movement" at the April 1946 party congress.[47] As the coming of the Cold War drove the communists to take up increasingly extreme attitudes, these sentiments became more pronounced.[48] Writing in 1948, Basso discerned between two mentalities within the labour movement. The communists were the hardened guardians of class interests, whilst the socialists were more open to "the needs of the larger masses."[49] Only in their combination could these two mentalities lead to true democracy. As Nenni put it in the run-up to the April 1948 parliamentary elections, the communist-socialist Popular Front

OLD AND NEW DEMOCRACY: PLACING THE ITALIAN ANOMALY... 161

offered a democratic solution for the popular masses—"If it fails, [...] we would be reduced to a choice between bolshevism and fascism."[50]

STRUCTURAL REFORMS

The PSI accepted, however, that the political unity of the working class was not sufficient to guarantee a democratic development by itself. To that end, other social groups—such as peasants, artisans, clerks, functionaries, intellectuals and crucially also the petit-bourgeoisie—that had for 20 years been the backbone of fascism needed to be won over.[51] However, that was no easy task. Basso commented that a peasant tended to vote whatever his priest told him to, whereas bourgeois society had been shown to be willing to take up arms to turn electoral results to its advantage. And even if a coalition around the working class managed to take power, it still faced some massive challenges. As the "tragic example" of the French Popular Front had demonstrated, a "capitalist offensive" could plunge a country into such an economic crisis as to prevent it from "reaping the fruits of universal suffrage." It was up to the socialists, then, to make sure that, unlike in interwar France, "the hundred plutocratic families" would be giving way to "the forty million" in post-war Italy.[52]

As the PSI programme laid down, this was to be achieved through "structural reforms"—land reform, industrial reform, banking reform, education reform and reform of the state. This language of reforms, however, presented a party branding itself as revolutionary with something of a theoretical conundrum. After all, how were the structural reforms proposed by the PSI any different from those measures carried through by social democratic reformists in most of Western Europe? According to Basso, the commonplace notion, i.e. that the old divide between revolutionary and reformist socialism had been overcome—with nobody wanting to revive the old capitalist order nor anyone calling for a violent take-over these days—was founded on a mistaken conception of revolution. Revolution was about bringing a new social class to power irrespective of whether that happened by the violence used during the Russian Revolution or by the peaceful reforms advocated by the PSI.[53]

The fundamental error reformists made, therefore, was to believe that social reforms within the existing capitalist power structures by themselves brought socialism closer. Quite the opposite was true as far as the Italian socialists were concerned.[54] Reforms carried through within the narrow confines of "bourgeois parliamentarism" only tended to strengthen the bourgeoisie's hold on society. For Basso, reformism amounted to handing over the lead of the revolutionary process to the petit-bourgeoisie. From Déat to De Man, the history of the socialist movement already knew "too many examples of where these deviations of classicism and the proletarian ideology could lead to."[55] The structural reforms championed by the PSI, in contrast, were intended to break the bourgeoisie's ability to turn formal democracy to its advantage. As Nenni worded it in early 1946, "a republic that does not at the same time give us agrarian reform, a republic that does not destruct those states within the state that are the large capitalist societies, that does not put those industrial, commercial and banking firms at the disposal of the people, would in reality be a new dress for a dance, that the bourgeoisie would give us to overcome its temporary problems."[56]

In this sense, structural reforms constituted a second liberation of the Italian people, which would be crucial if the country was going to be a true democracy. In a document the PSI published on entering government for the first time in May 1944, it argued that the new democracy the party was fighting for had nothing in common with old parliamentary democracy. It would be freed of the "bourgeois deformations that had disfigured and corrupted traditional democracy," whereas its economy would be "subordinated to the general interests of society" within the framework of a plan "elaborated by works councils, peasants, technicians, functionaries and clerks, by the liberal professions, by culture and by science."[57] This focus on liberating ordinary people from the shackles of bourgeois capitalism remained a constant in socialist thinking on democracy throughout the post-war years. In October 1945, Nenni declared that the PSI would demand that the Constituent Assembly got on with agrarian and industrial reform. For without land reform, "three-quarters of our country would remain subject to the agrarian caste, which has always been opposed to democracy." And if power within the factories did not shift from management to the works councils, "we might have freedom of expression and freedom of manifestation but the leadership of the state would remain in the hands of those former fascists that have now turned anti-fascists."[58] Similarly, Basso argued that workplace democracy represented what was truly new about democracy. New democracy, then, would solve the contradiction of bourgeois democracy, in which democracy stopped "at the gates of the factories, of the banks, of companies in general, everywhere where those magic words had been written: private property."[59]

Crushing the power structures on which bourgeois society was founded, however, was not the only reason for the PSI's insistence on a radical overhaul of socio-economic life: Just as important was its desire to teach the Italian people democracy after the experience of fascism and war. This concerned the country's peasant majority first and foremost. According to Basso, peasants only had a very basic understanding of their own political interests. If faced with such simple questions as whether they approved land reform, like in the June 1946 "People's Referendum" in Poland, they would come out overwhelmingly in favor. But come the time of parliamentary elections, those same peasants would vote for all the clerical and reactionary parties that wanted to take the land away from them.[60] Peasants were certainly not the only group, however, that was considered politically underdeveloped by the socialists. Even within the working class, there were significant pockets of "political analphabetism." Especially those women and youngsters who had not participated in the anti-fascist resistance were often disinterested in political problems, and the socialists knew all too well "that every anti-democratic movement had its roots in this absenteeism."[61] Participation in public life, then, was key to the moral re-education of these groups. It was about getting peasants, women and youngsters to attend those grassroots meetings (in factories or on the countryside) where their everyday problems were discussed so that they would gradually learn to translate these concrete points into more abstract ideas on the national political struggle whilst developing "a democratic conscience" in the process.[62]

In these efforts to implement structural reforms and re-educate the people, the PSI increasingly looked toward its Eastern European sister organizations for inspiration. In August 1947, a three-part series in *Avanti!* painted developments in post-war Czechoslovakia in distinctly rosy terms. One month later, after his visit to the country, Nenni was describing "the Polish road to socialism" as an interesting alternative for Italy. With a communist–socialist united front also facing a strong Catholic competition in Poland, he was particularly impressed by the far-reaching nature of its agrarian reform and industrial nationalizations.[63] And whereas Western European social democracy was already widely denounced at the January 1948 congress of the PSI, Basso was all praise about the fact that "the experience of the interwar period had inspired the people of Central and Eastern Europe to realize a new democracy, a structural democratic reform that had allowed workers and peasants to finally take the stage in political life as well as in their country's history."[64]

Conclusion

At the December 1947 congress of the Polish Socialist Party, its leader, Józef Cyrankiewicz, berated the French socialists entering into an anti-communist alliance with centre-right parties concluding that the Polish socialists were "wiser than the West European socialists by a whole historical period."[65] Of course, he did not mean the PSI by this because close relations between the Italian and Polish socialists had developed during the previous months. In fact, in a late 1947 note on the situation within the international socialist movement, Labour's International Secretary, Denis Healey, explained that the PSI was "seen as part of East Europe."[66] If this was the case, it certainly seems anachronistic to only compare the Italian socialists with their Western European counterparts and subsequently dismiss them as an anomaly. For a better understanding of what drove the post-war PSI, as well as what set the Italian socialists apart from their Western counterparts, we must include the history of the Eastern European socialist and social democratic parties in the equation.

There are many reasons for the striking parallels between the approaches advocated by the Italian socialists on one side and their comrades in countries—such as Hungary, Poland, and Rumania—on the other. Much like Italy, these were countries with backward rural economies, with large and frequently analphabetic peasant majorities, with strong Catholic and/or nationalist movements and without longer democratic traditions. Above all, in every single one of these countries the experience of right-wing authoritarian or fascist rule had lasted not, like in most of Western Europe, just half a decade nor even, like in Austria or Germany, a full decade; dating back all the way to the 1920s, it had lasted an entire generation.

This generational aspect, so clearly articulated in the above-mentioned quote by Cyrankiewicz, found its reflection in the composition of the leadership teams of the post-war socialist and social democratic parties. Whereas many of their sister parties were still being led by exponents of the interwar old guard, a group of mostly younger and (internationally at least) little-known leaders stood at the helm of the PSI and Eastern European parties. On one level, this was simply a consequence of the long duration and repressive nature of the regimes with which these parties had had to contend, which naturally made for a more significant turnover in their leaderships. However, it was also linked to the fact that many of the older leaders had been discredited after they had tried to find some sort of accommodation with right-wing rulers during the inter-war and war

OLD AND NEW DEMOCRACY: PLACING THE ITALIAN ANOMALY... 165

years.[67] The result was a profound generational mismatch between the younger and more revolutionary socialists in charge of the Italian and Eastern parties and the older and more moderate leaders of mainstream Western social democracy—with far-reaching consequences for the unity of the post-war international socialist movement. Or, as Healey wrote to Larock in the aftermath of the schism within Italian socialism, "These neo-Trotskyist 'impossibilist' movements among the young Socialists in many parts of Europe may easily prove more dangerous to the survival of democratic socialism than the Communist Parties themselves."[68]

NOTES

1. "Rapport au Bureau sur le "congres du scission" du parti italien." Fonds Max Buset, 77 Rapports de Victor Larock, Institut Emile Vandervelde, Brussels.
2. Callaghan, John T. *The Retreat of Social Democracy.* Manchester: Manchester University Press, 2000, ch. 1.
3. See e.g. Sabbatucci, Giovanni. *Il riformismo impossibile. Storia del socialismo italiano.* Rome/Bari: Laterza, 1991; Cafagna, Luciano. *Una strana disfatta. La parabola dell'autonomismo socialista.* Venice: Marsilio, 1996.
4. Colarizi, Simona. "I socialisti italiani e l'Internazionale Socialista." *Mondo Contemporaneo* 1/2 (2005), 1–62, 1.
5. Basso, Lelio. "Compiti nuovi." *Quarto Stato* 12 (15-07-1946).
6. Basso, Lelio. "Tre punti di chiarire." *Quarto Stato* 25/26 (30-01-1947 and 15-02-1947).
7. Cfr. Degl'Innocenti, Maurizio/Ciuffoletti, Zeffiro. *Storia del Psi III: Dal dopoguerra a oggi.* Rome/Bari: Laterza, 1993; Sabbatucci, Giovanni, ed. *Storia del socialismo italiano V: Il secondo dopoguerra, 1943–1956.* Rome: Il Poligono, 1981.
8. "Dalla dichariazione del Consiglio del Partito del settembre 1944." *Orientamenti: Bollettino di Commento e di Indirizzo Politico* I–II (18-01-1948), 9.
9. Pavone, Claudio. *Una guerra civile: Saggio storico sulla moralità della Resistenza, 1943–1945.* Turin: Bollatti Boringhieri, 1991.
10. On this euphoria (which quickly gave way to disillusionment) in three other Western European socialist and social democratic parties, see: Orlow, Dietrich. *Common Destiny: A Comparative History of the Dutch, French, and German Social Democratic Parties, 1945–1969.* New York/Oxford: Berghahn, 2000, 44–64.
11. Nenni, Pietro. "Motivi di inquietudine all'interno." *Avanti!,* 15.08.1944.

166 J. DE GRAAF

12. "Documento del Convegno Interregionale del PSIUPAI, novembre 1944." In Neri Serneri, Simone, ed. *Il partito socialista nella resistenza. I documenti e la stampa clandestina (1943–1945)*. Pisa: Nistri Lischi, 1988, 336.
13. Ibid.
14. Nenni, Pietro. "Il vero problema." *Avanti!*, 25.11.1944.
15. "La crisi del primo governo Bonomi. Dichariazione del Partito Socialista al Paese" [10.12.1944]. *Orientamenti: Bollettino di Commento e di Indirizzo Politico* I–II, 18.01.1948, 13–15; "Contro il governo Bonomi, febbraio 1945." In Neri Serneri, ed. *Il partito socialista*, 282.
16. "Intrasigenza socialista, febbraio 1945." In Neri Serneri, ed. *Il partito socialista*, 283–285.
17. "Discorso di Nenni al popolo di Milano" [22.07.1945]. Fondo Nenni, Busta 87, Fasc. 2191. Archivio Centrale dello Stato [ACS], Rome.
18. "Comitato Centrale. Seduta del 17 ottobre 1945." Fondo Nenni, Busta 87, Fasc. 2191. ACS, Rome.
19. Basso, Lelio. "Per una coscienza democratica." *Avanti!*, 29.08.1945.
20. During a meeting of the PSI Direzione, *Avanti!* editor Ignazio Silone reminisced about the collapse of the Weimar Republic and concluded that for the millions who had voted for the monarchy, the concept of a republic should quickly be provided with some content. "Riunione a Roma del 13 giugno 1946." Fondo Foscolo Lombardi. Partito Socialista Italiano, Direzione Nazionale, Busta 4, Fasc. 20. Istituto Storico della Resistenza in Toscana [ISRT], Florence.
21. "Riunione della Direzione – 6 Agosto 1946 (notturna)." Fondo Foscolo Lombardi. Partito Socialista Italiano, Direzione Nazionale, Busta 4, Fasc. 20. ISRT, Florence.
22. Ibid.
23. "Relazione dell'Ufficio Internazionale." Fondo Lelio Basso, Serie 15, Fasc. 7. Fondazione Lelio e Lisli Basso Isocco, Rome.
24. "Internationale socialistische bijeenkomst te Parijs tot herstel der Internationale op 18 Augustus 1947." Archief Partij van de Arbeid [Archive of the Dutch Labour Party], Map 2680. International Institute of Social History [IISH], Amsterdam.
25. See, for example, the open letter to a (fictional) member of the Labour Party by a Polish socialist leader, Hochfeld, Julian. "List do towarysza z Labour Party." *Przegląd Socjalistyczny* 4 (1946), as quoted by: Heumos, Peter ed. *Europäischer Sozialismus im Kalten Krieg: Briefe und Berichte 1944–1948*. Frankfurt a.M./New York: Campus, 2004, 129–139.
26. "International Socialist Conference at Clacton May 17th–20th 1946." Labour Party Archives [LPA], International Department [LP/ID], Box 3. Labour History Archive and Study Centre [LHASC], Manchester.

27. Cannavero, Alfredo. "Pietro Nenni, i socialisti italiani e l'Internazionale socialista tra Est ed. Ovest dopo la Seconda Guerra mondiale." Les Internationales et le problème de la guerre au XXe siècle. *Actes du colloque de Rome (22–24 novembre 1984)*. Rome: École Française de Rome, 1987, 252.
28. Healey to Matteotti, 03.11.1947. LPA, LP/ID, Box 9, LHASC, Manchester.
29. In a particularly heated exchange, Dutch delegate Koos Vorrink referred to the repression he had witnessed during his recent visits to Eastern Europe and asked the Eastern European socialists "how they could continue like this." "Protokoll der internationalen sozialistischen Konferenz Antwerpen 28 November – 2 Dezember 1947," Socialist International Archives, Box 236. IISH, Amsterdam.
30. Ibid.
31. Ibid.
32. "The Labour Party and Italy." LPA, LP/ID, Box 13, LHASC, Manchester.
33. Basso, Lelio. "Sul socialismo europeo." Fondo Lelio Basso, Serie 15, Fasc. 6. Fondazione Lelio e Lisli Basso Isocco, Rome.
34. Nenni, Pietro. *Che cosa è, che cosa ha fatto, che cosa vuole il Partito Socialista*, [unpublished, 1944] as quoted by Sandro Pertini in: Caretti, Stefano, ed. *Sandro Pertini. Dal delitto Matteotti alla Costituente. Scritti e discorsi: 1924–1946*. Manduria: Lacaita, 2008, 87.
35. On how the Western European bourgeoisie emerged strengthened rather than weakened from World War Two more generally, see: Conway, Martin. "The Rise and Fall of Western Europe's Democratic Age, 1945–1973." Contemporary European History 13: 1 (2004), 73 f.
36. "Le tesi di Bandiera Rossa, giugno 1944." Neri Serneri, *Il partito socialista*, 166.
37. "Il presidente del Partito alla Radio" [01-05-1945]. Fondo Nenni, Busta 87, Fasc. 2191. ACS, Rome.
38. Basso, Lelio. "Per una politica socialista." *Quarto Stato* 2, 15.02.1946.
39. On the eve of the April 1946 Party Congress, the leadership of the PSI published a document admitting that their struggles for Constituente and Republic belonged to the bourgeois rather than the socialist cycle of history. Yet, "one of the teachings of Marxism" was that "a bourgeois revolution could not be completed if the proletariat does not stand at its head." "Relazione politica della Direzione del Partito per il XXIV congresso nazionale." Orientamenti: Bollettino di Commento e di Indirizzo Politico I–II, 18.01.1948, 26.
40. "Al Congresso di Firenze." In Neri Serneri, Simone/Casali, Antonio/ Errera, Giovanni, eds. *Scritti e Discorsi di Sandro Pertini. Volume I, 1926–1978*. Rome: Presidenza del Consiglio dei Ministri, Dipartimento per l'Informazione e l'Editoria, 1992, 78–79.

168   J. DE GRAAF

41. "Internationale socialistische bijeenkomst te Parijs tot herstel der Internationale op 18 Augustus 1947." Archief Partij van de Arbeid [Archive of the Dutch Labour Party], Map 2680. IISH, Amsterdam.
42. Quoted by Braunthal, Julius. *Geschichte der Internationale, vol. III.* Hannover: Dietz, 1971, 170 f. A similar point was made in the abovementioned letter to a (fictional) member of the Labour Party by Polish socialist leader Julian Hochfeld. In it, he claimed that if the Tories would have won the 1945 General Election, Labour would just have had to wait for 5 years to get another shot at power: "Not so for us. We are convinced that, if we were to lose power, we would have to retake it not from conservatives but from fascists, and not at the ballot box but in an armed struggle." Hochfeld. "List do towarysza." Heumos, ed. *Europäischer Sozialismus,* 131.
43. "Intervento al Consiglio Nazionale del Partito Socialista." In Caretti, ed. *Sandro Pertini,* 149.
44. "Relazione della Direzione del Partito al 3° Consiglio Nazionale di Roma." *Orientamenti: Bollettino di Commento e di Indirizzo Politico* I–II, 18.01.1948, 17.
45. "Comitato Centrale. Seduta del 17 ottobre 1945." Fondo Nenni, Busta 87, Fasc. 2191. ACS, Rome.
46. "Intervento al Comitato Centrale." In Caretti, ed. *Sandro Pertini,* 186.
47. "Al congresso di Firenze." In Neri Serneri/Casali/Errera, eds. *Scritti e Discorsi,* 78 f.
48. Especially after the founding conference of the Cominform (Oct. 1947) had divided the world into war and peace camps, there was much apprehension within the PSI about the communists embarking on "a programme of agitations and sabotage." See the discussions within the PSI Direzione: "Riunione della Direzione (1^ e 2^ seduta del 15 ottobre 1947)." Fondo Foscolo Lombardi. Busta 5, Fasc, 41, ISRT, Florence.
49. Basso, Lelio. "Sul socialismo." Fondo Lelio Basso, Serie 15, Fasc. 6. Fondazione Lelio e Lisli Basso Isocco, Rome.
50. Partito socialista italiano. Congresso nazionale "Roma 19–22 gennaio 1948," 19/01/1948–22/01/1948, 360 f. Fondo Partito socialista italiano (Psi) – Direzione Nazionale. Serie 20: Congressi nazionali e internazionali. Sottoserie 1: Congressi nazionali. Fondazione di Studi Storici Filippo Turati, Florence.
51. "Relazione politica della Direzione del Partito per il XXIV congresso nazionale." Orientamenti: Bollettino di Commento e di Indirizzo Politico I–II, 18-01-1948, 28. On the significance of the middle classes (term interchangeably used for petit-bourgeoisie) not "succumbing to the capitalist bourgeoisie yet again" if Italy was to "become a true democracy," see also Nenni, Pietro. "Le classi nella lotta per la democrazia." *Avanti!,* 11.08.1945.

OLD AND NEW DEMOCRACY: PLACING THE ITALIAN ANOMALY... 169

52. Basso, Lelio. "Il discorso del compagno Basso: La secessione è un atto che non ha soltanto ragioni personalistiche, ma ragioni più profonde di mentalità e di sensibilità politica." *L'Idea* 10, 08.03.1947.
53. Basso, Lelio. "Socialismo al bivio." *Quarto Stato* 6/7, 30.04.1946.
54. Just how broadly this anti-reformist sentiment was shared within the postwar PSI is attested to by the fact that even Saragat affirmed that he and his allies were no reformists in an August 1946 session of the PSI Direzione. "Riunione della Direzione – 6 agosto 1946 (notturna)." Fondo Foscolo Lombardi. Partito Socialista Italiano, Direzione Nazionale, Busta 4, Fasc. 20. ISRT, Florence.
55. Basso, Lelio. "Socialismo al bivio." *Quarto Stato* 6/7, 30.04.1946.
56. "I problem interni e internazionali della democrazia italiana. Discorso pronunciato da Pietro Nenni a Palazzo Ducale il 3 febbraio 1946." Fondo Nenni, Busta 87, Fasc. 2191. ACS, Rome.
57. "La politica socialista dopo la crisi governativa, 1 maggio 1944." In Neri Serneri, ed. *Il Partito Socialista*, 149.
58. "Discorso di Nenni al popolo di Milano" [22.07.1945]. Fondo Nenni, Busta 87, Fasc. 2191. ACS, Rome.
59. Basso, Lelio. "Risposta a un invito." Quoted by: Rossi, Emanuele. *Democrazia come partecipazione: Lelio Basso e il PSI alle origini della Repubblica 1943–1947*. Rome: Viella, 2011, 243 f.
60. Basso, Lelio. "Socialismo europeo." *Quarto Stato*, 16, 15.09.1946.
61. Basso, *Per una coscienza*.
62. Ibid.
63. Rossi. *Democrazia come partecipazione*, 270–272.
64. Partito socialista italiano. Congresso nazionale "Roma 19–22 gennaio 1948," 19.01.1948–22.01.1948, 75. Fondo Partito socialista italiano (Psi) – Direzione Nazionale. Serie 20: Congressi nazionali e internazionali. Sottoserie 1: Congressi nazionali. Fondazione di Studi Storici Filippo Turati, Florence.
65. "Twenty-Seventh Congress of the Polish Socialist Party" [December 1947], The National Archive, London, FO 371/66097 N14846.
66. "European Socialism," LPA, LP/ID, Box 13, LHASC, Manchester.
67. The inter-war leadership of the Hungarian Social Democratic Party, for example, had not covered itself in glory by signing a pact with the right-wing authoritarian government of its country in December 1921. In return for being left in peace by the government domestically, the social democrats undertook to forsake on political strikes and support the government's foreign policy. Even if the Italian socialists obviously never worked with the fascist regime in their country, some of its older leaders managed to discredit themselves as well. Angelo Tasca, the anti-communist reformist who became one of the main leaders of the PSI (i.e. the exiled PSI in

France), after the announcement of the Molotov-Ribbentrop pact, fell from grace in 1940 after he threw in his lot with the Vichy regime. See Lorman, Thomas. "The Bethlen-Peyer Pact: A Reassessment." *Central Europe*, 1: 2 (2003), 147–162; De Grand, Alexander. "'To Learn Nothing and to Forget Nothing': Italian Socialism and the Experience of Exile Politics, 1935–1945." *Contemporary European History* 14: 4 (2005), 539–558.

68. Healey to Larock, 27.01.1947, LHASC, LPA, LP/ID, Box 3.

CHAPTER 8

Inheriting Horror: Historical Memory in French Socialists' and German Social Democrats' Fight for European Democracy, 1945–1958

Brian Shaev

When one is an insoluble part of a people, as the SPD is of the German people, that involves consequences. No one can free himself from the bond of belonging to a class or nation. It is like an inheritance — one takes over the debts as well as the assets. (—Kurt Schumacher to the International Socialist Conference in Zurich, 8 June 1947[1])

Two years after the end of the Second World War, Kurt Schumacher addressed a transnational conference of European socialists on behalf of his party, the German Social Democratic Party (SPD). Formally requesting the SPD's (re)admittance into the international socialist community, Schumacher spoke of the "debts" and "assets" that were his party's "inheritance." Schumacher was aware that before he and his international colleagues could begin to contemplate the future, there would be a frank and painful reckoning with the horrors of the recent past. Anticipating the

---

B. Shaev (✉)
Leiden University, Leiden, The Netherlands

© The Author(s) 2018   171
J. Späth (ed.), *Does Generation Matter? Progressive Democratic Cultures in Western Europe, 1945–1960*, Palgrave Studies in the History of Social Movements, https://doi.org/10.1007/978-3-319-77422-0_8

at-times hostile questions that were to come, Schumacher opened the meeting by binding past, present and future together in a metaphor of mutual obligation.

The concept of inheritance is a fruitful entry point for an analysis of how historical memory shaped the political culture not only of post-war German social democracy but of French socialism as well. To bequeath is to pass a heritage through time and between people, that is, between generations. "No one can free himself from [this] bond," Schumacher said. The sense of compulsion that the past imposed on the present in the period after the Second World War is at the heart of this chapter. The argument, however, proceeds a step further. Although the emphasis of Schumacher's remark is on the "insoluble" relationship between the SPD and the German people, he places the "bond of belonging to a class" alongside that of nation. As we shall see later in this text, this allegiance to multiple (if overlapping) communities was not a remark isolated to transnational discussions; it was a strong feature of post-war SPD leaders' domestic discourses as well. These dual allegiances also emerge in statements, both public and private, of post-war French socialist leaders.

The temporal and spatial characteristics of German social democratic and French socialist discourses on democracy in the decade after the Second World War bear so much in common that it is appropriate to analyse the party leaderships as a single generation of socialist politicians in post-war Europe. Most scholars of generation and memory continue to conceptualize their objects of study within national boundaries (except for recent comparative and transnational studies of the generation of 1968).[2] This leads to a general neglect of the possibility that, under specific sets of circumstances, transnational "memory communities" and generations may emerge. Jan Assmann writes that, in national memory communities, people "live in a shared world of symbolic meaning," accept the nation's "foundational memory" based on canonical texts and incorporate their personal experiences or "biographical memory" within the overarching memory culture.[3] In cases when memory is integral to a group's identity, Pierre Nora designates these "memory communities" with "debts and inheritances from the past," concepts that emerge in the quotation from Schumacher that opens this chapter.[4] Generation, meanwhile, "remains a highly ambiguous concept" in academic literature.[5] For Jürgen Reulecke, "generation and generationality are, in the end, not tangible entities but rather mental, often very zeitgeist-dependent constructs through which people, as members of a specific age group, are located or locate themselves historically."[6] The centrality of age and demography remains contentious in the literature on generation. Jean-François Sirinelli writes, "In political history, generation...appears [to have]...a chronologically elastic structure."[7] These authors are emblematic of their field in that they analyse generations as nationally bound entities, German in the case of Reulecke and French for Sirinelli.

Generation and memory studies have called attention to divisions within national spheres. Below the "macro-formation of one culture," according to Jan Assmann, one finds "an array of cultural microformations."[8] Historians of memory, such as Henri Rousso, have analysed political parties as having distinct memory cultures.[9] Scholars also agree that there was no homogenous memory discourse within Western European countries during the post-war period.[10] In France, the resistance mythology was claimed by socialists, communists and Gaullists, but they presented different narratives of recent French history and contrary visions for the future.[11] Although historians of West Germany have emphasized a "community of silence" in the 1950s, the SPD frequently objected to the prevailing memory discourse of the time.[12] Another set of historians have pointed to the importance of generational differences within political parties, for instance, the "'45ers" and "68ers" in the SPD and the post-war generation around French Socialist leader Guy Mollet, the Algerian War generation that arose in the late 1950s to oppose him and the broader generation of 1968 that then followed.[13]

Although a number of recent works have encouraged scholars to conceptualize historical memory in a European context, memory and generation studies have not really considered the impact of sustained transnational contact between sub-national groups, transnational exchanges and the possibility of the formation of transnational memory communities.[14] The international socialist community—its rituals, symbols and institutions—is an ideal subject to explore the European dimension of generation and memory. The present chapter is a step in this direction. Scholars of generation emphasise the importance of a "founding moment," especially for those who "experienced times of radical upheaval and new beginnings," that serves to foster a "common vision of historical events."[15] Social psychologists, for their part, have shown how experiences of collective trauma often serve as the strongest basis for bonds among group members.[16] This chapter explores how the chain of events from the collapse of Weimar democracy to the Second World War facilitated a convergence of socialist-memory cultures in post-war France and Germany.

French socialists and German social democrats often presented their experiences of exile, imprisonment, and torture during the Nazi and Vichy regimes as having resulted from their socialist identity in a European anti-fascist struggle. Party leaders shared much in common in their analyses of the rise of Nazism, their assessment of non-socialist political forces, and the trajectory of post-war West German and French democracy. From these memorial discourses, both parties asserted a democratic legitimacy to present a post-war program for economic and social transformation. As Schumacher claimed, "our legitimacy comes from history, from the past."[17] Expectations for the future are often at the margins of memory studies, but—as Jon Cowan writes about post-war France—"assumptions of continuity between past and future meant that debates over the nation's future essentially hinged on the politics of memory," a claim that is equally valid for West Germany.[18] This chapter explores how SPD and SFIO narratives of what went wrong in the past—the lessons that each party derived from those experiences for their present and the proposals they designed for the future—often bore more in common with one another than they did with other political forces within their own nations. The SPD and SFIO also made frequent reference to the histories of their neighbours when interpreting developments in their own country. At crucial moments when their post-war democracies appeared threatened, party leaders interpreted their politics in a wider European context rather than as being bound within national borders. Taken together, these commonalities demonstrate that is a worthwhile endeavour to analyse these politicians as a single generation in the history of European social democracy.

Historical Legitimacy in French Socialist and German Social Democratic Discourses Emerging from the Second World War

In a series of meetings in 1947, European socialists debated the (re)admittance of the SPD into their family of parties, then known as COMISCO, the predecessor of the Socialist International established in 1951. A dominant feature of these discussions was the SPD's (in)action in the events leading up to the Nazi conquest of power in 1932–1933 and the relative impotence displayed by the German anti-fascist resistance during the Third Reich. Socialist delegates from the Netherlands and, in particular, from central Europe turned the proceedings into a sort of tribunal, in which the SPD's leader, Kurt Schumacher, attempted to achieve legitimacy for his renascent party through a defence of the SPD's struggle and suffering during the preceding 15 years.

Schumacher pleaded for the understanding and sympathy of his socialist colleagues. The discussion focused at first on the SPD's decision to preserve its name, signalling organisational and ideological continuity with the inter-war and turn-of-the-century SPD. Marinus van der Goes van Naters, a Dutch delegate of the PvdA, a party that changed its name from a Socialist to a Labour party after the Second World War, pointedly demanded of Schumacher: "Is the SPD ready to acknowledge its pre-war failure and start as a new party?" In response, Schumacher conceded SPD errors, which he rarely did in public. He rejected, though, his Dutch colleague's link between inter-war failures and the necessity of renouncing his party's inheritance:

> *You must see that it was necessary to reassemble what forces were available and for this purpose the power of attraction of an old banner is stronger than any new organisation...I always belonged to the rebels in the old party, but to deny the old party on that account we will never do. The party made mistakes now and again, also tactical errors, but it was the party that strove for great principles which are today still demanded by the world and you should not make our failure your standard of judgment in all things. It is not always the better man who wins.[19]*

Here Schumacher received crucial support from French socialist representatives. Party leader Guy Mollet reminded his Socialist colleagues that his party had also resurrected its name and argued that this was no reason to exclude the SPD from international socialist meetings. In the end, COMISCO approved the (re)admittance of the SPD.

Although battles for historical legitimacy generally took place within national political arenas, the cataclysm and traumas of the Second World War transcended borders, destroyed national myths, discredited political movements of the right and hoisted to power a new set of political elites who competed with one another to articulate new discourses of national memory during a period of confusion and dislocation. Although the idea of a "Zero Hour" (*Stunde Null*) was a myth of the period, Nazi rule in Germany, the collapse of the French Third Republic and the "National Revolution" in France left ideological and mythological vacuums in Germany and in France. With fascism and collaboration having fallen into public disrepute, French socialists and German social democrats attempted to formulate, propagate and cement new memorial discourses to legitimate their parties' claims to political power. They sought, through repetition at party congresses, political rallies, in party presses and in parliamentary bodies to win normative status for their narrations of the past in order to achieve collective authority for the politics of their present and future.[20] Central to these rhetorical efforts were assertions by both parties that they were the most democratic of the political movements in their countries during both the inter- and post-war periods.

To make these assertions convincing, the post-war generation of SPD and SFIO leaders prevented the re-emergence of inter-war party leaders whose past actions had compromised their credentials as defenders of democracy. The SPD voted against the Enabling Act that marked the end of the Weimar Republic in 1933, but it remained overwhelmingly passive as Nazi storm troopers solidified the NSDAP's political victory by conquering the streets of Germany. Schumacher was well known for advocating violent resistance to the NSDAP as a leader of the republican Iron Front in 1931–1933, activities that led to his arrest and long-term imprisonment. Such actions, however, were those of a clear minority within the SPD. Schumacher did not make much of his own resistance activities after the war, but his ascent to leadership was in effect a retroactive endorsement of his activism during this fateful period and a condemnation of the impotency of the SPD leadership in the last years of the Weimar Republic. Schumacher's reaction to a German communist campaign in 1945 to malign a prominent official of the Weimar-era SPD, Carl Severing, who had preached non-resistance as Prussian Interior Minister in 1932 and who now sought a new leadership role in the post-war SPD, was an implicit rejection of the SPD's Weimar leadership. Schumacher refused to lend his own legitimacy, nor that of his party, to Severing's public efforts to defend himself.[21]

Although the SPD unanimously rejected the Enabling Act of 1933, thus allowing it to retrospectively claim credit for having opposed the Nazis in the Reichstag, SFIO deputies split their votes when—in the chaos of the French military defeat of 1940—the National Assembly convened in Vichy and voted full powers to Marshal Philippe Pétain. Although the Socialist tally did not break down completely along the factional lines of the late 1930s, for the most part a pacifist wing around party leader Paul Faure voted for Pétain's investiture and sought to integrate itself into the new institutions of the "National Revolution." Anti-fascists around parliamentary leader Léon Blum voted in opposition and provided the first cadres of the underground SFIO resistance. Emerging from the Second World War, the SFIO undertook the most profound post-war purge of any French political party.[22] Underground party leader Daniel Mayer pushed for the exclusion of all deputies who had voted for Pétain's investiture (the party later allowed a few to re-join if they had proven resistance credentials), all mayors who had remained in office under Vichy without explicit party approval, all socialists who had praised Vichy or the occupiers in any way and anyone known to have been involved in black-market activities.[23] These actions allowed the 1944 SFIO Congress to declare during the liberation of France, "The party has carried out a victory upon itself...It has chased from its breast traitors, cowards, weaklings."[24]

Post-war socialist leaders defended the democratic constitutions of their inter-war republics from the stigma of having failed to prevent the rise of dictatorships. The narrative developed in Blum's *À l'Échelle Humaine* set the contours around which the SFIO developed its critique of the Third Republic and its vision for a Fourth. Casting judgment on the politics of the Third Republic, Blum admitted that there were elements of "instability, of discontinuity, of inefficiency" but declared that, "Taken as a whole, the Third Republic, like the Second and the First, was an honest regime."[25] He saw the failures of the inter-war period not in democratic institutions but in those who directed them. Schumacher, for his part, said in 1946 that, "the Weimar constitution was undoubtedly the best in the world. How come this modern constitution worked so terribly[?]...it [was] due to the spirit [of the time] and the people who wielded it."[26] Fritz Erler, later an important SPD official, made a similar point in January 1947: "It was much less a sign of the weakness of the Weimar Constitution and much more of the Weimar Republic....Democracy in Germany did not surrender in 1919 during the building of the constitution, but rather in the years thereafter...".[27]

SFIO and SPD leaders put forward aggressive claims to lead their countries towards democratic futures by arguing that their parties had foreseen the dangers of fascism in the inter-war period. In the SFIO's narrative, France's property-owning class had committed treason because it preferred Adolf Hitler to Blum, who had led the Popular Front governments of 1936–1938. The underground party press declared in 1941 that the French military defeat of 1940 was a "catastrophe desired and prepared by [French fascists]."[28] In 1943, a clandestine socialist newspaper claimed that socialists had correctly understood the challenges of the inter-war period:

We are "men of the past"? Error: we are the men of the future. The truth is that in the past we were already the men of the future. We foresaw yesterday what would come to pass, we presented solutions that were not carried through and which, if they had been accepted, would have avoided this catastrophe...[29]

On 6 May 1945, Kurt Schumacher struck a similar tone in his first public speech since 1933. He recalled the SPD slogan of the 1930s that "Hitler means war" and claimed in countless speeches over the next year that the German people had not adequately heeded the SPD's warning.[30] Schumacher resurrected his inter-war rhetoric, invoking his belligerent 1932 speech to the Reichstag, in which he called the Nazis "Neanderthals" and Nazism the "pinnacle of human stupidity."[31] The SPD presented a social-democratic version of the "*Sonderweg*," Germany's "special path." Schumacher assigned an economic origin to Nazism, proclaiming that "German's large property class (*Großbesitz*) knew what it was doing! ... Heavy industry, armaments capital, militarism and all their vassals, who afterwards seek to distance themselves from what the Nazis tried to do, bear as mid-wives of Nazi tyranny the full responsibility for everything that happened."[32] "The Social Democratic Party," Schumacher told his international socialist colleagues in June 1947, "was the only party in Germany whose members made real sacrifices for freedom and democracy during the period of the [Weimar] Republic's crisis."[33]

The politics of memory were also central to socialist efforts to discredit other political groups. Socialists propagated their own narratives of these groups' histories. In his May 1945 speech, Schumacher portrayed a German liberal movement condemned by its historical failures: The 1848 revolutions marked the original sin of German liberalism when the German bourgeoisie sided with reactionary forces.[34] In December, he proclaimed that, "The great ideas of the great French Revolution have no place any more among our German liberals; they now only have sanctuary among the socialists."[35] Schumacher repeatedly attacked the German Communist Party (KPD) for targeting the SPD and not committing itself to the defence of Weimar democracy. He went so far as to claim that, "If the KPD had not sabotaged democracy together with the Nazis and the German Nationalists, we would have had no Third Reich and no Second World War." Nor did he spare the Christian Democratic Union (CDU), led by the former mayor of Cologne, Konrad Adenauer. In his June 1947 comments to COMISCO, Schumacher said that, "The CDU is the great collector (*Sammelbecken*) of property-owners, Nazis and reactionaries."[36]

The CDU and SPD engaged in a running war of words as they competed to become the largest party of post-war Germany. In response to CDU criticisms of the passivity of SPD inter-war leaders Otto Braun and Carl Severing, Schumacher responded with this criticism of the CDU's predecessor, the Centre Party, during the final years of Weimar:

> *...since Mr. Adenauer likes to speak so much of Braun and Severing—who negotiated for a governing coalition with the Nazis in summer 1932? Who wanted to rule together with the Nazis? It was the Centre Party and also that part of the Centre Party that Adenauer and his cohort represented. And finally, dear Assembly, Mr. [Franz] von Papen was also previously a Prussian local delegate of the Centre Party. ...the right-wing of the Centre Party, represented by Dr. Adenauer and his friends, is unteachable and is engaging in the same politics and the same hateful and objectionable methods with those who have already once destroyed democracy.*[37]

Schumacher concluded that, "democracy in Germany is today not much stronger than the Social Democratic Party."[38]

In France, SFIO leaders thought that socialism was "master of the hour" after the Second World War.[39] Their initial concern was to convince Free French leader Charles de Gaulle to declare publicly his support for democracy and overcome his disdain for political parties. As Mayer stated in 1944: "A democracy cannot live without parties, without the loyal competition of diverse political organisations."[40] By 1945, the party found itself locked in a dispute over the powers of the National Assembly vis-à-vis de Gaulle's executive. Socialist André Philip, who had joined de Gaulle in London exile, declared in frustration: "We want him [de Gaulle] to stay, but we also want him to get used to democracy."[41] Although Blum had called for a strong executive in *À l'Échelle Humaine*, the SFIO generally shared the republican consensus that equated republicanism with parliamentary rule. A presidential system, to the SFIO, meant "personal rule," in other words, a dictatorship based on the Bonapartist model. After de Gaulle resigned from his post as premier and gave a June 1946 speech denouncing the parliamentary system, Blum declared the need for a "Third Force" coalition charged with "republican defence" against the Gaullist right and communist left.

Soon after the ratification of a new constitution, the French Fourth Republic appeared endangered from the right and the left as de Gaulle hammered the government for inadequately defending French interests and the Communist Party adopted an aggressive attitude after the tripartite government ended in spring 1947. In summer, Socialist Premier Paul Ramadier spoke of the need to "defend the Republic" and warned darkly of "conspirators who…have formed associations intending to wield violence against the Republic."[42] Massive strikes broke out in French industry in 1948, which the government treated as an attempted *coup d'état* to overthrow democracy and install a soviet-style system on the model of the recent Prague coup in Czechoslovakia.[43] In Germany as well, vivid memories of the inter-war period and a wave of strikes led the SPD to worry that poor economic conditions could prove fatal for post-war democratization. With democracy seemingly under siege in France by 1947 and hardly begun in Germany, French socialists and German social democrats observed in dismay that their designs for economic democracy, which they considered a necessary prerequisite for political democracy, stalled as the political winds shifted to the right. Increasingly on the defensive within a few years of the end of the war, neither French nor German socialists were confident that their nations' futures would be democratic.

A New Beginning or Restoration? Socialist Doubts about French and German Democracy, 1949–1952

When West Germany held its first federal elections in August 1949, SPD leaders were convinced that a "restoration" of Germany's traditional, anti-democratic political culture was under way.[44] Party leaders argued that, without Allied interference, revolutionary elements in Germany would have enacted a more far-reaching and effective purge of the public administration and economy. Without such a purge, Schumacher declared, "for the second time the revolution threatens to wash away."[45] At party congresses, SPD officials lamented that U.S. and British occupying authorities had reinstated former Nazis to positions in the bureaucracy and police. Although they considered the underground Nazi movement to be incapable yet of "dramatic and dynamic action," they worried about the impact inter-party jockeying for the votes of former Nazis would have on the wider political culture.[46] The re-staffing of bureaucracies with people who had exhibited a marked hostility to the left during Weimar seemed to bode poorly for the inculcation of a new democratic spirit.

SFIO and SPD leaders often relied on a common set of recent historical examples to craft their assessment of German Christian democracy at the birth of the Bonn republic. Although Allied governments expressed relief that political forces programmatically committed to democracy won the vast majority of votes in the 1949 elections, the slight advance of the CDU/Christian Social Union (CSU) over the SPD caused consternation in both the SPD and the SFIO. The SFIO launched a press campaign calling for the SPD's inclusion in a grand coalition.[47] The examples of Christian dictatorships in Spain, Portugal and inter-war Austria shaped SFIO and SPD views of Christian democracy. Salomon Grumbach, the SFIO's leading expert on Germany, told the 1949 SFIO congress, "There is the Christian-Democratic Party, which may be a democratic party, but is far more Christian," and he explicitly compared developments in Germany with those in France, noting that former Pétainists were joining the Christian democratic (MRP) and Gaullist (RPF) parties.[48] Four days after the CDU/CSU victory, Schumacher cast this judgment: "Inside the Christian Democrats there is a large right-wing movement that is very reserved towards democracy. Also, their clerical core likes more the Christian state in the style of the Austria of [Engelbert] Dolfuss or [Kurt] Schuschnigg and of [Francisco] Franco's Spain."[49] Two years later, Grumbach presented the CDU through the prism of a dangerous, transnational Catholic political ascendancy in Western Europe.[50]

As occupation controls began to fall in Germany, a moderate yet clear recrudescence of neo-Nazi activities and far-right politics made international headlines from 1949 to 1952, shaking the politics of the young republic. A series of amnesty laws to free people from de-Nazification, the readmission of former Nazis into government administration and a public campaign for the pardoning of German war criminals represented a reassertion of right-wing elements in West German society who had kept a prudent silence during the early years of occupation. Most ominous of all was the emergence of a political party of former Nazis, the Socialist Reich Party (SRP), the rhetoric, means of mobilisation and organisational structure of which mimicked those of the NSDAP.[51] The SRP has received relatively little attention from historians, but its presence on the early democratic scene did much to shape the early political culture of the Bonn republic. After years arguing that Germans would more effectively de-Nazify the country if left to do it on their own, the SPD faced the situation that it was the occupation authorities, not the German government, that acted as the decisive agents in the suppression of neo-Nazi movements.[52] Abroad—as part of its campaign to regain full German sovereignty—the party argued that reports about neo-Nazism were sensationalist and exaggerated and that the far right did not represent a credible threat to German democracy. At home, however, social democrats criticized the lax attitude of the government, engaged in direct confrontations with the far right and fretted that neo-Nazism was gaining a foothold within the more establishment parties.

In November 1949, German Party deputy and former Nazi Party member Wolfgang Hedler gave a speech in which he claimed that Germans bore "minimal guilt" for the Second World War and that anti-Nazi German resisters were "national traitors." Most incendiary of all, he said, "It is possible to have differing opinions about the question of whether gassing the Jews was the means of choice. Maybe other ways could have been found to get rid of them."[53] A social democratic official recorded his comments and reported it to the party. In January 1950, Hedler was put on trial for disparaging the memory of German resisters, for insulting Jews and for inciting violence. The list of co-plaintiffs, including Schumacher and SPD deputy Jacob Altmaier, who was Jewish, propelled the trial into the international spotlight. Two of the three presiding judges had been former Nazi party members. They created a peculiarly narrow standard of guilt: whether or not Hedler's comments indicated that he approved the gassing of Jews. On this basis, the court acquitted Hedler. To SPD leaders, the Weimar practice of judges acting leniently towards right-wing agitators appeared to be reasserting itself.

Five days after the verdict, Schumacher asked, "Who will protect us against these judges, who, due to the will of local occupation authorities, are made up of at least 70 per cent former Nazis? ... Especially the judges who have lost all the respect of a large portion of the people and who carried out the work of the primitive Gestapo officers, must first earn our trust."[54] In March 1950, the SPD central committee dedicated a whole session to "Defence against Neo-fascism." The SPD's leader in Schleswig-Holstein told the meeting, "We must ensure that the police are with us and forbid any militarist organisation." Schumacher responded that, "the police are unreliable and the justice system is against us."[55] The same day as the Hedler verdict, the SPD introduced two bills into the Bundestag. The first, a "Law against the Enemies of Democracy," called for the imprisonment of those who threatened force against the republic, who "render[ed] the republic's flag contemptible or impugn[ed] the dignity of a group of people on the basis of race, belief, or [world view]," or insulted the memory of victims. The second bill would retroactively legalize the actions of those who had resisted Nazism in 1933–1945.[56]

The party executive decided to set up an internal office to track and respond to neo-Nazi movements. Personal notes from SPD Vice-Chairman Erich Ollenhauer's archive provide a snapshot of the SPD's assessment of neo-Nazism. He wrote that there were not sufficient laws to suppress these types of parties and that the state and police were proceeding with excessive hesitation: The "State must prove its authority … [because] Neo-fascist powers only recognize strength."[57] Local SPD chapters organised counter-demonstrations with other groups each time a SRP speaker came to town. Regional SPD interior ministers, after street brawls at SRP rallies, banned SRP leaders from speaking in Schleswig-Holstein and Lower Saxony, the largest bastions of far-right support in post-war West Germany. After SRP leader Fritz Dorls called the Bavarian Social Democratic Interior Minister Wilhelm Hoegner "the most despicable subject the German earth has ever brought forth" for attending the Nuremberg executions of German war criminals, the Bundestag lifted his immunity.[58] Dorls was placed on trial for slander, and Hoegner banned SRP rallies in Bavaria. In February 1950, Schumacher said that "the great sin of the Weimar Republic is repeating itself" and, due to its alleged reluctance to condemn right-wing movements, "The German middle is making the same mistake as during the Weimar Republic."[59] SPD leaders later welcomed the decision of the German constitutional court to ban the SRP in 1952.[60]

As they denounced anti-democratic groups in Germany, SPD leaders expressed even greater concern about political developments in France. In a September 1945 speech, Schumacher highlighted how democracy was more historically implanted in England and France than in Germany.[61] However, when the new Gaullist Party (RPF) achieved great success in the 1947 French municipal elections, Schumacher looked at events in France with foreboding: "What we must consider is the fact that a people with such a tradition of democracy, with four revolutions, voted…70% in its large cities for potential hangmen of democracy." Worst of all, he declared, "is the fatal parallels in France with the political situation of Germany in 1932."[62] The growing alienation between socialist parties and working-class voters, who tended to support communists in France and in Italy, augured poorly for European democracy: "Where developments have led to distance between workers and social democrats, the middle classes are not in a position to maintain democracy over the long term. We are experiencing that already in the rocking [taking place] in Italy and in France."[63]

In private, SFIO leaders largely agreed with this dire assessment. French socialists did not view France to be immune from the fate that befell interwar German democracy. Mollet echoed Schumacher's despair in September 1947 in a SFIO party executive meeting: "if we go on like this, in six

184 B. SHAEV

months we will all end up in concentration camps."[64] A year later he said that, "The present situation is quite similar to that of Germany in 1932."[65] That both SFIO and SPD leaders turned to the example of 1932 Germany to interpret events in late-1940s France indicates the weight that memories of Weimar's collapse exerted on their interpretations of the present. The analogy of the Weimar Republic had such strength that SFIO leaders at times debated tactics through contrary interpretations of the "lessons" of Weimar. In January 1949, the SFIO National Council discussed whether to continue participating in a Radical-led government that was steadily moving to the right. Édouard Depreux couched his opposition to participation by stating:

> *German Social Democracy was filled with good faith when, in agreement with the Catholic Centre to fight on two fronts against Hitler and the communists, it went from concession to concession until it accepted participation in [Chancellor Heinrich] Brüning's government, the social policy of which is not so different from a government directed by the Radicals in France. Result: a large part of the German proletariat marched to the communists.*[66]

Mollet defended participation with a counter-narrative: It was only after multiple elections and permanent agitation that Hitler seized power. For Mollet, forcing the dissolution of the French Assembly would only benefit communists and Gaullists.

Operating within national boundaries, few historians have analysed how revisionist and reactionary sentiment about the wartime experience peaked in France and Germany during the same years. In 1951, the French electorate returned an Assembly considerably to the right of its predecessor. The SFIO acquiesced uncomfortably as an amnesty bill for Vichy collaborators began emptying prisons during a period when neo-Pétainist sentiment reached an apogee. Observing events across the Rhine, Schumacher stated that without the U.S., France and Italy would already be dictatorships.[67] He called France "the weak point" of democracy in Europe. His analysis of the French election was apocalyptic, and he compared the SFIO's tactics with those of the Weimar-era SPD: It was "a Hitler election result. If the Socialists enter government or tolerate a minority government, the process of dissolution will take place."[68] Grumbach recalled that a sense of fatalism helped Hitler rise to power and warned his socialist colleagues privately that it could do so in France as well.[69] As support for a new de Gaulle government grew, Mollet told a party meeting, "That day the [SFIO] Directing Committee will have to call for a rebellion including everyone, including the [communists]. To accept de Gaulle is to accept a dictatorship. A popular demonstration could be effective even if broken."[70] The siren call of a new Popular Front—and the deep-seated resistance this eventuality evoked within the Cold War-era socialist party—complicated internal party discussions about how to effectively defend parliamentary democracy.

Historical memory of Europe's tumultuous inter-war period framed this generation of socialist leaders' understanding of the predicament facing French democracy. In September 1951, Mollet told the SFIO National Council, "De Gaulle's fascism is as dangerous for us as it was for the other democracies—even if it is different…[and] the comparison is misplaced in certain regards—the fascism of Hitler, the fascism of [Benito] Mussolini… it resembles more that of [Portuguese dictator António de Oliveira] Salazar…the day when Hitler was called to power, in Germany, it was after a quite similar electoral success…as that just achieved by the RPF."[71] Although hopes for a stable democratic regime in France rallied in the years that followed, worse was to come.

AN AUTHORITARIAN CONTAGION? THE CONSOLIDATION OF CHRISTIAN DEMOCRACY IN WEST GERMANY AND THE FALL OF THE FRENCH FOURTH REPUBLIC, 1953–1958

The CDU/CSU victory in the 1953 federal elections (its vote increased 14.2% to reach 45.2% as the SPD vote stagnated) unleashed a wave of fear in the SPD leadership that the CDU might use its newfound strength to eliminate the bases of democratic opposition in Germany. In the lead-up to the elections, Erler warned, "political Catholicism [has] a tendency towards authoritarian state-building."[72] The new party leader, Erich Ollenhauer, who replaced Schumacher after his death in 1952, stated, "We are closer today in the *Bundesrepublik* to an authoritarian system than to a free *Volksstaat*" due to "the authoritarian attitude of the government and above all of the head of government towards the parliament."[73] SPD leaders fretted that far right and unreformed Nazis were joining the Christian democrats, thereby "strengthen[ing] the restorative, nationalist and authoritarian politics of the CDU/CSU."[74] Ollenhauer's analysis in private party discussions was directly informed by the Nazi electoral success of 1933. He warned that the CDU would likely attempt a "synchronization process" [*Gleichschaltungsprozess*] to eliminate the independence of the trade unions, the press, the arts, and the state (*Land*) governments.[75] Faced with signs of "a totalitarian and war-like danger" as the government pressed for German rearmament, Ollenhauer called on the SPD to vigorously contest such efforts "before it is too late."[76] A few years later, the party opposed the banning of the Communist Party by the Constitutional Court, a ruling that followed a request by Adenauer's government. Ollenhauer told the SPD parliamentary group that the decision was "political foolishness that will in the long term bring only damage to democracy." Furthermore, "we must strongly protest that the implementation [of the ruling] by the police, the arrests, the house searches and police seizures in certain cases are being carried out in the spirit of the purges after the Reichstag fire of February 1933."[77]

Having shared the SPD's assessments of German democracy due to a similar understanding of the recent past in 1946–1951, the experience of SFIO leaders with Christian democracy in France, and its dealings with CDU politicians in international fora in the 1950s, led them to a contrary interpretation of the 1953 election. The SFIO leadership now considered the CDU to have proven its democratic credentials and welcomed its success at the polls. No doubt to avoid a confrontation with SPD delegates at a Socialist International meeting in February 1954, Mollet crossed out the following statement from his speech: "The vote of September 1953 was a great victory for democracy and for Europe. The democratic parties—our Social Democratic friends and Adenauer's CDU, won votes and seats to the detriment of nationalists and the Communist and Nazi parties have been practically struck from the political map."[78] This comment foreshadowed the amiable spirit of cooperation that Mollet developed with Adenauer during his tenure as French premier in 1956–1957. Lamenting the state of French politics in November 1957, Mollet told a socialist audience, "I dream of a [French] conservative party on...the German model."[79] The politics of memory, despite their resiliency, are never set in stone.

Although fears of renewed German militarism reached a crescendo in French politics during the European Defence Community debates of 1954, concerns for German democracy steadily lost their potency within the SFIO leadership during the 1950s. The SPD's reaction to the CDU's thumping victory of 1957, when the CDU/CSU became the first party in German history to reach an absolute majority, demonstrates that the SPD leadership, unlike SFIO leaders, continued to mistrust Adenauer. The party press stated, "German democracy must now pass its trial by fire" because "the electors of the Federal Republic have given the CDU an absolute majority and with it carte blanche to build one party rule."[80] Important elements within the party privately argued that such fears were exaggerated, but publicly the SPD sounded the alarm against Adenauer. In January 1958, Ollenhauer wrote, "The attempted *Gleichschaltung* of regional elections, the plans of the Interior Minister to build a state security office and Adenauer's dangerous line of thought that the opposition has no rights shows [that]…the governing party is orienting itself more and more in a conservative-restorative direction." Adenauer, the text went on, "is exploiting his position of power to build an authoritarian one-man-system in a centralized unity state and is therefore endangering democracy."[81]

It was France, however, that faced the most serious threat to parliamentary democracy. After a narrow victory in 1951 for pro-regime parties, the December 1955 national elections took place amidst a popular tax revolt led by Pierre Poujade. The small-town, lower middle–class demographics of the Poujadist movement and its violent anti-parliamentary rhetoric invited comparisons with inter-war fascism.[82] In October 1955, socialist Gérard Jaquet worried that little was needed to spark a fascist uprising.[83] After the election, Mollet gave a similar view: "We know well that in France there is a permanent fascist movement …" more dangerous than the Gaullists because it contains "the hardest, youngest, most aggressive elements. The immense danger I see in Poujadism are the violent demonstrations that it will provoke, that could lead to a new Popular Front directed by the [PCF] and the [Communist-aligned trade union] C.G.T."[84] In a dynamic that recalled 1934–1935, the leadership received reports of local SFIO chapters collaborating with Communists, portending a grassroots Popular Front from below. The perceived danger of the far right and left-wing unity efforts played a role in the SFIO's decision to lead a "Republican Front" governing coalition in January 1956. Whereas Mollet worried that "an impotent majority" led by the Socialists would be "suicide [for] the party and democracy," André Philip and Christian Pineau put forth the "republican defence" argument that, when the republic was in danger, the SFIO must come to its aid. Under party pressure, Mollet agreed to become premier.

Mollet's government was the longest lasting of the Fourth Republic, but it struggled to contain growing domestic discontent, runaway inflation, and an escalating war to maintain French rule in Algeria, the success of which many socialists believed vital to the survival of the regime. Other socialists broke with the government over Algeria, with Philip, for instance, accusing Mollet of "creating the psychological conditions that slowly formed in Germany after 1930 and brought about the basis of the fascist movement."[85] Mollet's government was followed by a series of short-lived, acrimonious coalitions in 1957–1958. Socialist participation in these ad hoc coalitions faced growing internal opposition.[86] Comments from disgruntled SFIO deputies were similar to the view Ollenhauer had expressed a few years earlier of the miniscule Italian Social Democratic Party (PSDI), which allied with Italy's Christian democratic-led government: "A Social Democratic Party that enters a coalition in which its political power is not necessary, but rather represents only an auxiliary resource, carries itself to its own grave."[87]

The prospect of a military "State within a State" à la Weimar had done much to shape the SPD's opposition to German rearmament in the 1950s. Now it reset the terms of debate within the SFIO. On 13 May 1958, the Algiers European population revolted against the government for allegedly preparing to abandon French Algeria. In the dramatic days and weeks of May–June 1958, much of the military leadership in Algeria rallied to its side. Facing a military revolt, the dominant historical analogy for Mollet was not Germany in 1932 but rather the attempted coup by Spanish General Francisco Franco in 1936 and the eventual victory of his forces in the ensuing Spanish Civil War. Jules Moch, again Interior Minister, reported that the army was in full revolt and that he had no faith that the metropolitan police would resist a military invasion of Paris. Backroom bargaining, rumours, and memories of the June 1940 Assembly investiture of Pétain combined to create a toxic mood in the party. As calls for "de Gaulle to power" mounted throughout the country, the socialist parliamentary group was furious to learn that its leadership had entered into secret negotiations with him. Whispers of "treason" punctuated socialist meetings. Many socialists saw Franco's image in de Gaulle, but Mollet now disagreed, saying that he preferred de Gaulle to a "Francoist government" or a "government of colonels."[88] Casting his eye over recent European history, Mollet reminded his colleagues that no internal revolution had overthrown a military regime in Europe without foreign intervention. Monnet's narrative of the Spanish Civil War's implications for France signalled his new openness to allying with de Gaulle to break the impasse in Algeria.

INHERITING HORROR: HISTORICAL MEMORY IN FRENCH SOCIALISTS... 189

In a climate of fear that paratroopers would soon land in Paris, Mollet and other leading politicians attained enough concessions from de Gaulle to maintain the pretence of republican legality for a transitional government. After 13 years of denouncing de Gaulle, Mollet now asked the SFIO to support his return to power. A series of tense meetings, in which some socialist deputies called for a broad anti-fascist coalition with the PCF, resulted in a 77–74 vote in de Gaulle's favour. However, a slim majority of SFIO deputies then voted against de Gaulle's investiture in the National Assembly on 1 June 1958. Mollet and two other Socialists entered de Gaulle's cabinet, to which the parliament granted full powers and charged with the task of writing a new constitution. Angry and bitter, a large number of SFIO deputies who opposed de Gaulle seceded to form the Autonomous Socialist Party (PSA), which later became the Unified Socialist Party (PSU). As the SPD's envoy to a PSA party congress reported to Ollenhauer, the socialists of the new party "think that democracy no longer exists (police measures, newspaper censorship, one-sided radio broadcasting, military intervention in political events)" and "fear—and say it openly—that de Gaulle is preparing a military dictatorship that will support itself strongly on the upper clergy of the Catholic Church."[89]

As the Fourth Republic collapsed, Ollenhauer warned party officials privately in June 1958 that, "the developments of the last ten years in France bear certain resemblances to the period between 1930 and 1932 in Germany."[90] The SPD sympathized with the SFIO's anti-Gaullist faction, but after Moch told Ollenhauer that he had lost authority over the police, the SPD leadership urged party members to restrain their criticism of Mollet. As events unfolded in France, Herbert Wehner said to the SPD central committee, "The strengthening appetite for authoritarian tendencies can also be a formidable problem for us," while Ollenhauer warned that "repercussions are to be feared in Germany."[91] In October, Ollenhauer said that "there are plenty of people [in Germany] who would very much like to imitate de Gaulle's example."[92] In the face of a possible civil war in France, the SPD could do little more than hope that the Fifth Republic would prove less authoritarian than it feared while girding itself against Adenauer's alleged wish "to be a second de Gaulle."[93] After the new French constitution created a presidential system to replace parliamentary rule, the SPD worried that events in France would act as a contagion in Germany, especially after Adenauer launched a campaign to move from the Chancellorship to the Presidency.[94] Ollenhauer told SPD officials,

190   B. SHAEV

"One must unfortunately say that the prospects that the November [1958] elections in France will result in a parliament that conforms to our conception of parliamentary democracy...is quite slim...what will this mean for Europe? What will this mean for Germany...? Our [Christian democrats] already have a lot of sympathy for a system in between democracy and dictatorship...and [will say] that we must now adjust our constitution..."[95] Memories of the inter-war years, when dictatorship spread from one European nation to the next, loomed large in the SPD's ominous analysis of events in France at the dawn of the Fifth Republic.

CONCLUSION

This chapter has demonstrated how a transnational collective memory of the inter-war period among the first generation of post-war SFIO and SPD leaders informed their analyses of democracy in France and in West Germany from 1945 to 1958. In private discussions, each party considered the other country's past, and that of other Western European countries, to be directly relevant to their understanding of political developments in their own nations. This generation of post-war SFIO and SPD leaders interpreted their recent traumas and the prospects for democratic futures not only within national but also within transnational and European perspectives. In addition, this chapter has argued that, under the influence of narratives of what happened in Europe in 1932–1945, the SPD and SFIO leaderships viewed their democracies to be under sustained threat for more than a decade after the war, a threat borne out by events in France in 1958 if not in Germany. The SFIO leadership gained confidence in West German democracy before the SPD, whose leaders looked to the future with caution and even pessimism through the 1950s. Historical experiences and narratives sustained a psychological atmosphere of fear, isolation and mistrust among the post-war generation of SPD leaders.

In 1959–1960, the pull of the past weakened within each party. The SPD abandoned its revolutionary program of social and economic transformation at its Bad Godesberg party congress in 1959. In 1960–1961, it began a public campaign to find "common ground" (*Gemeimsamkeit*) and stopped criticizing the "authoritarian" nature of Christian democracy, most dramatically when it took a moderate stance in the 1962 *Spiegel* affair after Adenauer's government threatened to bring treason charges against a leading magazine for publishing secret documents and for criticizing German defence policy. During the 1960s, the SPD presented itself to the German electorate as the "better party" rather than the only true democratic party. With the nomination of the youthful Willy Brandt as SPD candidate for chancellor in 1961, the SPD dampened the apocalyptic tone of its historical narratives and sought alliances with liberals and Christian democrats, thus paving the way for the party's participation in ruling coalitions from 1966 to 1982. The context of French politics shifted as well. Many socialists continued to denounce the authoritarian tendencies of de Gaulle's presidency, branded him a dictator-in-the-making, and hoped to restore parliamentary rule in France. In contrast, a larger group of socialists saw de Gaulle as the only person capable of resolving the Algerian War without destroying French democracy. In the mid-1960s the political culture of France and Germany changed as socialist leaders found themselves contesting new interpretations of the traumas and lessons of the inter-war period that were being aggressively put forth by the student generation of '68. Politics in Western Europe had entered a new era.

Notes

1. "Extract from the Proceedings of the International Socialist Conference, Zurich, 06–09.06.1947." Socialist International 235, International Institute for Social History (IISH). Quotation is in English.
2. Klimke, Martin/Scharloth, Joachim. "1968 in Europe: An Introduction." In id., eds. *1968 in Europe: A History of Protest and Activism, 1956–1977.* Basingstoke: Palgrave Macmillan, 2008, 2–7; Slobadian, Quinn. *Foreign Front: Third World Politics in Sixties West Germany.* Durham/NC: Duke University Press, 2012; and Varon, Jeremy. *Bringing the War Home: The Weather Underground, the Red Army Faction, and Revolutionary Violence in the Sixties and Seventies.* Berkeley: University of California Press, 2007.
3. Assmann, Jan. *Cultural Memory and Early Civilization: Writing, Remembrance, and Political Imagination.* Cambridge: Cambridge University Press, 2011, 37, 116.
4. Booth, W. James. "Communities of Memory: On Identity, Memory, and Debt." *The American Political Science Review* 93: 2 (1999), 249.
5. Prochnow, Jeanette/Rohde, Caterina. "Generations of Change. Introduction." *InterDisciplines* 2, 2011, 6.
6. Reulecke, Jürgen. "Generation/Generationality, Generativity, and Memory." In Nell, Astrid/Nünning, Ansgar, eds. *Media and Cultural Memory/Medien und kulturelle Erinnerung.* Berlin: De Gruyter, 2010, 119.

7. Sirinelli, Jean-François. "Génération et histoire politique." *Vingtième Siècle. Revue d'histoire* 22 (1989), 79.
8. Assmann, *Cultural Memory*, 120.
9. Rousso, Henry. *Le syndrôme de Vichy, 1944–1987.* Paris: Seuil, 1987, 12.
10. Lagrou, Pieter. *The Legacy of Nazi Occupation: Patriotic Memory and National Recovery in Western Europe, 1945–1965.* Cambridge: Cambridge University Press, 2004, 3.
11. Rousso, *Le syndrôme de Vichy*, 36.
12. Judt writes that, "with the rare exception of a statesmen like Kurt Schumacher…German public figures in the Forties and Fifties managed to avoid any reference to the Final Solution." Judt, Tony. *Postwar: A History of Europe Since 1945.* New York: Penguin Press, 2005, 809.
13. Sirinelli, *Génération*, 70–74; Bergounioux, Alain. "Générations socialistes." *Vingtième Siècle. Revue d'histoire* 22 (1989), 93–101; Jalabert, Laurent. "Aux origines de la génération 1968: Les étudiants français et la guerre du Vietnam." *Vingtième Siècle. Revue d'histoire* 55 (1997), 78 f.
14. See Assmann, Aleida. "Europe: A Community of Memory?" *GHI Bulletin* 40 (2007); the Introduction in François, Étienne/Schulze, Hagen, ed. *Deutsche Erinnerungsorte.* Munich: C.H. Beck, 2007, 2001; the final essay of Judt's *Postwar*; and Sierp, Aline. *History, Memory, and Trans-European Identity: Unifying Divisions.* New York: Routledge, 2014.
15. Sirinelli, *Génération*, 73; Reulecke, *Generation*, 119; Prochnaw/Rohde, *Generations of Change*, 5.
16. Tetlock, Philip E. "Social Psychology and World Politics." In *Handbook of Social Psychology (4th Edition)*, New York: McGraw-Hill, 1998, 896.
17. "Rede Dr. Schumacher SPD Kreisverein Husum 07.07.1946." Schumacher 37, Archiv der sozialen Demokratie (AdsD).
18. Cowan, Jon. "Visions of the Postwar: The Politics of Memory and Expectation in 1940s France." *History and Memory* 10: 2 (1998), 91–92.
19. "Extract from the Proceedings of the International Socialist Conference, Zurich, 06–09.06.1947."
20. In Knapp's analysis, a narrative about the past achieves collective authority when it has attained sufficient normative status. Knapp, Steven. "Collective Memory and the Actual Past." *Representations* 26 (1998), 123.
21. Reulecke, Jürgen, ed. *Arbeiterbewegung an Rhein und Ruhr: Beiträge zur Geschichte der Arbeiterbewegung in Rheinland-Westfalen.* Wuppertal: Peter Hammer, 1974, 426.
22. Castagnez-Ruggiu, Noëlline. *Socialistes en République: les parlementaires SFIO de la IVe République.* Rennes: Presses universitaires de Rennes, 2004, 21–31.
23. See Sadoun, Marc. *Les socialistes sous l'occupation: résistance et collaboration.* Paris: Presses universitaires des sciences politiques, 1982, 229–233.

INHERITING HORROR: HISTORICAL MEMORY IN FRENCH SOCIALISTS... 193

24. Congrès national extraordinaire des 9, 10, 11 et 12 novembre 1944, www. archives-socialistes.fr
25. Blum, Léon. *À l'Échelle humaine*. Paris: Gallimard, 1945, 57 f., 75.
26. "SPD-Kundgebung in Frankfurt." 25.06.1946 *Frankfurter Rundschau*. Schumacher 37 AdsD.
27. Erler, Fritz. "Über Verfassungsfragen." *Sozialistische Monatshefte*, January 1947. Emphasis in original.
28. Ibid., 183.
29. "La France de Demain: Une concentration des Partis sera-t-elle possible?" *Le Populaire*, 31.02.1943 in Mayer, 195.
30. "Wir verzweifeln nicht! Rede, gehalten vor sozialdemokratischen Funktionären am 6. Mai 1945," and August 1945, "Politische Richtlinien fuer die S.P.D. in ihrem Verhältnis zu den anderen politischen Faktoren". Schumacher 34 AdsD.
31. Schumacher. "Der entscheidende Gegensatz." *Volksblatt*, 08.02.1950, Schumacher 50 AdsD.
32. "Wir verzweifeln nicht!"
33. Sitzung des Kontakt-Komitees in Nürnberg am 30. Juni 1947, SI 349, IISH.
34. "Wir verzweifeln nicht!"
35. "Die Aufgaben der Sozialdemokratischen Partei." 01.12.1945 in Düsseldorf. Schumacher 35 AdsD.
36. Sitzung des Kontakt-Komitees in Nürnberg am 30. Juni 1947.
37. "Dr. Kurt Schumacher auf der Wahlkundgebung am 6. Oktober 1946 auf dem Burgplatz in Duisburg." Schumacher 39 AdsD.
38. "Rede Dr. Schumacher am Sonntag, dem 03.02.1946 in Köln." Schumacher 36 AdsD.
39. Quilliot, Roger. *La S.F.I.O. et l'exercice du pouvoir, 1944–1959*. Paris: Fayard, 1971, 26.
40. "La France de Demain: Une concentration des Partis sera-t-elle possible?" Mayer, 196.
41. Graham, Bruce Desmond. *The French Socialists and Tripartisme, 1944–1947*. Canberra: The Australian National University Press, 1965, 131.
42. *Journal Officiel de la République française. Débats parlementaires*, 02.07.1947 and 04.07.1947, 2638, 2756.
43. Shaev, Brian. "Workers' Politics, the Communist Challenge, and the Schuman Plan: A Comparative History of the French Socialist and German Social Democratic Parties and the First Treaty for European Integration." *International Review of Social History* 61: 2 (2016), 251–281.
44. Schumacher consistently called for a new beginning (*Neubau*) rather than restoration (*Wiederaufbau*). "Dr. Kurt Schumacher, Hannover: Was wollen die Sozialdemokraten? Neubau-nicht Wiederaufbau!" Schumacher 35 AdsD.

194   B. SHAEV

45. Kurt Schumacher "Hunger und Nationalismus". *Sopade* Nr. 38, 28.11.1946. Schumacher 39 AdsD.
46. See the speeches of Andreas Gayk, Herbert Kriedemann, Wilhelm Knothe, and Ernst Winter. *Protokoll des SPD-Parteitages Hannover 1946*, 10–11, 97, 172–6.
47. See the articles of Léon Blum and Salomon Grumbach in *Le Populaire* August–September 1949. Office Universitaire de Recherche Socialiste (OURS).
48. Congrès national, 16.07.1949. OURS.
49. "Die Sozialdemokratie in der Bundesrepublik." 18.08.1949. Schumacher 48 AdsD.
50. Conseil national. 16.09.1951. OURS.
51. Hansen, Henning. *Die Sozialistische Reichspartei (SRP): Aufstieg und Scheitern einer rechtsextremen Partei*. Düsseldorf: Droste, 2007, 10–11.
52. Frei, Norbert. *Adenauer's Germany and the Nazi Past: The Politics of Amnesty and Integration*. New York: Columbia Press, 2002, 1997, 263.
53. Ibid., 237–250.
54. "Dr. Schumacher sprach in Eisenwerk Wülfel am 20. Februar 1950." Schumacher 50 AdsD.
55. Parteivorstand 13.03.1950 in Bonn. AdsD.
56. Frei, *Adenauer's Germany*, 244–245.
57. Undated notes. Ollenhauer 180. AdsD.
58. Hansen, *Die Sozialistische Reichspartei*, 187.
59. Schumacher. "Presse-Konferenz am 24. März 1950", Schumacher 50 AdsD.
60. "Dr. Schumacher zur Entscheidung der Bundesregierung über die SRP." 04.05.1951, Schumacher 55 AdsD.
61. "Die Aufgaben der Sozialdemokratischen Partei." 01.12.1945 in Düsseldorf. Schumacher 35 AdsD.
62. "Referat Dr. Schumacher auf der Redakteurkonferenz der Parteipresse am 30.11.1947 in Hannover." Schumacher 43 AdsD.
63. "Rede Dr. Schumachers vor Parteivorstand und Parteiausschuss auf der Tagung vom 14.03.1950 in Bonn, Bundeshaus." Schumacher 50 AdsD.
64. Comité directeur, 06.09.1947. OURS.
65. Comité directeur, 08.09.1947. OURS.
66. Conseil national, 27.02.1949. OURS.
67. "Rede Dr. Schumacher vor Parteivorstand und Parteiausschuss auf der Tagung vom 13.04.1950."
68. Parteivorstand, 22–23.06.1951. AdsD.
69. Comité directeur, 12.09.1951. OURS.
70. Ibid.
71. Conseil national, 1er décembre 1951. OURS.

72. "Abschnitt Europäische Verteidigungsgemeinschaft—Europäische Politische Gemeinschaft." July 1953. Erler 9 AdsD.
73. "Referat des Vorsitzenden der Sozialdemokratischen Partei Deutschlands Erich Ollenhauer auf dem Wahlkongress der SPD am 10. Mai 1953 in Frankfurt/Main." Erich Ollenhauer 92, AdsD.
74. "Erklärung Erich Ollenhauers auf der SPD-Pressekonferenz am 07.09.1953." Erich Ollenhauer 98, AdsD.
75. Parteivorstand 8–9.09.1953.
76. "Das Ergebnis des 6. September." *Neuer Vorwärts*, 11.09.1953, Ollenhauer 98 AdsD.
77. "Gen. Ollenhauer. Fraktionssitzung auf September 11.09.56." Erich Ollenhauer 126 AdsD.
78. "G. Mollet 54 discours au Congrès de l'I.S. Les Autorités européennes." AGM 106 OURS.
79. Conseil National, Puteaux, 03.11.1957, OURS.
80. *Parlementarisch-Politischer Pressedienst*, 16.09.1956. Ollenhauer 136 AdsD.
81. "Eilt." January 1958. Ollenhauer 139 AdsD.
82. For the history of the Poujadist movement, see Dominique Borne. *Petits bourgeois en révolte ? Le mouvement Poujade*. Paris: Flammerion, 1977.
83. Groupe parlementaire socialiste, 06.10.1955, Archiv d'histoire contemporaine (AHC).
84. Comité directeur, 04.01.1956. OURS.
85. Comité directeur, 23.01.1957, OURS. Emphasis in original.
86. Groupe parlementaire socialiste, 09.10.1957 AHC.
87. "Ansprache von Erich Ollenhauer am Sonntag, dem 2. Aug 1953, 11,45 Uhr, im Sitzungsaal der SPD-Fraktion (Stadthalle-Hannover)." Ollenhauer 96 AdsD.
88. Lapie, Pierre-Olivier. *De Léon Blum à de Gaulle. Le caractère et le pouvoir.* Paris: Fayard, 1971. 800–801, 827–836.
89. Markscheffel, Günter. "Der Parteitag der französischen Sozialisten." *SPD-Pressedienst*, 15.09.1958, Parteivorstand 1958 AdsD; Markscheffel letter to Ollenhauer, 05.04.1960, Erich Ollenhauer 368 AdsD.
90. Rede Erich Ollenhauer auf der Parteiratsitzung vom 11. Juli 1958, Parteivorstand AdsD.
91. "Sitzung des Parteivorstandes am 9. Juni 1958 in Bonn." Parteivorstand AdsD.
92. "Parteiausschuss-Sitzung 24.10.1958." Erich Ollenhauer 143 AdsD.
93. "SPD-Bezirkskonferenz in Bielefeld: Ollenhauer fragt die Regierung nach ihrem Deutschlandplan." *Freie Presse*, 26.02.1959. Ollenhauer 145 AdsD.
94. "Politik aus der erster Hand," 15.04.1959, Ollenhauer 145 AdsD.
95. Rede Erich Ollenhauer auf der Parteiratsitzung vom 11. Juli 1958.

CHAPTER 9

Two "Difficult Outsiders"? Anti-fascism, Anti-Nazism and Democracy in Lelio Basso and Wilhelm Hoegner

Jens Späth

It might seem a bit strange to define Lelio Basso and Wilhelm Hoegner as two "difficult outsiders." Usually, we think of an outsider as someone who is isolated, detached or even excluded from activities or concerns of his or her community. However, can two of the most prominent socialist and social democratic politicians in Italy and Germany during the period after the Second World War be classified as such? Both men were leading figures within their parties: Basso as secretary general of the Italian Socialist Party (PSIUP) and Hoegner (SPD) as two-time and up to now the only Social Democratic prime minister of Bavaria. "Der schwierige Aussenseiter" was even the title of Hoegner's autobiography, which clearly flirted with this image.[1] Nevertheless, one could disagree with his self-perception. Historians in favor point to the difficult relationships both protagonists had with their parties and remind us e.g. of Basso's withdrawal from the *Partito Socialista Italiano*'s (PSI's) executive (*direzione*), its central committee and the entire party or of Hoegner's multiple thoughts of withdrawal.[2]

J. Späth (✉)
Universität des Saarlandes, Saarbrücken, Germany

© The Author(s) 2018   197
J. Späth (ed.), *Does Generation Matter? Progressive Democratic Cultures in Western Europe, 1945–1960*, Palgrave Studies in the History of Social Movements, https://doi.org/10.1007/978-3-319-77422-0_9

To access the complex topic of socialist and social democratic politics after 1945 in Italy and (West) Germany I suggest focusing on two key words: anti-fascism/anti-Nazism and democracy. Both shall serve as a central thread for the analysis of Basso's and Hoegner's policies up until the early 1960s. Geographically, the study allows us to compare anti-fascism in its country of origin with anti-Nazism in Germany as the country that overtook the former example, Fascist Italy, and became the dominant totalitarian power in Europe. To facilitate readability only, the general adjective "socialist" will be used when we talk about Italian socialists and German social democrats. What does anti-fascism in the post-war period mean? The definition of the term has changed several times[3] from political counter-movement to Italian fascism, then against right-wing dictatorships in general, and to German National Socialism in particular but also to the republican camp during the Spanish civil war.[4] After 1945, this common anti-fascist front line persisted in all new or re-founded political parties, but the term was increasingly replaced in Germany by "anti-communism" during the Cold War and the partition. The Italian socialists instead collaborated closely with the communists until 1956.[5] The central question of this paper will be how did Basso and Hoegner refer to anti-fascism in Italian and to anti-Nazism in Bavarian and West German democratic politics using different terms—which was due to the contemporary political situations in Italy and Germany—and what allows us to draw interesting conclusions for the respective party politics? From a socialist point of view, only a social democracy seemed acceptable. However, the theoretical problem of democracy and socialism, the not-finally-clarified attitude towards parliamentary democracy, and the ambitions to set up a people's democracy remained a constant challenge for Basso and Hoegner.

In its first section, the paper briefly summarizes the protagonists' experiences with fascism and National Socialism to better understand their discourse and actions. It raises the question as to what extent can we apply the concept of generation as communities of collective experience to both politicians?[6] Second, selected aspects of their political ideas and activities after 1945 will be discussed. Third, comparison of the political biographies of two significant democratic politicians addresses some similarities and differences between the post-war Italian and German political left and argues for a wider, more general perspective. Because Basso and Hoegner never met nor contacted each other—as far as the author knows—this is just about comparative history; transnational elements can be mostly excluded.

As far as the state-of-the-art concerns, the research on both politicians has produced various books and articles—yet a complete biography of the life of Lelio Basso by a single author is still missing. Two younger Italian scholars, Roberto Colozza and Emanuele Rossi, each published a partial, but thoughtful and innovative biography, together covering the period from 1943 to 1958. Rossi's book on *Democrazia come partecipazione* in particular touches the argument of democratization, which this paper deals with.[7] Even more recently, Chiara Giorgi and Giancarlo Monina came up with the first complete biography of Lelio Basso in two separate volumes.[8] In contrast, Wilhelm Hoegner has been the object of several articles and books, including the one and only biography written by Peter Kritzer in 1979.[9] This study tries an Italian/German–comparative perspective on both politicians highlighting the post-war period and combining an analysis of democratic politics with the memory of anti-fascism. The research on two single left-wing politicians is meant to be embedded into a larger perspective on socialist politics in Western Europe during the post-war period.[10] For this purpose, the extensive publications and private archives of Lelio Basso (in the foundation of the same name in Rome) and those of Wilhelm Hoegner (in the archive of the Institute for Contemporary History in Munich) have been exploited.

GENERATIONAL ASPECTS: BACKGROUND AND BELIEF SYSTEMS OF BASSO AND HOEGNER

Lelio Basso and Wilhelm Hoegner—the former secretary general of the PSI in 1947–1948 and the latter Bavarian Prime Minister for the *Sozialdemokratische Partei Deutschlands* (SPD) in 1945–1946 and again from 1954 to 1957—have many things in common: Both joined their respective political party after the First World War (Basso in 1921 and Hoegner in 1919); both studied law; both faced prison and exile during fascism and national socialism; both played a major part in re-founding the PSI in 1943 and the Bavarian SPD in 1946, respectively; both were members of constituent assemblies (Basso of the Italian and Hoegner of the Bavarian in 1946); both co-determined the post-war politics of their parties; both brought forward impressive scientific and journalistic works, and both concluded their political careers as highly esteemed moral authorities until their deaths in 1978 and 1980, respectively.

Nonetheless, we can find striking differences in their lives: Basso, 15 years younger than Hoegner, came from a liberal middle-class family in

200   J. SPÄTH

Liguria and enjoyed a profound education, earning university degrees in law and philosophy. In contrast, Hoegner, born in Munich in a modest railway man's family, was only able to attend high school to study at great costs and thanks to hard work and diligence. Although Basso's entry in the PSI at age 18 and his choice to study law occurred under the conviction of Marxist theory, Hoegner joined the SPD as an "emotional socialist" only in 1919, after having suffered from social injustice, humiliation and insults at an early age.[11] Despite his profound theoretical studies, the humanistic, intellectual Basso never lost contact with the working class. He was particularly capable of sparking enthusiasm in the young antifascist generation for democratic socialism—perhaps because he himself belonged to a "special generation" with society and not with family being the central reference.[12] Since the First World War as the watershed of the century, he pursued a radical pedagogical concept that defined politics as education and culture as historical consciousness. Although Hoegner remained faithful to the SPD for his whole life, Basso rubbed the party's executive the wrong way several times and was expelled in 1963. Another difference consists of the fact that Hoegner was two-time Bavarian Prime Minister and as well served as Secretary of State for Justice and Home Secretary, whereas Basso never held a government office. Last, but not least, Basso was internationally active in academics and justice, but Hoegner's focus remained rather limited to Bavaria, although also was a member of several transnational organisations.

In 1933, 45-year old Hoegner was forced to flee from the Nazis into Austrian and then Swiss exile, whereas Basso was imprisoned on the island of Ponza in 1928 at age 24. If we reason from generational group-building in a horizontal way by age-specific units of activity, our protagonists were part of different generations: Hoegner belonged to a demographic category and emotional community that grew up in Wilhelmine Germany. He unsuccessfully volunteered to fight in the German army during the First World War and played an active role in the first German democracy, then the Weimar Republic, both as Bavarian and German Member of Parliament. Basso had not yet had parallel experiences by this time. He also grew up in a constitutional monarchy, but Mussolini's march on Rome in 1922 and the beginning of the fascist state postponed Italian democratic and republican hopes for decades and anticipated his struggle with first authoritarian and then totalitarian regimes. One could even argue that the First World War, as a great historical event, created two new generations: an older one with their own fighting experiences, to which Hoegner belonged, and a

TWO "DIFFICULT OUTSIDERS"? ANTI-FASCISM, ANTI-NAZISM... 201

younger one—born between 1900 and 1910—without their own war experiences, to which Basso belonged.

Let us now look briefly at Basso's and Hoegner's activities from the 1920s to the end of the Second World War. It is well known that Basso studied Marxism thoroughly; this is shown, among other publications, his graduation thesis in law on liberty in Marxist theory. Leafing through his numerous articles in periodicals (49 total between 1923 and 1942)—such as *Critica sociale*, *Il Caffè*, *L'Avanti!*, *Coscientia*, *Quarto Stato* and *Pietre*—central topics include Marxism, socialism, liberalism, philosophy and democracy but also education, moral values, liberty and anti-fascism.[13] These key words all highly refer to his intellectual role model, Piero Gobetti, with whom he had collaborated on the political review *La Rivoluzione liberale* from 1922 to 1925. Promoting Gobetti's ideas to unite socialists, liberals and republicans even after his death, Basso founded the secret society *Giovane Italia* in 1927, which represented the first national Italian attempt to aggregate and mobilize all anti-fascist democrats and which can be regarded as a historic predecessor of *Giustizia e Libertà*.[14]

Notwithstanding his arrest in Milan in 1928, Basso studied philosophy on Ponza and graduated immediately after his return to Milan in 1931 with a thesis on the German religious scientist and theologian Rudolf Otto. In addition to working as a lawyer, he collaborated from 1934 onwards with a clandestine socialist group (*Centro Socialista Interno*) along with Rodolfo Morandi, Lucio Luzzatto and Eugenio Colorni. Arrested again in 1939–1940 and sent to the concentration camp of Colfiorito (Perugia), he finally prepared and founded the *Movimento di Unità Proletaria* (MUP) in January 1943, which aimed at uniting all proletarian classes. In August, the MUP merged with the PSI using the name *Partito Socialista Italiano di Unità Proletaria* (PSIUP).

Changing perspective once again, we might start in 1920 when the Bavarian public prosecutor Wilhelm Hoegner took office in Munich. Four years later, he was elected member of the Bavarian regional parliament, where he proposed a motion for a committee of inquiry on the Beer Hall Putsch of Hitler and Ludendorff of November 1923 and the acquittal of the main responsible persons in the following case. Even though the Bavarian *Landtag* accepted and confirmed Hitler's high treason in 1928, Hoegner continued to accuse similar crimes of further persons and the failure of justice.[15] Two years later, when he became a member of the Weimar parliament, the SPD politician from Bavaria defied the Nazis

202 J. SPÄTH

again. In his first speech in the Reichstag on 18 October 1930, he answered the National Socialist Georg Strasser, revealing the Italian example for National Socialism and showing the determination of the social democrats to defend German democracy against the fascist tyranny of the Fuehrer.[16] In another speech at the SPD regional party conference in Munich on 25 September 1932, he again compared Hitler's Nazi Germany with Mussolini's fascist Italy and called Hitler a "painting assistant" who had learned "to draw along Italian stencils".[17]

All at once, Hoegner was well-known in the whole Reich and became one of the most desired speakers for public manifestations. These two prominent acts and his rich journalistic activity (e.g. an article in the *Vorwärts* on "Der Nationalsozialismus: Sammelbecken des Bösen. Die faschistische Schlammflut") explain why the Nazis considered him to be one of their most hated and wanted enemies.[18] Of course, he voted with the entire SPD parliamentary party against the Enabling Act of 23 March 1933. Just some days later, the Bavarian political police carried out the order to take him in "protective custody" and dismissed him from public service. Hoegner was able to escape the Nazis during the next months with the help of luck and clues from his wife Anna. Only when the danger for his entire family became too big did some friends convince him to flee to another country. In July, he reached Austria, where he continued his anti-fascist activities as journalist and secretary of the Austrian Social Democratic Labour Party.[19] The change of regime in Austria forced him to flee again in February 1934, this time to Switzerland where he and his family persevered until Hitler's end.[20]

Of course, Hoegner remained as active there as his Nazi tormentors in the Third Reich: The security police added him to the list of SPD members of parliament and to the list of leading politicians of the system period (Marxists and communists). Furthermore, in October 1938, he was expatriated together with his wife and his children.[21] He was not allowed to work as a politician, lawyer or journalist in Switzerland. Therefore, he wrote fiction and poetry, was in correspondence with exiled SPD and other politicians in Switzerland and France and collaborated clandestinely with the SPD's executive in exile.[22] Only when the Second World War broke out, and particularly from 1943 onwards, did the envoy of the American secret service OSS, Allan W. Dulles, employ Hoegner to draft laws and constitutions for a democratic Bavarian and all-German state after Hitler. In a lively interchange with different personalities—such as Otto Braun, Heinrich Ritzel, Josef Wirth, Hans Nawiasky, Michael

Freiherr von Godin and Johann Jacob Kindt-Kiefer—Hoegner co-founded the working group "Das Demokratische Deutschland," which drew up a 22-page document for the future German political order. It drafted a European embedding of Germany, taking its responsibility for war and crimes of the Nazi regime, yet declined the collective guilt of the German people, postulated Christian and Humanistic values, a real and just peace and the exclusion of national socialists from public service. Hoegner also wrote a paper on a future Bavarian state built on a democratic administration from below.[23] He referred to many of these texts later when he was charged with various duties within the Bavarian government.

ANTI-FASCISM AND ITS COMMEMORATION

Analyzing just a few of Basso's and Hoegner's political concepts for the post-war period, we can easily see that not all goals and expectations were achieved. This seriously disappointed our protagonists and contributed to them feeling like outsiders. Let us now look briefly at two selected fields of politics that I consider as particularly suitable for showing similarities and differences between Basso and Hoegner and skip the more consensual topics of constitutions and education: (1) the way in which both commemorated fascism and national socialism; and (2) Basso's ideas on organizing party and society on one hand and Hoegner's efforts and achievements when he was in governmental offices on the other.

Basso entered the arena of national party politics in Italy in 1943 for the first time in his life. The chance to contribute building a new democratic order in his country in freedom and peace after the Second World War made him a true "45er."[24] He reflected continuously on the meaning of fascism and anti-fascism for the young democratic Italian Republic, which had been founded by a referendum in 1946. Although the fascist governmental system had broken down, he warned that some elements of the plutocracy continued to exist and tried, particularly within the *Democrazia Cristiana*, to preserve their privileges. "Sure, this movement won't call itself fascism [...] but substantially it will still be fascism, and the dangers of fascism are not those of nostalgic demonstrations of the past. We must not recognize fascism in these small rising movements which we always can crush. The danger, however, within the involution of the *Democrazia Cristiana*, within its government lies in the setting-up of a crystallization of interests which has dominated our country's life in the past and still does so today, determined to keep these positions whatever it costs,", said the secretary general of the PSI.[25] We are talking about January 1948. Six months later, at the 27th party congress, he explained why the united front of antifascists—including working classes, representatives of the progressive bourgeoisie, of capitalism and of former profiteers from fascism—had ceased to exist: Major forces had been interested only in a legal-political transformation of the system but not in a new social order. All those former profiteers "were only interested in splitting up fascism and its causes, in isolating the fight against fascism from the fight against the interior contradictions of capitalism, and in stopping the mass movement by leaving intact the structures of the old state." Furthermore, there had been too many compromises of the political left with other groups. "Thus, the people's front, which would have almost certainly been victorious if it had been set up in spring 1945, failed in 1948."[26]

At this point, some remarks about Basso's studies on the origins of fascism help to understand his anti-fascist activities during the post-war period. In a series of published articles and conference speeches, he underlined that usually anti-fascism had not analysed the socio-economic aspects of fascism in depth.[27] It therefore had promoted the cliché that fascism was identical with an anti-parliamentary dictatorship and anti-fascism with a parliamentary democracy. To fight fascism, the supporters of the legalistic perspective thought, it would be enough to fight for democratic principles. That was why the Western countries themselves emerged as "archetypes of democracy."[28] However, Basso argued with the results of his socio-economic analysis that fascism had not just been an "accident" or a "simple fact of moral degeneration" that ended ingloriously on 25 July 1943 with the resignation of Mussolini.[29] Instead, Basso identified fascism with "the expression of all our political immaturity, the accumulation of all our historic deficiencies, the shipwreck of our entire leading class" and said that "only a radical and profound devolution can strike at the root of this evil; only a vigilant consciousness and activity of all what is inherently 'fascist' in our society, in our life can help us to overcome the tragic past."[30] He spread these ideas in many articles, books and speeches at conferences and public manifestations, e.g. when he remembered the contribution of the former *Partito d'Azione*, of which many activists joined the PSI in 1947. This meant that from then on "the most lively part of the Italian militant culture", "a noble tradition of fighting for the triumph of democracy", "one of the most active and combative movements of antifascism" clearly demonstrated that "the battle for democratic socialism in Italy could only be fought within the PSI."[31] In several occasions, such as 25 April, the day

TWO "DIFFICULT OUTSIDERS"? ANTI-FASCISM, ANTI-NAZISM... 205

of liberation from Nazi occupation, Basso underlined the importance that anti-fascism and Resistance had for the contemporary Italian democratic republic.[32] He continued to do so in the 1960s and 1970s when anti-fascism, as Mariuccia Salvati puts it, had come out from parliamentary hall and from party dispute and had become an argument of research and political fight in the university lecture halls of a new generation that took a position of opposition towards the centre-left government.[33]

Just like in Italy, neo-fascist groups soon also emerged in the young democracies in the Federal Republic of Germany and in Bavaria.[34] Although (or probably) just because of personal insults and menaces,[35] Hoegner documented the activities of the radical right and the opposition against them in society, to which he contributed. He became involved in numerous societies for a peaceful and democratic coexistence and for international collaboration, such as the "Union of Europe" or "Moral Rearmament."[36] In January 1950, he gave a widely noted speech in the Bavarian Landtag on the activities of neo-national socialist groups.[37] There as well, as in a letter to his friend Heinrich Ritzel 3 years later, he underlined his conviction not to collaborate with former national socialists: "I wiped out the SRP [*Sozialistische Reichspartei*, successor organization of the NSDAP, forbidden in 1952] in Bavaria and I cannot allow it to come in again via the back stairs. [...] I cannot and do not want to have to do with disguised national socialists. Indeed, I don't have time for Adenauer as a person and politician but a major part of his followers can at least be called democrats. [...] So please don't take it bad if I still regard groups of the radical right in Bavaria as archenemies of democracy who would hang us every day if they could."[38]

Hoegner was conscious that it was insufficient to have more or less de-Nazified some professional groups and to have established democratic structures; it was also necessary to remember the national socialist crimes and to promote historical research. His most prominent involvement in this field constitutes his participation in the foundation of a memorial in the former concentration camp of Dachau.[39] On the inauguration ceremony on 30 August 1964, Hoegner said, "In the event of this day we remember the numerous victims claimed by two world wars and the persecution by National Socialism. [...] This former concentration camp Dachau will be extended as charge and admonition for future generations into a memorial for the victims of the national socialist mud flood."[40] Even in the 1970s, he thoroughly followed the events in society and continued his antifascist engagement in various ways.[41]

Theory (Basso) and Practice (Hoegner) of Democratic Governments

From 1944 to 1947, PSIUP (which was renamed PSI in 1947) was a member of the Italian all-parties government. "All-parties" means that the government was characterized by a broad anti-fascist basic consensus, which included communists and Christian democrats. Caught in between, the socialists considered fascism from a Marxist point of view primarily as a phenomenon of unsolved class struggles and economic crises of the capitalist systems and thus as precursor for fascist regimes. Therefore, Basso added that Italian fascism and German National Socialism could only be overcome by solving the capitalist socio-economic order.[42] After the end of fascist rule in Italy, Basso was concerned, along with his fellow party men, about a general amnesty for former fascists. Lifting the ban on their political participation too early could have allowed many of them to return into office and power.[43] The big manifestations against fascism and National Socialism of 1945 risked oblivion far too soon. Thereby, also major continuities from the totalitarian regimes—the continuities of great industries (in particular in Germany and Japan),[44] the continuities in bureaucracy, police, diplomacy and culture,[45] the parallels between capitalist forces that once supported fascism and now partially supported the *Democrazia Cristiana*, the preservation of many fascist laws[46] and, overall, a still-missing social renewal—would be overlooked. "As a synthesis and consequence of these mistakes resulted the entire structure of post-fascist politics which, instead of representing a break with the last twenty years, was completely dominated by the concern, however evident and justifiable among the old groups but to be repudiated decisively by the leftist parties, to ensure the political and juridical continuity with the old Sabaudian-fascist state and to suppress every attempt of renovation with formally legal and, of course, fascist diligence because the laws in vigor were fascist."[47]

To change these politics, Basso wanted the working classes to become fully conscious of their historical role. To realize his live theme, he described the necessary revolution as a long process towards "real" social democracy. He tried to harmonize liberty and participation, the individual and the community by supporting the equality of all Italians tirelessly not only in legal but especially in socio-economic terms. Therefore, Basso pinned his hopes on the democratic unity front with the communists of 1947–1948, which, in contrast to the former anti-fascist unity front,

TWO "DIFFICULT OUTSIDERS"? ANTI-FASCISM, ANTI-NAZISM... 207

included a profound socio-economic analysis of society.[48] Central elements of the unity front's programme consisted in a redistribution of wealth, especially a land reform, to make the Italian society more equal.[49] Basso saw the crisis caused by fascism as a great chance for a political and moral regeneration of a socialist and democratic society.[50] That is also why he studied the origins of fascism thoroughly during the first post-war decade.[51] He aimed at uniting the forces of the political left by creating a single proletarian party that should take over governmental power and then realize a socialist–democratic society.[52] Many contemporary socialists, such as Giuseppe Faravelli, declared this idea to be utopian.[53] However, Basso always answered that the social revolution would be a tedious task. He defined socialism as highest state of democracy and most ideal expression of the human's and citizens' chances.[54] Great hopes but little output: The democratic unity front, with common lists of socialists and communists, not only failed in the elections of 1948 but caused a splintering off the PSI by the right wing with Giuseppe Saragat and the foundation of a social democratic party.

Although Basso's ideas remained theoretical concepts, because the PSI found itself in opposition from 1947 to 1963, Wilhelm Hoegner had the chance to govern Bavaria twice as Prime Minister and to influence its politics as Justice and Home Secretary. Shortly after his appointment as Prime Minister by the American military government, he announced in a radio transmission in October 1945 that his major concern was to overcome National Socialism in politics, economy and culture.[55] Because he had drafted several laws for the future de-Nazification during his Swiss exile, he was well prepared to play an important role in this task.[56] With the "Gesetz zur Befreiung von Nationalsozialismus und Militarismus" ("Law for liberation from National Socialism and Militarism") (BefrG) of 5 March 1946, the Allies handed over the de-Nazification to German responsibility. As Prime Minister, Hoegner had the difficult task to control the application of the law in Bavaria. He regarded it as a "political great feat"[57] and hoped that the law would contribute to the "inner recovery" of the German people.[58] Although sometimes he spoke out for leniency against hangers-on, later on he declared a rigid application of the liberation law necessary because he was increasingly disappointed in people's lacking remorse.[59] Obviously, many difficulties arose concerning the application of the law. Nevertheless, Hoegner's acting as a mediator between the claims of the military government and the rather slackening members of his cabinet guaranteed that the law did not fail completely.[60]

208   J. SPÄTH

When Hoegner resigned in December 1946, he looked back on 15 months of extensive democratic reconstruction in Bavaria. He had not only been responsible for the implementation of the denazification; he had also established a state commissioner for Jewish affairs.[61] He and the chief public prosecutor, Friedrich Leistner, had participated as the only German testimonials in the execution of 10 principal war criminals at the international military trial in Nurnberg on 15 October 1946.[62] Furthermore, elements of a fair social order (as in social basic rights) and of direct democracy, as well as institutions to promote civic and political education, had been set up. Of particular interest for historians is the foundation of the Institute for Bavarian History at the Ludwig-Maximilians-University of Munich in 1947. Hoegner could claim to be responsible for the denazification of primary schools, and universities, for the reintroduction of religion as school subject as well as the creation of new organizations for young people and popular colleges.[63]

During his second term of office as Bavarian Prime Minister, at the head of a four-party coalition from 1954 to 1957, Hoegner continued his democratic initiative in educational and scientific matters. It is true: He failed to establish new models of teacher training because of the opposition of the Catholic Church, which insisted on closed-training institutions for religious schools. However, he managed to move the Max Planck Institut for physics and astrophysics from Göttingen to Munich and to build a teaching reactor for exploring the peaceful use of nuclear energy. He also promoted science and research and became involved in the foundation of the scientific council of the Federal Republic of Germany.[64]

Conclusions and Outlook

Both Basso and Hoegner were personalities that were able to give antifascism a meaning, even after the end of the totalitarian regimes, by fighting for strong social democracies in the future. Around 1943–1945, in their violent experiences with the World War(s), Basso and Hoegner shared the same spirit even though they did not belong to the same generation in an age-specific sense: Basso had been a child during the First World War, whereas Hoegner had consciously lived through it. The exile, however, put them on a similar emotional level, making them two representatives of a new democratic, republican and social generation after 1945. Other patterns of order, such as nation, were historically burdened by guilt, whereas this new generation interrupted the fascist and Nazi history, demanded a new beginning and promised to work for a better future. If we think of "generation" as community of experience and expectations, Hoegner and Basso were very close to each other.[65] After various transformations in the political systems from constitutional monarchies, the Weimar Republic, authoritarian and totalitarian regimes, after 1945 they could finally try to realize democratic and peaceful politics for decades. The zeitgeist was on their side and was clearly marked by socialist ideas. In the years between 1945 and 1947, everything seemed possible.

The triad of equality, liberty and civil and social rights as leading values describes the democratic programme of both politicians accurately. However, whereas Basso remained the brilliant intellectual who combined theoretical research and revolutionary political struggle, Hoegner was more a man of governmental implementation of his never-ending hopes for a just and truly democratic society. Due to personal characteristics, national and international politics as well as different histories, the PSI represented the by-far most radical Western European socialist party after the social democrats split off in 1947. Therefore, they clung longer and more fundamentally to the Marxist doctrine than the Social Democrats in Germany or the *Section Française de l'Internationale ouvrière*.[66] We could call this a hybrid position of the PSI between being a mass party and a party of political reforms.

Ultimately, the (auto-)definition of Hoegner and Basso as "difficult outsiders" remains a matter of opinion. I argue that both persons can be defined as such, but they are by far not the only ones within their parties. In addition, Basso and Hoegner were outsiders in several moments of their lives because they also fought for democratic and social societies within totalitarian regimes. It was especially these personalities that young democratic states could count on after the Second World War. What about the break of 1945? Lacking greater democratic experience before fascism, Basso adopted e.g. the concept of the anti-fascist unity front to that of a proletarian unity front. Having instead been an active politician of the Weimar republic, Hoegner continued to fight for social democracy: de-Nazification without criminalizing the masses, constitutional reforms stressing federalism, democratic education of the youth and the construction of a social and co-operative constitutional state: these were Hoegner's lessons that he had earned from Weimar.[67]

Coming back to the memory of the past within socialist party politics, we must note considerable differences in the process of auto-definition as anti-fascists in Germany and Italy after 1945. The common anti-fascist *koine* of the 1930s seemed to have gone lost. Sure, socialists in both countries remembered the fascist and Nazi crimes as well as the resistance against it in various forms and media. However, national specifics—such as the people's front in Italy, the German division or anti-fascism as founding myth of the GDR—might explain why different cultures of memory developed that included the republican founding myth born out of the resistance and excluded the partial collaboration with totalitarian regimes in Italy. Instead, it led to a more reluctant use of the anti-fascist past in the Federal Republic of Germany because of the instrumentalization of the term in the GDR.

With the peaceful transition from monarchy to republic in Italy, with democratic parliamentary elections and highly progressive constitutions in both Italy and Germany, anti-fascism freed itself from being just an anti-movement against fascism and National Socialism and began its constructive phase. Nonetheless, with this the shared belief, the anti-fascist basic consensus, the existing minimum of values and aims seemed to be exhausted. Since the outbreak of the Cold War, anti-totalitarianism or, expressed in a positive way as renunciation of violent revolutions and the use of democratic means only, became the fundamental difference between communist and socialist anti-fascists. Although not only Basso and the PSI, but also Hoegner and the SPD, fought for people's democracies with an as-high-as-possible participation of the working class, the German social democrats showed themselves quite early on to be happy with just improving the liberal democracy into an increasingly more social one.

Notes

1. Hoegner, Wilhelm. *Der schwierige Aussenseiter. Erinnerungen eines Abgeordneten, Emigranten und Ministerpräsidenten.* Munich: Isar, 1959.
2. For Basso, see Colozza, Roberto. *Lelio Basso. Una biografia politica (1948–1958).* Rome: Ediesse, 2010, especially 96 f.; for Hoegner, see Hoegner, *Aussenseiter*, 334; Kritzer, Peter. *Wilhelm Hoegner. Politische Biographie eines bayerischen Sozialdemokraten.* Munich: Süddeutsche Zeitung Verlag, 1979, 268.
3. In German, the term appeared for the first time in 1926 in the book of the Austrian social democrat Deutsch, Julius—*Antifaschismus. Proletarische Wehrhaftigkeit im Kampfe gegen den Faschismus.* Vienna: Wiener Volksbuchhandlung—in 1926 and around 1930 when German communists aimed at building a unity front against the NSDAP. Still, the best

TWO "DIFFICULT OUTSIDERS"? ANTI-FASCISM, ANTI-NAZISM...   211

overview study is Grunenberg, Antonia. *Antifaschismus – Ein deutscher Mythos*. Reinbek: Rowohlt, 1993. The most valuable contributions to Italian historiography were made by Collotti, Enzo, ed. *Fascismo e antifascismo. Rimozioni, revisioni, negazioni*. Rome/Bari: Laterza, 2000; De Bernardi, Alberto/Ferrari, Paolo, eds. *Antifascismo e identità europea*. Rome: Carocci, 2004; De Bernardi, Alberto. *Discorso sull'antifascismo*. Milan: Mondadori Bruno, 2007. For Britain and France, see Droz, Jacques. *Histoire de l'antifascisme en Europe 1923–1939*. Paris: La Découverte, 1985; Cerutti, Mauro. *Le Tessin, la Suisse et l'Italie de Mussolini. Fascisme et antifascisme 1921–1935*. Lausanne: Payot, 1988; Wolikow, Serge, ed. *Antifascisme et nation*. Dijon: Editions universitaires de Dijon, 1998; Hähnel-Mesnard, Carola, ed. *L'antifascisme revisité. Histoire, idéologie, mémoire*. Paris: Editions Kime, 2009; Vergnon, Gilles. *L'Antifascisme en France. De Mussolini à Le Pen*. Rennes: PU Rennes, 2009; Copsey, Nigel/Olechnowicz, Andrzek, eds. *Varieties of Anti-Fascism. Britain in the Inter-War Period*. Basingstoke/New York: Palgrave Macmillan, 2010.

4. The same appears to theoretical studies on fascism and fascisms, respectively: International research has underlined that fascism was not only a specific Italian but a European, if not global, phenomenon that can be compared with other totalitarian structures, such as Marxist–Leninist systems. See Griffin, Roger. *The Nature of Fascism*. London, New York: Routledge, 2006 (first London 1991); Dippper, Christof/Hudemann, Rainer/Petersen, Jens, eds. *Faschismus und Faschismen im Vergleich. Wolfgang Schieder zum 60. Geburtstag*. Cologne: SH-Verlag, 1998; Gregor, A. James. *The Faces of Janus. Marxism and Fascism in the Twentieth Century*. New Haven/London: Yale University Press, 2000; Mann, Michael. *Fascists*. Cambridge: Cambridge University Press, 2004; Bauerkämper, Arnd. *Der Faschismus in Europa 1918–1945*. Stuttgart: Reclam, 2006; Wippermann, Wolfgang. *Faschismus. Eine Weltgeschichte vom 19. Jahrhundert bis heute*. Darmstadt: Primus, 2009.

5. See Cattaruzza, Marina, ed. *La nazione in rosso. Socialismo, comunismo e "Questione nazionale", 1889–1953*. Soveria Mannelli: Rubbettino, 2005; Mattera, Paolo. *Il partito inquieto. Organizzazione, passioni e politica dei socialisti italiani dalla Resistenza al miracolo economico*. Rome: Carocci, 2004; Sebastiani, Pietro. *Laburisti inglesi e socialisti italiani. Dalla ricostituzione del PSI (UP) alla scissione di Palazzo Barberini da Transport House a Downing Street (1943–1947)*. Rome: FIAP, 1983.

6. For an excellent introduction, see Jureit, Ulrike. "Generation, Generationality, Generational Research, Version: 02.0." In *Docupedia-Zeitgeschichte*, 09.08.2017; http://docupedia.de/zg/Jureit_generation_v2_en_2017 (08.09.2017).

212 J. SPÄTH

7. Colozza, Roberto. *Lelio Basso. Una biografia politica (1948–1958)*. Rome: Ediesse, 2010; Rossi, Emanuele. *Democrazia come partecipazione. Lelio Basso e il PSI alle origini della Repubblica 1943–1947*. Rome: Viella, 2011; Luciani, Simona, ed. *Bibliografia degli scritti di Lelio Basso. Introduzione di Enzo Collotti*. Florence: L. S. Olschki, 2003.

8. Giorgi, Chiara. *Un socialista del Novecento. Uguaglianza, libertà e diritti nel percorso di Lelio Basso*. Rome: 2015; Giancarlo Monina, Lelio Basso, leader globale. Un socialista nel secondo Novecento, Rome: Carocci, 2016.

9. Kritzer, *Wilhelm Hoegner*; see also Kronawitter, Hildegard. "Bayerischer Patriot, Gefühlssozialist und erfolgreicher Ministerpräsident: Wilhelm Hoegner." *Einsichten und Perspektiven* 2 (2005), 34–57; most recently Späth, Jens. "Un antifascista e democratico particolare: il socialdemocratico bavarese Wilhelm Hoegner." *Diacronie. Studi di Storia Contemporanea* 9:1 (2012), http://www.studistorici.com/2012/02/13/spath_numero_9/ (08.09.2017).

10. See e.g. the permanent Italian interdisciplinary seminar "Le culture del socialismo italiano (1957–1976)", which was coordinated by the foundation Giacomo Brodolini in Milan and Rome since 2009. Furthermore, research on Italian socialism notes trends of international comparative and entangled history, e.g. Scirocco, Giovanni. *Politique d'abord. Il PSI, la guerra fredda e la politica internazionale (1948–1957)*. Milan: Unicopli, 2010.

11. See the eulogy of Christian Ude, former mayor of Munich, on Prof. Heribert Prantl in occasion of the presentation of the Wilhelm-Hoegner prize 2011, URL: http://www.spd-landtag.de/downl/PK11/111009WHP_Ude.pdf (08.09.2017).

12. Giorgi, *Basso*, 11.

13. See e.g. "L'educazione della classe lavoratrice e le riforma Gentile." *Critica sociale*, 1–15 ott. 1923, n. 19, 300–302; "Al di là del fascismo." *Il Caffè*, 1 ott. 1924, n. 7, 2; "La crisi della democrazia." *La Rivoluzione liberale*, 20 set. 1925, n. 33,133 f.; "Liberalismo-democrazia-socialismo. La polemica sull'origine della democrazia." *Pietre*, ott. 1926, n. 7, 193–199.

14. Sedita, Giovanni. *La "Giovane Italia" di Lelio Basso. Prefazione di Mauro Canali*. Rome: Aracne, 2006.

15. Concerning the Beer Hall Putsch, see Hoegner, *Aussenseiter*, 20–37, 43–48. In 1928, Hoegner published two leaflets entitled "Hitler und Kahr. Die bayerischen Napoleonsgrößen von 1923," which compared Hitler's planned march on Berlin with that of Napoleon from Elba on Paris.

16. Hoegner, Der Volksbetrug der Nationalsozialisten. Rede des Reichstagsabgeordneten Dr. Wilhelm Hoegner, Berlin 1930, pp. 14, 16.

TWO "DIFFICULT OUTSIDERS"? ANTI-FASCISM, ANTI-NAZISM... 213

17. Hoegner, *Aussenseiter*, 67.
18. Quoted after ibid., 87.
19. Seefried, Elke. "Sozialdemokraten und Sozialisten im österreichischen Exil 1933/34." *Zeitschrift für Geschichtswissenschaft* (50) 2002, 581–602. For the impressive description of the crossing of the Alps, see Hoegner, *Aussenseiter*, 120–123.
20. Concerning the exile in Austria and Switzerland, see ibid., 127–141 and 141–185.
21. All references in: Schumacher, Martin/Lübbe, Katharina/Schröder, Wilhelm Heinz, eds. *Die M.d.R. Die Reichstagsabgeordneten der Weimarer Republik in der Zeit des Nationalsozialismus. Politische Verfolgung, Emigration und Ausbürgerung, 1933–1945. Eine biographische Dokumentation.* Düsseldorf: Droste, ³1994, Nr. 634, 207 f.
22. For minor writings in the exile, see Kritzer, *Hoegner*, 124–129; Liechti, Urs [=Wilhelm Hoegner]. *Wodans Wiederkunft. Ein lustiger Reisebericht aus einer traurigen Zeit.* Zürich: Jean Christophe, 1936; Ritter, Hans [=Wilhelm Hoegner]. *Politik und Moral.* Zürich: Jean Christophe, 1937; Ritter, Georg [=Wilhelm Hoegner], "Katholische Kirche und totaler Staat." *Rote Revue, Sozialistische Monatsschrift* 16: 10 (1937), 323–333; id. "Lehren der Weimarer Republik." *Schweizer Monatshefte* 25: 1 (1945); Ritter, Rudolf [=Wilhelm Hoegner] "Die deutsche Frage." *Schweizer Monatshefte* 24: 8 (1944).
23. Institut für Zeitgeschichte München (IfZ), NL Hoegner, ED 120-2-18+19: Otto Braun to Hoegner, Ascona 06.06.1944; ED 120-2-26+27: Braun to Ritzel, Ascona 21.09.1944; ED 120-13-138-147: In the folder "Union deutscher Sozialisten in der Schweiz 1945," there is a manuscript entitled "Hauptpunkte einer deutschen Nachkriegspolitik. Programmbeitrag," written by a SAP- or ISK-group in Switzerland, to which probably Anna Siemsen belonged in 1942/43; ED 120-12-70-91: Das Demokratische Deutschland, Bern/Leipzig 1945; see also Hoegner, *Aussenseiter*, 166–172.
24. Concerning the term "45er," see the article by Dominik Rigoll, 47–67.
25. See Basso's speech as secretary general of the PSI at the 26th party congress in Rome in January 1948, which was partially reprinted in the *Avanti!* Issue of 20.01.1948.
26. "Discorso di Lelio Basso al XXVII Congresso." *Avanti!* 28.06.1948.
27. Enzo Collotti to Pietro Nenni, 27.12.1960, Archivio Centrale dello Stato Roma, Archivio Nenni, b. 22, fasc. 1241, letter 1, in which the promotion committee asked Nenni to give a lesson about socialism in exile and the international collaboration on 27.03.1961 within the scope of "Lezioni sulla storia d'Italia dal 1918 al 1948". The first lecture on the origins of fascism was given by Lelio Basso. Further socialists involved were Vittoria

214   J. SPÄTH

Foa on fascist economics, Leo Valiani on the crisis of European democracy, Riccardo Bauer on antifascism and the origins of the Italian Resistance until 1943, Franco Venturi on the political problems, the relations between the parties and the relations with the Allies in the Italian Resistance, and Ferruccio Parri on the period from the Resistance up to the Republic and the Constitution.

28. Basso, Lelio. "Ciclo totalitario (1)." *Quarto Stato* 10: 11 (1949), 3–8.
29. Franceschini, Claudia. *Le idee costituzionali della Resistenza*. Roma 1997, 255.
30. Basso, Lelio. "Come prima, peggio di prima." *Avanti!*, 01.08.1943, now in: Basso, Lelio. *Due totalitarismi. Fascismo e Democrazia cristiana*. Milan: Garzanti, 1951.
31. See e.g. Lelio Basso, Manuscript on the history of the PSI from its origins until 1957, 1958, Fondazione Basso, Fondo Lelio Basso, serie 2, b. 9, fasc. 18. See also id., Antifascismo ieri e oggi, 1961, Fondazione Basso, Fondo Lelio Basso, serie 15, attività politica, b. 7, fasc. 34.
32. See e.g. the socialist press on the 9th anniversary of the liberation in *Avanti!* issue 58of 25.04.1954, in which Basso wrote an article on p. 3 entitled "La Costituzione è nata dalla Resistenza". Because most of his leading party followers were in various Italian cities, Basso held the main speech on the values of the Resistance at the manifestation in Cagliari; see Fondazione Basso, Fondo Lelio Basso, ser. 1, scritti, 1.40.
33. Salvati, Mariuccia. "Lelio Basso protagonista e interprete della Costituzione." In Monina, Giancarlo, ed. *La via alla politica. Lelio Basso, Ugo La Malfa, Meuccio Ruini protagonisti della Costituente*. Milan: Franco Angeli, 1999, 38; Salvati, Mariuccia/Giorgi, Chiara, eds. *Lelio Basso. Scritti scelti. Frammenti di un percorso politico e intellettuale (1903–1978)*. Rome: Carocci, 2003, 16 f. Cf. also Basso's writings of this period, in: ibid.: *Perché il fascismo*, 1976, pp. 102–113; Uno strumento del fascismo, 1955, pp. 235–238; Norimberga dimenticata, 1976, pp. 297–299.
34. IfZ, NL Hoegner, ED 120-62-58: Ritzel to Hoegner, Bonn 13.04.1951; for tumults after a lecture on the German collective guilt by pastor Martin Niemöller at the University of Erlangen in January 1946 see Kritzer, *Hoegner*, 319–321; see also IfZ, NL Hoegner, ED 120-56-74+75: Letter and newspaper article (Stuttgarter Zeitung 20.01.1950) from Adolf Julius Merkl to Hoegner, Tübingen, 01.02.1950.
35. IfZ, NL Hoegner, ED 120-108-19: resolution of the association of the victims of the Nazi regime against menaces of former Nazis, Augsburg, 19.01.1950. In an assembly of more than 200 former members of the NSDAP in the Cafe Luitpold in Augsburg in November 1949, somebody said: "Dr. Hoegner is a bastard!"

TWO "DIFFICULT OUTSIDERS"? ANTI-FASCISM, ANTI-NAZISM... 215

36. IfZ, NL Hoegner, ED 120-88-16: The review *Echo der Woche* wanted to set up committees called "Demokratische Aktion" "with the scope to disturb and to break up neo-Nazi and other assemblies of extreme-rightist groups"; ED 120-90-29-40: leaflet of the relief association "Freiheit für Rudolf Hess e.V."; ED 120-327-64-83: leaflet documenting the constituent assembly of the association of the victims of the Nazi regime; ED 120-65-5-11: Letter Udo Rukser to Heinrich Ritzel, Chile, 03.06.1947 containing a leaflet that promoted the idea of a European Germany and opted against a German Europe; ED 120-101-111: SPÖ (Dr. Adolf Schärf and Franz Rauscher) to Hoegner, Wien, 12.02.1946; ED 120-349-170+171: Distinguished Visitors Attending World Assembly and ED 120-349-193-205: Die moralische Aufruestung. Der Vormarsch einer weltumspannenden Idee; ED 120-349-316-329: Diary of Hoegner's trip to the USA, 28 May-18.06.1948. The movement was founded in 1921 as the Oxford movement. In 1938, it took its contemporary name "Moral Rearmament" (MRA) and established its central seat in Caux/Switzerland in 1946. Hoegner, who was a member of the "Gemeinschaft der Freunde der MRA e.V." in Bonn, later distanced himself from the movement when he eventually recognised that it was primarily sponsored by American high finance. See Kritzer, *Hoegner*, 270–272.

37. See ibid., 318 f.

38. IfZ, NL Hoegner, ED 120-62-76: Hoegner to Ritzel, München, 25.07.1953. Concerning the confrontation with the SRP see Kritzer, *Hoegner*, 322 f. Even in the following years, the topic remained of current interest for him, as a letter of Hoegner to the "Volksbund für Frieden und Freiheit", München, 14.03.1960 shows: "To me it seems important to fight against bolshevism and also against neo-Nazism." See IfZ, NL Hoegner, ED 120-108-44.

39. IfZ, NL Hoegner, ED 120-93-2-98: correspondence concerning the establishment of a memorial in the former concentration camp Dachau. The International Dachau Committee wrote in a report in 1964 regarding the content of the museum that the memorial should address first of all "the young generation and all those who did not know about, let alone felt the entire dimension of Nazi terrorism"; it should "force people to wake up and reflect and to call on the individual responsibility"; and it should clarify "why and how things could have gotten so far." See IfZ, NL Hoegner, ED 120-93-52: extract of the report about the museum in Dachau by the Comité International de Dachau, Büro München, 06.06.1964.

40. IfZ, NL Hoegner, ED 120-93-76-79: Speech of Hoegner at the commemoration ceremony in Dachau, 30.08.1964.

216 J. SPÄTH

41. IfZ, NL Hoegner, ED 120-78-154-161: documents and press review concerning the exhibition "Antifaschistischer Widerstand in Deutschland 1933–1945" in Munich.
42. Recent research has underlined the antidemocratic attitude and anti-system spirit of the liberal Italian state. See Settembrini, Domenico. "L'evoluzione delle sinistre antisistema negli anni del centrismo." In ib., ed. *Socialismo, marxismo e mercato. Per un bilancio dell'idea socialista.* Lungro: Marco, 2002, 200–203.
43. Anonymous letter to Basso proposing to declare null and void the purge, Milano, 28.12.1953, in: Fondazione Basso, Fondo Lelio Basso, serie 25, fasc. 9.
44. Lelio Basso, Conferenza dell'On. Basso tenuta nella sede del PSI in Piazza Calderini a Bologna, 03.09.1949, Fondazione Basso, Fondo Lelio Basso, serie III, b. 1, f. 1.
45. Basso, Lelio. "Atene e Roma." *Avanti!*, 10.01.1945: "Great parts of the fascist bureaucracy and police were left untouched. The diplomatic service was only renewed to a small extent and very slowly. Many former fascist leaders continue living peacefully."
46. Basso, Lelio. "Intervento al XXXI Congresso del P.S.I." *Avanti!*, 03.04.1955.
47. Basso, Lelio. "Dall'unità antifascista all'unità democratica." *Socialismo 7*: 12 (1947), 141.
48. Ibid., 143.
49. Basso, Lelio. "Prospettive del Fronte Democratico Popolare." *Socialismo* 3: 4 (1948), 2–4.
50. Luciani, Simona. *Bibliografia degli scritti di Lelio Basso.* Florence: Leo S. Olschki, 2003, VII.
51. Ibid., X f.
52. That is what Nenni called "dal governo al potere." See Settembrini, *L'evoluzione*, 206.
53. Faravelli to Rossi, Lugano, 13.04.1945, in: Masini, Pier Carlo/Merli, Stefano, eds. *Il socialismo al bivio. L'archivio di Giuseppe Faravelli, 1945–1950. Annali della Fondazione Giangiacomo Feltrinelli* 20 (1988–89), 34 f.
54. Collotti, Enzo/Ajmone, Fiorella, eds. *Ripensare il socialismo. La ricerca di Lelio Basso.* Milan: Mazzotta, 1988, 15 f.
55. Hoegner, *Aussenseiter*, 209–211.
56. See the drafts and bills, partially in English, in: IfZ, NL Hoegner, ED 124-8-10: elimination of Nazis from the economy; 124-14-17: continuity of shops run by former Nazis; 124-21-24: declaration of the secretary of economics, Dr. Lange; 124-35-37: bill to compensate for Nazi crimes; 124-50-54: draft of bill for indemnification measures; 124–55: bill to do penance for Nazi crimes. See also Hoegner, *Aussenseiter*, 216–220.

57. Niethammer, *Entnazifizierung*, 326.
58. Hoegner, *Aussenseiter*, 231–233; IfZ, NL Hoegner, ED 120-124-3-7: problem how to cope with Nazis, legal drafts.
59. Kritzer, *Hoegner*, 234 f.
60. Hoegner, *Aussenseiter*, 208.
61. Ibid., 271.
62. Ibid., 265–271.
63. Ibid., 282.
64. Ibid., 321 f., 330–332.
65. See Koselleck, Reinhart. "'Erfahrungsraum' und 'Erwartungshorizont'. Zwei historische Kategorien." In id., ed. *Vergangene Zukunft. Zur Semantik geschichtlicher Zeiten.* Frankfurt a.M.: Suhrkamp, 1979, 349–375.
66. Berman, Sheri. *The Primacy of Politics, Social Democracy and the Making of Europe's Twentieth Century.* Cambridge: Cambridge University Press, 2006, 192–195.
67. Niethammer, *Entnazifizierung*, 215–217.

CHAPTER 10

European Socialism and the French–German Reconciliation

Christine Vodovar

According to most historians, the Elysée Treaty or Treaty of French–German Friendship, signed in 1963, was above all a common-interest alliance and a step in an on-going process of rapprochement between France and Germany, which had been formally started in 1950. However, it has been introduced as and it is still celebrated as the consecration of the Franco–German reconciliation. Indeed, if the treaty is not a starting point, it must be considered a turning point for two reasons: first, because it built a framework for Franco–German cooperation, which is still in force today, laying the foundations for organizations that aimed at reconciliation between the two peoples at all levels; and second, and more importantly, because its promoters gave it immediately and voluntarily a mythical connotation and they commemored it over the years by rituals and celebrations.[1]

European Socialists immediately criticized both this use of the theme of reconciliation and its personification in de Gaulle and Adenauer. Once won't hurt, the Sozialdemokratische Partei Deutschlands (SPD) and the Parti Socialiste—Section Française de l'Internationale Socialiste (SFIO) published a joint statement in July 1962[2]; just as, in March 1963,

---

C. Vodovar (✉)
LUISS Guido Carli, Rome, Italy

© The Author(s) 2018   219
J. Späth (ed.), *Does Generation Matter? Progressive Democratic Cultures in Western Europe, 1945–1960*, Palgrave Studies in the History of Social Movements, https://doi.org/10.1007/978-3-319-77422-0_10

220 C. VODOVAR

the *Bureau de liaison des partis socialistes de la Communauté européenne* (BLPSCE).[3] These documents were very general and merely expressed some principles without determining the attitude of the parties in advance. They represented an attempt to standardize the positions of (a part of)[4] European Socialists. Their common criticism was based on two arguments. On one hand, they denied the treaty's authors the paternity of the Franco–German reconciliation, instead claiming for themselves the honours of a historic undertaking. There is not one paragraph of the BLPSCE's communiqué that does not recall that the reconciliation of French and German people started long before 1963 and that it has always been one of the main preoccupations of European Socialists.[5] In contrast, they insisted on the opposition between two alternative conceptions of Europe: (1) the Gaullist conception of a Europe of nations, independent of the two blocks, where decisions are made by the governments or directly by the Franco–German tandem and hence the realization of the Franco-German rapprochement in a bilateral context; and (2) the socialist conception of a Europe of peoples that goes beyond nationalism and the limited framework of national sovereignty inserted within a broader system of alliances; hence a reconciliation of the French and German peoples as "at once the way and the aim of the constitution of a European Community."[6]

However, such a common understanding and will were far from being achieved at the end of the Second World War. In fact, despite a stated desire for reconciliation, considered a necessary but insufficient condition for the establishment of a peaceful and democratic order in Europe, divergences and mutual distrust prevailed mostly on the convergence of opinion. This joint effort at the time of the Elysée Treaty did not go beyond the stage of a statement of principle: The SPD ratified the treaty after the addition of the preamble, whereas the SFIO voted against it. An amendment to the resolution of the SFIO's Congress of 1963, in which Léon Boutbien proposed to ratify the treaty anyway, was unanimously rejected.[7]

How can we explain these divergences? Do they correspond to different conceptions of peace and collective security, or do they refer primarily to interest calculations? What is the importance of memory and the system of collective representations of socialists? On this last point, and following the main problematic of this volume, this chapter will pay particular attention to try to answer the question of whether generations matter as far as the French–German reconciliation is concerned. As pointed out by many scholars, the concept of "generation" is quite fluid and flexible. We will recall four elements of the definition of a political generation. First, the demographic element, i.e. a political generation usually—if not always—belongs to the same age group. Second, the ideological and cultural element, i.e. these people have, at least in front of some specific political issues, similar political ideas and even emotive reactions. Third, this background is the result of a common past experience and, more specifically, the result of the experience of a common founding event. Last, all these elements represent a tool for mobilization. Saying that, and privileging an empirical approach, we will wonder to what extent did the experience of two world wars and of the assertion of authoritarian and totalitarian regimes contribute to shaping common representations and expectations? And to what extent did it politically mobilize these parties starting in 1945, and did it contribute to the creation of a generation effect and a new political culture?[8]

This article focuses on German, French and Italian Socialist parties.[9] In fact, they belonged to the same political family[10] and took part, even if sometimes discontinuously, in the same international organizations and networks where they tried to make their views compatible.[11] In addition, they operated in countries that had experienced similar political developments even if their international position in 1945 was different. Finally, these countries, especially France and Germany, had fought each other violently in the previous decades. Hence, the position of these protagonists is not the same: The SFIO and the SPD were obviously directly involved in the issue of Franco–German reconciliation, whereas the Italian parties could be considered a kind of participant–observer.

Contentious Memories

In the aftermath of the Second World War, French, Italian and German Socialist leaders tried to build a common memory of the conflict, especially by denying the principle of collective responsibility of the German people. This refusal responded primarily to a double political necessity. On one hand, it was necessary to avoid the mistakes of the first post-war period and to pave the way for a future reconciliation, which all of them considered necessary for the establishment of a lasting peace. The SPD and the Italian Socialist Party of Proletarian Unity (PSIUP), which belonged to defeated countries, were fighting for a "fair" peace. However, the SFIO expressed the same arguments: "Any policy that aims to charge the entire German people, irrespective of legitimate returns or reparations, for the criminal politics of its torturers, would lead to dire recurrence."[12] To ensure the security of the continent, without resorting to a Carthaginian peace that would inevitably arouse a sense of revenge, Germany had to be inserted into an international community "powerful enough to re-educate, discipline and, if necessary, master it" in order to eventually restore its full sovereignty.[13]

However, the desire to absolve the German people from all liability also sought to exalt and give credibility to the existence of a socialist resistance to Nazism. This allowed each party to deny any responsibility for the rise of dictatorial or totalitarian regimes in the name of this universality because these regimes were born against a labour movement that was, by nature, uninvolved in them. This provided a moral and political backing for socialists and thus served to legitimize them. In that way, they should appear as the most capable of ensuring democratic rehabilitation in their country.[14] This was based on an interpretation of Nazism resulting from an encounter between extremist leaders and the bourgeoisie. The use of Marxist keys for understanding illustrated the difficulties many socialists had in understanding these new types of regimes. However, it also allowed for the denial of any specificity to Nazism and the consideration of fascism and Vichy as expressions of the same phenomenon. In the German and Italian cases, socialists continued to claim their participation in fighting against Nazism and "Nazi-fascism." They presented themselves as victims or martyrs of these regimes and tried to establish a great part of their legitimacy on that assumption.[15] Even when Italian socialists distinguished the Italian responsibility from the German one, they still referred to "Hitlerian" Germany.[16] This point is less evident in the French situation because in 1945 no one challenged the SFIO's position in the political system and its contribution to the Liberation anymore. However, this had not always been the case. There was a time in which French Socialists needed to forget and to live down their ratification of the Munich Agreement, the vote of the full powers to Pétain by more than a half of its senators and deputies and the collaboration of some of its most illustrious representatives with Vichy. Thus, it is not a coincidence that, in 1941, Blum proposed the following analysis:

> In Italy, it is the bourgeoisie which invented and arose Fascism, before installing it in power; in France, it applauded or pretended to applaud the 'National Revolution' [...]. It does not matter for the bourgeoisie if the 'National-socialisms' or the 'National Revolutions' declaim against capitalism, without indeed harming it, providing that they [the 'National-socialisms' or the 'National Revolutions'] crush the only opponent of whom

it [the bourgeoisie] was frightened [...]. Shrugged off the socialism by Nazism and its substitutes, it [the bourgeoisie] counts on the movement of history to cancel Nazism in its turn.[17]

However, such a construction of memory ran into several obstacles and failed in building a common position. First, it never succeeded in imposing on the individual memory of many socialists, mostly German and French. Mistrust, even hostility, remained the main feature of the perception of the other until at least the mid-1950s. And with few exceptions, it also concerned the relations between the two parties.[18] Indeed, the Blumist denial of collective responsibility was imposed gradually in the *Populaire* from the end of 1946 and finally in 1948. Even so, the SFIO still had in its ranks—following the example of the Labour Party and of a part of the international socialist movement—supporters of a firm policy towards Germany. They did not always identify with the official party line.

The example of Vincent Auriol is emblematic because he had been, after the First World War, one of the main spokespersons of the SFIO as far as the Treaty of Versailles is concerned and—since the Second World War—one of the few socialists who really "thought" of Europe. Born in 1884, close to Blum, former Minister of the Popular Front, future first president of the Fourth Republic, future opponent to the European Defence Community (EDC), Auriol was particularly anxious to keep Germany "under supervision" from all points of view. He was firmly convinced that there was originally a problem of mentality and education. In *Hier ... Demain*, written in 1943, he explicitly condemned "the German people who, blinded by the self-conceit of Hitler and intoxicated by his power, had been in the grip of pride and violence." For this reason, "no confidence would, for a long time, have had in it and, during that time, it would be necessary to keep it strictly under observation and supervision."[19] He confirmed his thoughts on 23 November 1944 when the Consultative Assembly of Algiers addressed the foreign policy issues: "Germany would assume the consequences of the actions of its masters."[20]

Another significant example is that of Guy Mollet because of his leadership after 1946. Born in 1905, he belongs to another (demographic) generation compared with Auriol. He did not participate in the First World War, but he suffered the consequences with the death of his father, who was gassed during the conflict. His ideological orientation and socio-professional profile are also quite different from those of Auriol. Whereas the latter—a lawyer and a publicist—was a notable from southwest France, close to Jaurès and Blum, and used to tread upon the corridors of high politics, Mollet was an English teacher from northern France whose prewar activism was essentially within the SFIO, in the leftist tendencies. General Secretary of the Socialist Party since 1946, Mollet "converted" to Europe in the late 1940s. However, although the construction of Europe became one of his key policy objectives, and although he belonged to the restricted group of those who were really interested in Germany (he had an extensive correspondence with Ollenhauer), he continued to have a great distrust of the neighbouring country. This is shown, for example, by his hostility to Carlo Schmid (he refused to sit in an Assembly with him), whose mother was French and who worked during the war in the legal department of the German administration in Lille. Another example is his assertion at the Director Committee of the SFIO on 4 October 1950, in which he stated that Boutbien "is very generous when he says: 'we have fought against Nazis, not against Germans'. Such an attitude allows many Germans to reject the collective responsibility of Germany. We can't forget that one of the main elements of neo-Nazism could be the military resurgence of Germany."[21]

Nevertheless, it is undoubtedly the episode of the EDC that illustrates best how the attitude of the French Socialists towards their neighbour remained ambiguous and based on an extreme distrust of a revival of German power, both economic and military. No socialist accepted willingly the prospect of German rearmament, whatever shape it should take. The "cédistes" chose the lesser of two evils and then sought to transform a constraint into an opportunity for European integration. As for the "anti-cédistes," they were an extremely heterogeneous group. Some were motivated by nationalist or patriotic feelings, others by internationalist and pacifist feelings, others because of their conception of collective security (these ones were called "atlanticists," i.e. supporters of close relations between Europe and the USA but against the rearmament of Germany), again others because of a violent anti-German feeling.[22] However, historians agree to consider that their choice was primarily motivated by individual reasons, often instinctive and emotional.[23] In any case, the cleavage between "cédistes" and "anti-cédistes" did not refer either to demographic generations or to common experiences. Indeed, Felix Gouin and Paul Ramadier, who were "adults" in 1914, voted in favour of the ratification, whereas Vincent Auriol, André Le Troquer and Salomon Grumbach (the main specialist of Germany within the SFIO) voted against it. Among

EUROPEAN SOCIALISM AND THE FRENCH–GERMAN RECONCILIATION   225

those who were 20 years old just before or just after the First World War, the conclusion is the same: Marcel-Edmond Naegelen, Jules Moch, Robert Lacoste, Daniel Mayer and Robert Verdier voted against; André Philip, Jean Le Bail, Guy Mollet and Christian Pineau were in favour. Among those who were born during or after the war, Alain Savary and Gérard Jaquet voted in favour, whereas Léon Boutbien voted against. Noelline Castagnez has shown well that, as far as the socialist deputies of the Fourth Republic are concerned, veterans of the Great War, pacifists of the interwar period, deportees and prisoners of the Second World War and members of the resistance all split up quite equally into "cédistes" and "anti-cédistes." Therefore, their past experience did not structure a joint mobilization in favour of or against the treaty.[24] They kept from this period only two markers of a common identity in relation to our subject: (1) an extreme distrust of Germany and Germans in general; and (2) an absolute priority given to defence issues as the result of both a bad conscience born with the ratification of the Munich Agreement and the marginalization of the SFIO's most peaceful tendencies during the clandestine period.

As in the French case, the willingness towards reconciliation of German Social Democrats never succeeded in imposing completely on individual memory. Furthermore, mistrust, even hostility, towards France was fed by the French foreign policy towards Germany as well as by the attitude of the French occupation authority towards the SPD and Schumacher. In any case, Social Democrats had difficulty accepting the image of a dominating France: Not only, at least until the mid-1950s, did the memory of the exile in France, the passivity of France in fighting against Nazism, the "betrayal" of Munich and especially the detention of hundreds of activists in camps and their delivery to the Germans continue to prevail among many of them,[25] but they also saw a gap between the international aspirations of France and the resizing of its power status upon Liberation.[26] As Paterson pointed out, at all the first steps of the European integration, the opposition of the SPD was based in part on the suspicion and prejudices against France that were widespread within much of the party.[27]

CONTENTIOUS INTERESTS

In fact, the difference between the international statuses of the three countries represented a second obstacle to reconciliation. Indeed, if the denial of collective responsibility of the German people referred to the issue of the existence of the Socialist parties, the intensity of this

226   C. VODOVAR

requirement of legitimisation was not comparable and weighed differently on the attitude of the parties because of the two modes already mentioned earlier of the political transition: the timing of the reconstruction of political systems and the political space in which the legitimisation must be affirmed. In essence, in 1945 nobody challenged France on its national independence, its winner status and its capacity to decide the future of Germany—and the SFIO intended to exploit all these elements legitimately[28]—whereas the SPD belonged to a defeated country under Allied administration and without sovereignty. The aspiration to "full sovereignty" and reunification was pervasive until the Paris Agreements and contributed much to the political choices of the SPD. The Italian case from this point of view was at an intermediate level: Italian Socialists had to face a deficit of legitimacy due to the political consequences of the war, but Italy recovered its "full sovereignty" over most of its territory by December 1945. However, the political forces still faced the delicate question of peace treaties—signed in February 1947 and ratified by the Constituent Assembly in late July—which included Italy's renunciation of its colonies, the loss of border areas and the creation of the Free Territory of Trieste, whose area A, slightly modified, passed under Italian civil administration only in October 1954.[29]

This difference of international status, as well as the lessons that the different parties thought themselves to have learned from the past because they eventually determined different priorities, prevented these parties from converging on a common position as far as French–German relations are concerned. The SPD and, at least initially, the PSIUP aspired above all to recover their full sovereignty and to be treated equally with their counterparts in the name of their externality to Fascism and Nazism and to prevent the recurrence of the errors of Versailles. However, SFIO, which shared the same principles as its neighbours, at least in its official propaganda, as we have seen, aspired to play a role in international balance and in particular to control Germany, giving priority to a requirement of security and defence.

SFIO Against German Militarism

In fact, until the early 1950s, French Socialists were primarily concerned with avoiding any revival of German militarism. They considered a long military occupation of Germany in order to have direct control and to make reforms deemed necessary for its democratization. The SFIO still supported this principle in 1947–1948 even though it became increasingly critical of the policy conducted in the French Zone of Occupation (FZO) by the French authority. In addition, the SFIO did not intend to give up war reparations, which should have been done especially through the internationalization of the Ruhr for the benefit of disaster states and through the exploitation by France of the Saar mines. However, unlike the French government, the SFIO opposed any dismemberment or fragmentation.[30] Indeed, the priority given to the control of German militarism and the concern for reparations fit into the framework of a more articulated scheme of the German question and collective security. This was not purely defensive and punitive but had to, eventually (even if the date was never specified), "allow republican and revolutionary Germany to enter with equal rights with the other nations in the international community."[31] With the beginning of the Cold War, the scheme took shape around two elements: the supervision of Germany within a democratic European Union and the rise of German socialism.[32]

However, although the Cold War gradually placed the Soviet threat at the forefront of socialist concerns, the perception of a German threat did not disappear. From 1948, as part of an explicit Western choice (the hopes of the third international force had been postponed), Europe became more than ever the solution for the German problem: the only way to keep Germany from swinging to the Soviet camp and/or recovering its hegemony whether political, military or economic. The reluctance of French Socialists to accept the Schuman Plan and the "Little" Europe must be interpreted in that perspective. In fact, British participation was insistently required to prevent a Franco–German head-to-head. In addition, it could strengthen, at least until 1951, the influence of socialism in Europe. The position of Mollet in favour of the EDC Treaty, approved by the majority of the party, is a good illustration of the reluctance of French socialists. Mollet was hostile to a German rearmament within the North Atlantic Treaty Organization (NATO), which would mean that Germany would have "all the attributes of sovereignty…with a national army at the service of a government in control of its destiny." He called for the implementation of the European project: a project that favoured an integrated Germany in a European structure to an integrated German army in NATO or a reunified Germany under the banner of neutrality, which was the SPD position supported by some "anti-cédistes" within the SFIO.[33] The preference given to integration rather than reunification obviously fed the criticism of the SPD.

From the failure of the EDC and the signature of the Paris Agreements, and without breaking with its previous developments, the European view of the SFIO acquired a new dimension. Originally, it was mainly the result—partly desired, partly compelled—of a willingness to supervise Germany. However, from 1954–1955, West Germany became a full partner with France just when the Socialist Party got ready to take command of the government. In addition, France was grappling with a process of decolonization with great consequences in political, economic and financial fields. The SFIO paid dearly for it: The prime minister from 1956 to 1957, Guy Mollet, had been particularly criticized for his Algerian policy within his own party, resulting in the eventual split of 1958 and the birth of the *Parti Socialiste Autonome*. In addition, both the Algerian emergency and the Suez crisis favoured the SFIO's isolation on an international level. They also proved the extent of the international resizing of France to French public opinion. In this general context, French socialists tried to insert Europe into a more complex perspective. On one hand, it became more autonomous from the German question and the organization of peace; in contrast, it was a critical element of the economic and social projects of the SFIO. One episode is significant of this new trend: When Jean Monnet asked Guy Mollet to participate in his Action Committee for the United States of Europe in 1955, Mollet subordinated his participation to that of the German Social Democrats. At the end of July, just after the end of the IV congress of the Socialist International (SI), Ollenhauer joined the committee and brought with him the SPD. Within the SI, dominated in the early 1950s by the "anti-community" group (composed of the Labour party, the Scandinavian socialist parties and the SPD who, for different reasons, opposed the European integration process), a convergence of views was starting to be outlined between the SFIO, the socialist parties of the Benelux Union and the SPD, which considered Europe fertile ground for developing a new economic and social mode different from that of the Labour and Scandinavian parties. More than ever, Europe would realize what nation–states were no longer able to do.[34] The evolution of the SPD, as far as Europe is concerned, and the settlement of the Saar's disputes helped to accelerate and deepen this convergence of views with the SPD.

SPD Against the French Hegemony

At least until the mid-1950s, the SPD was extremely critical of France and did not hesitate to come forward as a victim of its policy. As already pointed out, the SPD based its post-war politics on a fundamental imperative: national unity, territorial integrity of Germany (in its 1937 borders), recovery of full sovereignty and, therefore, equality of rights with its partners, especially the European ones. The SPD was not denying France its own requirements—or indeed the demilitarization or "de-Nazification" of Germany—but it considered that they had to be separated from the issue of sovereignty. For example, the SPD would have accepted an international control on the Saar if this had remained united to Germany and if Germany had participated in the Saar control.[35] In such a view, the SPD did not appreciate either the management of the FZO or the attempts of the French government to reduce the German territory. In particular, the Saar question had been the main bone of contention, especially because it related directly to the priorities of the SPD, which interpreted this question as a disguised form of annexation.[36] The Council of Europe, the ECSC and the EDC were then considered initiatives devised by France to extend an unacceptable situation and to establish its hegemony in Europe, especially as long as the UK was not involved. The SPD was not against Europe: In 1946, the party took back the 1925 programme and reaffirmed that a European organization would be the base for the organization of peace. In addition, it included in its ranks people who were less intransigent than the party leader in this field. However, because of its priorities, the SPD opposed the method undertaken for organizing Europe in the late 1940s and early 1950s. Consistent with its views, and even though it supported in principle an organization based on transfers of sovereignty, the SPD opposed the supranational nature of these projects and rather considered that the Federal Republic of Germany (FRG) would access equal rights within an intergovernmental framework more easily: Rather than putting a lot into European integration with a non-discriminatory position in view (Adenauer's policy), Schumacher was hoping to get equal rights and national unity within the borders of 1937, gambling on the need to anchor Germany to the West, which had been required by Westerners. In this context, the spirit of the Pleven plan could not be "the one of reconciliation." The hostility of the SPD concerned, amongst other things, the alleged discriminatory claims of France because they prevented the FRG from having the same rights as the other members. Although it was anti-communist and anti-Soviet, unlike the PSI, the priority given to the reunification and the equality of rights brought the SPD to claim a position of neutrality for Germany, offering to negotiate the non-rearmament of Germany in exchange for unification. The integration into a collective security system should happen once all attempts to negotiate with the East had been exhausted.[37]

This uncompromising position was due in great part to the leadership of Schumacher and to the fact that, as Paterson pointed out, his followers were in large proportion refugees, even if there were some exceptions. Paul Löbe, Wilhelm Kaisen and Ernst Reuter, for instance, were in favour of the Council of Europe.[38] However, the experience of exile and persecution of most of the party leaders encouraged German Social Democrats to assert their national identity.[39] This position, nevertheless, was gradually crumbling within the party: In 1950, some voices were opposed to the anti-European intransigence of the majority of the party, and, in 1954, the "cédistes" within the SPD strengthened after the failure of the Berlin conference. However, they failed to impose themselves as far as the Paris Agreements were concerned, especially because the agreement package of Mendes France ruined their attempts to separate the Saar question from the rest. After a unanimous rejection of the Saar settlement in London, the party split again on the admission of West Germany into NATO and the creation of the Western European Union. However, this evolution brought the party to approve the Treaties of Rome. Consistent with its previous positions, the SPD justified its membership amongst the others, arguing that it "had no longer evidence of the politics of the winners."[40]

As for Italian and French Socialists, the years 1955–1957 were in fact crucial and must be considered as a turning point. On one hand, the new status of the countries after the Paris and London Agreements and the Saar's settlement changed the context in which the French–German reconciliation would happen. In contrast, thanks to the predominance of economic and social issues in relation with European integration after the failure of the EDC, Italian socialists and German Social Democrats found a way to get closer to Europe. Even if their proposals did not always coincide, these evolutions made the dialogue easier and brought French, German and Italian socialist leaders to think about a new model of development.

Italian Socialism and Its Divisions

Even if they were less directly affected by the German problem, from both the memorial and the political points of view, the position of the Italian Socialists is nevertheless interesting for understanding the importance of international status in the approach to the problem. Unlike the SFIO, the Italian Socialists had no real program for Germany in the aftermath of the war, and there are very few documents in Italian archives on this issue. Italy did not have its say in the peace settlement and was primarily concerned with its own fate, which depended, like that of Germany, on the good will of the victors. With the signature of the peace treaties in 1947, both the recovery of full sovereignty and the permanence of some pending cases—including the exclusion of the United Nations, the fate of the ex-colonies and the question of Trieste—did not determine the same attitudes as they did in Germany or France. In any case, the PSIUP split into two formations in January 1947. The pro-Communist wing of the party took the name of "Italian Socialist Party" (PSI) and lined up gradually with the positions of the Italian Communist Party (PCI), especially in international politics. Excluded from COMISCO after its support of the Czech coup, the PSI found itself isolated internationally and developed an uncompromising opposition to all stages of European integration until the Treaties of Rome. This opposition was not based on a strategy to obtain a revision of the international status of Italy as it was for the SPD. They used at least four arguments to justify their position, which was basically the one of the Soviets. First, the Schuman Plan and the Pleven Plan were, above all, the illustration of American interference in Europe, a "crusade tool against the other half of Europe"[41]: "the whole architecture of European initiatives is based on the following assumption: the United States – as part of their usual imperialistic policy [...] – concentrate much of their efforts on Western Europe in order to transform it in a profitable appendage to the expansion of its own [...] economy, and to transform it [...] in an advanced base for the military assault against USSR and People's Democracies."[42] In that sense, the "Little Europe" had "the same roots as the Europe of Hitler, with the contribution, that time, of the American capital."[43] Second, the ECSC and the ECD would have ensured French–German, even German hegemony in Western Europe; they established a kind of French–German dictatorship, with American's patronage, against the USSR.[44] Third, they were a way to give the full possession of their faculties back to Germans, and so they favoured a resurgence of German militarism. In the minds of Italian Socialists of the PSI, especially after the EDC proposal, West Germany remained trapped by its old demons, especially if compared with East Germany, and "did not demonstrate to the world, […] that it has become a democratic country, a country that got out from the ominous influences that twice inspired the executioner of European youth."[45] Last, but not least, in the interpretation of the leaders of the PSI, the ECSC and EDC will perpetuate the division of Germany, and thus the division of the world, and as such could not serve peace. In fact, for the PSI, the German question was a priority, but their proposal was the Soviet solution: a neutralized and united Germany in Europe guaranteed by a renewed American–Soviet agreement: "Two solutions are today taken into consideration […]: the American one […] that aims to the signature of contracts with the FRG, i.e. a separate peace with Western Germany and its integration in a European army and, indirectly, in the Atlantic Pact. The other solution, the Soviet one […] aims to rebuild a united Germany, independent and apart from any military alliance, with an army limited to the strict exigencies of its own defence." The Soviet solution "moves from the idea of a possible pacific coexistence between the two regimes […], subject to everybody who effectively wants peace and who wants to create its international conditions, and above all, in Europe, a Germany apart from the blocks, European centre of international equilibrium and equidistance rather than outpost of a military alliance."[46] Whereas from the mid-1950s the PSI tried to distance itself from the PCI—in a context of relaxation in international relations—and thanks to the focus on economic issues, it started to change very gradually its mind about Europe (much less on the German question). It voted in favour of Euratom and abstained on the European Economic Community (EEC). However, it remained critical of these initiatives, still denouncing their limitation to Western Europe, their technocratic character, their conservative orientation, the German economic supremacy. Nevertheless, it was possible—even necessary—to act within the institutions to try to change them.[47] The PSI also tried to get back in touch with West European Socialists, especially with the Labour Party but also the SPD, with whom Riccardo Lombardi— in charge of the international office of the PSI since January 1959—wanted to have some exchanges of opinions about the European Common Market. These contacts were not easy because the SPD's chosen intermediary was the Italian Social Democratic Party (PSDI) and because the SPD was critical about the PSI's pro-Soviet orientations and, especially, about the PSI's position on German reunification. These contacts remained complicated also because of the very negative reception of the Bad Godesberg's program within the PSI.[48]

The position of the Italian Social Democrats is more interesting for comparison. In fact, unlike their former companions, they attached great importance to Europe. Since the treaty of Peace of 1947, they insisted on the necessity of a quick reinstatement of Germany and, within the Socialist international movement, a quick reinstatement of the SPD.[49] They always had the sensation of a community of destiny for European people and especially for the Italians and Germans as testified by the comments of the Zurich conference where the PSI—which was still at this time the Italian representative at the conference—voted against the reinstatement of Germany as a full member: "The German problem is the centre of the European problem [...], and this is even more evident from the Italian point of view [...] The great new fact is the possibility to build Europe, and this possibility has at its heart, the economic and moral recovery of the Germans."[50] Contrary to the PSI, who saw the European integration as an obstacle to the resolution of the German question, the Social Democrats considered it as its solution: "The scheme of the European army must serve, for want of resolution of the German question, to make the solution easier, integrating the forces of the new German democracy [...] for the common defence and for the defence of Germany itself [...], of whom we all recognize the danger if it rearms itself on national and nationalistic basis."[51] The split of the PSIUP in January 1947 had been consummated on the question of the relationship with the Communists. In any case, although they were very heterogeneous amongst themselves, the two tendencies that met within the Socialist Party of Italian Workers (PSLI) also shared the deep aspiration to create a Federal European Union. "Critica sociale" was the expression of a democratic and humanist socialism, heir to Turati, and joined the PSLI because of its "right-wing" criticism of the alliance with the Communists. The members of "Critica sociale" aspired to the construction of a Federal and "Third Force" Europe to ensure a lasting peace by international agreements and the centre of a democratic and progressive project. "Iniziativa socialista" was made up of young people who had grown up under fascism and who were more ideological and inflexible than the others. They joined the PSLI because of a "left-wing" criticism of the alliance with the communists. They aspired to a Federal Europe but rather as the result of a revolutionary and autonomous action of the masses, to prevent war and to build a new world. Therefore, at the time of the split, the majority of the supporters of Europe in the PSIUP joined the PSLI, the European sensibility of which was much more assertive than that of the SFIO, as shown by the lively debates accompanying the ratification of the accession of Italy to NATO. The PSLI gradually abandoned the prospect of a "Third Force" Europe, as did the SFIO, but it paid dearly with various splits and reconstructions. In 1949, the left wing of the PSLI—which disagreed with the "atlanticist" choice of its leadership—the "autonomists" of the PSI (i.e. the members who were against the close alliance with the PCI but who refused to join the PSLI in 1947) and the Union of Independent Socialists, created in February 1948 by Ignazio Silone merged into the Unit Socialist Party (PSU). Finally, the PSLI and the PSU merged into the PSDI in 1951–1952.[52] The position of the Italian Social Democrats on European integration was more akin to that of the SFIO rather than to that of the SPD in the late 1940s and early 1950s. They voted in favour of all the first stages of European integration. Nevertheless, the European perspective of the PSLI, the PSU and then the PSDI differed from that of the SFIO on a fundamental point: the perception of a general decline of Europe that made the German problem a simple aspect of the European view of the Italian Social Democrats. The European integration was not primarily a way to control Germany but rather a means for Italy—and West Germany—to reintegrate into the international context and to be considered a full partner to the other countries of Western Europe. Therefore, the EDC was an instrument for preventing an "autonomous" German rearmament, but it was primarily meant to give Europe a strong political impetus through the establishment of a European Political Community (EPC) that would allow it "to solve the problems of Europe."[53] The distance from the SFIO is clear on this point because the SFIO opposed the EPC. The absence of the British did not prevent most French Socialists from establishing specialized communities based on the example of the ECSC. However, it made the construction of a political community more difficult because this would have definitely sanctioned the division of Western Europe and left France in a head-to-head with Germany. This could also explain why the PSDI opposed the Elysée Treaty. In line with the positions of the socialist parties in the European Community, the Elysée Treaty was in contradiction with their conception of Europe. It also threatened the international assertion of Italy.[54] Last, as was the case for France, it is difficult to find a generational effect in the attitude of Italian socialism as a whole towards Europe and the "reconciliation" if one considers its divisions. In fact, except for "Iniziativa Socialista"—the members of which belonged quite clearly to the same generation but who represented just a marginal part of Italian socialism—the experiences of the inter-war period and of the war did not determine a common mobilization in favour of Europe and reconciliation. These resulted more from ideological and strategic choices than from generational effects, considering both from the point of view of the demography as well as past experiences or memory. At most, we can observe that the transfer of interest from issues of defence to those of economics and society, as well as the evolution of internal politics, favoured a larger consensus of Italian socialism towards Europe.

CONSTRAINING POLITICAL SYSTEMS

The international status of the various countries in the aftermath of the war determined different priorities. Nevertheless, conflicting interests or different points of view could bring these parties to converged solutions, such as European integration. This is basically the bet made by the fathers of Europe. It is also why the PSDI and the SFIO could appear as the German, Italian or French Christian Democrats allies. In addition, the agreement of 1954–1955, the settlement of the Saar and the focus on economic integration surely made the dialogue easier. Indeed, their positions were still partly different, as the vote of the Elysée Treaty highlights, and refer to a final explanatory variable: the place of these parties in their different political systems and the strategies they planned.

All the parties we considered herein aspired to govern after the war. They all focused on national interest and used a "nationalist" discourse. This "nationalist" fervour was stronger in Germany and in Italy because they had a more stringent political necessity than France. The Italian Socialists intended to delegitimize the Monarchy, which—together with the bourgeoisie and without or against the people—had made the Risorgimento and promoted Fascism. Liberation was an opportunity they had never really had to carry out given the unity of their nation; hence, the image of Liberation as a "Second Risorgimento", the one the popular masses brought to salvation by the PSIUP.[55] The German Social Democrats had another necessity: They intended to learn from their first experience of power and erase the image of the "stateless" party, which had stuck with them since the time of Weimar. Excluded, like the Italian Socialists, from the process of national unification, they had a first opportunity to embody the nation after the First World War. That is why, because of his quality as an opponent and "martyr" of the Nazis—and by virtue of an unsuspected democratic faith—Schumacher exalted the nation in his speeches at the risk of shocking his interlocutors.[56] The SFIO situation is once again different because of the terms of the political transition. If in 1945 the French Socialists insisted less than the SPD or the PSIUP on the national character of their struggle, it is because—on one hand—their existence and their place in the political system was less questioned and—in contrast on the other hand—the unity of the nation was embodied by de Gaulle and the Socialists having formed a de facto alliance with the General in 1943, a "honeymoon" that came to an end in 1945.[57]

It must be noted, however, that in the socialist's mind, this use of a "nationalistic" discourse did not conflict with their internationalist ideals: If the nations had become socialist—which means democratic—why, indeed, should they not agree at an international level? In fact, all had the feeling that the time had come for Socialism in Europe as the victory of the Labour Party in England in 1945 seemed to confirm. However, the prospect of a socialist victory across Europe disappeared, and the socialist parties we considered either never governed alone or were opposition parties. In addition, European integration became, since its first steps, a strong element of legitimization, and a positive attitude towards it was a requirement for who wanted to govern.

Thus, although it proposed solutions different from those of the government, the SFIO eventually ratified the German policy by France (including the Saar). In addition, the acceptance, albeit reluctant, of Little Europe was also partly the result of government choices made by the SFIO. We can also assume that questions of strategy played an important role during the episode of the EDC, i.e. at a time when the SFIO sought out and hesitated between a kind of new version of The Third force and a left-oriented alternative strategy. In any case, the weight of domestic issues became even clearer after de Gaulle's return to power. Indeed, the French Socialists vehemently opposed the Gaullist version of Franco–German reconciliation for questions, which as we have seen, were in part ideological: the opposition of two very different conceptions of European integration. Nevertheless, it should be noted that in 1959, but even more in 1962, Europe was one of the main arguments of the Socialists against de Gaulle, an argument that brought together the political parties of the Fourth Republic, which were now openly hostile to de Gaulle's leadership. When, during the ratification of the Elysée treaty, they were accused of being less accommodating than the German Social Democrats, French Socialists argued that the addition of a preamble on the model of that of the

Bundestag—obviously inconceivable to the French government—would have allowed the Socialists to ratify the treaty.[58]

In the aftermath of the war, the SPD—in the prospect of free elections and having in mind the memory of Weimar—considered the territorial integrity of Germany, national unity and equality of rights the cardinal points of its foreign policy. It used them as the main theme of the 1949 campaign and then used them again in the controversy with the government. Its opposition party's status strengthened its ideological rigidity and intransigence, which was fed by the attitude of France, especially regarding the Saar and the Ruhr. From the mid-1950s, after the settlement of the Saar issue and the recovery of sovereignty, the line of the SPD gradually changed, as was evidenced in particular by the acceptance of the Treaties of Rome and finally by the ratification of the Elysée Treaty. As for the PSI, this evolution was also the result of electoral considerations. As shown, in part, by the result of the elections of 1953, the uncompromising position of the late 1940s and early 1950s had not yielded good results, and the deputies were pressing to change the line of the party and adapt it to the evolution of the public opinion, especially that of the young, which was increasingly more attracted to Europe. Some of the main future specialists of international issues within the party—such as Herbert Wehner, Fritz Erler and Karl Mommer—began to consider the advantages of Europe in terms of consensus. They belonged to another demographic generation and were more pragmatic than Schumacher; they also had experience within the European structures and networks. In addition, Erich Ollenhauer, the new leader of the party after Schumacher's death, was in less of a position to resist to these pressures than his predecessor. Finally, trade unions, who had voted in favour of ECSC, were also lobbying the party leaders to adopt a more positive attitude towards the economic integration of Europe.[59] The ratification of the Elysée Treaty crowned the work done by the Social Democrats in the late 1950s and early 1960s to revise their doctrine and to give credibility to a government program. More than Bad Godesberg, the speech of Wehner in the Bundestag on 30 June 1960—by which the SPD officially recognized the integration of the FRG into NATO as well as the commitments made in the context of Western Europe—marked a turning point and illustrated the willingness of the party to walk out of its political isolation for the first time since 1949. After obtaining the addition of the preamble, it was difficult and politically absurd for the SPD not to ratify the Elysée Treaty.

238 C. VODOVAR

In Italy, the political system's balance and the game of political alliances were even more important than in France or Germany for understanding the positioning of the various parties because of the traditional use of international policy issues for the purpose of internal politics.[60] As part of the government area, the PSLI, and then the PSDI, supported the policy of its allies and considered the entire European construction not only a way for Italy to assert itself on an international level but also a condition of membership in the Western camp and a way to stabilise internal politics. The PSI, which joined the opposition in 1947 in close alliance with the communists and took on a position of supposed neutrality (in reality pro-Soviet), criticized both Europe as a product of American imperialism, supported by the Christian Democrats and the Vatican, and the aspirations to a Europe "Third Force," which had once been supported by the Social Democrats. The turning point of 1955, in which the PSI accepted the Atlantic Pact and started to pay more attention to European integration, was primarily the result of a change in domestic political strategy, namely, the attempt—in a context of relaxation in international relations—to split from the PCI and to approach the government. The vote in favour of Euratom and the abstention regarding the EEC was also, and especially, a choice of political strategy. As for German Social Democrats, the trade unions were pressing to adopt a positive attitude towards Europe. As in Germany, the acceptation of European integration was a source of legitimation. If the opposition of the PSI to the Elysée Treaty kept ideological tones (among other things, the Franco–German axis was seen as the culmination of a return of reaction in Europe), however, their arguments tended to echo those of the PSDI, i.e. a different vision of Europe and the refusal of a French–German hegemony on Europe that would marginalise Italy.

Conclusion

The SPD, the SFIO and, to a lesser extent because they felt less directly concerned, the PSIUP (and its various derivatives, with the exception of the PSI in its pro-Soviet phase) repeatedly stressed, since 1945, their commitment to the French–German reconciliation as the basis for a pacified European space. However, it had been necessary to wait for the Elysée Treaty to see all express a common position of principle[61] (but still negative against the Gaullists' projects) and for reasons that are still sometimes different.

In fact, if the French-German reconciliation and its various concrete steps were all (usually) missed occasions to let European socialism speak with one voice, it was in part because they had to consider not only contentious memories, but also contentious national interests at a time when they were perfecting integration into their respective political systems and claimed to rule the destinies of their country.

Scholars have already underlined the fact that the Second World War, probably because of the diversity of the experiences, did not really represent a turning point as far as "political" generations are concerned. At the same time, however—and this was the hypothesis of this chapter—the common desire to build a peaceful and reconciled world based on the memory of the past, as well as the membership of common transnational institutions, could have given way to a common mobilization in favour of European integration. However, it did not despite the joint statements of 1963 recalled in the introduction. After 1955, the changes were more the results of a new general context (equal partners, predominance of economic and social issues, new internal strategy) than the result of a generational turnover, except in the German situation, in which the strong leadership of Schumacher after the war gave more sense to this variable. This chapter can definitively confirm that the past experiences (authoritarian/totalitarian regime and the war) did not form, in the first decades after the war, a shared political culture able to mobilize socialist parties to share a common perspective as far as Europe was concerned.

These conclusions bring us to a last methodological consideration concerning political generation. As said before, the use of the concept of "generation", especially in political history, is very fluid. It appears even more fluid as far as more countries are concerned. In fact, at least for the years taken into consideration, a "generational effect" may be found on very limited groups of people or, indeed, individuals. In contrast, the comparison highlights the fact that the renewal of the elite, from a demographic point of view, is different, thus making a transnational approach quite complicated. In contrast, the comparison highlights that the national context was still, in 1945, an important element in forging political culture.

NOTES

1. See Soutou, Georges-Henri. *L'Alliance incertaine. Les rapports politico-stratégiques franco-allemands.* Paris: Fayard, 1996; Schoenborn, Benedikt. *La Mésentente apprivoisée. De Gaulle et les Allemands, 1963–1969.* Paris: PUF, 2007; Defrance, Corine/Pfeil, Ulrich, ed. *La France, l'Allemagne et le Traité de l'Elysée, 1963–2013.* Paris: CNRS, 2012; Id. *Entre Guerre*

240   C. VODOVAR

Froide et intégration européenne: reconstruction et rapprochement, 1945–1963. Villeneuve d'Ascq: Presses Universitaires du Septentrion, 2012; Martens, Stephan/Thorel, Julien, ed. *Les Relations franco-allemandes: bilan et perspectives.* Villeneuve d'Ascq: Presses Universitaires du Septentrion, 2012; Ziebura, Gilbert. *Les Relations franco-allemandes dans une Europe divisée: mythes et réalités.* Pessac: Presses Universitaires de Bordeaux, 2012; Delori, Mathias. *La Réconciliation franco-allemande par la jeunesse.* Brussels: P. Lang, 2016.

2. "Déclaration commune SPD-SFIO," in Fondation Jean Jaurès (FJJ), Fonds Pontillon (FP), 8 FP7/151, «position du SPD sur le Traité de Paris», ed. in *Le Populaire*, 03.07.1962.

3. "Les partis socialistes européens de la Communauté européenne prennent position sur le traité franco-allemand." *Courrier socialiste européen* 14.03.1963, FJJ, FP, 8 FP7/151.

4. The BLPSCE is made up of the parties from the member countries of the Community. As for the resolutions of the Socialist International (SI), they all adopted a very general tone on European integration. On the BLPSCE, see Devin, Guillaume. "L'Union des partis socialistes de la Communauté européenne. Le socialisme communautaire en quête d'identité." in *AA. VV. I Socialisti e l'Europa.* Milan: Franco Angeli, 1989, 265–290; about the divisions of international Socialism, see id. *L'Internationale socialiste. Histoire et sociologie du socialisme international, 1945–1990.* Paris: PFNSP, 1993, 250–280.

5. See *Les partis socialistes européens.* See also the resolution of the 54th National Congress of the SFIO (June 1963): "In 1945, while General de Gaulle thought that the dismemberment of Germany and the incorporation of the Saarland into France was the best formula on which the relationships between the two countries must be based, the Socialist party approved alone [...] the necessity to work towards a French-German rapprochement, that excluded any will of revenge and that was based on friendship and trust." *Bulletin Intérieur (BI)* 129 (1963). See also the speech of Erich Ollenhauer at the Bundestag, 07.02.1963, in which he alluded to "the efforts of the German Social Democracy to realize a French-German understanding long before the First World War."

6. *Les Partis socialistes européens*, 2.

7. Only 4 of more than 3000 representatives approved the amendment, see *BI*, 16.

8. About the concept of political generation, see Whittier, Nancy. "Political Generations, Micro-Cohorts and the Transformation of Social Movements." *American Sociological Review* 62 (1997), 760–778; Sirinelli, Jean-François. "Génération et histoire politique." *Vingtième Siècle* 22 (1989), 67–80; Mannheim, Karl. *Le Problème des générations.* Paris: Nathan, 1990.

9. After the split of the Italian Socialist Party of Proletarian Unity (PSIUP) in January 1947, Italian Socialism was mainly represented by the Socialist Party of Italian Workers (PSLI), the Italian Socialist Party (PSI) and, since May 1949, the Unit Socialist Party (PSU). In 1951/1952, the PSLI and the PSU merged into the Italian Social Democrat Party (PSDI). Consequently, Italian socialism was represented by the PSDI and the PSI until the second half of the 1960s.

10. See a definition of "political families" in Rémond, René. "Conclusions." In *Les Familles politiques en Europe Occidentale au XIXe siècle*. Rome: EFR, 1997. See also Orlow, Dietrich. *Common Destiny*. New York: Berghahn Books, 2000.

11. While the SPD was reinstated late, in November 1947, the PSI was relegated, in March 1948, to the rank of observer member of the Comisco, then expelled in May 1949. Since 1948, Italian socialism was represented by the Social Democrats, first the PSLI and the PSU, and then the PSDI. The PSI would join the SI again in 1966 after reunification with the PSDI. See Colarizi, Simona. "I socialisti italiani e l'Internazionale socialista, 1947–1958." *Mondo Contemporaneo* 2 (2005); Steininger, Rolf. "L'Internazionale socialista e la SPD dopo la seconda guerra mondiale." in AA.VV., *I socialisti e l'Europa*. Milan: Franco Angeli, 1988; Devin, *L'Internationale socialiste*.

12. "Le socialisme et l'Allemagne." *Le Populaire*, 10.10.1944. On the PSIUP, see Sacerdote, Gustavo. "L'altra Germania." *Avanti!*, 31.07.1945.

13. Blum, Léon. *A l'échelle Humaine*. Paris: Gallimard, 1945, 176; and "Le problème allemand." *Le Populaire,* July 1943. See also Loth, Wilfried. "Les projets de politique extérieure de la résistance socialiste en France." *Revue d'histoire moderne et contemporaine* 1954, 544–569.

14. It is not a coincidence that these parties, especially the SPD and the SFIO, particularly insisted on their internal efforts of purging, see the speech of Schumacher at the conference of Zurich in June 1947 (minutes of the conference, June 6–7, 1947, International Institute of Social History, Amsterdam); see also Castagnez, Noëlline/Morin, Gilles. "Le parti issu de la résistance." In AA.VV., *Le Parti socialiste entre résistance et république*. Paris: Publications de la Sorbonne, 2000, 37–59.

15. See the speech of Kurt Schumacher at the conference of Zurich, *cit.*

16. According to Pietro Nenni, Italy was no more than a "Mediterranean appendix of Hitlerian Germany," "Il nefasto 9 settembre" *Avanti!* 17.06.1944; Umberto Calosso refers to the "Hitlerian war," «Il segreto dell'Unità» *Avanti!* 21.11.1944. See also Vodovar, Christine. "La Resistenza nel dibattito politico in Francia e in Italia: il caso dei socialisti (1944–1948)." In Craveri, Piero/Quagliariello, Gaetano, eds. *La Seconda Guerra Mondiale e la sua memoria*. Soveria Mannelli: Rubbettino, 2006, 491–528.

242   C. VODOVAR

17. See Blum, *A l'Echelle humaine*, 93.
18. Regarding the relations between the SPD and the SFIO after 1945 see Dohrmann, Nicolas. *Les relations entre la SFIO et le SPD dans l'immédiat après guerre, 1945–1953.* Thèse de doctorat, Ecole Nationale des Chartes, Paris, 2003; Bombois, Sophie. *La SFIO et l'Allemagne, mémoire de maitrise.* Université de Paris 1 1991; Cahn, Jean-Paul. *Le Parti social-démocrate allemand et la fin de la Quatrième République française, 1954–1958.* Bern: P. Lang, 1996.
19. Auriol, Vincent. *Hier ... Demain.* Paris: Charlot, 1945, 206.
20. *Le Populaire*, 24.11.1944. See also Auriol, Vincent. *Journal du Septennat.* Paris: Taillandier, 2003.
21. See the minutes of the Directive Committee, 04.10.1950, Office Universitaire de Recherche Socialiste (OURS), Paris. Concerning Mollet's attitude towards Germany, see Guillaume, Sylvie. "Guy Mollet et l'Allemagne." In AA.VV., *Guy Mollet, un camarade en république.* Lille: PUL, 1987.
22. See Morin, Gilles. "Les oppositions socialistes à la CED: les acteurs du débat." *Les cahiers IRICE* 4 (2009). On SFIO and the EDC Treaty, see also Loth, Wilfried. "The French Socialist Party 1947–1954." In Griffith, Richard T., ed. *Socialists Parties and the Question of Europe in the 1950's.* Leiden: E.J. Brill, 1993, 25–42.
23. See Bossuat, Gérard. "La campagne de Daniel Mayer contre la CED." *Matériaux pour l'histoire de notre temps* 50–52 (1998), 33–45; Castagnez, Noëlline. *Socialistes en République. Les parlementaires SFIO de la IVe République.* Rennes: PUR, 2004, 293–299; Lafon, François. *Guy Mollet.* Paris: Fayard, 2006, 417–429; Quilliot, Roger. *La SFIO et l'exercice du pouvoir.* Paris: Fayard, 1972.
24. See Castagnez, *Socialistes en République*, 293–299. See also Bergounioux, Alain. "Générations socialistes?" *Vingtième siècle* 22 (1989), 93–102.
25. For example, Rudolf Hilferding, Johanna Kirchner and Rudolf Breitscheid, that had been handed over to the Gestapo in February 1941. See Cahn, *Le Parti social-démocrate*, 18 f.; see also Dorhmann, *Les relations entre la SFIO et le SPD.*
26. See the article by Karl Mommer in *Neuer Vorwärts*, 08.02.1952, quoted in Cahn, *Le Parti social-démocrate*, 19.
27. See Paterson, William E. *The SPD and European Integration.* Farnborough: Saxon House, 1974, 65 f.
28. See the report by Daniel Mayer, October 1945.
29. Regarding the importance of these elements on the Italian and German governments, see Rusconi, Gian Enrico. *Germania Italia Europa. Dallo stato di potenza alla "potenza civile."* Bologna: Il Mulino, 2003, 215–239.

30. See *Problèmes d'aujourd'hui: programme d'action du Parti socialiste, 1946*. Paris: Editions de la liberté, 1946, 66–72; "Programme d'action adopté par le Conseil national du PS-SFIO." *Le Populaire*, 08.12.1946, 4. These programs included, among other things, the establishment of a federal state, measures of socialization, decartelization and land reform, correctional work. However, the SFIO evolved and increasingly held account of SPD needs and interests, see on this Dohrmann, *Les relations entre la SFIO et le SPD*.
31. "Le socialisme et l'Allemagne." Declaration by Daniel Mayer at BBC, *Le Populaire*, 10.10.1944.
32. See Blum, Léon. "Le problème allemand." *Le Populaire*, 24.07.1947; Mollet, Guy. "Une seule issue: L'Internationale." *Le Populaire*, 18.09.1947.
33. See Directive Committee, 12.12.1951 and 07.05.1952; and the set of articles in *Le Populaire*, entitled "L'Europe unie," December 1952.
34. See, on this Devin, *L'Internationale socialiste*; Cruciani, Sante. *L'Europa delle sinistre. La nascita del Mercato commune attraverso I casi francese e italiano, 1955–1957*. Rome: Carocci, 2007.
35. See Schmid, Carlo. "Germany and Europe. The German Social Democratic Program." *Foreign Affairs* 30: 1/4 (1951/1952), 531–544.
36. See Cahn, Jean-Paul. "Un problème bilatéral aux ramifications européennes: la question sarroise (1949–1956)." In Knopper, Françoise/Ruiz, Alain, eds. *Politique européenne et question allemande depuis la paix de Westphalie*. Toulouse: PUM, 1999, 137–162.
37. See Schmid, *Germany and Europe*; Cahn, Jean-Paul. "Le Parti social-démocrate allemand et l'idée européenne, du congrès de Heidelberg à la chute du gouvernement Helmut Schmidt." In AA.VV., *La République Fédérale d'Allemagne et la construction de l'Europe*. Paris: Éditions du Temps, 2000, 157–177; Id. *Le Parti social-démocrate allemand*, 47–73; Guillaume, Sylvie. "L'idée européenne chez les sociaux-démocrates allemands de 1945 aux années soixante-dix." In Knopper/Ruiz, eds. *Politique européenne*; Gougeon, Jean-Pierre. *La Social-démocratie allemande, 1830–1996*. Paris: Aubier, 1996, 289–304.
38. The three men belonged to the same demographic generation as they all had experiences from the First World War. Löbe (1875–1967) and Reuter (1889–1953) had been SPD deputies before 1933 and were then deported. Löbe then decided to remain in Germany and had contact with the resistance whereas Reuter went into exile in Turkey.
39. See Paterson, *SPD and European Integration*.
40. Quoted in Cahn, *Le Parti social-démocrate allemand et l'idée européenne*.
41. See the speech by Lelio Basso at the National Assembly, 13.12.1954, 15011.

244 C. VODOVAR

42. See *Propaganda socialista*, 15.05.1953. Regarding the PSI and Europe, see Scirocco, Giovanni. *Politique d'abord. Il Psi, la guerra fredda e la politica internazionale (1948–1957)*. Milan: Unicopli, 2010; Di Nolfo, Ennio. "The Italian Socialists." In Griffith, ed. *Socialists Parties*; Picinini, Iacopo. "L'opposizione socialista alla Comunità europea di difesa (1950–1952)." *Ricerche storiche* 1 (2006); Vodovar, Christine. "The impossible Third force. Italian and French socialism and Europe, 1943–1963." In AA.VV., *European Parties and the European Integration Process, 1945–1992*. Brussels: P. Lang, 2015, 45–62.

43. See the speech by Lelio Basso, *op. cit.*, 15011. See also Riccardo Lombardi who compared the Bonn Treaty to the Monaco Agreements, 12.06.1952, 38818; see also Mario Marino Guadalupi, 14.12.1954, 15146–15148

44. See the speeches at the National Assembly by Riccardo Lombardi (12.06.1952, 38809–38820), Amerigo Bottai (16.06.1952, 38848), Lelio Basso (13.12.1954, 15022) and Riccardo Lombardi (09.10.1963, 2534).

45. See Fenoaltea, Giorgio. "Perché Adenauer è venuto a Roma." *Mondo Operaio*, 03.04.1954; see also Decleva, Enrico. *La politica estera: dal frontismo alla riscoperta dell'Europa*. In AA.VV., *Storia del PSI*, vol. III. Padua: Marsilio, 1980, 29; Scirocco, *Politique d'abord*, 116–118.

46. See Vecchietti, Tullio. "Germania al bivio." *Mondo Operaio*, 17.05.1952.

47. See Scirocco, *Politique d'abord*, 254–261; Felsini, Daniela. "1943–1957, Il PSI e l'integrazione europea." *Anali dell'Istituto Ugo La Malfa* 2 (1987).

48. See Nencioni, Tommaso. "Tra neutralismo e atlantismo. La politica internazionale del Partito socialista italiano 1956–1966." *Italia contemporanea* 260 (2010), 444 f. and 465.

49. Treves, Paolo. "Ritorno all'Internazionale." *L'Umanità*, 19.01.1947; Cialdea, Basilio. "Una soluzione socialista per la Germania." *L'Umanità*, 22.04.1947.

50. "Compagni tedeschi." *L'Umanità*, 06.07.1947.

51. See the speech by Paolo Treves at the National Assembly, 05.10.1951, 31043.

52. Concerning the western choice of the PSLI, see De Felice, Alessandro. *La socialdemocrazia e la scelta occidentale dell'Italia*. Catania: Boemi, 1999.

53. See Zagari, Mario. "Il socialismo italiano e l'europeismo. Testimonianza." In AA.VV., *I socialisti e l'Europa*. Milan: Franco Angeli, 1988.

54. See Giuseppe Saragat, speech of 23.02.1963, ed. in BLPSCE, *Document d'information*, PS/CE/13/63, in FJJ, FP, 8FP7/151.

55. See Vodovar, *La Resistenza nel dibattito politico*.

56. See Edinger, Lewis J. *Kurt Schumacher: A Study in Personality and Political Behaviour*. Stanford: Stanford UP, 1965; Vardys, Vytas Stanley. "Germany's Postwar Socialism: Nationalism and Kurt Schumacher, 1945–1952." *Review of Politics* 27: 2 (1965).

EUROPEAN SOCIALISM AND THE FRENCH–GERMAN RECONCILIATION   245

57. Regarding the relations between the socialists and de Gaulle, see Crémieux-Brilhac, Jean-Louis. "Les combattants socialistes de la France Libre." In Guidoni, Pierre/Verdier, Robert, eds. *Les Socialistes en résistance, 1940–1944.* Paris: Seli Arslan, 1999, 77; Id. *La France Libre.* Paris, Gallimard, 1996; Rousselier, Nicolas. "L'idée de la France selon les socialistes (été 1944-janvier 1946)." In AA.VV., *Le Parti socialiste entre résistance et république,* 61–74.

58. See the resolution of the 54th National Congress (June 1963); see also "note à Guy Mollet: attitude de la SPD vis à vis du traité franco-allemand." In FJJ, FP, 8 FP7/151.

59. See Paterson, *The SPD and European Integration;* D'Ottavio, Gabriele/Bernardini, Giovanni. "SPD and European integration. From scepticism to pragmatism, from pragmatism to leadership, 1949–1979." In AA.VV., *European Parties,* 29–44.

60. See on this point Scirocco, *Politique d'abord,* 13–24.

61. The PSI was not yet a member of the BLPSCE, but it adopted the same position.

CHAPTER 11

Conclusions: Five Dimensions of Generation Around 1945

Jens Späth

In the introduction, we stressed the ubiquity of the term "generation" on one hand and the fluidity and vagueness of the analytical concept on the other. There is a disproportionate gap between popular self-ascriptions in all modern societies and precise methodological instruments in science. Are we really talking about the same thing when we use the term "generation"? We most certainly are not. To contribute to a profound understanding of generational studies, all articles presented in this volume have tried to address generational issues from an international and transnational perspective. They have focused on a specific moment in time, i.e. the immediate period after the Second World War in Western Europe, Western Germany, Italy and France in particular. To summarize some important results of these contributions, I suggest grouping them into five central dimensions of generation around 1945.

J. Späth (✉)
Universität des Saarlandes, Saarbrücken, Germany

© The Author(s) 2018   247
J. Späth (ed.), *Does Generation Matter? Progressive Democratic Cultures in Western Europe, 1945–1960*, Palgrave Studies in the History of Social Movements, https://doi.org/10.1007/978-3-319-77422-0_11

Generation as an Open Question

First, Karl Mannheim's distinction between generational location and generational cohesion/generational unity still represents a sound starting point for reflections on generational issues. Having the same age and operating as age-specific action entities does not automatically mean that certain age cohorts belonged to a particular generation. Moreover, conflicts are not always directed against the fathers either, which means that youth is not an exclusive characteristic of a generation. Before defining themselves as such, people usually need a common experience background, a common cultural context, a common perception of events as well as a chronological contemporaneity that shapes their attitudes, thoughts and actions. Only if they show a generational consciousness and respond uniformly to events and living conditions might we talk about generational units that go beyond a mere generational connectedness.[1] These situations change, and therefore we have several different political generations in the age of extremes marked by key reference events such as both World Wars or Fascism and National Socialism. As Andreas Wirsching suggests, generations in the twentieth century became less ideologically and politically dominated after 1945 and were characterized rather by tendencies of post-heroism on one hand and mass-culture, consumerism and leisure on the other. Later, a younger generation criticized the centralized mass democracies.

The importance of bringing together different layers of time, i.e. the past and the future, has been elaborated in numerous studies since Reinhart Koselleck's reflections on experience and expectation.[2] Some of the chapters presented in this volume have emphasized that generations were both communalities of experience and of expectation (Brian Shaev, Jens Späth). Even if generations as mental units are ambivalent, age and demography continue to matter thus making political generations "chronologically elastic."[3] Others have stressed the *longue durée* and emphasized that political cultures and specific interpretations of the past were more significant for generational issues than for simple age-cohorts (Maurizio Cau, Gabriele D'Ottavio). Although Gabriele D'Ottavio identifies generation as an actual driving force of scientific progress in political sciences in Germany and Italy after 1945, he emphasizes the specific cultural traditions reaching back to Weimar and clarifies that this progress cannot be explained just in terms of Westernization and Americanization.

As applies to history in general, there were winning and losing generations. Although we probably agree that the 68ers must be considered

CONCLUSIONS: FIVE DIMENSIONS OF GENERATION AROUND 1945   249

winners in history, there were people in the immediate post-war period that might be characterized as a "lost generation." Christian Blasberg suggests that the Italian liberal, Nicolò Carandini, was such an individual. Although he showed responsibility and a willingness to contribute to democratic reconstruction, he was not able to take the leading position within the liberal party after 1945. He described himself as part of a "mature and experienced generation" arguing for institutional reforms without breaking completely with the liberal tradition because liberalism had a very positive assessment in Italy before the rise of Fascism. However, age 50 years and thus already a "senior" among the young liberal generation, the younger party members considered him to be a part of the inflexible political system of Cavour and therefore not a trustworthy representative of liberty and justice in the fight against conservative monarchists.

THE INITIALIZING EVENTS: THE WORLD WARS

As we saw in the introduction, generations are usually formed around disruptive events: a crisis, a natural catastrophe or a war. Throughout the chapters presented in this volume, both World Wars have served for establishing a certain order of human groupings. Scholars of various disciplines agree that the First World War marked a watershed in the twentieth century. Jens Späth, in his contribution, asked if the First World War created two new generations: an older one born in the last third of the nineteenth century with personal active fighting experiences and a younger one born after 1900 without such experiences. In his case study, he explored to what extent one can apply the generational concept as a collective experience community to the Bavarian social democrat Wilhelm Hoegner as representative of the older generation and to the Italian socialist Lelio Basso as representative of the younger generation.

This chapter, among others, has raised the question of whether 1945 represented a break or a continuity in generational terms. What references did those scholars have who had studied during Fascism and National Socialism and then took leading positions in the post-war societies? Applying it to the legal and political sciences in Italy and West Germany, Maurizio Cau and Gabriele D'Ottavio came to rather differentiated conclusions. As Cau states for the legal sciences, the German debate was dominated by different doctrinal and cultural options and less by opposing generational blocs. In Italy, however, the generational factor was of importance. There it was the reason for and the effect of accelerated change, of

250   J. SPÄTH

common values and a generational perspective, but not the expression of homogeneous positions. In Germany, there was no generational break among legal scientists by 1945, whereas in Italy an antagonism of two generational units characterized the debate on the most recent past, in particular until the Italian Constitution came into effect in 1948. As for the political sciences, it was essential in both Germany and Italy to help these losers of the Second World War to reverse their backwardness regarding state sciences. Especially in Italy, where the first generation of political scientists failed to resist the ideologization of Fascism, this became a political, cultural and generational value in itself. Although the second generation of political scientists in Italy built on their *resistenza* experience and developed a rather positivistic approach after 1945, their German colleagues struggled with their status as remigrants from exile and primarily introduced US American methods of thinking (D'Ottavio).

THE CONTENT: DEMOCRACY

According to Andreas Wirsching, the older generation with roots in the nineteenth century played a crucial role in the democratic reconstruction after the Second World War. Against the background of the age of totalitarianism, they were able to revive older political traditions and give them a new shape after 1945. In contrast to the generation born around 1900, they were significantly less vulnerable to the temptations of totalitarian thinking. The Fascists and Nazis, for example, searched for career opportunities and power through violent means, whereas the communists and socialists declared anti-fascism as their generational leitmotiv, set up resistance, were persecuted and forced into exile. These radical and extremist tendencies of the generation born around 1900 diminished after the Second World War and became socially integrated into post-war societies. By now, the generation of pre-war democrats got their second chance and soon found itself in leading positions, benefitting as well from allied support. The definition and understanding of, as well as the relation to, democracy became crucial for political scientists in Italy and Germany. After 1945, they primarily aimed at immunizing the young generation against any totalitarianism by means of a democratic education (D'Ottavio).[4]

For the older generation, it was easier to accept democracy and pluralism. They were usually part of the liberal and well-educated middle classes or the rational leaders of the labour movement before 1914. Having

CONCLUSIONS: FIVE DIMENSIONS OF GENERATION AROUND 1945   251

created a pragmatic faith in progress, they believed in the social-development processes provided by reforms. A typical example was the "generation Friedrich Ebert," which was socialized before the outbreak of the First World War and was therefore biographically and psychologically more independent than the younger generation. Referring to Charles Maier, these findings of a political culture dominated by the traditions of the nineteenth century confirm a sort of second "recasting bourgeois Europe" after 1945.[5] The consensus of the older generation, which had suffered from oppression and violence during the post-war period, definitely replaced the ideological bipolarity of the inter-war period.

GENERATION-BUILDING: THE 45ERS

If we assume that generation-building always happens in a horizontal way by age-specific action units, we would have to strictly distinguish the older generation born in the last third of the nineteenth century from the younger generation born around 1900. Thus, we would exclude that both could be part of the democratic, republican and social generation described previously, which in 1945 interrupted the history of National Socialism and Fascism by replacing old and heavily burdened concepts of order, such as "nation," with a democratic new beginning, European integration and working for a better future. Especially the non-compromised members of the younger generation, such as Lelio Basso, were able to inspire a young anti-fascist generation in Italy with democratic socialism. This was possible because they were part of a specific generation that took its references from society and not from family (Späth).

Therefore, could we call all those who were involved in democratic (re-)construction processes in Western Europe after the Second World War "45ers" despite the large age differences between cohorts? And might the "45ers" be characterized as a generation of resistance? After all, of those born around 1900, the generation of the Hitler Youth emerged as well. In his article, however, Dominik Rigoll insists that the decisive characteristic of the generation-building of the "45ers" consisted of having taken part in resistance movements. Though we very rarely find generational self-ascriptions of former resistance fighters—the term "generation" does not appear, for example, in Eugen Kogon's writings—Rigoll suggests using the term "45ers" as an analytical instrument to understand the development of West Germany up to the 1980s and 1990s. They saw themselves as a strategic group and part of a pan-European generation of anti-Nazis. As other contributions have already confirmed (Wirsching, Shaev, Späth), not age but the role played in the European civil war (1914–1945) and in the democratic-reconstruction process was most important for their generational consciousness. Thus, the "45ers" are not a generation in itself but rather a generation for itself whose communicative building of generationality and generational unity were directed against supporters of Fascism and National Socialism (Rigoll).

THE TRANSNATIONAL SPHERE

Directly connected to the last aspect are questions regarding the transnational dimension of generations: Can we talk about a European generation of resistance by 1945? Although we have national resistance (and liberation) movements in France and Italy that cooperated on various transnational levels, a similarly broad movement did not develop within Nazi Germany. The French generation of resistance addressed its consciousness against the generation of their fathers, in particular, who had failed to avoid a German occupation in 1940. Contrary to this French generation of resistance born in illegality due to the German aggression, German "45ers" did not dispose of the same audience as the French resistance literature did. That is why authors such as Heinrich Böll or Hans Werner Richter, who could have had an effect on the new beginning, were called the "lost generation." In the end, it is tempting to regard the "45ers" as a transnational generational unity that consisted of the political generation of resistance and two opposing generations: the first of those who actively supported the allied powers and the second of those who remained neutral (Dominik Rigoll). Subsuming several and sometimes antagonistic units within one generation might be a solution to dealing with the "45ers" in further research.

Jan de Graaf argues in this direction as well. He confirms that the battle between older leading party politicians and younger challengers over how to deal with the experience of right-wing dictatorships can not only be observed in the liberal sphere but also in the debates on socialist post-war politics. It is essential to remember that Italian Fascism lasted for an entire generation and thus lasted far longer than Fascist regimes in Germany, Austria and other Western European countries. Whereas almost exclusively elder socialists were in leading positions in these latter countries, in Italy and central-eastern Europe a young and internationally far less known generation was ready to take over from their discredited party comrades. Polish socialists, for example, regarded themselves as "wiser than the West

European socialists by a whole historical period."[6] This helps to explain the generational disharmony between younger revolutionaries and elder moderates in Europe, which threatened the unity of the international socialist community after 1945.

Christine Vodovar remains rather sceptical of the question of whether generation mattered in the Franco–German reconciliation process. She characterizes the conflict on a European Defence Community not as generational or motivated by common experiences but marked by a deep distrust of Germany and a marginalization of the socialist peace movement in the interwar-period. As for Italy, she stresses the importance of ideology and strategy rather than a generational effect of Italian socialists concerning Europe and reconciliation. Although she admits that the common desire for peace and a coming to terms with the past, combined with cooperation in transnational institutions (such as the European-integration process), could have mobilized Western European socialists after the Second World War, this only happened in the 1960s when a new generation of younger politicians took the leading positions. Before then, common experiences had not formed a common political culture in socialist parties—or if they did, then they did so only in very limited groups and individuals.

Despite of heterogeneous political discourses in Western Europe and the distinct memory cultures of each political party, one could also imagine two or more national political groups as a single generation. Whereas de Graaf and Vodovar might have preferred the term "age cohorts" for their case studies, Brian Shaev thinks of a generation as a self-aware and interconnected action unity with a community-generating notion. He crosses national borders and investigates the Franco–German socialist relations as transnational memory communities after 1945. Although he identifies visible generational differences within both parties, he stresses the negatively formative character of the interwar-period, which was absolutely discredited by the end of the Second World War. The transnational memory of the SFIO and the SPD touched their understanding of democracy and led mutual interferences to tackle the legacy of the past in a transnational (in other words, European) way toward the future in order to strengthen democracy. Although the French socialists showed optimism earlier, the German social democrats took more time to get out of their timid, isolated and mistrusted position.

Although the contributions herein have focused on various aspects in three different countries, they all confirm that new political cultures existed in Western Europe after 1945. Their manifestations were manifold and included trends toward post-heroism and toward mass culture; the latter has facilitated vibrant research activities and current projects referring to the term "popular culture."[7] However, the most important manifestation was democracy. Even if we concede that national narratives dominated the history of post-war democracies, grown out of distinct political cultures, we can identify common elements of democratization by examining transnational personal networks, discourses and border-crossing biographic experiences more closely. Leading progressive politicians in France, Italy and Western Germany, who often belonged to a democratic generation rooted in the late nineteenth century, shared common values. These manifested themselves in substantially convergent definitions, experiences and practices of democracy and led to a notion of "Europeanness" never seen before in history. Although their political backgrounds and their lives under dictatorship and occupation had been extremely diverse, they could rely on their networks and tactical experiences created and collected over a long period of time. Many of the politicians, scientists and intellectuals of this generation presented in this volume operated as key actors and initiators of numerous constitutions, bills and further normative texts in the transitional period.

These findings suggest once more that generation matters not only to structure history but especially when it comes to discussing how collective resources should be distributed within societies. At the same time, we should take the approach of constructing an artificial order seriously and always question if generation is really a helpful category for dividing history into periods. Generation seems to be especially appropriate when other patterns of order, such as "nation," have been discredited as was the case by 1945. Its future-oriented character facilitated a break with the past and a request for a new beginning. Applying structured research methods horizontally rather than vertically and referring to society rather than to family, the chapters confirm that the democratization process developed within a "transnational praxis," which meant first of all a transatlantic context until the 1960s.[8] Opening up comparative and transnational perspectives, the contributions also show the potential and limitations of Europeanizing the continent's history. Although memory and generation studies often remain within a national framework, the disruptive event of the Second World War represents an ideal starting point from which to conceptualize cultural, political and scientific communities and institutions, with all their rituals and symbols, as transnational units. By stressing comparisons, transfers and entanglements, by conceiving of (Western)

Europe beyond binational frameworks and by considering the *longue durée* of the protagonist's lives in the late nineteenth and most of the twentieth century, the articles can be seen as small laboratories of how to write European history today.[9]

NOTES

1. Mannheim, Karl. "Das Problem der Generationen." *Kölner Vierteljahreshefte für Soziologie* 7 (1928), 309–311.
2. Koselleck, Reinhart. *Vergangene Zukunft. Zur Semantik geschichtlicher Zeiten.* Frankfurt a.M.: Suhrkamp, 1988, 349–375.
3. Sirinelli, Jean-François. "Génération et histoire politique." *Vingtième Siècle. Revue d'histoire* 22 (1989), 79.
4. See now also Detjen, Joachim. *Politische Erziehung als Wissenschaftsaufgabe. Das Verhältnis der Gründergeneration der deutschen Politikwissenschaft zur politischen Bildung.* Baden-Baden: NOMOS, 2016.
5. Maier, Charles. *Recasting Bourgeois Europe. Stabilization in France, Germany and Italy in the Decade after World War I.* Princeton: PUP, 1975.
6. See the quote in Jan de Graaf's contribution in this volume.
7. See e.g. Hüser, Dietmar/Pfeil, Ulrich, eds. *Populärkultur und deutsch-französische Mittler: Akteure, Medien, Ausdrucksformen.* Bielefeld: transcript, 2015; id. *Populärkultur transnational – Lesen, Sehen, Hören, Erleben in europäischen Nachkriegsgesellschaften der langen 1960er Jahre.* Bielefeld: transcript, 2017.
8. Bauerkämper, Arnd. "Demokratisierung als transnationale Praxis. Neue Literatur zur Geschichte der Bundesrepublik in der westlichen Welt." *Neue Politische Literatur* 53 (2008), 57–84.
9. See Leonhard, Jörn. "Comparison, Transfer and Entanglement, or: How to write Modern European History today?" *Journal of Modern European History* 14: 2 (2016), 149–163.

BIBLIOGRAPHY

The bibliography only contains secondary sources. For archival sources and published press articles, please consult the footnotes.

AA.VV, ed. *I socialisti e l'Europa*. Milan: Franco Angeli, 1989.

Acham, Karl/Nörr, Knut W./Schefold, Betram, eds. *Erkenntnisgewinne, Erkenntnisverluste. Kontinuitäten und Diskontinuitäten in den Wirtschafts-, Rechts- und Sozialwissenschaften zwischen den 20er und 50er Jahren.* Stuttgart: Steiner, 1998.

Améry, Jean. *Karrieren und Köpfe. Bildnisse berühmter Zeitgenossen.* Zürich: Thomas Verlag, 1955.

———. *Geburt der Gegenwart.* Olten/Freiburg: Walter, 1961.

Andreotti, Giulio/Delleani, Vincio. *Visti da vicino. Vol. 2.* Milan: Rizzoli, 1982.

Andro, Gaïd. *Une génération au service de l'État.* Paris: Société des études robespierristes, 2015.

Angster, Julia. *Konsenskapitalismus und Sozialdemokratie. Die Westernisierung von SPD und DGB.* Munich: Oldenbourg, 2003.

Arculeo, Antonella, ed. *La scienza politica in Italia. Materiali per un bilancio.* Milan: Franco Angeli, 1984.

Ardagh, John. *The new French revolution.* New York: Secker & Warburg, 1968.

Arndt, Hans-Joachim. *Die Besiegten von 1945. Versuch einer Politologie für Deutsche samt Würdigung der Politikwissenschaft in der Bundesrepublik Deutschland.* Berlin: Duncker & Humblot, 1978.

Assmann, Aleida. *Erinnerungsräume. Formen und Wandlungen des kulturellen Gedächtnisses.* Munich: C.H. Beck, 1999.

© The Author(s) 2018

J. Späth (ed.), *Does Generation Matter? Progressive Democratic Cultures in Western Europe, 1945–1960*, Palgrave Studies in the History of Social Movements, https://doi.org/10.1007/978-3-319-77422-0

258 BIBLIOGRAPHY

———. *Der lange Schatten der Vergangenheit. Erinnerungskultur und Geschichtspolitik.* Munich: C.H. Beck, 2006.

———. "Europe: A Community of Memory?". *Bulletin of the GHI Washington* 40 (2007), 11–25.

——— /Frevert, Ute. *Geschichtsvergessenheit – Geschichtsversessenheit. Vom Umgang mit deutschen Vergangenheiten nach 1945.* Stuttgart: DVA, 1999.

Assmann, Jan. *Cultural Memory and Early Civilization. Writing, Remembrance, and Political Imagination.* Cambridge: CUP, 2011.

Auriol, Vincent. *Hier ... demain.* Paris: Charlot, 1945.

———. *Journal du septennat, 1947–1954.* Paris: Tallandier, 2003.

Balzer, Friedrich-Martin, ed. *Wolfgang Abendroth, wissenschaftlicher Politiker. Bio-bibliographische Beiträge.* Opladen: Leske + Budrich, 2001.

Bartole, Sergio. *Interpretazioni e trasformazioni della Costituzione repubblicana.* Bologna: Il Mulino, 2004.

Basso, Lelio. *Due totalitarismi. Fascismo e democrazia cristiana.* Milan: Garzanti, 1951.

Bauerkämper, Arnd, ed. *Demokratiewunder. Transatlantische Mittler und die kulturelle Öffnung Westdeutschlands 1945–1970.* Göttingen: Vandenhoeck & Ruprecht, 2005.

———. *Der Faschismus in Europa 1918–1945.* Stuttgart: Reclam, 2006.

———. "Demokratisierung als transnationale Praxis. Neue Literatur zur Geschichte der Bundesrepublik in der westlichen Welt." *Neue Politische Literatur* 53 (2008), 57–84.

Becker, Jean-Jacques. *Histoire politique de la France depuis 1945.* Paris: Colin, 1989.

Behr, Hermann. *Vom Chaos zum Staat. Männer, die für uns begannen 1945–1949.* Frankfurt a.M.: Verl. Frankfurter Bücher, 1961.

Benjamin, Walter/Bonola, Gianfranco/ Ranchetti, Michele. *Sul concetto di storia.* Bologna: Il Mulino, 1997.

Berger, Stefan/Nehring, Holger, eds. *The history of social movements in global perspective. A survey.* London: Palgrave Macmillan, 2017.

Berghahn, Volker R. *America and the intellectual cold wars in Europe.* Princeton, N.J.: Princeton Univ. Press, 2001.

Berghoff, Hartmut/Jensen, Uffa/Lubinski, Christina/Weisbrod, Bernd, eds. *History by generations. Generational dynamics in modern history.* Göttingen: Wallstein, 2013.

Bergounioux, Alain. "Générations socialistes." *Vingtième Siècle. Revue d'histoire* 22 (1989), 93–101.

Bergsträsser, Arnold. *Weltpolitik als Wissenschaft. Geschichtliches Bewußtsein und politische Erziehung.* Cologne/Opladen: Westdt. Verl., 1965.

Berman, Sheri. *The primacy of politics. Social democracy and the making of Europe's twentieth century.* Cambridge: CUP, 2006.

BIBLIOGRAPHY   259

Bernardi, Alberto de. *Discorso sull'antifascismo*. Milan: B. Mondadori, 2007.
——— /Ferrari, Paolo, eds. *Antifascismo e identità europea*. Rome: Carocci, 2004.
Berstein, Serge, ed. *Le parti socialiste entre résistance et République*. Paris: Publications de la Sorbonne, 2000.
Béthouart, Bruno. "Le Mouvement Républicain Populaire. L'entrée des catholiques dans la République française." In Gehler, Michael/Kaiser, Wolfram/Wohnout, Helmut, eds. *Christdemokratie in Europa im 20. Jahrhundert. Christian democracy in 20th century Europe = La démocratie chrétienne en Europe au XXe siècle*. Vienna: Böhlau, 2001, 313–331.
Blasberg, Christian. "La crisi del PLI. I liberali tra CLN e qualunquismo." In Monina, Giancarlo, ed. *1945–1946. Le origini della Repubblica*. Soveria Mannelli: Rubbettino, 2007, 169–201.
———. *Die Liberale Linke und das Schicksal der Dritten Kraft im italienischen Zentrismus, 1947–1951*. Frankfurt a.M.: P. Lang, 2008.
———. "Liberali per il centrosinistra: Radicali e Democrazia liberale." *Ventunesimo Secolo* 15:7 (2008), 57–80.
———. "Nicolò Carandini." In Berzi, Gianpietro, ed. *Dizionario del liberalismo italiano. Vol. II*. Soveria Mannelli: Rubbettino, 2015, 247–251.
Bleek, Wilhelm, ed. *Schulen der deutschen Politikwissenschaft*. Opladen: Leske + Budrich, 1999.
———. *Geschichte der Politikwissenschaft in Deutschland*. Munich: C.H. Beck, 2001.
Blomert, Reinhard, ed. *Heidelberger Sozial- und Staatswissenschaften. Das Institut für Sozial- und Staatswissenschaften zwischen 1918 und 1958*. Marburg: Metropolis-Verl., 1997.
———. *Intellektuelle im Aufbruch. Karl Mannheim, Alfred Weber, Norbert Elias und die Heidelberger Sozialwissenschaften der Zwischenkriegszeit*. Munich: Hanser, 1999.
Blum, Léon. *A l'échelle humaine*. Paris/Montréal: Gallimard L'Arbre, 1945.
Bobbio, Norberto. *Gaetano Mosca e la scienza politica*. Rome: Academia nazionale dei Lincei, 1960.
———. "Politische Theorie und Forschung in Italien." In Stammer, Otto, ed. *Politische Forschung. Beiträge zum zehnjährigen Bestehen des Instituts für politische Wissenschaft*. Cologne/Opladen: Westdt. Verl., 1960, 65–80.
———. "Teoria e ricerca politica in Italia." *Il Politico* 25 (1961), 215–233.
———. *Profilo ideologico del Novecento italiano*. Torino: Einaudi, 1969.
———. *Saggi sulla scienza politica in Italia*. Bari: Editori Laterza, 1969.
——— /Papuzzi, Alberto, eds. *Autobiografia*. Rome: GLF editori Laterza, 1999.
Bohnenkamp, Björn. *Doing Generation. Zur Inszenierung von generationeller Gemeinschaft in deutschsprachigen Schriftmedien*. Bielefeld: transcript, 2011.
Bombois, Sophie. *La SFIO et l'Allemagne*. Mémoire. Université de Paris 1. Paris, 1991.

260 BIBLIOGRAPHY

Bommarius, Christian. *Das Grundgesetz. Eine Biographie.* Berlin: Rowohlt, 2009.

Booth, William J. "Communities of Memory: On Identity, Memory, and Debt." *The American Political Science Review* 93: 2 (1999), 249–263.

Borne, Dominique. *Petits bourgeois en révolte? Le mouvement Poujade.* Paris: Flammarion, 1977.

Bösch, Frank. *Die Adenauer-CDU. Gründung, Aufstieg und Krise einer Erfolgspartei; 1945–1969.* Stuttgart/Munich: DVA, 2001.

Bossuat, Gérard. "La campagne de Daniel Mayer contre la CED." *Matériaux pour l'histoire de notre temps* 50–52 (1998), 33–45.

Böttcher, Karl W. "Die junge Generation und die Parteien." *Frankfurter Hefte* 1948: 3, 756–761.

Boyer, Marc. *Histoire du tourisme de masse.* Paris: Presses Univ. de France, 1999.

Braun, Bernd. "Die „Generation Ebert"." In Schönhoven, Klaus/Braun, Bernd, eds. *Generationen in der Arbeiterbewegung.* Munich: Oldenbourg, 2005, 69–86.

Braunthal, Julius. *Geschichte der Internationale, Vol. III.* Hannover: Dietz, 1971.

Brizzi, Riccardo. *Il governo Mendès France.* Bologna: CLUEB, 2010.

Broszat, Martin, ed. *Zäsuren nach 1945. Essays zur Periodisierung der deutschen Nachkriegsgeschichte.* Munich: Oldenbourg, 1990.

Buchstein, Hubertus. *Demokratiepolitik. Theoriebiographische Studien zu deutschen Nachkriegspolitologen.* Baden-Baden: Nomos, 2011.

Bülow, Birgit v. *Die Staatsrechtslehre der Nachkriegszeit. (1945–1952).* Berlin: Berlin-Verl. Spitz, 1996.

Buruma, Ian. *Year Zero. A History of 1945.* New York: Atlantic Books Ltd, 2013.

Caciagli, Mario. "Il dibattito politologico nella Repubblica Federale Tedesca." *Rivista italiana di scienza politica* 6 (1976), 561–587.

Cafagna, Luciano. *Una strana disfatta. La parabola dell'autonomismo socialista.* Venice: Marsilio, 1996.

Cahn, Jean-Paul. *Le Parti socialdémocrate allemand et la fin de la quatrième République Française (1954–1958).* Bern: Lang, 1996.

——— /Fritsch-Bournazel, Renata, eds. *La République Fédérale d'Allemagne et la construction de l'Europe. (1949–1963).* Paris: Éd. du Temps, 2000.

Callaghan, John. *The retreat of social democracy.* Manchester: Manchester Univ. Press, 2000.

Cannavero, Alfredo. "Pietro Nenni, i socialisti italiani e l'Internazionale socialista tra Est ed Ovest dopo la Seconda Guerra mondiale." In École Française de Rome, ed. *Les internationales et le problème de la guerre au XXe siècle. Actes du colloque … (Rome, 22–24 novembre 1984).* Rome: École Française de Rome, 1987, 241–264.

Capozzi, Eugenio. *Il sogno di una costituzione. Giuseppe Maranini e l'Italia del Novecento.* Bologna: Il Mulino, 2008.

Capuzzo, Paolo. *Genere, generazione e consumi. L'Italia degli anni Sessanta.* Rome: Carocci, 2003.

BIBLIOGRAPHY 261

Carandini, Nicolo. *Il partito liberale e i problemi italiani. Discorso tenuto in Roma il 3 settembre 1944.* Bari: Laterza, 1944.
———. *Il punto di vista liberale.* Rome: Arti poligrafiche Imperia, 1943.
———. *L'Unità Europea e il Congresso dell'Aja. Discorso tenuto alla Manifestazione federalistica di Firenze, 13 giugno 1948.* Rome: Athenais, 1948.
———. *Responsabilità europea. Discorso tenuto al Teatro Sistina di Roma il 4 novembre a chiusura della campagna per la petizione in favore di un patto d'unione federale europea.* Rome: Emer, 1950.
———. *The Alto Adige. An experiment in the devaluation of frontiers.* Rome: "Il Mondo", 1958.
Carandini Albertini, Elena. *Passata la stagione. Diari 1944–1947.* Florence: Passigli, 1989.
——— *Dal terrazzo. Diario 1943–1944.* Bologna: Il Mulino, 1997.
———. *Le case, le cose, le carte. Diari 1948–1950.* Padova: Il poligrafo, 2007.
Cardini, Antonio. *Mario Pannunzio. Giornalismo e liberalismo; cultura e politica nell'Italia del Novecento, 1910–1968.* Naples: Edizioni scientifiche italiane, 2011.
Caretti, Stefano/Degl'Innocenti, Maurizio, eds. *Sandro Pertini e la bandiera italiana.* Manduria: Lacaita, 1998.
Castagnez-Ruggiu, Noëlline. *Socialistes en République. Les parlementaires SFIO de la IVe République.* Rennes: Presses Univ. de Rennes, 2004.
Cattaruzza, Marina, ed. *La nazione in rosso. Socialismo, comunismo e questione nazionale, 1889–1953.* Soveria Mannelli: Rubbettino, 2005.
Cerne, Marina, ed. *I 60 anni della SIOI. Cronache e memorie, 1944–2004. Prefazione di Umberto La Rocca.* Naples: ES, 2005.
Cerutti, Mauro. *Le Tessin, la Suisse et l'Italie de Mussolini. Fascisme et antifascisme 1921–1935.* Lausanne: Payot, 1988.
Chauveau-Veauvy, Yves. *Génération AFN. [Algérie 1956–1962].* Turquant: Àpart du temps, 2009.
Colarizi, Simona. "I socialisti italiani e l'Internazionale socialista, 1947–1958." *Mondo Contemporaneo* 2 (2005), 5–66.
Coleman, Peter. *The liberal conspiracy. The Congress for Cultural Freedom and the struggle for the mind of postwar Europe.* New York: Free Pr, 1989.
Collotti, Enzo/Ajmone, Fiorella, eds. *Ripensare il socialismo. La ricerca di Lelio Basso.* Milan: Mazzotta, 1988.
——— /Boldrini, Arrigo. *Fascismo e antifascismo. Rimozioni, revisioni, negazioni.* Rome: Laterza, 2000.
Colozza, Roberto. *Lelio Basso. Una biografia politica; (1948–1958).* Rome: Ediesse, 2010.
Comparato, Vittor I./Lupi, Regina/Montanari, Giorgio E., eds. *Le scienze politiche. Modelli contemporanei.* Milan: Franco Angeli, 2011.
Confino, Alon. *The work of memory. New directions in the study of German society and culture.* Urbana: University of Illinois Press, 2002.

262 BIBLIOGRAPHY

———. *Histories and memories of twentieth-century Germany*. Bloomington: Indiana University Press, 2005.

Conway, Martin. "The Rise and Fall of Western Europe's Democratic Age, 1945–1973." *Contemporary European History* 13: 1 (2004), 67–88.

——— /Patel, Kiran K., eds. *Europeanization in the twentieth century. Historical approaches*. Basingstoke: Palgrave Macmillan, 2010.

Conze, Werner/Lepsius, Mario R., eds. *Sozialgeschichte der Bundesrepublik Deutschland. Beiträge zum Kontinuitätsproblem*. Stuttgart: Klett-Cotta, 1983.

Copsey, Nigel/Olechnowicz, Andrzej, eds. *Varieties of anti-fascism. Britain in the inter-war period*. Basingstoke: Palgrave Macmillan, 2010.

Covatta, Luigi, ed. *Storia del partito socialista. Dalla guerra fredda all'alternativa*. Venezia: Marsilio, 1980.

Cowan, Jon. "Visions of the Postwar: The Politics of Memory and Expectation in 1940s France." *History and Memory* 10: 2 (1998), 68–101.

Crémieux-Brilhac, Jean-Louis. *La France libre. De l'appel du 18 juin à la Libération*. Paris: Gallimard, 1996.

Crisafulli, Vezio. "La sovranità popolare nella Costituzione italiana." In Orlando, Vittorio E., ed. *Scritti giuridici in memoria di V.E. Orlando, Vol. 1*. Padova: CEDAM, 1955, 407–463.

Croce, Benedetto/Galasso, Giuseppe. *Storia d'Europa nel secolo decimonono*. Milan: Adelphi, 1999.

Cruciani, Sante. *L'Europa delle sinistre. La nascita del Mercato comune europeo attraverso i casi francese e italiano (1955–1957)*. Rome: Carocci, 2007.

D'Ottavio, Gabriele. "Democracy in Transition. The Development of a Science of Politics in Western Europe after 1945." In Pombeni, Paolo, ed. *The historiography of transition. Critical phases in the development of modernity: (1494–1973)*. New York/London: Routledge, 2016, 183–198.

——— /Bernardini, Giovanni. "SPD and European integration. From scepticism to pragmatism, from pragmatism to leadership, 1949–1979." In Bonfreschi, Lucia/Orsina, Giovanni/Varsori, Antonio, eds. *European parties and the European integration process, 1945–1992*. Brussels: P. Lang, 2015, 29–44.

Daniel, Ute. "Die Erfahrungen der Geschlechtergeschichte." In Bos, Marguérite, ed. *Erfahrung: alles nur Diskurs? Zur Verwendung des Erfahrungsbegriffs in der Geschlechtergeschichte. Beiträge der 11. Schweizerischen HistorikerInnentagung 2002*. Zürich: Chronos-Verl., 2004, 59–69.

De Grazia, Victoria. *Irresistible empire. America's advance through twentieth-century Europe*. Cambridge, Mass.: Harvard Univ. Press, 2005.

Defrance, Corine/Pfeil, Ulrich. *Entre guerre froide et intégration européenne. Reconstruction et rapprochement ; 1945–1963*. Villeneuve d'Ascq: Presses Univ. de Septentrion, 2012.

——— /Pfeil, Ulrich, eds. *La France, l'Allemagne et le traité de l'Elysée*. Paris: CNRS, 2012.

BIBLIOGRAPHY 263

Degl'Innocenti, Maurizio/Ciuffoletti, Zeffrio. *Storia del PSI. Dal dopoguerra a oggi*. Rome/Bari: Laterza, 1993.

Delori, Mathias. *La réconciliation franco-allemande par la jeunesse. La généalogie, l'événement, l'histoire (1871–2015)*. Brussels: P. Lang, 2016.

Delporte, Christian. "Au miroirs des médias." In Rioux, Jean-Pierre/Sirinelli, Jean-François, eds. *La culture de masse en France de la Belle Epoque à aujourd'hui*. Paris: Hachette, 2006, 305–351.

Detjen, Joachim. *Politische Erziehung als Wissenschaftsaufgabe. Das Verhältnis der Gründergeneration der deutschen Politikwissenschaft zur politischen Bildung*. Baden-Baden: Nomos, 2016.

Devin, Guillaume. *L'internationale socialiste. Histoire et sociologie du socialisme international (1945–1990)*. Paris: Presses de la Fondation Nationale des Sciences Politiques, 1993.

Di Nolfo, Ennio. "The Italian Socialists." In Griffiths, Richard T., ed. *Socialist parties and the question of Europe in the 1950's*. Leiden/New York: E.J. Brill, 1993, 90–98.

Di Nucci, Loreto. *Nel cantiere dello Stato fascista*. Rome: Carocci, 2008.

Dipper, Christof/Hudemann, Rainer/Petersen, Jens, eds. *Faschismus und Faschismen im Vergleich. Wolfgang Schieder zum 60. Geburtstag*. Vierow: SH-Verl., 1998.

Doering-Manteuffel, Anselm. *Wie westlich sind die Deutschen? Amerikanisierung und Westernisierung im 20. Jahrhundert*. Göttingen: Vandenhoeck & Ruprecht, 1999.

———. *Das doppelte Leben. Generationenerfahrungen im Jahrhundert der Extreme*. Stuttgart: Steiner, 2013.

Dohrmann, Nicolas. *Les relations entre la SFIO et le SPD dans l'immédiat après guerre, 1945–1953*. Paris: Ecole Nationale des Chartes, 2003.

Domenach, Jean-Marie. "Le modèle américain." *Esprit* 28 (1960), 1219–1232.

Dorn, Walter L. *Inspektionsreisen in der US-Zone. Notizen, Denkschriften und Erinnerungen aus dem Nachlaß*. Munich: Oldenbourg, 1973.

Droz, Jacques. *Histoire de l'antifascisme en Europe. 1923–1939* Paris: La Découverte, 2001.

Durand, Jean-Dominique. *Christian democrat internationalism. Its action in Europe and worldwide from post World War II until the 1990s. vol. 2: The Development 1945–1979: the Role of Parties, Movements, People*. Brussels: Lang, 2013.

Echternkamp, Jörg/Martens, Stefan, eds. *Experience and memory. The Second World War in Europe*. New York: Berghahn, 2010.

Edinger, Lewis J. "Post-totalitarian Leadership. Elites in the German Federal Republic." *The American Political Science Review* 54: 1 (1960), 58–82.

———. *Kurt Schumacher. A study in personality and political behavior. [With portraits.]*. Stanford: Stanford Univ. Press, 1965.

264 BIBLIOGRAPHY

Eggebrecht, Axel, ed. *Die zornigen alten Männer. Gedanken über Deutschland seit 1945.* Reinbek: Rowohlt, 1979.

Epstein, Catherine. "The Politics of Biography: The Case of East German Old Communists." *Daedalus* 128: 2 (1999), 1–30.

———. *The last revolutionaries. German communists and their century.* Cambridge, MA: Harvard Univ. Press, 2003.

Espagne, Michel, et al. "Forum II: How to Write Modern European History Today? Statements to Jörn Leonhard's JMEH-Forum." *Journal of Modern European History* 14: 4 (2016), 465–490.

Esposito, Carlo. *La Costituzione italiana.* Padova: Saggi, 1954.

Farr, James/Seidelman, Raymond, eds. *Discipline and history. Political science in the United States.* Ann Arbor, Mich.: University of Michigan press, 1993.

Felice, Alessandro de. *La socialdemocrazia e la scelta occidentale dell'Italia, 1947–1949. Saragat, il PSLI e la politica internazionale da Palazzo Barberini al Patto atlantico.* Catania: Boemi, 1998.

Felice, Renzo de. *Storia degli ebrei italiani sotto il fascismo.* Torino: Einaudi, 1961.

———. "L'Italia postfascista vista da Parigi e da Londra: Pagine di diario di Leone Cattani, febbraio-marzo 1947." *Storia Contemporanea* 15 (1984), 973–1014.

Felsini, Daniela. "1943–1957, Il PSI e l'integrazione europea." *Annali dell'Istituto Ugo La Malfa* 2 (1987).

Filippone-Thaulero, Giustino. "Diario 1944–1945 di Nicolò Carandini." *Nuova Antologia* 2146 (1983).

Fisichella, Domenico. "Alle origini della scienza politica italiana. Gaetano Mosca epistemologo." *Rivista italiana di scienza politica* 3 (1991), 447–470.

Fogt, Helmut. *Politische Generationen. Empirische Bedeutung und theoretisches Modell.* Opladen: Westdt. Verl., 1982.

Forner, Sean A. *German intellectuals and the challenge of democratic renewal. Culture and politics after 1945.* Cambridge: CUP, 2014.

Forsthoff, Ernst. *Lehrbuch des Verwaltungsrechts: 1. – Allgemeiner Teil.* Munich/Berlin: C.H. Beck, 1950.

———. *Einleitung zum Bonner Grundgesetz.* Heidelberg: Rothe, 1953.

Fouque, Antoinette. *Génération MLF. 1968 – 2008.* Paris: Des Femmes Antoinette Fouque, 2008.

Fraenkel, Ernst. *Das amerikanische Regierungssystem. Eine Politologische Analyse.* Wiesbaden: VS Verl. für Sozialwissenschaften, 1960.

Franceschini, Claudia. *Le idee costituzionali della Resistenza. Atti del Convegno di studi Roma 19 20 e 21 ottobre 1995.* Rome: Presidenza del Consiglio dei Ministri Dipart. per l'Informazione e l'Editoria, 1997.

François, Étienne/Schulze, Hagen, eds. *Deutsche Erinnerungsorte.* Munich: C.H. Beck, 2007.

Frei, Norbert. *Adenauer's Germany and the Nazi Past. The Politics of Amnesty and Integration.* New York: Columbia University Press, 2002.

———. *Vergangenheitspolitik. Die Anfänge der Bundesrepublik und die NS-Vergangenheit*. Munich: C.H. Beck, 2012.

Fröhlich, Claudia/Kohlstruck, Michael. "Einleitung." In Fröhlich, Claudia, ed. *Engagierte Demokraten. Vergangenheitspolitik in kritischer Absicht*. Münster: Westfälisches Dampfboot, 1999, 14–18.

Frosini, Tommaso E. *Maranini e la costituzione tra mito e realtà*. Roma: Ideazione, 1996.

Galante Garrone, Alessandro. *Calamandrei*. Milan: Garzanti, 1987.

Galizia, Mario, ed. *Forme di stato e forme di governo. Nuovi studi sul pensiero di Costantino Mortati*. Milan: Giuffrè, 2007.

——— /Grossi, Paolo, eds. *Il pensiero giuridico di Costantino Mortati*. Milan: Giuffrè, 1990.

Galli, Giorgio. *Il bipartitismo imperfetto. Comunisti e democristiani in Italia*. Bologna: Il Mulino, 1967.

Garner, Curt. "Remaking German democracy in the 1950s. Was the civil service an asset or a liability?" *German Politics and Society* 6 (1997), 16–53.

Gatzka, Claudia C. ""Demokratisierung" in Italien und der Bundesrepublik. Historiographische Narrative und lokale Erkundungen." In Levsen, Sonja/Torp, Cornelius, eds. *Wo liegt die Bundesrepublik? Vergleichende Perspektiven auf die westdeutsche Geschichte*. Göttingen: Vandenhoeck & Ruprecht, 2016, 145–165.

Gay, Peter. "Weimar Culture. The Outsider as Insider." In Fleming, Donald/Bailyn, Bernard, eds. *The intellectual migration. Europe and America, 1930 – 1960*. Cambridge, MA: Belknap Press, 1969, 11–93.

Gemelli, Giuliana. *The Ford Foundation and Europe, 1950's–1970's. Cross-fertilization of learning in social science and management*. Brussels: European Interuniversity Press, 1998.

Gentile, Francesco/Grasso, Pietro G./Ferrari, Giuseppe, eds. *Costituzione criticata*. Naples: Edizioni scientifiche italiane, 1999.

Geppert, Dominik, ed. *The postwar challenge. Cultural, social, and political change in Western Europe, 1945–58*. Oxford: Oxford Univ. Press, 2003.

Gerland, Kirsten/Möckel, Benjamin/Ristau, Daniel, eds. *Generation und Erwartung. Konstruktionen zwischen Vergangenheit und Zukunft*. Göttingen: Wallstein, 2013.

Gibas, Monika. "'Bonner Ultras', 'Kriegstreiber' und 'Schlotbarone'. Die Bundesrepublik als Feindbild der DDR in den fünfziger Jahren." In Satjukow, Silke/Gries, Rainer, eds. *Unsere Feinde. Konstruktionen des Anderen im Sozialismus*. Leipzig: Leipziger Universitätsverlag, 2004, 75–106.

Giorgi, Chiara. *Un socialista del Novecento. Uguaglianza, libertaÁ e diritti nel percorso di Lelio Basso*. Rome: Carocci, 2015.

Giorgi, Maria de/Antoni, Carlo, eds. *Il movimento liberale italiano. (Roma, 1943–1944)*. Galatina: Congedo, 2005.

266 BIBLIOGRAPHY

Glazman, Wolf. *De génération en génération. Les enfants de la Shoah.* Paris: Harmattan, 2009.

Gotto, Bernhard. "Enttäuschung als Politikressource. Zur Kohäsion der westdeutschen Friedensbewegung in den 1980er Jahren." *Vierteljahrshefte für Zeitgeschichte* 62 (2014), 1–33.

Gougeon, Jacques-Pierre. *La social-démocratie allemande 1830–1996. De la révolution au réformisme.* Paris: Aubier, 1996.

Grabas, Christian/Nützenadel, Alexander, eds. *Industrial policy in Europe after 1945. Wealth, power and economic development in the Cold War.* Basingstoke: Palgrave Macmillan, 2014.

Grabert, Herbert. *Sieger und Besiegte. Der deutsche Nationalismus seit 1945.* Tübingen: Verl. d. Dt. Hochschullehrer-Ztg, 1966.

Grace, Nancy M./Skerl, Jennie, eds. *The transnational beat generation. [Beat Generation Symposium held at the Columbia College Chicago in the October 2008].* New York, NY: Palgrave Macmillan, 2012.

Graham, Bruce D. *The French socialists and tripartisme, 1944–1947.* Toronto: The University of Toronto Press, 1965.

Grand, Alexander de. "To Learn Nothing and to Forget Nothing: Italian Socialism and the Experience of Exile Politics, 1935–1945." *Contemporary European History* 14: 4 (2005), 539–558.

Grandi, Aldo. *La generazione degli anni perduti. Storie di Potere operaio.* Torino: Einaudi, 2003.

Grassi Orsini, Fabio/Nicolosi, Gerardo, eds. *I liberali italiani dall'antifascismo alla Repubblica.* Soveria Mannelli: Rubbettino, 2008.

Gregor, James. *The faces of Janus. Marxism and fascism in the twentieth century.* New Haven/London: Yale University Press, 2010.

Gregorio, Massimiliano. "Quale costituzione? Le interpretazioni della giuspubblicistica nell'immediato dopoguerra." *Quaderni Fiorentini per la storia del pensiero giuridico moderno* (2006), 849–913.

Griffin, Roger. *The nature of fascism.* London: Routledge, 2006.

Griffo, Maurizio. "Sull'origine della parola 'partitocrazia'." *L'Acropoli* 4 (2007), 396–409.

Grossi, Paolo. *Scienza giuridica italiana. Un profilo storico, 1860–1950.* Milan: Giuffrè, 2000.

Großmann, Johannes. *Die Internationale der Konservativen. Transnationale Elitenzirkel und private Außenpolitik in Westeuropa seit 1945.* Munich: Oldenbourg, 2014.

Guidoni, Pierre/Verdier, Robert, eds. *Les socialistes en Résistance. 1940–1944; combats et débats.* Paris: Arslan, 1999.

Günther, Frieder. "Ein Jahrzehnt der Rückbesinnung. Die bundesdeuscthe Staatsrechtslehre zwischen Dezision und Integration in den Fünfziger Jahren." In Henne, Thomas/Riedlinger, Arne, eds. *Das Lüth-Urteil aus*

BIBLIOGRAPHY **267**

(rechts-) historischer Sicht. Die konflike um Veit Harlan und die Grundrechtsjudikatur des Bundesverfassungsgerichts. Berlin: Berliner Wissenschafts-Verlag, 2005, 301–314.

———. *Denken vom Staat her. Die bundesdeutsche Staatsrechtslehre zwischen Dezision und Integration 1949–1970.* Munich: Oldenbourg, 2009.

Habermas, Jürgen. *Stichworte zur "Geistigen Situation der Zeit".* Frankfurt a.M.: Suhrkamp, 1979.

Habicht, Hubert, ed. *Eugen Kogon – ein politischer Publizist in Hessen. Essays, Aufsätze, Reden zwischen 1946 und 1982.* Frankfurt a.M.: Insel Verl., 1982.

Hähnel-Mesnard, Carola, ed. *L'antifascisme revisité. Histoire, idéologie, mémoire : dossier = Nogmaals antifascisme : geschiedenis, ideologie, gedachtenis.* Paris/ Brussels: Éditions Kimé; Éditions du Centre d'études et de documentation Mémoire, d'Auschwitz, 2009.

Hanhimäki, Jussi M./Westad, Odd A., eds. *The Cold War. A history in documents and eyewitness accounts.* Oxford: Oxford Univ. Press, 2004.

Hansen, Henning. *Die Sozialistische Reichspartei (SRP). Aufstieg und Scheitern einer rechtsextremen Partei.* Düsseldorf: Droste, 2007.

Heinsohn, Nina/Moxter, Michael, eds. *Enttäuschung. Interdisziplinäre Erkundungen zu einem ambivalenten Phänomen.* Paderborn: Wilhelm Fink, 2017.

Henkel, Michael. *Hermann Hellers Theorie der Politik und des Staates. Die Geburt der Politikwissenschaft aus dem Geiste der Soziologie.* Tübingen: Mohr Siebeck, 2012.

Herbert, Ulrich. *Best. Biographische Studien über Radikalismus, Weltanschauung und Vernunft; 1903–1989.* Bonn: Dietz, 1996.

———. "NS-Eliten in der Bundesrepublik." In Loth, Wilfried/Rusinek, Bernd-A, eds. *Verwandlungspolitik. NS-Eliten in der westdeutschen Nachkriegsgesellschaft.* Frankfurt a.M.: Campus-Verl., 1998, 93–115.

Hessel, Stéphane. *Engagiert Euch!* Berlin: Ullstein, 2011.

———. *Tanz mit dem Jahrhundert.* Berlin: List, 2011.

Hessisches Ministerium für Erziehung und Volksbildung. *Die politischen Wissenschaften an den deutschen Universitäten und Hochschulen. Gesamtprotokoll der Konferenz von Waldleiningen vom 10. und 11. September 1949.* Frankfurt a.M.: Verl. Neue Presse, 1949.

———. *Über Lehre und Forschung der Wissenschaft von der Politik. Gesamtprotokoll d. Konferenz von Königstein im Taunus vom 15. u. 16. Juli 1950.* Wiesbaden: Verl. Neue Presse, 1950.

Heumos, Peter, ed. *Europäischer Sozialismus im Kalten Krieg. Briefe und Berichte 1944–1948.* Frankfurt a.M.: Campus-Verl., 2004.

Heyde, Veronika. *De l'esprit de la Résistance jusqu'à l'idée de l'Europe. Projets européens et américains pour l'Europe de l'après-guerre (1940–1950).* Brussels: P. Lang, 2010.

268 BIBLIOGRAPHY

Högner, Wilhelm. *Der Volksbetrug der Nationalsozialisten. Rede.* Berlin: Dietz, 1930.

———. *Der schwierige Außenseiter. Erinnerungen eines Abgeordneten Emigranten und Ministerpräsidenten.* Munich: Isar-Verl., 1959.

Hölscher, Lucian. *Die Entdeckung der Zukunft.* Göttingen: Wallstein, 2016.

———. "Historische Zukunftsforschung – neueste Literatur." *Neue Politische Literatur* 61: 1 (2016), 47–62.

Horn, Gerd-Rainer/Kenney, Padraic, eds. *Transnational moments of change. Europe 1945, 1968, 1989.* Lanham, Md.: Rowman & Littlefield, 2004.

Hurrelbrink, Peter. *Der 8. Mai 1945. Befreiung durch Erinnerung ; ein Gedenktag und seine Bedeutung für das politisch-kulturelle Selbstverständnis in Deutschland.* Bonn: Dietz, 2005.

Hüser, Dietmar, ed. *Populärkultur transnational. Lesen, Hören, Sehen, Erleben im Europa der langen 1960er Jahre.* Bielefeld: transcript, 2017.

——— /Pfeil, Ulrich, eds. *Populärkultur und deutsch-französische Mittler. Akteure, Medien, Ausdrucksformen = Culture de masse et médiateurs franco-allemands.* Bielefeld: transcript, 2016.

Hütter, Hans W./Rösgen, Petra, eds. *Endlich Urlaub! Die Deutschen reisen: [Begleitbuch zur Ausstellung im Haus der Geschichte der Bundesrepublik Deutschland, Bonn, 6.6. – 13.10.1996].* Cologne: DuMont, 1996.

Ipsen, Hans P. *Über das Grundgesetz.* Hamburg: Selbstverl. der Univ., 1950.

———. *Staatsrechtslehrer unter dem Grundgesetz. Tagungen ihrer Vereinigung 1949–1992.* Tübingen: Mohr, 1993.

Jackson, Julian. *France. The dark years, 1940–1944.* Oxford: Oxford Univ. Press, 2001.

Jalabert, Laurent. "Aux origins de la génération 1968: Les étudiants français et la guerre du Vietnam." *Vingtième Siècle. Revue d'histoire* 55 (1997), 69–81.

Jannazzo, Antonio. *Croce e il prepartito della cultura.* Rome: Carocci, 1987.

Jones, Larry E. *German liberalism and the dissolution of the Weimar party system, 1918–1933.* Chapel Hill/N.C: University of North Carolina Press, 1988.

Judt, Tony. *Postwar. A history of Europe since 1945.* New York: The Penguin Press, 2005.

Jureit, Ulrike. "Generation, Generationality, Generational Research. Version: 2.0, 09.08.2017." In *Docupedia-Zeitgeschichte* http://docupedia.de/zg/Jureit_generation_v2_en_2017 (08.09.2017).

———. *Generationenforschung.* Stuttgart: Vandenhoeck & Ruprecht, 2006.

——— /Wildt, Michael, eds. *Generationen. Zur Relevanz eines wissenschaftlichen Grundbegriffs.* Hamburg: Hamburger Edition, 2005.

Kalyvas, Stathis. *The rise of Christian democracy in Europe.* Ithaca: Cornell University Press, 1996.

Kershaw, Ian. *To hell and back. Europe, 1914–1949.* London: Penguin Books, 2015.

BIBLIOGRAPHY   269

Kleßmann, Christoph. "1945 – welthistorische Zäsur und „Stunde Null". Version: 1.0, 15.10.2010." In *Docupedia-Zeitgeschichte* http://docupedia.de/zg/1945 (10.04.2017).

Klimke, Martin/Scharloth, Joachim, eds. *1968 in Europe. A history of protest and activism, 1956–1977.* New York, NY: Palgrave Macmillan, 2008.

Knapp, Steven. "Collective Memory and the Actual Past." *Representations* 26 (1998), 129–149.

Kogon, Eugen. "Beinahe mit dem Rücken zur Wand." *Frankfurter Hefte* 9 (1954), 641–645.

———. *Gesammelte Schriften.* Weinheim/Berlin: Beltz Quadriga, 1997.

Koppe, Françoise/Ruiz, Alain, eds. *Politique européenne et question allemande depuis la paix de Westphalie.* Toulouse: Presses Univ. du Mirail, 1999.

Koselleck, Reinhart. *Vergangene Zukunft. Zur Semantik geschichtlicher Zeiten.* Frankfurt a.M.: Suhrkamp, 1988.

Kössler, Till. *Abschied von der Revolution. Kommunisten und Gesellschaft in Westdeutschland, 1945–1968.* Düsseldorf: Droste, 2004.

Kracauer, Siegfried. *Das Ornament der Masse.* Frankfurt a.M.: Suhrkamp, 1963.

Krauss, Marita. *Heimkehr in ein fremdes Land. Geschichte der Remigration nach 1945.* München: C.H. Beck, 2001.

Krige, John. *American hegemony and the postwar reconstruction of science in Europe.* Cambridge, MA: MIT Press, 2006.

Kritzer, Peter. *Wilhelm Hoegner. Politische Biographie eines bayerischen Sozialdemokraten.* Munich: Süddt. Verl., 1979.

Kronawitter, Hildegard. "Bayerischer Patriot, Gefühlssozialist und erfolgreicher Ministerpräsident: Wilhelm Hoegner." *Einsichten und Perspektiven* 2 (2005), 34–57.

Kuisel, Richard F. *Seducing the French. The dilemma of Americanization.* Berkeley: Univ. of California Press, 1993.

Lafon, François. *Guy Mollet. Itinéraire d'un socialiste controversé : (1905–1975).* Paris: Fayard, 2006.

Lagrou, Pieter. *The legacy of Nazi occupation. Patriotic memory and national recovery in Western Europe; 1945–1965.* Cambridge: CUP, 2004.

Lanchester, Fulco. *I giuspubblicisti tra storia e politica.* Turin: Giappichelli, 1998.

———. "I costituzionalisti italiani tra Stato nazionale e Unione Europea." *Rivista Trimestrale di Diritto Pubblico* 4 (2001), 1079–1104.

———, ed. *Passato e presente delle facoltà di scienze politiche.* Milan: Giuffrè, 2003.

Lanfranchi, Enrico. *Un filosofo militante. Politica e cultura nel pensiero di Norberto Bobbio.* Torino: Boringhieri, 1989.

Lapie, Pierre-Olivier. *De Léon Blum à de Gaulle. Le caractère et le pouvoir.* Paris: Fayard, 1971.

Latini, Carlo/Vita, Vincenzo. *Il Sessantotto. Un evento, tanti eventi, una generazione.* Milan: Franco Angeli, 2008.

270 BIBLIOGRAPHY

Laudani, Raffaele. *Franz Neumann, Herbert Marcuse e Otto Kirchheimer. Il nemico tedesco. Scritti e rapporti riservati sulla Germania nazista (1943–1945)*. Bologna: Il Mulino, 2012.

Lebow, Richard Ned/Kansteiner, Wulf/Fogu, Claudio, eds. *The politics of memory in postwar Europe*. Durham N. C.: Duke university press, 2006.

Leggewie, Claus/Lang, Anne. *Der Kampf um die europäische Erinnerung. Ein Schlachtfeld wird besichtigt*. Bonn: Bundeszentrale für Politische Bildung, 2011.

Leonhard, Jörn. "Comparison, Transfer and Entanglement, or: How to write Modern European History today?" *Journal of Modern European History* 14: 2 (2016), 149–163.

Lepsius, Mario R. *Denkschrift über die Lage der Soziologie und Politikwissenschaft. Im Auftrag der Deutschen Forschungsgemeinschaft*. Wiesbaden: Steiner, 1961.

Levsen, Sonja. "Authority and Democracy in Post-War France and West Germany (1945–1968)." *Journal of Modern History* 89: 4 (2017), 812–850.

Liechti, Urs. *Wodans Wiederkunft. Ein lustiger Reisebericht aus einer traurigen Zeit*. Zürich: Jean Christophe-Verlag, 1936.

Lietzmann, Hans J. *Politikwissenschaft im "Zeitalter der Diktaturen". Die Entwicklung der Totalitarismustheorie Carl Joachim Friedrichs*. Opladen: Leske + Budrich, 1999.

Llanque, Marcus. *Souveräne Demokratie und soziale Homogenität. Das politische Denken Hermann Hellers*. Baden-Baden: Nomos, 2010.

Loader, Colin. *The intellectual development of Karl Mannheim. Culture, politics, and planning*. Cambridge et al.: CUP, 1985.

Loewenstein, Karl. "Über den Stand der politischen Wissenschaften in den Vereinigten Staaten." *Zeitschrift für die gesamte Staatswissenschaft* 106: 2 (1950), 349–361.

Lombardo, Antonio. "Sociologia e scienza politica in Gaetano Mosca." *Rivista italiana di scienza politica* 1: 2 (1971), 297–323.

Longo, Oddone, ed. *Albertini, Carandini. Una pagina della storia d'Italia*. Venice: Istituto veneto di scienze lettere ed arti, 2005.

Lorman, Thomas. "The Bethlen-Peyer Pact: A Reassessment." *Central Europe* 1: 2 (2003), 147–162.

Loth, Wilfried. "Les projets de politique extérieure de la résistance socialiste en France." *Revue d'histoire moderne et contemporaine* (1954), 544–569.

Lübbe, Hermann. "Fortschritt als Orientierungsproblem." In Podewils, Clemens G., ed. *Tendenzwende? Zur geistigen Situation der Bundesrepublik*. Stuttgart: Klett-Cotta, 1975, 9–24.

Luciani, Simona, ed. *Bibliografia degli scritti di Lelio Basso*. Florence: L. S. Olschki, 2003.

Lucifero, Falcone/Lucifero, Alfredo/Perfetti, Francesco, eds. *L'ultimo re. I diari del ministro della Real Casa*. Milan: Mondadori, 2002.

Maase, Kaspar. *Grenzenloses Vergnügen*. Frankfurt a.M.: Fischer, 1997.

BIBLIOGRAPHY 271

Maier, Charles S. *Recasting bourgeois Europe. Stabilization in France, Germany and Italy in the decade after World War I.* Princeton, NJ: Princeton Univ. Press, 1975.

Maier, Hans. "Die Lehre der Politik in den deutschen Universitäten vornehmlich zum 16. bis 18. Jahrhundert." In Oberndörfer, Dieter, ed. *Wissenschaftliche Politik. Eine Einführung in Grundfragen ihrer Tradition und Theorie.* Freiburg i.Br.: Rombach, 1962, 59–116.

———. "Zur Lage der politischen Wissenschaft." *Vierteljahreshefte für Zeitgeschichte* 10: 3 (1962), 273–285.

Mangoldt, Hermann v. "Zum Beruf unserer Zeit für die Verfassungsgebung." *Die öffentliche Verwaltung* 74 (1948), 51–53.

———. "Die Grundrechte." *Die öffentliche Verwaltung* 75 (1949), 261–263.

———. "Grundrechte und Grundsatzfragen des Bonner Grundgesetzes." *Archiv für öffentliches Recht* 75 (1949), 273–290.

Mann, Michael. *Fascists.* Cambridge: CUP, 2004.

Mannheim, Karl. "Das Problem der Generationen." *Kölner Vierteljahreshefte für Soziologie* 7 (1928), 157–185, 309–330.

———. *Ideology and utopia.* London/New York: Routledge, 1997.

———. *Collected works. Essays on the sociology of knowledge.* London: Routledge, 1998.

——— /Wolff, Kurt H. *Wissenssoziologie. Auswahl aus dem Werk.* Neuwied am Rhein: Luchterhand, 1970.

Margalit, Avishai. *The ethics of memory.* Cambridge, MA: Harvard Univ. Press, 2002.

Margalit, Gilad. *Guilt, suffering, and memory. Germany remembers its dead of World War II.* Bloomington, IN: Indiana University Press, 2010.

Martens, Stéphan/Thorel, Julien, eds. *Les relations franco-allemandes. Bilan et perspectives à l'occasion du 50e anniversaire du traité de l'Élysée.* Paris: Septentrion, 2012.

Masala, Antonio. *Il liberalismo di Bruno Leoni.* Soveria Mannelli: Rubbettino, 2003.

Mattera, Paolo. *Il partito inquieto. Organizzazione, passioni e politica dei socialisti italiani dalla Resistenza al miracolo economico.* Rome: Carocci, 2004.

Mauch, Christof, ed. *The United States and Germany during the twentieth century. Competition and convergence.* Cambridge et al.: CUP, 2010.

Mayer, Daniel. *Les Socialistes dans la Résistance.* Paris: Presses Univ. de France, 1968.

Meineke, Stefan. *Friedrich Meinecke. Persönlichkeit und politisches Denken bis zum Ende des Ersten Weltkrieges.* Berlin, New York: De Gruyter, 1995.

Ménager, Bernard, ed. *Guy Mollet. Un camarade en République.* Lille: Presses Univ. de Lille, 1987.

Merkel, Wolfgang. *Systemtransformation. Eine Einführung in die Theorie und Empirie der Transformationsforschung.* Wiesbaden: VS Verl. für Sozialwissenschaften, 2010.

272 BIBLIOGRAPHY

Meyer, Henning. *Le changement de la "culture de mémoire" française par rapport à la Deuxième guerre mondiale à partir de trois "lieux de mémoire": Bordeaux, Caen et Oradour-sur-Glanne. Der Wandel der französischen "Erinnerungskultur" des Zweiten Weltkriegs am Beispiel dreier "Erinnerungsorte" : Bordeaux, Caen und Oradour-sur-Glane.* [S.l.]: [s.n.], 2006.

Möckel, Benjamin. *Erfahrungsbruch und Generationsbehauptung. Die "Kriegsjugendgeneration" in den beiden deutschen Nachkriegsgesellschaften.* Göttingen: Wallstein, 2014.

Mohr, Arno. *Politikwissenschaft als Alternative. Stationen einer wissenschaftlichen Disziplin auf dem Wege zu ihrer Selbständigkeit in der Bundesrepublik Deutschland 1945–1965.* Bochum: Studienverl. Brockmeyer, 1988.

Möllers, Christoph. *Der vermisste Leviathan. Staatstheorie in der Bundesrepublik.* Frankfurt a.M.: Suhrkamp, 2008.

Monina, Giancarlo. *Lelio Basso, leader globale. Un socialista nel secondo Novecento.* Rome: Carocci, 2016.

Mori, Maria T. *Di generazione in generazione. Le italiane dall'Unità a oggi.* Rome: Viella, 2014.

Morin, Gilles. "Les oppositions socialistes à la CED. Les acteurs du débat." *Les cahiers IRICE* 2: 4 (2009), 83–100.

Mosca, Gaetano. *Elementi di scienza politica.* Rome: Bocca, 1896.

———/Kahn, Hannah D./Livingston, Arthur, eds. *The Ruling class. (Elementi di scienza politica).* New York: McGraw-Hill, 1939.

Moses, Anthony D. *German intellectuals and the Nazi past.* Cambridge: CUP, 2007.

Moses, Dirk. "The Forty-Fivers. A Generation between Fascism and Democracy." *German Politics and Society* 17 (1999), 94–126.

Müller, Jan-Werner. *Contesting democracy. Political ideas in twentieth-century Europe.* New Haven, CT: Yale University Press, 2011a.

Müller, Tim B. "Frieden durch Demokratie? Intellektuelle im Dienst der US-Regierung vom Zweiten Weltkrieg zum Kalten Krieg." In Dülffer, Jost, ed. *Frieden durch Demokratie? Genese, Wirkung und Kritik eines Deutungsmusters.* Essen: Klartext, 2011b, 147–166.

Münkler, Herfried. "Heroische und Postheroische Gesellschaften." *Merkur. Deutsche Zeitschrift für europäisches Denken* 61 (2007), 742–752.

Naschold, Frieder. *Theorie der Demokratie.* Stuttgart: Kohlhammer, 1971.

Naumann, Michael. *Der Strukturwandel des Heroismus. Vom sakralen zum revolutionären Heldentum.* Königstein/Ts.: Athenaeum, 1984.

Naumann, Werner. *Nau-Nau gefährdet das Empire?* Göttingen: Plesse, 1953.

Nehring, Holger. ""Generation" as a Political Argument in West European Protest Movements during the 1960s." In Lovell, Stephen, ed. *Generations in twentieth-century Europe.* Basingstoke: Palgrave Macmillan, 2007, 57–78.

Nencioni, Tommaso. "Tra neutralismo e atlantismo. La politica internazionale del Partito socialista italiano 1956–1966." *Italia contemporanea* (2010), 438–470.

BIBLIOGRAPHY 273

Nietzsche, Friedrich. *Untimely meditations*. Cambridge: CUP, 1997.
Nolte, Paul. *Was ist Demokratie? Geschichte und Gegenwart*. Munich: C.H. Beck, 2012.
Nora, Pierre. "La génération." In Nora, Pierre, ed. *Les lieux de mémoire, Vol. 3*. Paris: Gallimard, 1992, 931–971.
Novelli, Claudio. *Il Partito d'Azione e gli italiani. Moralità, politica e cittadinanza nella storia repubblicana*. Milan: Nuova Italia, 2000.
Orlando, Vittorio E./Grassi, Fabio. *Discorsi parlamentari*. Bologna: Il Mulino, 2002.
Orlow, Dietrich. *Common Destiny. A Comparative History of the Dutch, French, and German Social Democratic Parties, 1945–1969*. New York, NY: Berghahn, 2000.
Orsina, Giovanni. *L'alternativa liberale. Malagodi e l'opposizione al centrosinistra*. Venice: Marsilio, 2010.
Palano, Damiano. *Geometrie del potere. Materiali per la storia della scienza politica italiana*. Milan: V&P, 2005.
Palmier, Jean-Michel. *Weimar in exile. The antifascist emigration in Europe and America*. London/New York: Verso, 2006.
Parment, Anders. *Generation Y in consumer and labour markets*. New York: Routledge, 2012.
Pasquino, Gianfranco, ed. *La scienza politica di Giovanni Sartori*. Bologna: Il Mulino, 2005.
────── /Regali, Marta/Valbruzzi, Marco, eds. *Quarant'anni di scienza politica in Italia*. Bologna: Il Mulino, 2013.
Patel, Kiran K./Reichardt, Sven. "The dark side of transnationalism social engineering and Nazism, 1930s–40s." *Journal of contemporary history* 51: 1 (2016), 3–21.
Paterson, William E. *The SPD and European integration*. Westmead: Saxon House, 1974.
Pavone, Claudio. *Una guerra civile. Saggio storico sulla moralità nella Resistenza*. Torino: Bollati Boringhieri, 1991.
Payne, Stanley G. *A history of Fascism, 1914–1945*. Madison Wis. et al.: Univ. of Wisconsin Press, 1995.
Pertini, Alessandro/Caretti, Stefano, eds. *Dal delitto Matteotti alla Costituente. Scritti e discorsi; 1924–1946*. Manduria: Lacaita, 2008.
Picinini, Iacopo. "L'opposizione socialista alla Comunità europea di difesa (1950–1952)." *Ricerche storiche* (2006).
Pombeni, Paolo. *Vittorio Emanuele Orlando. Lo scienziato, il politico e lo statista*. Soveria Mannelli/Rome: Rubbettino/Senato della Repubblica, 2003.
Portinaro, Pier P. "Una disciplina al tramonto? La Staatslehre da Georg Jellinek all'unificazione europea." *Teoria politica* (2005), 3–33.
Prochnow, Jeanette/Rhode, Caterina. "Generations of Change. Introduction." *InterDisciplines* 2 (2011), 1–10.

274 BIBLIOGRAPHY

Quagliariello, Gaetano/Campochiaro, Emilia, eds. *La legge elettorale del 1953*. Bologna: Il Mulino, 2003.

Quaglioni, Diego. "Ordine giuridico e politico in Vittorio Emanuele Orlando." In Carta, Paolo/Cortese, Fulvio, eds. *Ordine giuridico e ordine politico. Esperienze lessico prospettive*. Padova: CEDAM, 2008, 3–25.

Quilliot, Roger. *La S. F. I. O. et l'exercice du pouvoir, 1944–1958*. Paris: Fayard, 1972.

Raphael, Lutz. *Imperiale Gewalt und mobilisierte Nation. Europa 1914–1945*. Munich: C.H. Beck, 2011.

Rauch, André. *Vacances en France de 1830 à nos jours*. Paris: Hachette, 2001.

Rausch, Helke. "«Allemagne, année zero?»". Dénazifier et democratiser (1945–1955)." In Tournès, Ludovic, ed. *L'argent de l'influence. Les fondations américaines et leurs réseaux européens*. Paris: Autrement, 2010, 125–142.

Reichardt, Sven/Zierenberg, Malte. *Damals nach dem Krieg. Eine Geschichte Deutschlands 1945 bis 1949*. Munich: DVA, 2008.

Rémond, René. "Conclusions." *Les familles politiques en Europe occidentale au XIXe siècle. Actes du colloque international ; (Rome, 1er – 3 décembre 1994)*. Rome: École Française de Rome, 1997.

Reulecke, Jürgen, ed. *Arbeiterbewegung an Rhein und Ruhr. Beiträge zur Geschichte der Arbeiterbewegung in Rheinland-Westfalen*. Wuppertal: Hammer, 1974.

———, ed. *Generationalität und Lebensgeschichte im 20. Jahrhundert. [Ergebnisse eines Kolloquiums veranstaltet vom 18. bis 21. Juli 2001]*. Munich: Oldenbourg, 2003.

———. "Generation/Generationality, Generativity, and Memory." In Erll, Astrid/Nünning, Ansgar, eds. *A companion to cultural memory studies*. Berlin: De Gruyter, 2010, 119–125.

Riccardi, Luca, ed. *Nicolò Carandini. Il liberale e la nuova Italia (1943–1953)*. Florence: Le Monnier, 1993.

Ridola, Paolo. "Gli studi di diritto costituzionale." *Rivista Trimestrale di Diritto Pubblico* (2001), 1262.

Rigoll, Dominik. "Erfahrene Alte, entradikalisierte Achtundsechziger. Menschenrechte im roten Jahrzehnt." In Frei, Norbert/Weinke, Annette, eds. *Toward a New Moral World Order? Menschenrechtspolitik und Völkerrecht seit 1945*. Göttingen: Wallstein, 2013, 182–192.

———. *Staatsschutz in Westdeutschland. Von der Entnazifizierung zur Extremistenabwehr*. Göttingen: Wallstein, 2013.

———. "Den Wald vor lauter Bäumen. Jean Améry und die Niederlage der 45er." In Bielefeld, Ulrich/Weiss, Yfaat, eds. *Jean Améry. "... als Gelegenheitsgast, ohne jedes Engagement"*. Paderborn: Fink, 2014, 105–118.

Rimoli, Francesco. "I manuali di diritto costituzionale." *Rivista Trimestrale di Diritto Pubblico* 4 (2001), 1412–1413.

BIBLIOGRAPHY 275

Rioux, Jean-Pierre/Sirinelli, Jean-François. *La culture de masse en France. De la belle époque à aujourd'hui.* Paris: Hachette, 2006.

Risso, Linda. "The [Forgotten] European Political Community, 1952–1954." In *EFPU Conference Paper 2004* http://www.lse.ac.uk/internationalRelations/centresandunits/EFPU/EFPUconferencepapers2004/Risso.doc (08.01.2017).

Rogari, Sandro. "Il "Cesare Alfieri" da Istituto a Facoltà di Scienze Politiche." In Rogari, Sandro, ed. *L'Università degli studi di Firenze, 1924–2004. Atti della tavola rotonda di presentazione del volume, Firenze, 17 dicembre 2004.* Florence: Firenze University Press, 2005, 677–739.

Roger, Philippe. *Rêves et cauchemars américains. Les Etats-Unis au miroir de l'opinion publique française (1945–1953).* Villeneuve d'Ascq: Presses Univ. du Septentrion, 1996.

Rossi, Emanuele. *Democrazia come partecipazione. Lelio Basso e il PSI alle origini della Repubblica, 1943–1947.* Rome: Viella, 2011.

Rousso, Henry. *Le syndrome de Vichy (1944–1987).* Paris: Ed. du Seuil, 1987.

Rusconi, Gian Enrico. *Germania, Italia, Europa. Dallo stato di potenza alla "potenza civile".* Torino: Einaudi, 2003.

Sabbatucci, Giovanni. *Storia del socialismo italiano Vol. V: Il secondo dopoguerra (1943–1955).* Rome: Il Poligono, 1981.

———. *Il riformismo impossibile. Storie del socialismo italiano.* Rome: Laterza, 1991.

Sack, Daniel. *Moral re-armament. The reinventions of an American religious movement.* New York: Palgrave Macmillan, 2009.

Sadoun, Marc. *Les socialistes sous l'occupation. Résistance et collaboration.* Paris: Presses de la Fondation Nationale des Sciences Politiques, 1982.

Salvadori, Massimo L. "Il liberalismo di Bobbio tra etica, politica e progresso sociale." In Salvadori, Massimo L., ed. *Liberalismo italiano. I dilemmi della libertà.* Rome: Donzelli, 2011, 153–168.

Salvati, Mariuccia. "Lelio Basso protagonista e interprete della Costituzione." In Monina, Giancarlo, ed. *La via alla politica. Lelio Basso, Ugo La Malfa, Meuccio Ruini protagonisti della Costituente; atti della giornata di studio, Roma, 19 dicembre 1997.* Milan: Franco Angeli, 1999, 33–84.

——— /Giorgi, Chiara, eds. *Scritti scelti. Frammenti di un percorso politico e intellettuale: 1903–1978.* Rome: Carocci, 2003.

Sartori, Giovanni. *Democrazia e definizioni.* Milan: Il Mulino, 1957.

———, ed. *Antologia di scienza politica.* Bologna: Il Mulino, 1970.

———. *Parties and party systems. A framework for analysis.* Cambridge: CUP, 1976.

———. "Norberto Bobbio e la scienza politica." *Rivista italiana di scienza politica* 1 (2004), 7–11.

Sassoon, Donald. "Politics." In Fulbrook, Mary, ed. *Europe since 1945.* Oxford: Oxford Univ. Press, 2000, 14–52.

276 BIBLIOGRAPHY

Schildt, Axel. "Der Beginn des Fernsehzeitalters. Ein neues Massenmedium setzt sich durch." In Schildt, Axel/Sywottek, Arnold, eds. *Modernisierung im Wiederaufbau. Die westdeutsche Gesellschaft der 50er Jahre.* Bonn: Dietz, 1993, 477–492.

———. *Moderne Zeiten. Freizeit Massenmedien und "Zeitgeist" in der Bundesrepublik der 50er Jahre.* Hamburg: Christians, 1995.

———. *Zwischen Abendland und Amerika. Studien zur westdeutschen Ideenlandschaft der 50er Jahre.* Munich: Oldenbourg, 1999.

———, ed. *Annäherungen an die Westdeutschen. Sozial- und kulturgeschichtliche Perspektiven auf die Bundesrepublik.* Göttingen: Wallstein, 2011.

Schilling, René. *"Kriegshelden". Deutungsmuster heroischer Männlichkeit in Deutschland 1813–1945.* Paderborn: Schöningh, 2002.

Schmid, Carlo. "Germany and Europe. The German Social Democratic Program." *Foreign Affairs* 30: 1 (1951/52), 531–544.

Schoenborn, Benedikt. *La mésentente apprivoisée. De Gaulle et les Allemands, 1963–1969.* Paris: Presses Univ. de France, 2007.

Schulz, Andreas/Grebner, Gundula, eds. *Generationswechsel und historischer Wandel.* Munich: Oldenbourg, 2003.

Schumacher, Martin/Lübbe, Katharina/Joseph, Angela, eds. *M.d.R., die Reichstagsabgeordneten der Weimarer Republik in der Zeit des Nationalsozialismus. Politische Verfolgung, Emigration und Ausbürgerung 1933–1945. Eine biographische Dokumentation.* Düsseldorf: Droste, 1994.

Scirocco, Giovanni. *Politique d'abord. Il PSI, la guerra fredda e la politica internazionale (1948–1957).* Milan: Unicopli, 2010.

Sebastiani, Pietro. *Laburisti inglesi e socialisti italiani. Dalla ricostituzione del PSI (UP) alla scissione di Palazzo Barberini, da Transport House a Downing Street, 1943–1947.* Rome: F.I.A.P, 1983.

Sedita, Giovanni. *La "Giovane Italia" di Lelio Basso.* Rome: Aracne, 2006.

Seefried, Elke. "Sozialdemokraten und Sozialisten im österreichischen Exil 1933/34." *Zeitschrift für Geschichtswissenschaft* 50 (2002), 581–602.

———. *Zukünfte. Aufstieg und Krise der Zukunftsforschung 1945–1980.* Berlin/Boston: De Gruyter, 2015.

Seidman, Michael. *Workers against work. Labor in Paris and Barcelona during the popular fronts.* Berkeley/Oxford: University of California Press, 1991.

Serneri, Simone N., ed. *Il partito socialista nelle resistenza. I documenti e la stampa clandestina (1943–1945).* Pisa: Nistri Lischi, 1988.

———. /Casali, Antonio/Errera, Giovanni, eds. *Scritti e Discorsi di Sandro Pertini. Vol. I, 1926–1978.* Rome: Presidenza del Consiglio dei Ministri Dipart. per l'Informazione e l'Editoria, 1992.

Setta, Sandro. *Croce. Il liberalismo e l'Italia postfascista.* Rome: Bonacci, 1979.

———. *L'uomo qualunque. 1944–1948.* Rome/Bari: Laterza, 2000.

BIBLIOGRAPHY 277

Settembrini, Domenico. "L'evoluzione delle sinistre antisistema negli anni del centrismo." In Settembrini, Domenico, ed. *Socialismo marxismo e mercato. Per un bilancio dell'idea socialista*. Lungro di Cosenza: Marco, 2002, 200–203.

Shaev, Brian. "Workers' Politics, the Communist Challenge, and the Schuman Plan: A Comparative History of the French Socialist and German Social Democratic Parties and the First Treaty for European Integration." *International Review of Social History* 61: 2 (2016), 251–281.

Sierp, Aline. *History, Memory, and Trans-European Identity. Unifying Divisions*. Hoboken: Taylor and Francis, 2014.

Sirinelli, Jean-François. "Génération et histoire politique." *Vingtième Siècle* 22 (1989), 67–80.

Slobodian, Quinn. *Foreign front. Third World politics in sixties West Germany*. Durham, NC: Duke University Press, 2012.

Söllner, Afons. "Normative westernization? The impact of remigres on the foundation of political thought in post-war Germany." In Müller, Jan-Werner, ed. *German ideologies since 1945: studies in the political thought and culture of the Bonn Republic*. New York et al.: Palgrave Macmillan, 2003, 40–60.

———. *Deutsche Politikwissenschaftler in der Emigration. Studien zu ihrer Akkulturation und Wirkungsgeschichte*. Wiesbaden: Westdt. Verl., 1996.

——— /Gwinner, Sabine, eds. *Zur Archäologie der Demokratie in Deutschland. Vol. 1: Analysen politischer Emigranten im amerikanischen Geheimdienst, 1943–1945*. Frankfurt a.M.: Fischer, 1982.

———, eds. *Zur Archäologie der Demokratie in Deutschland. Vol. 2: Analysen von politischen Emigranten im amerikanischen Außenministerium 1946–1949*. Frankfurt a.M.: Fischer, 1986.

Soutou, Georges-Henri. *L'alliance incertaine. Les rapports politico-stratégiques franco-allemands 1954–1996*. Paris: Fayard, 1996.

Späth, Jens. "Un antifascista e democratico particolare: il socialdemocratico bavarese Wilhelm Hoegner." *Diacronie. Studi di Storia Contemporanea. 9: 1 (2012)*. http://www.studistorici.com/2012/02/13/spath_numero_9/ (08.09.2017).

Spernol, Boris. *Notstand der Demokratie. Der Protest gegen die Notstandsgesetze und die Frage der NS-Vergangenheit*. Essen: Klartext, 2008.

Spinelli, Altiero/Levi, Lucio/Rossi, Ernesto, eds. *Il Manifesto di Ventotene*. Milan: Corriere della Sera, 2011.

Stambolis, Barbara. *Leben mit und in der Geschichte. Deutsche Historiker Jahrgang 1943*. Essen: Klartext, 2010.

Steininger, Rolf. *Autonomie oder Selbstbestimmung? Die Südtirolfrage 1945/46 und das Gruber-De-Gasperi-Abkommen*. Innsbruck/Vienna et al.: Studien-Verl., 2006.

Stephan, Alexander, ed. *The Americanization of Europe. Culture diplomacy and anti-Americanization after 1945*. New York: Berghahn, 2006.

278 BIBLIOGRAPHY

Stolleis, Michael. *Geschichte des öffentlichen Rechts in Deutschland Vol. 3: Weimarer Republik und Nationalsozialismus.* Munich: C.H. Beck, 2002.
———. *Geschichte des öffentlichen Rechts in Deutschland Vol. 4: Staats- und Verwaltungsrechtswissenschaft in West und Ost 1945–1990.* Munich: C.H. Beck, 2012.

Strath, Bo/Pakier, Małgorzata, eds. *A European memory? Contested histories and politics of remembrance.* New York: Berghahn, 2010.

Tetlock, Philip E. "Social Psychology and World Politics." In Gilbert, Daniel T./Fiske, Susan T./Lindzey, Gardner, eds. *The handbook of social psychology.* Boston/New York: Oxford Univ. Press, 1998, 868–912.

Uhl, Heidemarie. *Zivilisationsbruch und Gedächtniskultur. Das 20. Jahrhundert in der Erinnerung des beginnenden 21. Jahrhunderts.* Innsbruck et al.: Studien-Verl., 2003.

Valois, Georges. *L'Homme qui vient. Philosophie de l'autorité.* Paris: Nouvelle Librairie Nationale, 1923.

Vardys, Stanley. "Germany's Postwar Socialism: Nationalism and Kurt Schumacher, 1945–1952." *Review of Politics* 27 (1965), 220–244.

Varon, Jeremy. *Bringing the war home. The Weather Underground the Red Army Faction and revolutionary violence in the sixties and seventies.* Berkeley, Calif.: Univ. of California Press, 2007.

Varsori, Antonio. "Il Congresso dell'Europe dell'Aja (7–10 maggio 1948)." *Storia Contemporanea* 21 (1990), 478.

Vergnon, Gilles. *L'antifascisme en France. De Mussolini à Le Pen.* Rennes: Presses Univ. de Rennes, 2009.

Vodovar, Christine. "The impossible Third force. Italian and French socialism and Europe, 1943–1963." In Bonfreschi, Lucia/Orsina, Giovanni/Varsori, Antonio, eds. *European parties and the European integration process, 1945–1992.* Brussels: P. Lang, 2015, 45–62.
———. "La Resistenza nel dibattito politico in Francia e in Italia: il caso dei socialisti (1944–1948)." In Craveri, Piero, ed. *La seconda guerra mondiale e la sua memoria. [gli atti del Convegno La Seconda Guerra Mondiale e la Sua Memoria, svoltosi a Napoli ... il 17 – 18 settembre 2004].* Soveria Mannelli: Rubbettino, 2006, 491–528.

Weber, Petra. *Carlo Schmid, 1896–1979. Eine Biographie.* Munich: C.H. Beck, 1996.

Weber, Werner. *Weimarer Verfassung und Bonner Grundgesetz.* Göttingen, 1949.
———. *Spannungen und Kräfte im westdeutschen Verfassungssystem.* Stuttgart: Vorwerk, 1951.
———. *Die Verfassung der Bundesrepublik in der Bewährung.* Göttingen: Musterchmidt-Verlag, 1957.

Wehler, Hans-Ulrich. *Deutsche Gesellschaftsgeschichte. Vol. 5: Bundesrepublik und DDR 1949–1990.* Bonn: Bundeszentrale für Politische Bildung, 2009.

BIBLIOGRAPHY   279

Weisbrod, Bernd. "Generation und Generationalität in der Neueren Geschichte." *Aus Politik und Zeitgeschichte* 8 (2005), 3–9.
Weiß, Hermann. "Ideologie der Freizeit im Dritten Reich. Die NS-Gemeinschaft „Kraft durch Freude"." *Archiv für Sozialgeschichte* 33 (1993), 289–303.
Whittier, Nancy. "Political Generations, Micro-Cohorts and the Transformation of Social Movements." *American Sociological Review* 62 (1997), 760–778.
Wieviorka, Olivier. "La génération de la résistance." *Vingtième Siècle* 22 (1989), 111–116.
———. *Nous entrerons dans la carrière. De la Résistance à l'exercice du pouvoir.* Paris: Seuil, 1995.
Wildt, Michael. *Generation des Unbedingten. Das Führungskorps des Reichssicherheitshauptamtes.* Hamburg: Hamburger Edition, 2002.
Winter, Jay. "Thinking about Silence." In Ben-Ze'ev, Efrat/Ginio, Ruth/Winter, Jay, eds. *Shadows of war. A social history of silence in the twentieth century.* Cambridge: CUP, 2010, 3–31.
Wippermann, Wolfgang. *Faschismus. Eine Weltgeschichte vom 19. Jahrhundert bis heute.* Darmstadt: Wiss. Buchges, 2009.
Wirsching, Andreas. *Vom Weltkrieg zum Bürgerkrieg? Politischer Extremismus in Deutschland und Frankreich 1918–1933/39. Berlin und Paris im Vergleich.* Munich: Oldenbourg, 1999.
———. "8. Mai und 27. Januar 1945. Zwei Tage der Befreiung?" In Conze, Eckart/Nicklas, Thomas, eds. *Tage deutscher Geschichte. Von der Reformation bis zur Wiedervereinigung.* Munich: DVA, 2004, 239–255.
———. "Massenkultur in der Demokratie. Zur Entwicklung von Kultur und Gesellschaft in der Bundesrepublik und Frankreich nach 1945." In Miard-Delacroix, Hélène/Hudemann, Rainer, eds. *Wandel und Integration. Deutsch-französische Annäherungen der fünfziger Jahre.* Munich: Oldenbourg, 2005, 379–396.
———. "Politische Generationen, Konsumgesellschaft, Sozialpolitik. Zur Erfahrung von Demokratie und Diktatur in Zwischenkriegszeit und Nachkriegszeit." In Doering-Manteuffel, Anselm, ed. *Strukturmerkmale der deutschen Geschichte des 20. Jahrhunderts.* Munich: Oldenbourg, 2006, 43–64.
———. "Demokratie als „Lebensform". Theodor Heuss (1884–1963)." In Hein, Bastian/Kittel, Manfred/Möller, Horst, eds. *Gesichter der Demokratie. Porträts zur deutschen Zeitgeschichte.* Munich: Oldenbourg, 2012, 21–35.
Woldring, Hendrik E. S. *Karl Mannheim: the development of his thought. Philosophy, sociology and social ethics, with a detailed biography.* New York: St. Martin's Press, 1987.
Wolikow, Serge, ed. *Antifascisme et nation. Les gauches européennes au temps du Front Populaire.* Dijon: Ed. Univ. de Dijon, 1998.
Wuermeling, Henric L. *Die weisse Liste. Umbruch der politischen Kultur in Deutschland 1945.* Frankfurt a.M./Berlin: Ullstein, 1988.

280 BIBLIOGRAPHY

Zanuttini, Annalisa. "L'organizzazione del partito radicale (1955–1962)." In Vallauri, Carlo, ed. *L'arcipelago democratico. Organizzazione e struttura dei partiti negli anni del centrismo (1949–1958)*. Rome: Bulzoni, 1981.

Zeldin, Theodore. *France 1848–1945. Intellect and pride*. Oxford: Oxford Univ. Press, 1950.

Ziebura, Gilbert. *Les relations franco-allemandes dans une Europe divisée. Mythes et réalités*. Pessac: Presses Univ. de Bordeaux, 2012.

Index[1]

A

Abendroth, Wolfgang, 53, 54, 58, 104
Abensour, Miguel, vi
Adenauer, Konrad, 16, 17, 33, 49, 55, 56, 65, 133, 178, 179, 186, 187, 189, 190, 219, 229
Africa, v
Albertini, Elena, 142
Albertini, Luigi, 121
Albertz, Heinrich, 53, 54, 58
Algeria, 187, 188
Altmaier, Jacob, 182
Americanization, 5, 9, 15, 18, 40, 106–110
American Secret Service Office of Strategic Services, 97
Améry, Jean, 17, 53, 54, 59–65
Amorth, Antonio, 79, 84, 92n46
Anno zero metaphor, 74

Anschütz, Gerhard, 75
Anti-fascism, 8, 9, 21, 32, 37, 52, 55, 57, 65, 101, 104, 120–124, 130, 136, 138, 155, 162, 174, 176, 189, 198–206, 208–210, 214n27, 250, 251
Anti-Nazism, 49, 52, 59, 182, 198, 252
Antologia di Scienza Politica, 103
Antoni, Carlo, 102, 103
Aragon, 63
Assmann, Jan, 172, 173
Assolombarda, 136
Auriol, Vincent, 16, 33, 223, 224
Austria, 12, 164, 252
Authoritarianism, 12, 29, 62, 82, 152, 164, 169n67, 185, 187, 189–191, 209, 221, 239
Avanti!, 214n32

---

[1] Note: Page numbers followed by 'n' refer to notes.

© The Author(s) 2018   281
J. Späth (ed.), *Does Generation Matter? Progressive Democratic Cultures in Western Europe, 1945–1960*, Palgrave Studies in the History of Social Movements, https://doi.org/10.1007/978-3-319-77422-0

282 INDEX

B
Badiou, Alain, vi
Badoglio, Pietro, 123
Barile, Paolo, 85
Basso, Lelio, 20, 21, 153–163, 197–210, 214n32, 251
Baudissin, Wolf Graf von, 53–57
Bauer, Riccardo, 214n27
Bavaria, 58, 183, 205, 207
Behemoth, 54
Behr, Hermann, 50, 56
Belgium, 31, 60
Benelux, 16
Benjamin, Walter, 71
Berger, Stefan, 15
Bergstraesser, Arnold, 18, 104, 105, 109
Birth of the Present, 61, 64
Bismarck, Otto von, 36
Blasberg, Christian, 19, 249
Blum, Léon, 33, 132, 176, 177, 179, 222–224
Bobbio, Norberto, 18, 98, 99, 101, 102, 107
Böckenförde, Ernst-Wolfgang, 77
Böll, Heinrich, 53–56, 63, 252
Bolshevism, 31, 161, 215n38
Bonaparte, Napoleon, 36
Boneschi, Mario, 137
Bonn Charter, 82
Bourdieu, Pierre, vi
Bourgeoisie, 20, 34, 60, 62, 119, 152, 154, 158–163, 167n35, 167n39, 168n51, 178, 204, 222–223, 235, 251
Boutbien, Léon, 220, 224, 225
Bracher, Karl-Dietrich, 105
Brandt, Willy, 65
Braun, Otto, 179, 202
Braunthal, Julius, 168n42
Breitscheid, Rudolf, 242n25
British Labour Party, 157, 159
Broszat, Michael, 51

Brüning, Heinrich (bitte nicht kursiv setzen), 184
Bulgaria, 160
Bundesprüfstelle für jugendgefährdende Schriften (Federal inspection authority for writings posing a risk to young people), 58
Bundesverfassungsgericht (Federal Constitutional Court), 77, 83
Bureau de liaison des partis socialistes de la Communauté Européenne (Liaison Office of Socialist Parties of the European Community) (BLPSCE), 220

C
Calamandrei, Piero, 85
Calogero, Guido, 137
Calosso, Umberto, 241n16
Capograssi, 92n46
Carandini, Elena, 126
Carandini, Nicolò, 19, 119–142, 249
Casati, Alessandro, 123, 124
Cassandro, Giovanni, 144n27
Castagnez, Noelline, 225
Cattaneo Institute, 107
Cattani, Leone, 123, 126, 138, 141, 142, 146n56, 149n111
Cau, Maurizio, 17, 248, 249
CDU, *see* Christlich Demokratische Union (German Christian Democratic Party)
Centro Socialista Interno, 201
Charles, Noel, 126
Christian Democracy, 35, 127, 135, 138, 181, 185–190
Christian Democratic Union (Germany), 35
Christian Social Union (CSU), 181, 185, 186
Christlich Demokratische Union (German Christian Democratic

INDEX **283**

Party) (CDU), 55, 57, 178–179, 181, 185–187
Clay, Lucius D., 97
CLN, see *Comitato di Liberazione Nazionale*
CNR, *see Conseil National de la Résistance*
Coercion, 32
Cold War, 9, 55, 57, 60, 63–66, 106, 131, 133, 139, 152, 154, 156, 160, 185, 198, 210, 227
Collaboration, 5, 8, 9, 37, 51, 56, 60, 62, 65, 132, 175, 187, 198, 201, 202, 205, 210, 222
Collective authority, 176, 192n20
Collective communities, 6
Collective destiny, 12
Collective experience, 14, 198
Collective memory, 14, 21, 36–38, 190
Collective security, 21, 220, 224, 227, 230
Collective trauma, 173
Colorni, Eugenio, 201
Colozza, Roberto, 199
Cominform conference, 168n48
COMISCO, *see* Committee of the International Socialist Conferences
Comitato di Liberazione Nazionale (CLN), 124–126
Committee for Political and Social Science (Italy), 107
Committee of the International Socialist Conferences (COMISCO), 174, 175, 178, 231
Communism, 14, 17, 19, 20, 31, 32, 34, 50, 52, 56, 63, 106, 125, 127, 133, 136, 137, 140, 152, 153, 155–157, 160, 179, 184–186, 198, 206, 207, 210, 233, 238, 250

Comparative historical research, 15
Concentration camp, 54, 55, 58, 66, 104, 184, 201, 205
Confindustria, 136
Confino, Alon, 38
Conseil national de la Résistance (CNR) (National Council of the Resistance) (CNR), 65, 66
Constitutional cultures, 71–86
    dragging past into post-war era, 73–74
    German case, 74–78
    implementation, and legal science point of view, 81–85
    Italian case, 78–81
Consulta nazionale (National Consultation), 71, 100
Contentious interests, 225–226
Continuity in rupture, 71–86
Conway, Martin, 16
Costamagna, Carlo, 79
Coudenhove-Kalergi, Richard, 64
Council of Europe, 64, 131, 229, 230
Cowan, Jon, 174
Crisafulli, Vezio, 78–80, 85
Crispi, Francesco, 158
Croce, Benedetto, 122–124, 127, 128, 130, 136, 142, 143n9, 143n19, 144n28, 145n46, 146n47
Crosa, Emilio, 79, 84, 92n46
CSU, *see* Christian Social Union
Cultural diplomacy, 106
Cyrankiewicz, Józef, 164
Czechoslovakia, 22, 130, 152, 157, 163, 180

D
Dachau concentration camp, 54, 205, 215n39
"Das Demokratische Deutschland", 203

284 INDEX

De Felice, Renzo, 138, 148n102, 149n111
De Gasperi, Alcide, 16, 33, 124, 128, 132, 141, 147n79
De Gaulle, Charles, 40, 62, 66, 129, 139, 179, 185, 188, 189, 191, 219, 236, 240n5
De Graaf, Jan, 19, 252, 253
De Man, Henri, 162
Déat, Marcel, 162
Democratic political cultures, 11–14
Democratization, 11–13, 15–18, 55, 57, 97, 180, 199, 227, 254
Democrazia come partecipazione, 199
Democrazia Cristiana (Italy), 35, 203, 206
Democrazia e definizioni ("Democracy and Definitions"), 103
Denazification, 14, 49, 50, 55, 57, 59, 75, 97, 181, 205, 207–209, 229
De Nicola, Enrico, 33
De Oliveira Salazar, António, 185
De Ruggiero, Guido, 101
Denmark, 31
Depreux, Édouard, 184
Der Monat journal, 106
Der Ruf, 36
Die zornigen alten Männer. Gedanken über Deutschland seit, 53
Dirks, Walter, 61
Doering-Manteuffel, Anselm, viii, 12
Dolfuss, Engelbert, 181
Domenach, Jean Marie, 41
Dorls, Fritz, 183
D'Ottavio, Gabriele, 18, 248–250
Drath, Martin, 89n21
Duguit, Léon, 80
Dulles, Allan W., 202

E
Ebert, Friedrich, 33
Echternkamp, Jörg, 14

Eco, Umberto, 124, 126
ECSC, *see* European Coal and Steel Community
EDC, *see* European Defence Community
EEC, *see* European Economic Community
Eggebrecht, Axel, 53, 55, 57, 59
Ehmke, Horst, 77
Ehrenburg, Ilja, 64
Einaudi, Luigi, 16, 33, 131, 136, 142
Elementi di scienza politica, 95
Elysée Treaty of 1963, 21, 219, 220, 234–238
Embarking on a Career. From the Resistance to the Conduct of Power, 64
Engaged democrats, 26n53
Engelmann, Bernt, 53–55, 58
EPC, *see* European Political Community
Erfahrungsraum (space of experience), 10
Erhard, Ludwig, 60
Erler, Fritz, 177, 185, 237
Erwartungshorizont (horizon of expectation), 10
Esposito, Carlo, 79, 80, 85
Esprit magazine, 41
Euratom, 232, 238
European Coal and Steel Community (ECSC), 133, 229, 231, 232, 234, 237
European Defence Community (EDC), 133, 134, 141, 223, 224, 227–230, 232, 234, 236, 253
European Economic Community (EEC), 232, 238
Europeanization of memory, 11
European memory, 14
collective, 14
Europeanness, 254

INDEX   285

European Political Community (EPC), 134, 147n79, 234
European socialism and French–German reconciliation, 219–239
European social movement, 8

F
Fabian, Walter, 53
Faravelli, Giuseppe, 207
Fascism, 6, 9, 10, 15, 17, 18, 20, 21, 29, 31, 32, 35–37, 60, 72, 80, 90n24, 98, 100–102, 121, 126, 142, 151–154, 156, 158–161, 163, 164, 175, 177, 185, 187, 188, 198–200, 202, 206–208, 210, 211n4, 213n27, 222, 226, 233, 235, 249–252
  and anti-fascism, 203–205
Faure, Paul, 176
Federal Republic of Germany (FRG), 35, 50, 82, 86, 229, 237
Ferrara, Giovanni, 137
Ferrara, Mario, 135
Fifth Republic (French), 189
Fioravanti, Maurizio, 90n24
First World War, 33, 159, 200
Flaiano, Ennio, 119
Flechtheim, Ossip K., 53, 54, 57
Foa, Vittoria, 214n27
Fogt, Helmut, 90n30
Ford Foundation, 106
Forner, Sean, viii
Forsthoff, Ernst, 76, 77, 82
Fourth Republic (French), 31, 35, 62, 66, 179, 225, 236
  fall of, 185–190
Fraenkel, Ernst, 104, 105, 109
France, 4–6, 9, 11–13, 15–17, 21, 22n7, 29–31, 33–35, 37, 38, 40, 51, 52, 54, 60–66, 120, 128–130, 132–134, 139,

149n111, 160, 170n67, 211n3, 247, 252, 254
  See also specific entries
France, Mendès, 134, 147n82
Franco, Francisco, 181, 188
Frankfurt, 108
Frankfurter Allgemeine Zeitung, 37
Frankfurter Hefte, 35, 50
Free Territory of Trieste, 226
French Christian democracy, 35
French socialism, 171–191
French Zone of Occupation (FZO), 227
Friedrich, Carl J., 18, 97, 104, 111n15
Fröhlich, Claudia, 26n53
FZO, *see* French Zone of Occupation

G
Galli, Giorgio, 108, 115n60
Garibaldi, Giuseppe, 36
Gay, Peter, 98
GDR, *see* German Democratic Republic
German Democratic Republic (GDR) (East Germany), 6, 22, 63, 75, 87, 210
Germanness, 134
German socialism, 171–191
Germany, 6, 9, 12, 13, 15, 21, 29, 33–36, 39, 51, 61, 72, 74, 81, 86, 87n3, 159, 160, 164, 250, 252
  See also Federal Republic of Germany; Historical memory; Modern political science, in Italy and Germany
  See also specific entries
Gestapo, 54, 242n25
Giannini, Amedeo, 79, 84
Giannini, Massimo Severo, 78, 79
Giolitti, Giovanni, 136
Giorgi, Chiara, 199

286 INDEX

Giovane Italia, 201
Giustizia e Libertà, 201
Gobetti, Piero, 201
Godin, Michael Freiherr von, 202–203
Goebbels, Joseph, 50
Goltz, Anna von der, vii
Gouin, Felix, 224
Grabert, Herbert, 50
Grass, Günter, 51, 58
Graziano, Luigi, 99, 100, 112n27
Great Britain, 30–31, 61, 96, 120,
  129–132, 134, 138, 139, 141,
  149n111, 153, 159, 183, 236
Greece, 54, 128
Greenberg, Udi, viii
Gregorio, Massimiliano, 92n49
Grumbach, Salomon, 181, 184, 224
Grundgesetz (Basic Law), 81–83,
  91n37, 91n41

H

Habermas, Jürgen, vi, 51, 53
Hague, The, 131
Hariou, Maurice, 80
Hassell, Ulrich von, 129
Healey, Denis, 164
Hedler, Wolfgang, 182
Heller, Hermann, 75, 78, 88n14,
  89n19, 89n20, 89n21,
  91n32
Hennis, Wilhelm, 77
Herbert, Ulrich, 6
Hesse, Konrad, 77
Hessel, Stéphane, 66
Heuss, Theodor, 33
Hier ... Demain, 223
Hirschhausen, Ulrike von, 16
Historical memory, 171–191
Historical monumentalism, 36
Historiography, vi, 4, 5, 7, 9, 15–17,
  50, 73, 211n3

Hitler, Adolf, 54, 60, 61, 63, 96, 97,
  130, 178, 184, 185, 201
Hitler Youth generation, 17, 51, 59,
  251
Hochfeld, Julian, 166n25, 168n42
Hochschule für Politik, 106
Hoegner, Wilhelm, 20, 21, 183,
  197–210, 249
Hoen, Reinhard, 75
Holland, 60
Hölscher, Lucian, 23n12
Holstein, 88n14
Huber, Ernst Rudolf, 75
Hungarian Social Democratic Party,
  169n67
Hungary, 22, 159, 160, 164
Huxley, Julian, 61

I

Ideology and Utopia, 95
Il Mondo, 133, 134, 136, 138, 139
India, v
Indignant Old Men, The, 53, 64
Iniziativa Socialista, 233, 234
Institut für Politikwissenschaft, 106
Integrated Western European history,
  15–22
Ipsen, Hans Peter, 75, 82
Italian socialism, 21, 152, 165,
  212n10, 231–235, 241n9,
  241n11
Italy, 4–6, 9, 11–13, 15–19, 29–31,
  33–35, 37, 39, 72, 81, 83, 86,
  98, 133, 183, 184, 188, 209,
  210, 222, 226, 231, 234, 235,
  238, 247, 249–254
  constitutional culture in, 78–81
  new generation of political scientists
    in, 99–103
  See also Modern political science, in
    Italy and Germany; *Partito*

Socialista Italiano (Italian Socialist Party)
See also specific entries
Ivanovitch, Ivan, 60

J
Japan, 12
Jaquet, Gérard, 187, 225
Jaurès, Jean, 224
Jellinek, Walter, 75
Judt, Tony, 192n12

K
Kaisen, Wilhelm, 230
Kaiser, Joachim, 51
Kalyvas, Stathis, 13
Kant, Immanuel, 13
Kaufmann, Erich, 75, 88n14
Kelsen, Hans, 75, 77, 89n19, 91n32, 102
Kennedy, John F., 139
Kindt-Kiefer, Jacob, 203
Kirchheimer, Otto, 97, 104
Knapp, Steven, 192n20
Koellreuter, Otto, 75
Koestler, Arthur, 64
Kogon, Eugen, 17, 50, 53–57, 59, 61, 63, 66, 104, 251
Kogon 45ers, 52, 58, 66
Kommunistische Partei Deutschlands (German Communist Party) (KPD), 178
Königstein, 108
Koptjajewa, Antonina, 60
Korean War, 133
Koselleck, Reinhart, 5, 248
Kössler, Till, 35
KPD, *see* Kommunistische Partei Deutschlands (German Communist Party)

Kracauer, Siegfried, 40
Kraft durch Freude ("Strength Through Joy") organization, 39
Kritzer, Peter, 199

L
Labour Party (Great Britain), 236
Laclau, Ernesto, vi
Lacoste, Robert, 225
Lanchester, Fulco, 90n25
La Rivoluzione liberale, 201
Larock, Victor, 151, 165
Latin America, v, 12
Lavagna, Carlo, 78, 79, 85
Le Bail, Jean, 225
Le Troquer, André, 224
Leggewie, Claus, 14
Legitimacy, ii, v, 13, 38, 41, 82, 84, 93, 121, 125, 221, 222, 226, 236, 238, 174–180
Leibholz, Gerhard, 75, 77, 83, 88n14, 89n17, 91n32
Leistner, Friedrich, 208
Lenin, Wladimir Iljitsch, 31
Leoni, Bruno, 99, 101, 102
L'Europeo, 132
Lewis, Sinclair, 60
Liberalism, 18, 19, 32, 33, 102, 120–123, 125, 127, 131, 136, 137, 140–142, 148n90, 178, 249
See also New Liberalism
Liberalization, 5
Libonati, Franco, 138
Löbe, Paul, 230, 243n38
Loewenstein, Karl, 18, 104, 108
Lombardi, Riccardo, 232
Lübbe, Hermann, 53
Lucifero, Falcone, 126, 145n37
Ludendorff, Erich, 201
Ludwig-Maximilians-University, 208
Luzzatto, Lucio, 201

288 INDEX

M

Maier, Charles, 34, 251
Maier, Hans, 99, 105
Malagodi, Giovanni, 135, 136
Malraux, André, 63, 64
Mangoldt, Hermann von, 83, 91n41
Mann, Thomas, 61, 96
Mannheim, Karl, 3, 18, 65, 79, 95, 96, 98, 248
Maranini, Giuseppe, 101, 102
Marcuse, Herbert, 97
Marshall Plan, 131
Martens, Stefan, 14
Marxism, 104, 200–202, 206, 222
Mass culture, 16, 30, 38–41, 248, 254
Matteotti, Giacomo, 151
Matteotti, Matteo, 151
Maunz, Theodor, 75
Mayer, Daniel, 82, 177, 179, 225
Memory studies, 171–191, 221–225
Mendès France, Pierre, 134, 230
MFE, *see Movimento Federalista Europa* (European Federalist Movement)
Miele, Giovanni, 78, 79
Missiroli, Mario, 120
MLI, *see Movimento Liberale Italiano* (Independent Liberal Movement, Italy)
Moch, Jules, 188, 225
Modern political science, in Italy and Germany, 93–110
Mohl, Robert von, 82
Mohr, Arno, 100
Mollet, Guy, 19, 173, 175, 183–185, 187–189, 223–225, 227, 228
Mommer, Karl, 237
Monina, Giancarlo, 199
Monnet, Jean, 133
Moral dignity, 37
Moral purity, 37
Moral Rearmament, 205, 215n36
Moral re-education, 163

Moral responsibility, 11, 38
Morandi, Rodolfo, 201
Mortati, Costantino, 78–81, 85, 91n35
Mosca, Gaetano, 18, 95
Moses, A. Dirk, viii, 6, 14, 51
Mouffe, Chantal, vi
Mounier, Emmanuel, 61
Mouvement Républicain Populaire (French Christian Democratic Party) (MRP), 181
Movimento di Unità Proletaria (Italian Proletarian Unity Movement) (MUP), 201
Movimento Federalista Europa (European Federalist Movement) (MFE), 128, 131
Movimento Liberale Indipendente and Movimento Liberale Italiano (Independent Liberal Movement) (MLI), 123, 135–137
Movimento Liberale Italiano (Independent Liberal Movement, Italy) (MLI), 123
MRP, *see Mouvement Républicain Populaire* (French Christian Democratic Party)
Mulino publishing group of Bologna, 107
Multiple temporality, 17
Münkler, Herfried, 36
MUP, *see Movimento di Unità Proletaria* (Italian Proletarian Unity Movement)
Mussolini, Benito, 31, 37, 101, 158, 185, 200, 204

N

Naegelen, Marcel-Edmond, 225
National Association of Political Science, 115n63
National memory communities, 172

INDEX   289

National Socialism, 9, 15, 18, 21, 29,
55, 65, 198, 199, 202, 203,
205–207, 210, 249, 251, 252
National Socialist Party, 76
*Nationalsozialistische Deutsche
Arbeiterpartei* (National Socialist
German Workers' Party)
(NSDAP), 181, 205, 210n3
NATO, *see* North Atlantic Treaty
Organization
Naumann, Werner, 50
Nawiasky, Hans, 75, 83, 202
Nazism, 36, 57, 63, 130, 178
Nehring, Holger, 15
Nenni, Pietro, 20, 120, 154–158, 160,
162, 163
Neo-fascism, 140, 154, 182, 183,
205, 135–137
Netherlands, The, 31, 174
Neu Beginnen (New Beginning)
group, 54, 74
Neues Wiener Tagblatt, 54
Neumann, Franz, 54, 97, 104
New Liberalism, 19, 121, 122, 125,
127, 128, 134, 135, 138
Nicolosi, Gerardo, 122
Niethammer, Lutz, vii, 50
Nietzsche, Friedrich, 36
Nitti, Francesco Saverio, 127
Nora, Pierre, 172
Normativism, 77, 80, 82–84, 88n14,
105, 109, 110, 176, 254
North Atlantic Treaty Organization
(NATO), 227, 230, 234, 237
Norway, 31
NSDAP, *see* *Nationalsozialistische
Deutsche Arbeiterpartei* (National
Socialist German Workers' Party)

O
Oertzen, Peter von, 77
Olivetti Foundation, 106

Ollenhauer, Erich, 182, 185–189,
224, 228, 237, 240n5
Original 45ers, 49–66
Amérys and, 59–64
as transnational generational unit,
65–66
West German perspectives and,
53–59
Orlando, Vittorio Emanuele, 71, 79,
84, 90n24, 91n31, 92n46, 124,
127, 144n30
Otto, Rudolf, 201

P
Paid vacation, 38–39
Palano, Damiano, 99
Pannella, Marco, 137, 138, 143n1
Pannunzio, Mario, 123, 124, 136,
138, 141
Panunzio, Sergio, 79
Papen, Franz von, 179
Paris Agreements, 230
Parri, Ferruccio, 214n27
Parti communiste français
(French Communist Party)
(PCF), 187
Parti socialiste autonome (French
Autonomous Socialist Party)
(PSA), 228
Parti Socialiste Unifié (French Unified
Socialist Party) (PSU), 241n9,
241n11
Partito Comunista Italiano (Italian
Communist Party) (PCI), 108,
231, 232, 234, 238
Partito d'Azione (Action Party, Italy)
(PdA), 123, 129, 204
Partito Liberale Italiano (Italian
Liberal Party) (PLI), 123–128,
135–137, 142, 145n32
*Partito Socialista dei Lavoratori
Italiani* (Italian Socialist Workers

290 INDEX

Party) (PSLI), 233, 234, 238, 241n9, 241n11, 244n52
Partito Socialista Democratico Italiano (Italian Social Democratic Party) (PSDI), 232, 234, 235, 238, 241n9, 241n11
Partito Socialista Italiano (Italian Socialist Party) (PSI), 151–165, 197, 199, 200, 204, 206, 207, 209, 210, 214n31, 230–234, 237, 238, 241n9, 241n11, 244n42, 245n61
  new democracy and, 153
  structural reforms and, 161–163
Partito Socialista Italiano di Unità Proletaria (Italian Socialist Party) (PSIUP), 197, 201, 206, 221, 226, 231, 233, 235, 236, 238, 241n9, 241n12
Patel, Kiran Klaus, 16
Paterson, William E., 225, 230
PCF, *see Parti communiste français* (French Communist Party)
PCI, *see* Partito Comunista Italiano (Italian Communist Party)
PdA, *see Partito d'Azione* (Action Party, Italy)
Pechel, Rudolf, 61
Pertini, Sandro, 159, 160
Pétain, Philippe, 176, 177, 188
Philip, André, 179, 187, 188, 225
Piccardi, Leopoldo, 137
Piccioni, Attilio, 33
Pineau, Christian, 187, 225
Pleven Plan, 133, 231
PLI, *see Partito Liberale Italiano* (Italian Liberal Party)
Poland, 22, 130, 160, 163, 164
Political generation, 4, 6, 7, 220–221, 239, 248, 252
  definition of, 90n30
Political systems, 12, 31, 32, 94, 105, 107–109, 209, 222, 226, 249

constraining, 235–239
Popular Front (France), 160, 161
Portraits of Famous Contemporaries, 64
Portugal, 12
Positivism, 77
Post-heroism, 36–38
Potsdam Agreement, 49
Poujade, Pierre, 187
Prague Coup (1948), 157
Pre-fascism, 31, 78, 90n25, 123, 124, 141
Preuss, 88n14
Primi Chiarimenti, 121, 123
PSA, *see Parti socialiste autonome* (French Autonomous Socialist Party)
PSDI, *see* Partito Socialista Democratico Italiano (Italian Social Democratic Party)
PSI, *see Partito Socialista Italiano* (Italian Socialist Party)
PSIUP, *see Partito Socialista Italiano di Unità Proletaria* (Italian Socialist Party
PSLI, *see Partito Socialista dei Lavoratori Italiani* (Italian Socialist Workers Party)

Q
Quaritsch, Helmut, 77
Queuille, Henri, 33

R
Radbruch, Gustav, 75
Ramadier, Paul, 133, 180, 224
Ranelletti, Oreste, 79, 92n46
Rassemblement du peuple français (Rally of the French people) (RPF), 181, 183, 185
"Realtà", 122
Rechtsstaat (rule of law), 80, 82

INDEX 291

Remigrants, role in West Germany, 104–107
Renger, Annemarie, 56
Resistance, 9–11, 17, 32, 34, 37, 51–55, 60–66, 73, 86, 107, 122, 124, 155, 163, 173, 174, 176–177, 185, 205, 210, 214n27, 214n32, 222, 225, 243n38, 250–252
Resistance prestige, 34
Reulecke, Jürgen, 172, 173
Reuter, Ernst, 230, 243n38
Riccardi, Luca, 127, 146n54
Richter, Hans Werner, 63, 252
Rigoll, Dominik, 17, 19, 251, 252
Rinser, Louise, 55, 56
Risorgimento, 121, 122, 127
Ritter, Joachim, 105
Ritzel, Heinrich, 202
Rockefeller Foundation, 106
Rodotà, Stefano, 137
Romano, Santi, 79, 80, 90n24
Roseman, Mark, vii
Rossi, Emanuele, 137, 199
Rossi, Ernesto, 137
Rostand, Jean, 61
Rousset, David, 63
Rousso, Henri, 173
RPF, *see Rassemblement du peuple français* (Rally of the French people)
Ruffini, Francesco, 136
Ruiz, Arangio, 100
Ruling Class, The, 95
Rumania, 160, 164

S
Salazar, António de Oliveira, 185
Salvati, Mariuccia, 205
Sänger, Fritz, 53, 54, 57
Saragat, Giuseppe, 124, 159, 169n54, 207

Sartori, Giovanni, 18, 99, 101–103, 107
Sartre, Jean Paul, 62–64
Savary, Alain, 225
Scalfari, Eugenio, 137
Scheuner, Ulrich, 76, 77
Schmid, Carlo, 104, 224
Schmitt, Carl, 31, 75, 77, 81, 82, 88n14, 91n32
Schneider, Hans, 77
Schnur, Roman, 77
Schröder, Louise, 56
Schumacher, Kurt, 16, 33, 104, 171, 172, 174–185, 225, 229, 230, 236, 237, 239
Schuman, Robert, 16, 33
Schuman Plan, 231
Schuschnigg, Kurt, 181
Schwarz, Peter, 105
Second World War, 36, 65, 98, 174–180
  as civilizational rupture, 7–11
Section française de l'Internationale ouvrière (French section of the workers' International (SFIO), 174, 176, 177, 179–181, 183–190, 209, 219–226, 231, 234–236, 238, 240n5, 241n14, 242n18, 242n22, 243n30, 253
  against German militarism, 226–228
Sécurité Sociale, 65
Severing, Carl, 179
Shaev, Brian, 20, 248, 252, 253
SI, *see* Socialist International
Silone, Ignazio, 166n20, 234
Sirinelli, Jean-François, 173
Smend, Rudolf, 77, 88n14, 89n17, 89n19, 91n32
Socialism, *see specific entries*
Socialist International (SI), 228, 240n4
Socialist internationalism, 19
Social-liberalism, 19, 121, 141, 142

292 INDEX

Social marginalization, 17, 34
Social movements, v–vii, 7, 8, 15
  See also specific entries
Social psychologists, 173
Social renewal, 57, 206
Social solidarity, 35
Söllner, Alfons, 96
Sontheimer, Kurt, 105
Southeast Asia, v
Sovereignty, 8, 79, 82, 84, 92n46,
  131, 132, 134, 181, 220, 222,
  226, 227, 229, 231, 237
Soviet Communist Party, 11
Soviet Union, 5, 128, 130, 131, 133,
  139, 140, 153
*Sozialdemokratische Partei
  Deutschlands* (German Social
  Democratic Party) (SPD), 56, 57,
  171–191, 199–202, 210,
  219–221, 225–234, 236–238,
  241n11, 241n14, 242n18,
  243n30, 243n38, 253
Sozialistische Reichspartei Deutschlands
  (Socialist Reich Party) (SRP),
  181, 183, 205
Spadolini, Giovanni, 120
Spain, 159, 160
Späth, Jens, vii, 20, 21, 248, 249, 251,
  252
SPD, *see Sozialdemokratische Partei
  Deutschlands* (German Social
  Democratic Party)
Spender, Stephen, 61
"Spoken into the Wind", 59
SRP, *see Sozialistische Reichspartei
  Deutschlands* (Socialist Reich
  Party)
Staatslehre, 74, 76, 78, 88n10, 88n13,
  88n14, 88n15, 89n21, 91n37
Staatsrechtslehre, 75, 76
Stahl, Friedrich Julius, 82
Strasser, Georg, 202

Studi politici magazine, 99, 103
Sweden, 31
Switzerland, 54

T
Tasca, Angelo, 169n67
Tempi Moderni journal, 106
Teusch, Christine, 55
Third Force, idea of, 130–133, 135,
  137, 138
Third Reich, 54, 58, 61, 174
Third Republic, 35, 51
Thoma, Richard, 75
Tilly, Charles, vii
Tocqueville, Alexis de, 41
Togliatti, Palmiro, 124
Totalitarianism, 9, 12, 14, 18, 29–41,
  72, 99, 105, 250
  mass culture and, 38–41
  post-heroism and, 36–38
Transgenerational collective destiny,
  12
Transnational communalities, 9
Transnational praxis, 254
Triepel, Hans, 75, 83
Troisième Force campaign, 132, 133
Truman Doctrine, 156
Turkey, 243n38

U
Über den Begriff der Geschichte (*On
  History*), 71
Umberto II, King of Italy, 124, 126
Unione Democratica Nazionale
  (National Democratic Union)
  (UDN), 127
"Union of Europe", 205
Union of European Federalists (UEF),
  132
Union of Independent Socialists, 234

INDEX 293

United Kingdom, *see* Great Britain
United States of America, 5, 54, 61, 96, 106, 107, 128, 131, 132, 134, 138–141, 147n69, 148n104
Uomo Qualunque, 128

V

Valiani, Leo, 137, 146n59, 214n27
Valois, Georges, 31
Van der Goes van Naters, Marinus, 175
Ventotene Manifesto, 128
Venturi, Franco, 214n27
Verdier, Robert, 225
Vereinigung der deutschen Staatsrechtslehrer (Association of German Constitutional Law Professors), 75, 83
Vichy, 6, 9, 29, 51, 170n67, 174, 176, 177, 184, 222
Victimhood, *see* Post-heroism
Victor Emanuel III, King of Italy, 123
Vodovar, Christine, 21, 241n16, 253
Von Godin, Michael Freiherr, 202–203
von Oertzen, Peter, 77
Vorrink, Koos, 167n29

W

Weber, Alfred, 12, 97
Weber, Werner, 77, 81, 82, 91n38
Wehler, Hans-Ulrich, 12
Wehner, Herbert, 189, 237
Weimar Republic, 32, 74, 76, 88n14, 91n32, 96, 99, 160, 166n20, 173, 176–178, 183, 184, 200, 201, 209
Weisbrod, Bernd, viii, 7
Wessel, Helene, 55
West Germany, 5, 9, 11, 12, 16, 18, 21, 30, 33, 34, 56, 65, 104–107, 247, 254
Westernization, 5, 9, 18, 94, 105, 248
See also Americanization
Wieviorka, Olivier, 17, 51, 52, 64
Wirsching, Andreas, 16, 248, 250, 252
Wirth, Josef, 202

Y

Yugoslavia, 128

Z

Zero Hour (*Stunde Null*), 175
Žižek, Slavoj, vi

CPSIA information can be obtained
at www.ICGtesting.com
Printed in the USA
LVHW06*1609240518
578385LV00005B/5/P